Provinces of the Revolution

Provinces of the Revolution

Essays on Regional Mexican History
1910 - 1929

Edited by Thomas Benjamin & Mark Wasserman

University of New Mexico Press

Albuquerque

Library of Congress Cataloging-in-Publication Data

Provinces of the Revolution : essays on regional Mexican history,
1910–1929 / edited by Thomas Benjamin
and Mark Wasserman. — 1st ed.
p   cm.
Includes bibliographical references.
ISBN 0-8263-1205-5
1. Mexico—Politics and government—1910–1946.
2. Mexico—History—Revolution. 1910–1920.
3. Peasantry—Mexico—Political activity—History—20th century.
4. Mexico—History, Local.
I. Benjamin, Thomas, 1952–
II. Wasserman, Mark, 1946–
F1234.P96   1990
972.08'16—dc20   89-77647

Maps 2 through 7 are reproduced from Antonio García Cubas, *Atlas
metódico para la enseñanza de la geografía de la República Mexicana (1910)*

Contents

Maps

Abbreviations

CNA	Comisión Nacional Agraria National Agrarian Commission
CNC	Confederación Nacional Campesina National Peasant Confederation
CROM	Confederación Regional Obrera Mexicana Mexican Regional Labor Confederation
CNOP	Confederación Nacional de Organizaciones Populares National Confederation of Popular Organizations
CTM	Confederación de Trabajadores de México Confederation of Mexican Workers
LNC	Liga Nacional Campesina National Peasant League
PAN	Partido Acción Nacional National Action Party
PNR	Partido Nacional Revolucionario National Revolutionary Party
PRI	Partido Revolucionario Institucional Institutional Revolutionary Party
PRM	Partido de la Revolución Mexicana Party of the Mexican Revolution

Political Chronology of the Mexican Revolution

1910.   Porfirio Díaz reelected. Francisco I. Madero proclaims the
               Plan de San Luis Potosí. Revolution begins.

1911.   Díaz retired and exiled. Madero elected president.

1912.   Rebellions by Pascual Orozco and Félix Díaz defeated.

1913.   Madero deposed and assassinated. Victoriano Huerta seizes
               the government. He is opposed by the Constitutionalists,
               led by Venustiano Carranza, and the peasant movement in
               the South, led by Emiliano Zapata.

1914.   The United States intervenes in Mexico, occupying
               Veracruz. The Constitutionalists defeat Huerta, then split
               into factions led by Carranza and Pancho Villa.

1915.   Carrancistas defeat Villa.

1916.   In response to Villa's raid on Columbus, New Mexico, the
               United States invades northern Mexico.

1917–1920.   Presidency of Venustiano Carranza.

1917.   Promulgation of new Constitution.

1919.   Zapata assassinated.

1920.   Alvaro Obregón deposes Carranza. Adolfo de la Huerta
               serves as interim president. Obregón elected president.
               Villa retires to ranch.

1920–1924.   Presidency of Alvaro Obregón

1923.   Rebellion of Adolfo de la Huerta defeated.

1924–1928.   Presidency of Plutarco Elías Calles.

1926–1929.   Cristero Rebellion.

1928.   Obregón reelected, but is assassinated before taking office.

1928–1934.   Maximato. Calles rules behind the scenes.

1928.   Presidency of Emilio Portes Gil.
Rebellion of Francisco Serrano and Arnulfo Gómez.

1929–1932.   Presidency of Pascual Ortiz Rubio.

1929.   National Revolutionary Party (PNR) organized by Calles.

1932–1934.   Presidency of Abelardo Rodríguez.

1934–1940.   Presidency of Lazaro Cárdenas.

1936.   Calles exiled.

1938.   Cárdenas expropriates property of international oil companies in Mexico.
The PRN reorganized as the Mexican Revolutionary Party (PRM). The last important rebellion, that of Saturnino Cedillo, defeated.

1940.   Manuel Avila Camacho elected president.

Provinces of the Revolution

An Introduction

Mark Wasserman

The last two decades have brought a decided shift in focus to the study of the Mexican Revolution. Historical interest has moved from the national to the state and local levels. The dominant theme has been the struggle for hegemony between the evolving Mexican national government and state-level political leaders or factions. Regional historians maintain that the only path to understanding the revolution is to look at it through the regions, not from the perspective Mexico City and environs. At the same time, historians have rediscovered the popular origins and movements of the revolution. Since many of the popular movements were local or regional, these two trends have meshed rather nicely. Neither the new regional history nor the new social history of the revolution are without corollaries or controversy. The purpose of this essay is to try to bring some order (*¿orden y progreso?*) to these two trends and to fit the essays in this volume into this new spectrum.

Enmeshed in these two foci is, of course, the central question of revisionism. Not everyone agrees that the Mexican Revolution was a revolution. Nor is everyone agreed on what it (whatever the "it" is) wrought. In simplest terms, the argument boils down to this: Did the Mexican Revolution cause profound change and, if it did, in what form and for whom? Regional history and the history of popular movements (often, but not always, overlapping) are crucial in this discussion, for it is in the regions that the historiographical civil war (as was the revolution itself) is being fought. The evidence (or proof) for the competing revisionist and antirevisionist (traditional) interpretations lies in regional histories. [1]

The first focal point, the evolution of the state, provides one of the foundations of revisionist history, for, above all, the revisionists have argued for the continuity of the Porfiriato and the postrevolutionary epoch of 1920 to 1940. The struggle between the central government and state-based elites is fundamental to the issue of continuity. The major thrust of both the Porfirian and the revolutionary states, the revisionists maintain, was the establishment of a

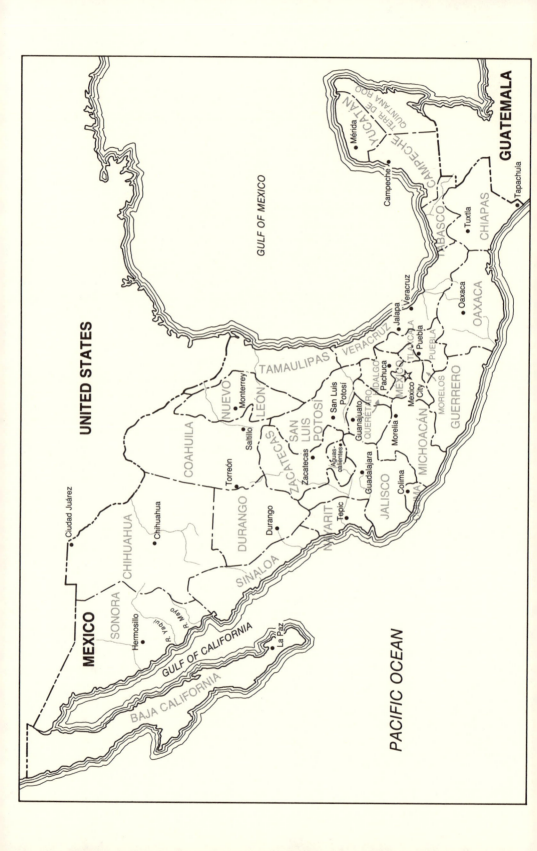

dominant central government. According to this argument, the revolutionary state crushed regional autonomy and established a neo-Porfirian state.[2] The second issue, the popular component of the revolution, is even more hotly argued, for it is the center of revisionism—with tradition (Tannenbaum) proposing that the revolution was popularly based and the revision maintaining that it was not.[3] The debates are linked, of course, for inherent in the argument against popular participation is the supposition that there was no revolution at all.

Until recently the revisionists held the upper hand. Lately, Friedrich Katz has cogently argued that the revolution comprised a number of popular movements.[4] Alan Knight, moreover, claims that "irrespective of its outcome (and I would argue it wrought many, if not always obvious changes in Mexican society), the revolution had one classic feature of the 'Great Revolutions': the mobilisation of large numbers of people who had hitherto remained on the margin of politics . . . . the popular movement in Mexico . . . might meet defeat, but in defeat it profoundly affected Mexican society and its subsequent evolution; the 'world turned upside down' was not the same world once it had been righted again."[5] In other words, we should not view the revolutionary and postrevolutionary eras as a linear progression in which "the benign process of the revolution towards social justice is replaced by the malign—or neutral—advance of the state towards national integration and centralized bureaucracy." This "discounts the pressures—including the popular pressures—acting upon the state . . . it gives a false homogeneity to Mexican history since the revolution . . ."[6] "But it was the popular movement, deriving from the countryside and significantly, though not exclusively, impelled by agrarian resentments, which was the heart of the revolution, and without which the revolution would have constituted no more than a form of 'middle class', anti-oligarchical political protest, liable to absorption and co-option, as in the comparable cases of Argentina or Chile."[7] The revolution was thus popular in two senses. It was fought by varied popular elements, particularly peasants. In addition, popular elements, peasant and proletariat, exerted considerable influence in the process of state formation, especially during the 1920s and 1930s. While neither Katz nor Knight rolled back revisionism entirely, they certainly caused it pause. They well point out that the events of 1910 to 1920 were complicated, and there is substantial evidence to indicate that indeed a revolution actually took place.

Mexican revolutionary historiography has come to rely on two sets of social science theories that shed light on the struggle between center and periphery and popular participation: theories on the evolution of the state and general theories of revolution, particularly peasant revolution.

The parameters of the discussion of the role of *the* state in revolution and its aftermath have been set generally by Nora Hamilton, who maintains that the "revolution of 1910 destroyed the pre-existing state apparatus and enabled the revolutionary leadership to form a new state within the context of structural options resulting from Mexico's prior development as well as new forces, alliances, and conflicts emerging from the revolution itself. The constitution of 1917 incorporated the ideal of a strong interventionist state."[8] Hamilton, however, concerns herself primarily with the comparison between the Porfirian state, defeated in the revolution, and the Cárdenas and post-Cárdenas state. To take this analysis and telescope it to the 1910–20 and 1920–30 (actually 1934) period is a fundamental mistake.[9]

The general (perhaps ephemeral) problems of definition of the state, state autonomy, and class–state relations aside, the main issues for the 1910 to 1929 era concern the strength of the Mexican state. These years were a continuation of the long process of political centralization begun by Benito Juárez and continued with some success by Porfirio Díaz. The revolution was to some considerable extent a manifestation of this struggle in its rawest form. Successive regimes—Madero, Huerta, Carranza—struggled unsuccessfully to assert control over the regions. Obregón and Calles were more successful, but at enormous cost. Violence and rebellion continued through the 1920s. Moreover, for all their success at centralization, neither Obregón and Calles could ultimately bring all of Mexico under their control. Satrapies continued to exist even on the central plateau. Saturnino Cedillo's San Luis Potosí and Tomás Garrido Canabal's Tabasco were only two of the most obvious examples.[10]

Nonetheless, as Alan Knight maintains, "the ultimate achievement of the revolution lay in its creation of a powerful state, just as committed to development and centralisation as its Porfirian predecessor, though employing more effective means to this end."[11] This does not mean that the revolution was not popularly based, nor does it mean that the process of building a strong state was linear, a steady process without its ups and downs. In fact, the most violent stages of the revolution, from 1913 to 1916, destroyed the old state, forcing the revolutionaries to build another from scratch. And it was not much easier after 1916, given the rebellions, coups, and the strength of the regional *caudillos*. No one can deny the importance of the state and the state-building process from 1917 to 1929, but the construction experienced many delays and the state was not nearly omnipotent. The 1920s (and the 1930s too, I would argue) were a period of transition.

The issue of popular participation rests primarily on the role of the peasantry (although during the 1920s the working class exerted considerable influence through labor unions). Both Katz and Knight have constructed typologies of peasant movements in the revolution. Katz has divided the revolutionary peasantry into four groups: free villages, tribal communities on the frontier, hacienda residents, and small landowners.[12] Knight has found two types: "middle peasants" who produced agrarian revolts, and "peripheral peasants" who produced Serrano movements.[13] Since these focus on the revolutionary era 1910 (and before) to 1919, I propose a third categorization to incorporate the 1920s: (1) Indian, most importantly the on-going struggles of the Yaqui in Sonora and the Mayo in Sinaloa; (2) ranchero, small landholder-led, the leaders of which have been called peasant bourgeoisie, the notable, studied illustrations of which are in Hidalgo and Guerrero; (3) village-based, of which the Zapatistas are the most obvious but not the only example; (4) rural movements from above, notably those of Salvador Alvarado and Felipe Carrillo Puerto in Yucatán, Adalberto Tejeda in Veracruz, Emilio Portes Gil of Tamaulipas, and Saturnino Cedillo of San Luis Potosí.[14] Typologies are complicated further during the 1920s, because the different rural groups began to war with one another. A fifth group, landless rural dwellers, began to organize in the 1920s, a development that threatened the other rural groups because they demanded land for themselves.

Much has been written about the first three categories, so for the purposes of this essay let us concentrate on the fourth. Heather Salamini has determined that there were two types of revolutions from above that were led by different types of leaders, the personalist *caudillo* and the populist-bureaucratic *caudillo*.[15] Saturnino Cedillo, the classic personalist *caudillo*, based his power on his charisma, military prowess, and patronage. He retained an army of small landowners beholden to him for their land.[16] Salvador Alvarado was, perhaps, the first of the populist breed. "The general's program was geared to impress upon workers and campesinos that all the benefits they received . . . resulted directly from state action. In turn, the state demanded their support . . . . Workers and campesinos would give their support by incorporating themselves into organizations created and controlled by the revolutionary government and by channeling their demands through the state apparatus."[17] After redressing the worst abuses of workers and peasants, the state sought to harmonize class relations. Alvarado would not stand for initiatives outside his perview. During the 1920s Felipe Carrillo Puerto, Adalberto Tejeda, and Emilio Portes Gil emerged as regional leaders who offered their own revolutionary social and economic programs and set about to expand their political power, not through exploitation of their charismatic talents, familial ties, or military exploits, but "through political manipulation of the state bureaucracy."[18] This new breed, born of the middle class, organized peasants and workers to serve as their political support. Eventually, their creation of radical political parties brought them into conflict with the central government. Tejeda and Carrillo Puerto successfully held off the central government under Obregón for prolonged periods in the 1920s.

The popular movement was as varied as Mexico's regions. Knight sees that

a fundamental . . . feature of the Mexican Revolution was . . . an agrarian rebellion against a landlord class which, for all its wealth, had lost its legitimacy in the eyes of the peasantry and was unable to defend its interests in the civil war. . . . where popular protest was weak . . . the landlord interest could defend itself. This divergent pattern cannot be explained solely or even primarily in terms of superior repressive power, which simply did not exist. It depended in part on the absence of popular grievances or organizational capacity, in part on the legitimacy of these elites, which was in turn nourished by ideology, clientilism, local "patriotism", and even shared objectives. [19]

In some places, like certain areas of Oaxaca in 1911, there were no appreciable peasant grievances so there were no rebellions.

Knight describes the character of peasant protest:

grievances were parochial, particular, poorly articulated, yet laden with moral sentiment; in absence of peaceful, institutional forms of redress, they were now settled violently and directly; and would continue to be until some fundamental reform—no mere nominal change of president—were undertaken. [20]

He pictures the popular movement as "predominantly rural, plebian, illiterate, parochial in outlook, displaying (for all its radical programmes) backward-looking, nostalgic traits, and a commitment to political authority that was local, personal, and traditional/charismatic."[21] Most interestingly, Knight also maintains that the revolution "evolved a logic of its own, which cannot be related to social origins or ideologies of participant groups. . . . As different political solutions were attempted, as regimes (national and local) came and went, as battle was joined at all the different levels of conflict—ideological, regional, ethnic, class, and clientilist— . . . so the various social actors departed from their original characterisations and—to varying extents—were taken over by the drama." The logic of the revolution "implies no a priori pattern, no grand Hegelian design; it suggests, rather, the whole complex of crises, events, options and opportunities which confronted participants and over which they felt themselves to have little control."[22]

What Knight is getting at here amounts to two things. First, there is an explicit connection between the localities and the regions and the popular movement. Second, there is a crucial interplay of local–regional events and persons with national (and international) events and trends.

Viewing the four stages of the revolution from 1910 to 1929—Madero, 1910–13; Huerta, 1913–14; Constitutionalist, 1915–1920; and Consolidation, 1920–29—from the regions and the popular movements born in them, the revolution becomes clearer. Our two foci then become the key elements in an interpretation of the revolution both in its stages and as a whole.

When historians analyzed Madero's downfall from a national perspective, they attributed it to the strenuous efforts of hacendados, old regime military officers, foreign and native entrepreneurs, and foreign diplomats. But when looking at his demise from the perspective of the regions, others found, as did William Beezley, that Madero fell "because of regional differences in the revolutionary movement . . ." He "never commanded a disciplined, integrated, rebel band or political party that could mobilize the people. Madero, moreover, failed to take control of formal networks into the backlands."[23] This was not just a case of blaming the victim. Beezley had discerned from his studies of Chihuahua and Coahuila that Madero never had control of the regions and, as a consequence, was vulnerable to Victoriano Huerta's coup.

Beezley hits the theme of popular rebellion when he pinpoints the reason for Madero's demise. "The simple fact is that Madero's Anti-reelectionist movement did not reach the simple and humble people . . . but if the revolt were to accomplish anything, if Madero were to remain in power, he had to mobilize these rural villagers."[24] Beezley identifies Madero's failure to gain access to informal networks between villagers and the outside world (priests, schoolteachers, itinerant peddlers, bandits, militia officers) except in Chihuahua (where of course his revolution had won the day and defeated Díaz) as the base of his overall failure. The Mexican Revolution "was no more than a series of regional struggles."[25]

Alan Knight adds that Madero's fall "was brought about by a combination of direct popular challenge, and the indirect effects of this challenge upon the political nation, notably the federal army."[26] Madero's government was bled to death by regionally or locally based popular rebellions.[27] Its strength, resolve, legitimacy, and resources were drained, leaving it vulnerable to Huerta's coup in 1913.

Ironically, according to Beezley, Madero had planned all along to "roll back centralized authority by restoring autonomy to the states and communities." Madero planned to delegate to the state governors the responsibility and the opportunity to reconstruct Mexico."[28] But state autonomy was doomed for a number of reasons. First, the states did not have any money. Second, some forms of reform required national commitment. Local and state governments were ill-equipped to battle large companies, for example.

The historiographical analysis of the counterrevolution under Victoriano Huerta has proceeded similarly to that of Madero. The view from Mexico City had Huerta swept away by Woodrow Wilson's intransigent opposition and the shaky alliance between Villa, Obregón and Carranza. For Knight, however, Huerta's problem was the same as Madero's: he could not control the regions. Huerta could not defeat "endemic popular revolt" based in the regions, notably Sonora, Chihuahua, and Coahuila. The dictator faced the recalcitrant regions without Porfirio Díaz's skills of persuasion, and employed only militarization and repression. And these tactics were insufficient to maintain him in power.

The defeat of Huerta led to a condition of "warlordism," or the triumph of the regions. "Only Carranza's Constitutionalists, led predominantly by petty bourgeois caudillos from Sonora and other northern states, seemed ultimately capable of filling the political vacuum that existed in the center." The Carrancistas, according to Gilbert Joseph, were "empowered by a long-term strategy for integrating Mexico's political and economic future within a centralized revolutionary state . . ."[29] Carranza put in place trusted northern pro-consuls. This move served well for a while, but neither Villa nor Zapata were defeated; nor, over the long term, could the pro-consuls be trusted. While Cándido Aguilar, the First Chief's son-in-law, could be depended upon, Salvador Alvarado in Yucatán, for one, showed himself too radical and independent and had to be transferred.

Alvaro Obregón had a somewhat better time of it, but it is hardly arguable that the central government exerted total control in the states during his presidency (1920–1924). As Ian Jacobs describes for Guerrero: "Rival groups jockeyed for power and influence in the state while the federal government struggled to reassert its control."[30] Jacobs sees the 1920s in terms of the "relentless process of the reestablishment of central political control over the state."[31] Relentless though it may have been, it was not entirely successful. Obregón was only able to keep the Figueroa family in check in Guerrero by virtue of his relations with a younger generation of Guerrerense revolutionaries, whom he set against it. During Obregón's presidential term, the Figueroas and Neris fought it out for control of the state. In this battle, we can see also the emergence of the basic outlines of Obregón's political strategy to offset regional political families with agrarista and labor support. The Figueroas based their support on their military power and their control over the federal military and local volunteer forces. The Neris were backed by agrarian and labor support. Much like Porfirio Díaz before him, Obregón ruled by dividing. This was a far cry indeed from an all-powerful state. A perusal of Ernest Gruening's classic *Mexico and Its Heritage* provides additional evidence of the internecine fights in the states during the early 1920s.[32] The de la Huerta rebellion in 1923 was, to a large extent, a regionally based uprising. The Figueroas, who had lost out to Obregón's allies, for example, joined the rebels.

The defeat of de la Huerta did not end the struggle by any means. Calles, from 1925 to 1927, undertook a full-scale effort to exert federal government control over the states in which he deposed twenty-five governors.[33] In Chihuahua, the future "jefe máximo" thwarted the emerging dynasty of the Almeida family, whose members barely escaped with life and limb during a successful coup against them.[34] Even the hard-nosed Calles, however, could not move either Tomás Garrido Canabal or Saturnino Cedillo.

While centralization had made enormous progress by the end of the 1920s and the founding of the Partido Nacional Revolucionario in 1929 would help even more, the Mexican state was a long way from being all powerful. It would take Cárdenas to defeat Garrido and Cedillo. Even with the demise of Cedillo in a pointless rebellion in 1938, the Cardenista state resembled more the Porfirista state, founded more firmly on alliances with regional bosses than on omnipotence. Cárdenas, most importantly, improved on Obregón's great innovation in state-building by carrying the popular element to its zenith of influence. Squarely relying on agrarian and labor-union support to counterbalance the army and other opposition, Cárdenas, as Obregón before him, used popular support to strengthen the national state against regional power holders. The crucial struggle to form the Mexican state was, therefore, inseparable from the popular aspect of the revolution. In the end, it was the popular classes who enabled the national state to triumph. The organizations of the popular classes, labor unions, and peasant leagues looked to the national government for support; for the interests of state and local elites—no longer, if they had ever been, revolutionaries—directly conflicted with their own aspirations to better wages and the acquisition of land. The national state needed the assistance of popular organizations in the regions in its struggle to bring under control these very same elites. Cárdenas rewarded the popular classes, but, on the whole, the state would prove an ungrateful beneficiary in the years that followed.

In the end, we reach three conclusions. First, historians, in the backlash of disillusionment following the harsh repression of the 1960s and the end of the economic miracle in 1980, have underestimated the extent of popular participation in the revolution, both during its violent stage, 1910 to 1920, and its transition stage, 1920 to 1940. Peasants were both the soldiers of the violent revolution and the pillars of the new state. The closer one examines the regions in revolution, the more important the popular classes become. The 1920s were an era of transition, when peasants acted as warriors in various national (though regionally based) rebellions and innumerable local conflicts and also as organized backers of the first populist *caudillos* like Adalberto Tejeda and then of the national state led by Lazaro Cárdenas. Second, the national, centralized state did not emerge until late in the Cárdenas era. There was no state at all from 1914 to 1917. The 1920s were a period of transition, featuring regionally based *caudillos* in conflict with centralizing presidents, Obregón and Calles, who, while making some inroads, had to rely as much on wile as force to maintain control. Third, the evolution of the state and the popular revolution were inextricably entwined. It was not until the popular rebellion was "tamed," so to speak, and channeled from violence in the regions and localities to organized leagues and political parties that the strong national state emerged. Obregón began this process with his land redistribution program and support of the Confederación Regional de Obreros Mexicanos (CROM). Cárdenas perfected the strategy. Thus, the revisionists are, at least, partially wrong; for it was not the lack of popular revolution that led to the formation of the bourgeois (or corporatist) state, but rather the fact that the popular movement was channeled from regional violence into a revolution from above.

In Part I, contributors David LaFrance, John Tutino, and Thomas Benjamin examine the Madero, Huerta–Carranza, and Obregón–Calles stages, respectively, to place the popular and regional aspects of the revolution in comparative perspective. LaFrance maintains that the rebellions in Hidalgo, San Luis Potosí, and the Huasteca, like those of the Zapatistas and Yaquis, erupted from profound agrarian discontent. In agreement with Beezley and Knight, he concludes that Madero's failure resulted from his inability to address locally based popular grievances. Tutino explains the success and failures of the warring factions in the 1913 to 1917 period in terms of their regional and popular origins. The regional support of the Zapatistas and Villistas proved to be both their greatest strengths and fatal weaknesses. In particular, their differing views of land reform prevented any lasting alliance between the two movements.

To Benjamin, the 1920s were an era of weak central government that permitted some states to conduct radical experiments. Most of the nation did not want Mexico City to rule. Consequently, Obregón, and to a lesser extent Calles, could not have governed without the support of radical and reformist state bosses. None of the "laboratories of revolution," however, radically changed the social fabric. Ironically, the popular organizations they created were used ultimately to defeat the very reform they advocated.

Part II explores the revolution in six states: Yucatán, San Luis Potosí, Oaxaca, Tamaulipas, Chihuahua, and Tlaxcala. Gilbert Joseph and Allen Wells seek to explain why, despite considerable contention among rival elite factions and the existence of continuing and significant unrest in the countryside, there was no generalized rebellion in Yucatán. Unlike people in other regions, especially in the north, Yucatecan dissidents did not unite, even temporarily, to produce the Maderista revolt. It would take Salvador Alvarado and eight thousand troops to bring the revolution to the peninsula in 1915.

In Romana Falcón's view, the period from 1913 to 1917 was the time with the greatest potential for radical reform. Central authority was at its lowest ebb. If popular grievances engendered the revolution, then reform would have manifested itself on the local level. Although she concludes that local upheavals in San Luis Potosí originated from rural protests, reform initially was delayed by the exigencies of the armed struggle—the hardest fighting took place during these years—and was later ended by Carranza.

The Oaxacan Sovereignty Movement, according to Paul Garner, was another product of the struggle between central and state authority. More so than in other regions, though, it was a political struggle. There was no agrarian revolt in Oaxaca. Like Knight, Garner argues that revolutionary labels often depended more on local or regional than national issues.

Heather Salamini reiterates the theme presented in earlier works that the weakness of central authority during the 1920s spawned a new kind of civilian-led populism. Using reform as a political tool, state governor–*caudillos* built power bases. Ironically, by harnessing the popular movement, labor unions, and peasant leagues they created a transitional stage to centralization. Calles and Cárdenas, through the revolutionary party, swept away the populist *caudillos* in the 1930s, taking over their peasant and worker organizations. Cárdenas made the popular sector the pillar of his regime.

In Chihuahua, politics during the 1920s played out as a three-tiered struggle: the first between factions to control local politics and keep state authorities from extending their power; the second at the state level between rival groups and the third between state factions and the national regime. I conclude that even by 1930 the federal government had not exerted control in Chihuahua, leaving the state in chaos. Here, as elsewhere, reform was used as a political tool.

Raymond Buve analyzes a similar interplay of local, state, and national politics in Tlaxcala during the 1920s. He maintains that a ruling group emerged there that established a "dependent cacicazgo" with strong central government support. Civilian politicians brokered the divisions between villages (or ejidos) to perpetuate themselves in power. The popular movement was divided and then controlled.

Part III consists of two broad-ranging essays by Stuart Voss and Thomas Benjamin that draw together the strands of regionalism and revolution. To Voss the revolutionary years from 1910 to 1940 saw the culmination of two long-standing conflicts over who was to rule Mexico and thus accrue the benefits of its economic resources and on what geographic scale these social interests were to be best served. The struggle ended with the victory of centralization and the suppression of reform under Manuel Avila Camacho. Benjamin concludes the volume with an overview of the development of regional historiography.

Notes

1. Recent discussions of revolutionary historiography include: William H. Beezley, "The Mexican Revolution: A Review," *Latin American Research Review* (hereafter cited as *LARR*) 13:3 (1978): 299–306; Thomas Benjamin, "The Leviathan on the Zócalo: Recent Historiography of the Post-Revolutionary Mexican State," *LARR* 20:3 (1985): 195–217; Alma M. García, "Recent Studies in Nineteenth and Early Twentieth Century Regional Mexican History," *LARR* 22:2 (1987): 255–66; Mark T. Gilderhaus, "Many Mexicos: Traditions and Innovations in Recent Historiography," *LARR* 22:1 (1987): 204–13; John M. Hart, "The Dynamics of the Mexican Revolution: Historigraphical Perspectives," LARR 19:3 (1984): 223–31; Simon Miller, "Recent Studies of the Porfiriato," *Bulletin of Latin American Research* 6:1 (1988): 83–87; Paul Vanderwood, "Building Blocks but Yet No Building: Regional History and the Mexican Revolution," *Mexican Studies/Estudios Mexicanos* 3:2 (Summer 1987): 421–32.

2. Roger D. Hansen, *The Politics of Mexican Development* (Baltimore: Johns Hopkins Press, 1971), 166–67. See also the discussions of the evolution of the Mexican state in Nora Hamilton, *The Limits of State Autonomy: Post-Revolutionary Mexico* (Princeton: Princeton University Press, 1982), 174–79 and D. A. Brading, "Introduction," in *Caudillo and Peasant in the Mexican Revolution*, ed. Brading (Cambridge: Cambridge University Press, 1980), 8–9.

3. Frank Tannenbaum, *The Mexican Agrarian Revolution* (Washington, D.C.: The Brookings Institution, 1929), 186–87. Ramón Eduardo Ruiz, *The Great Rebellion: Mexico, 1905–1924* (New York: Norton, 1980), ix. See also David C. Bailey, "Revisionism and the Recent Historiography of the Mexican Revolution," *Hispanic American Historical Review* 58:1 (February 1978): 62–79.

4. Friedrich Katz, *The Secret War in Mexico: Europe, the United States, and the Mexican Revolution* (Chicago: University of Chicago Press, 1981), 3–49 and passim.

5. Alan Knight, "The Mexican Revolution," *History Today* 30 (May 1980): 28.

6. See the review essay by Alan Knight, "Review of Gilbert M. Joseph, *Revolution from Without: Yucatán, Mexico, and the United States, 1880–1924* (Cambridge: Cambridge University Press, 1982); Ian Jacobs, *Ranchero Revolt: The Mexican Revolution in Guerrero* (Austin: University of Texas Press, 1983); W. Dirk Raat, *The Mexican Revolution: An Annotated Guide to Recent Scholarship* (Boston: G. K. Hall, 1982); and Gene Z. Hanrahan, *Blood Below the Border: American Eye-Witness Accounts of the Mexican Revolution* (Salisbury, N.C.: Documentary Publications, 1982), in the *Journal of Latin American Studies* 16 (November 1984): 526.

7. Alan Knight, "Peasant and Caudillo in Revolutionary Mexico, 1910–17," in *Peasant and Caudillo in the Mexican Revolution*, 19.

8. Hamilton, *The Limits of State Autonomy*, 3.

9. Alan Knight, "The Mexican Revolution: Bourgeois? Nationalist? Or Just a 'Great Rebellion,' " *Bulletin of Latin American Research* 4: 3 (1985): 5, 12–15.

10. Dudley Ankerson, *Agrarian Warlord: Saturnino Cedillo and the Mexican Revolution in San Luis Potosí* (DeKalb: Northern Illinois University Press, 1984); Romana Falcón, *Revolución y caciquismo: San Luis Potosí, 1910–1939* (México: El Colegio de México, 1984); Alan M. Kirshner, *Tomás Garrido Canabal y el movimiento de las Camisas Rojas* (México: Sepsententas, 1976); Lorenzo Meyer, *El conflicto social y los gobiernos del Maximato, Historia de la Revolución Mexicana: Periodo 1928–1934* (México: El Colegio de México, 1978), 287–319.

11. Knight, "Peasant and Caudillo, 19–20.

12. Friedrich Katz, "Peasants in the Mexican Revolution," in *Forging Nations: A Comparative View of Rural Ferment and Revolt* ed. Joseph Spielburg and Scott Whiteford (East Lansing: Michigan State University Press, 1976).

13. Knight, "Peasant and Caudillo," 21–37; Alan Knight, *The Mexican Revolution* (Cambridge: Cambridge University Press, 1986), 1:151–70.

14. Evelyn Hu DeHart, *Yaqui Resistance and Survival: The Struggle for Land and Autonomy, 1821–1910* (Madison: University of Wisconsin Press, 1984); Jacobs, *Ranchero Revolt*; Frans J. Schryer, *The Rancheros of Pisaflores* (Toronto: University of Toronto Press, 1980); Joseph, *Revolution from Without*; Heather F. Salamini, *Agrarian Radicalism in Veracruz, 1920–1938* (Lincoln: University of Nebraska Press, 1971); Salamini, "Tamaulipas," in this volume.

15. Heather F. Salamini, "Revolutionary Caudillos in the 1920s: Francisco Mújica and Adalberto Tejeda," in *Caudillo and Peasant in the Mexican Revolution*, 170.

16. Dudley Ankerson, "Saturnino Cedillo, a traditional caudillo in San Luis Potosí 1890–1938," in *Peasant and Caudillo in the Mexican Revolution*, 140–41.

17. Joseph, *Revolution from Without*, 111.

18. Salamini, "Revolutionary Caudillos," 171.

19. Knight, *The Mexican Revolution*, 2: 88.

20. Ibid., 2: 54.

21. Ibid., 1: 301.

22. Ibid., 1: 302.

23. William H. Beezley, "Madero: The 'Unknown' President and His Political Failure to Organize Mexico," in *Essays on the Mexican Revolution: Revisionist Views of Its Leaders*, ed. George Wolfskill and Douglas W. Richmond (Austin: University of Texas Press, 1979), 13.

24. Beezley, "Madero," 12.

25. Ibid., p. 13.

26. Knight, *The Mexican Revolution*, 1: 467.

27. Of course, we have to be careful here to realize that not all local movements were popularly based. Counterrevolutionaries rebelled in the localities and regions as well. Sometimes, as Knight often reminds us, local and regional rebellions had a logic of their own, responding to specific alignments and issues on those levels. It was not unlikely that popular and reactionary groups could ally as they did in Chihuahua in 1912 in the revolt of Pascual Orozco.

28. Beezley, "Madero," 6.

29. Joseph, *Revolution from Without*, 94.

30. Jacobs, *Ranchero Revolt*, 112.

31. Ibid.

32. Ernest Gruening, *Mexico and Its Heritage* (New York: The Century Co., 1928), 393–493.

33. Jean Meyer, *Estado y sociedad con Calles. Historia de la Revolución Mexicana: Periódo 1924–1928* (México: El Colegio de México, 1977), 182.

34. See Chapter 9.

Part I

Regionalism and the Mexican Revolution

2

Many Causes, Movements, Failures, 1910–1913

The Regional Nature of Maderismo

David LaFrance

It may seem trite to state once again that Mexico is, even today, a nation of regions despite the efforts of regimes from that of Benito Juárez in the ninetenth century to today's ruling party, the Institutional Revolutionary Party (PRI), to wield all-embracing and effective control from the national level. Therefore, a view of Mexican history from a regional perspective can provide a very different and instructive view of the nation's development.

One of the earlier, and at least for a while, seemingly more effective efforts to tame and corral Mexico's regions was that of the dictator Porfirio Díaz (1876–1911). As time would prove, however, Díaz's policies did not eliminate this phenomenon. Instead, many of his developmental policies actually exacerbated longtime centrifugal tendencies. The intrusion of increasing central government control and modern economic capitalistic practices disrupted more traditional political and economic structures and tied previously quite autonomous areas more closely to the vicissitudes of the policies of Mexico City and world markets. By the first decade of this century, regional elements of all socioeconomic stripes had begun to question and even challenge Díaz's threatening ways.

Little that was concrete could be achieved, however, to redress the threat to regional interests by the Díaz regime, as indicated by the early failures of the so-called "precursor movement" after 1900, until exogenous economic and political circumstances (the impact of the United States economy and the debate over Díaz's successor) changed later in the decade. These factors, then, allowed for the birth of competing political movements, including that of Francisco I. Madero, himself the son of a frustrated and economically threatened regional elite family. Madero's call for political reform (leavened only lightly with socioeconomic content) quickly garnered support from large numbers of regional elements.

Madero's political and then revolutionary support enabling him to overthrow the Díaz dictatorship came primarily, although not exclusively, from two regions of the country. The most important was that composed of the five contiguous northwestern states of Chihuahua, Sonora, Sinaloa, Durango, and Coahuila. The second principal region was that of the five adjoining central states of Guerrero, Morelos, Puebla, Tlaxcala, and Veracruz. Other areas, especially western and southeastern Mexico, proved to be much less involved in the Maderista movement between 1909 and 1911.

Madero's rise to power in 1911 meant the establishment of at least nominally Maderista governments in all the nation's states. Nevertheless, continuing opposition to Madero, from the Porfirian right and then increasingly from the left as the revolutionary cum president proved incapable (and unwilling) to undertake significant changes, soon undermined the new government. In this case, too, the most serious rebel movements to challenge the administration came from the northwestern and central states that had earlier provided Madero with his main base of support. Again, other parts of the country boasted only marginal insurrections against the central government. Although not immediately nor directly successful, these anti-Madero movements did help to weaken the regime, thus nurturing the February 1913 coup d'etat headed by General Victoriano Huerta that finally toppled Madero from power. In turn, ironically, Huerta in 1913 and 1914, and then Venustiano Carranza from 1915 to 1920, would have to face armed challenges to their governments from, again, these same two regions of the country.

Origins

At the risk of oversimplification, two phenomenon can be posited as the principal factors causing the Madero revolution, capitalistic penetration of the economy and society and increasing central government control of the political system. Each had far-reaching and complex repercussions, and their impact was greatest in the northwestern and central regions of the country, the areas where the Maderistas were strongest.

Capitalistic penetration of the country during the Porfiriato had several important economic and social effects. It tied Mexico's economy more closely to the outside world (especially the United States). This linkage led to severe dislocations in 1905 when Mexico devalued its silver-based currency, the peso, and switched to the gold standard, and again after 1907 when economic depression in the United States hurt the Mexican mining, textile, and agricultural sectors with thousands of people suddenly out of work. The opening of foreign markets to Mexico's natural resources, mainly foodstuffs and minerals, combined with the introduction of the railroad, prompted the rapid commercialization and modernization of agriculture and mining, the disruption of traditional economic practices, the loss of village lands, rising prices, and the shortage of basic commodities. The competition of foreign investment and the presence of many non-Mexicans in the country provoked a nationalistic reaction (including attacks on foreigners). The creation of a select domestic elite, allied with foreign interests at the expense of other nationals, especially hurt certain key provincial upper-class interests. Meanwhile, the middle class chafed under inequitable taxes and limited economic opportunities while the lower classes, both urban and rural, struggled to survive under generally deteriorating conditions.

Díaz's program of political centralization also had significant repercussions that led to the alienation of regional elements. A smoothly functioning "investment-worthy" modern state could not tolerate troublesome autonomous regions. Central government interference in state and local affairs meant the imposition of outsiders, encouraged abusive and corrupt authorities, and frustrated politically ambitious locals not allied with the regime. It also threatened the integrity of the pueblo (particularly *municipio libre*) and led to strict enforcement of the universally hated levy.

These two factors alone, capitalistic advances and political centralization, however, are not enough to explain fully why Maderismo took solid root in the northwest and center of the country. Indeed, other areas of the nation also underwent similar experiences, yet failed to back the movement strongly. The Maderistas also prospered, then, where the liberal movement, including its later more radical manifestation, the Partido Liberal Mexicano (PLM), had been most active between 1900 and 1910. Although unsuccessful in toppling the Díaz regime, the PLM offered a coherent alternative political and socioeconomic program (much of which eventually would be incorporated, unofficially at least, into the Maderista program); forced the authorities to step up their repression, thus exposing even more clearly the contradictions within the regime and alienating more people; organized principally urban workers; and trained an armed cadre that would play an important role in the Madero revolution. Another factor was the activities of the Protestant, and especially the Methodist, church in the northwest and center of the nation. Its calls for civil rights and constitutional liberties appealed to many. Probably the most well-known Protestant of the revolution was Pascual Orozco, but many other insurgents, especially old-line liberals already wary of or hostile to the Catholic church, came under Protestant influence. A mobile work force also seems to have been a prerequisite for successful political organizing. In those areas where workers had the option of geographic and occupational mobility, they were much more aware of their condition and surroundings, less dependent upon the largess of bosses and owners, able to make mutually beneficial contacts, and generally more willing to get involved in political activity. Students, too, played an important role in the movement; often the offspring of provincial urban elites, they gained theoretical knowledge and political experience in the state capital and then went home to proselytize their family and friends. Finally, it is evident that the Maderistas prospered most where there existed strong local leaders willing to risk themselves for the cause. This type of person, like Abraham González in Chihuahua and Aquiles Serdán in Puebla, seems to have been most prevalent in the northwest and center, perhaps because of coincidence but more likely as a result of the circumstances in which they lived, for both were from old middle-class families marginalized from the Díaz regime. [1]

The north of Mexico has long been recognized as a region apart from the remainder of the country. It exhibited several historically well-defined characteristics that help to explain why it was the most rebellious region throughout the Madero period as well as during the entire revolution. Distant and quite isolated from the influence of central Mexico and lacking a large sedentary Indian population, the north developed without the same degree of constraint that the Catholic church, state, and hacienda imposed on other areas of the country. With labor scarce and mobile and formed by a frontier mentality, there existed a large degree of socioeconomic and geographical mobility and opportunity for the self-made man. Many of these people came to resent the closed Porfirian system. Although influenced by United States economic and political liberalism (many having visited or lived north of the border), they disliked foreign monopolization of large sectors of the economy. To these elements, then, the calls for political change by Madero, himself a northerner, had much appeal. [2]

In Chihuahua, the focal point of the Maderista revolution in the northwest, monopolization of economic and political life by the Terrazas-Creel family and the intrusion of the railroad caused deep-seated discontent among a cross-section of society from the middle class and small landowners to the workers. The PLM also added to the widespread local tension by provoking harsh government crackdowns. After 1905 the state suffered greatly from widespread encroachment on communal and municipal lands following the implementation of the Municipal Land Law of that year. Then, after 1907, the international economic turndown hurt industry and agriculture while poor weather only exacerbated the difficult situation. Indeed, Mexico's close and dependent economic relationship with the United States became very evident after the 1907 crisis; and the inability of the U.S. to absorb Chihuahua's discontented and unemployed laborers forced many to return to or remain at home where they joined the revolutionary armies. A good example of this type of worker was José Inéz Salazar, who found employment on both sides of the border as a miner, railroad hand, foreman, and smuggler before joining the PLM and then the Maderistas in 1910. Meanwhile, middle-class leadership emerged in the persons of Abraham González, Silvestre Terrazas, and, in the volatile and mountainous western part of the state, Pascual Orozco.[3]

In neighboring Sonora, the foreign-aided economic boom of the Porfiriato had uneven and divisive effects. It barely touched such traditional centers of economic and political power as Alamos and Hermosillo, but had a large impact on other areas like Guaymas and Navajoa. The latters' economic fortune, however, was not accompanied by a corresponding increase in political power, thus causing a breach between the new rich and the old political elite. These upstarts, along with disaffected lower-middle-class elements who also benefited from the boom but resented the powerful and wealthy traditional bourgeoisie in the state, united to initiate the Madero movement. One of its principal leaders, hacendado José María Maytorena, led a group of fellow wealthy landowners, professionals, and petty entrepreneurs against the regime. Their major grievances were the government's policies of encouraging foreign developers in the state and the carrying out of Indian extermination campaigns, both of which endangered the elite's precarious labor supply. Anti-foreign sentiment took its most concrete manifestation in the form of attacks on Chinese who dominated petty commerce in many northwestern towns.[4]

Durango, another northwestern state leavened with liberal influence and anti-Americanism as a result of large United States investments in mines and haciendas, also played an important role in the Madero period. Foreign control of mining tied Durango to the world silver market, which collapsed after 1895. New investments in agriculture also accelerated the growth of capital-intensive joint-stock companies destroying the old paternalistic hacendado–client relationship heretofore predominant on the state's haciendas. This process resulted in the rise of a mobile wage labor system and the displacement of peasants who then joined the revolutionary armies. Díaz's protection of foreign investors at the expense of middle-class interests also alienated this key sector of the state's society.[5]

In Coahuila, Madero's home state, discontent also existed, especially among rancheros and the urban petty bourgeoisie who resented the unequal tax structure, foreign economic intrusion, and the monopolization of the political system by Díaz cronies. Unemployment among rural workers, inadequate and unequal educational and health services, and threats to village autonomy by large landowners also agitated the lower classes. As in other areas of the northwest, the 1907 economic downturn combined with the 1910 drought, which drastically cut food supplies for rural dwellers, added to the tension. Here foreigners, too, became targets of a rising nationalistic backlash as peons singled out Spanish-owned businesses and ranches. Finally, the defeat of Madero-backed Venustiano Carranza for the governorship in 1909 by a Díaz-imposed candidate, Jesús del Valle, gained many supporters for the Maderista cause.[6]

The cotton-growing Comarca Lagunera, located along the Coahuila–Durango border, became a particularly fecund seedbed of revolutionary activity. Anti-foreign sentiment, caused by the monopolistic concession Díaz granted to the Tlahualilo Company, abounded as this British and United States–owned concern competed for water, labor, and markets with Mexican producers and exploited the area's workers. Small landowners and Indian villagers also resented the encroaching cotton hacienda (both national and foreign-owned), while landless agricultural laborers experienced the insecurity of intermittent work, low wages, and high prices. Many workers in the region had experience in the United States or along the international border and were considered by owners to be more "uppity" than their less worldly colleagues. Here, too, the 1907 depression hit hard as Mexico's textile industry slumped. Both the PLM and Madero found large numbers of supporters in the Laguna, and recruits from the area formed a key element in Madero's army. In fact, Madero cut his own political teeth in the Laguna in 1905 when he organized groups backing an anti-Díaz candidate for the governorship of Coahuila. His activity gained him respect and helped establish his reputation as a "man of the people."[7]

Sinaloa, a state of sharp contrasts and inequalities, also produced a large and active Maderista contingent by 1910. There, modern coastal plantations, many of whose owners felt closed out of the Díaz political system, encroached on traditional Indian communities. The isolated and backward mountain areas consisted of small marginal farmers and miners, the latter of whom severely felt the economic downturn of 1907 and the threat of large foreign operators who were moving into the area. In the urban areas, such as Culiacán and Mazatlán, there existed a growing but frustrated middle class. Two important elements of this middle sector, professionals and students, teamed up in 1909 to back the journalist José Ferrel for the governorship. In a clearly rigged contest, however, he was defeated by the Díaz-imposed hacendado and industrialist, Diego Redo, thus adding to the discontent and tension in the state.[8]

Unlike the north and particularly the northwest, the second major region of Maderista activity, the center, was a more traditional area where the state,

Catholic church, and hacienda generally wielded a constraining influence on society. Nevertheless, certain parts of the region, especially the sierras of Guerrero and Puebla; the Guerrero, Morelos, and Puebla lowlands; the Atoyac River valley; and the industrialized zones of Puebla, Tlaxcala, and Veracruz demonstrated many of the same characteristics of the northwest that provided the basis for a strong Maderista movement: capitalistic penetration, political centralization, the influence of the liberal movement and the Protestant church, a mobile work force, activist students, and a strong leadership.

In Guerrero, two distinct foci of activism developed to join the Maderista movement. In the northern highlands, middle-class dissidents (professionals, small merchants, students, intellectuals, rancheros, and some hacendados), influenced by the liberal movement, joined together to protest the Díaz government's encroaching political power and the imposition of outsiders. Led by the Figueroa brothers, a prosperous ranchero family, they wanted to return to the halcyon days of greater local and regional autonomy of the nineteenth century when they dominated the political scene. In the coastal lowlands, where commercial tropical crops were produced by haciendas and small leaseholders, resentment ran strongly among the peasantry, especially against Spanish owners. Here, adherence to the Maderista cause would be slower to develop than in the sierra and would eventually take the form of Zapatismo.[9]

In Morelos, an aggressive planter class attempted to take advantage of an expanding world sugar market (stimulated in large part by the introduction of the railroad), while simultaneously warding off increasing domestic and international competition. By 1908 the state had become the third largest sugar-producing area of the world (after Hawaii and Puerto Rico), but this growth came at the expense of Morelos's peasants and their villages, eighteen of which disappeared between 1884 and 1905 as haciendas gobbled up land and imported new labor-saving capital equipment. Hacendado control of the economic and political systems of the state alienated other groups, too, including small merchants, students, intellectuals, and professionals. Movement into Madero's ranks came quickly following the 1909 gubernatorial election in which, as in other states, Díaz once again imposed an official candidate, this time the planter-backed Pablo Escandón, over the favorite of the "outs," Francisco Leyva.[10]

The Maderista movement in Puebla made early and strong gains, especially in the central part of the state delimited by the Atoyac River valley. There, mainly urban elements (middle-class professionals, artisans, shopkeepers, workers, and students), formed by a tradition of protest and mobility, resented the heavy-handed and corrupt rule of the longtime (since 1892) gov-

ernor, Mucio Martínez. Limited political opportunity and deteriorating economic conditions (Puebla was very dependent upon a depressed textile industry
between 1907 and 1910), combined with poor crops, agitation by the PLM,
and the message of the Protestant church, had an important impact. Of particular influence on the success of the Maderistas in Puebla was the leadership
of the shoemaker, Aquiles Serdán. In the southern lowlands of the state, geographically an extension of neighboring Morelos, villagers also faced the relentless incursion of the sugar hacienda. The mountainous northern area of the
state, as opposed to the south, did not so much fear and suffer from the loss
of land as from threats to its traditionally autonomous and isolated way of life
by outside political forces and capitalistic intruders, such as the railroad and
the huge Necaxa hydroelectric project which supplied power to Mexico City
and surrounding states.[11]

To a large degree, central and southern Tlaxcala was an extension of central Puebla, with both states sharing the Atoyac River valley, an area in transition to a capitalistic industrial economy. Here, nearly everyone chafed under
the deadening hand of Governor Próspero Cahuantzi (who served a total of
twenty-six years in office). Hacendados and the urban elite were hurt especially hard by the 1907–1910 depression. Industrial workers, artisans, and
campesinos, influenced by the PLM, the Protestant church, and a hatred for
Spanish-owned factories, farms, and shops, formed the backbone of the
Maderista movement in the area under the local leadership of Juan Cuamatzi,
a collaborator of Serdán.[12]

In Veracruz, Maderista support was mostly confined to the industrial areas
of Orizaba–Río Blanco and Atoyac, located in the highlands along the Puebla
border. There, textile-mill hands, like their counterparts in Puebla and Tlaxcala,
labored under generally harsh and deteriorating conditions, often for foreign
(mainly French and Spanish) owners and bosses. Influenced by the PLM and a
tradition of protest (remember the Río Blanco strike and killings of 1906–1907),
these workers early on took an active part in the movement.[13]

At this point the question must be asked why, if other regions of the country also experienced some of these same phenomenon, such as capitalistic penetration and political centralization, did they not also form a strong and active
base of support for Madero? There seems to be no totally satisfactory answer,
but a brief examination of several factors helps to shed light on the problem.

In some isolated areas of Mexico, especially the southeast and west, only a
minimum of outside information reached most of the populace, thus greatly
reducing the opportunities for political consciousness and mobilization. In
Chiapas and Tabasco, for example, people commonly remained ignorant of

the revolution until 1913 and 1914, when the Maderista phase had already ended.[14] Even where word of the upheaval was received, such as in Mascota (via mule driver), a town located in the mountains of Jalisco, its isolation from the centers of Maderista activity made any political action difficult. The community, in fact, did not even receive its first revolutionaries until 1913. Consequently, Porfirian institutions and practices there continued to function uninterrupted through the Madero years.[15] Indeed, one student of the revolution estimates "that perhaps about 71 percent (the percentage of Mexicans living in communities smaller than 2,500 inhabitants in 1910) of the population in revolutionary Mexico may have been unaffected by the revolution during its violent phase."[16] Surely the percentage was even greater during the Madero years.

Isolation also certainly played a key role in Yucatán where Maderista activity was quite circumscribed. Nevertheless, here, where the henequén industry represented a high degree of foreign capitalistic influence and the Molina and Peón families maintained centralized control over the state, other factors also kept political activity to a minimum. The overwhelmingly repressive power of the hacendados and their allies in the state and local governments thwarted any attempt to organize the campesino. The strength of the hacienda system came largely at the expense of the village, meaning that the rural workers' almost complete dependence on the hacienda aided the owners in maintaining control. Yucatecan elites also easily shed their pro-Díaz sentiments and nominally joined the Maderista cause, thus preempting middle-class challenges to the upper classes or efforts to organize the lower ones. Consequently, Yucatán did not feel the full brunt of the revolution until 1915, with the arrival of the Constitutionalist armies from the north.[17]

Other areas, too, experienced little political activity during the Madero period, mainly because of the dominant nature of the hacienda. Even in the face of a serious deterioration in their standard of living, for example, the campesinos of the German-owned coffee plantations of the Soconusco area of Chiapas remained relatively subdued. Similar circumstances also existed in Campeche, Tabasco, and southern Veracruz.[18] Even in Tlaxcala, a state whose central and southern zones were highly politicized, peasants in the north remained largely impotent in the face of the powerful pulque hacienda.[19]

Another factor impeding political activity was due to people relatively satisfied with (or at least not conscious of) their lot. In Oaxaca, peasants generally were docile because most land remained part of traditional village holdings; coffee and cochineal production (the state's two most important commercial crops) were labor intensive and efficiently grown on small plots. Only in the areas of Tuxtepec and La Cañada, where sugar and tobacco were important, did haciendas take over large amounts of village lands, thereby provoking violence during the Madero period.[20]

Relative satisfaction, leading to a minimum of political protest, can also be found in other areas. The state of Mexico, which shares borders with the activist central states discussed above, took little part in the Maderista movement. Nearly all revolutionary influence in the state came from the outside, mainly from the Zapatistas to the south. Throughout the nineteenth century, the state remained relatively stable as the takeover of indigenous lands mostly had taken place a hundred years earlier, still leaving property for many people which the paternalistic state and local officials tended to protect against further encroachment. People in less prosperous circumstances had the opportunity to migrate to nearby Mexico City or to other areas of the state. The economic difficulties of the Porfiriato had only minimal impact on consumers as prices rose less than at the national rate; supplies of basic foodstuffs remained adequate; and mines and industry, well capitalized by large concerns, avoided serious downturns. In general, Mexico City, the nation's seat of power, exercised a conservative and stabilizing force on the state.[21]

Nuevo León, which shares a border with the activist states of the northwest, also seems to follow the pattern of the state of Mexico. There, a tradition of land division existed before the Porfiriato, while industrialization, urbanization, and access to opportunities outside the area (in this case, the United States) undermined the tendency found elsewhere for political agitation. Much the same can also be said of Aguascalientes.[22]

A final, more all-embracing explanation for agrarian rebellion or its absence has to do with the relative security experienced by peasants. Rural elements, according to the theory, are disposed to tolerate poor, even exploitative, conditions within a dependent situation (Yucatán, for example) as long as their lot is basically predictable and stable. When insecurity arises, however, campesinos will opt to struggle for their independence (in Morelos or Chihuahua, for example).[23]

Revolution

For over a year, from the spring of 1909 to the summer of 1910, Madero attempted, at least publicly, to seek a peaceful route to power by challenging Díaz in the June 1910 presidential election. During the campaign Madero visited twenty-two states, some more than once, taking advantage of the widespread discontent in many parts of the nation to gain and organize support.

Local efforts, overcoming such obstacles as internal divisions, official perse-cution, and the lack of funds, proved to be quite successful as several hun-dred Anti-Reelectionist political clubs composed of thousands of members were formed, with the great majority, although not all, in the northwestern and central regions of the country.

All things considered, Díaz allowed Madero a relatively free hand to carry out his opposition electoral campaign; for many months, the dictator was more concerned with the movement nominally led by the general and former Nuevo León governor, Bernardo Reyes, than the young, somewhat eccentric, and seeminly harmless Madero. It was not until April 1910, when Madero presided over a highly successful national Anti-Reelectionist convention held in Mexico City, that Díaz began to take his challenger more seriously. After that date, both Madero and his followers came under increasing harassment, culminating in Madero's June 1910 arrest in Monterrey.

Before Madero's incarceration, which proved Díaz's insincerity in claiming to want a free and fair election, local Anti-Reelectionist leaders in the center and in the northwest, many of whom were in close contact with the PLM, pressed Madero to shed his electoral façade and choose the revolutionary option. Even as early as late 1909 the Anti-Reelectionist club in the mining town of Cananea, Sonora, initiated plans to rebel in June 1910. The plot failed, how-ever, when someone notified the police. In Puebla, Aquiles Serdán attempted a trio of May 1910 uprisings in the Puebla-Atlixco-Tlaxcala area. Because of poor organization and especially the lack of arms, only one of the rebellions got off the ground, that led by Juan Cuamatzi in Tlaxcala. It too came to naught, however, when a hostage escaped and warned the government. Then, in June 1910, Sinaloan Anti-Reelectionist activist Gabriel Leyva, goaded into rebellion by the authorities, was soon caught by the Rurales and "shot while trying to escape." He provided the Maderistas with their first martyr.[24]

While being held by the government in the city of San Luis Potosí during the summer of 1910, Madero finally came to the decision to head an armed revolution against Díaz. In early October, dressed as a railroad mechanic (rail-road workers in many areas of central and northern Mexico cooperated closely with the Maderistas carrying messages and, later, arms), he escaped to San Antonio, Texas, where supporters from around the country awaited him. In the southern Texas city Madero and his aides drew up the Plan de San Luis Potosí, calling for revolution on 20 November 1910. Named by Madero to head armed movements and to form governments in their respective states, the conspirators then returned to Mexico.

On 12 November, police captured two of Madero's principal agents in Mexico City and confiscated documents outlining the revolutionary conspiracy for all of central Mexico. Subsequent arrests in Tlaxcala brought to light even more detailed plans for the Puebla-Tlaxcala-Veracruz region under the general leadership of Aquiles Serdán. Serdán, who had contacts with Maderistas and the PLM from Guerrero to Veracruz, was to head a rebellion from his home in the center of the city of Puebla in coordination with other uprisings in the region. When the local authorities moved to arrest Serdán and his immediate followers, he decided to revolt two days ahead of schedule on 18 November. The rebellion failed and Serdán was killed.

Serdán's defeat and death had repercussions for the Madero revolution not only in Puebla but throughout the nation. First, it provided the movement with a second and even more well-known martyr. Second, it meant the loss of one of Madero's most influential and effective adherents. Third, it undermined any chance of a successful rebellion on 20 November. Fourth, the subsequent governmental crackdown on the mainly urban-based movement forced it to the countryside, where it became more decentralized, increasingly divided, and subject to control and manipulation by rural caciques who often were more committed to their own agendas than to Maderista principles and objectives. As a result, to the ideological and class divisions already apparent within the ranks of the movement were now added the cultural differences between city and countryside, often expressed in terms of the modern versus the traditional. Finally, Serdán's death and the movement's relocation to the rural areas also set back the revolutionaries' timetable. In all areas of the country, except along the Sierra Madre Occidental in the northwest, the movement would not show sure signs of recovery until February and March 1911.[25]

The heart of the rebellion in the northwest was located in the western sierra of Chihuahua, sometimes referred to as the cradle of the revolution. The movement in the area must be credited principally to Pascual Orozco, a twenty-eight-year-old mule driver with many connections, including the PLM, in the predominantly mining and lumbering region. Orozco took up arms on 19 November 1910, and, along with allies in other areas, such as the Arrietas in Durango, managed to hold the government forces to a stalemate over the next several weeks. Orozco''s success eventually convinced Madero to reconsider his decision to give up the revolution and seek permanent sanctuary abroad. By the time Madero did return from exile in Texas in mid-February 1911, the Maderista rebels controlled the Sierra Madre Occidental from the United States border to Tepic and Zacatecas. They even had begun to challenge Diaz's army in the lowlands, such as the Comarca Lagunera and along the Chihuahua City–Ciudad Juarez railway line.[26]

By February, rebels in the center of Mexico were also beginning to show renewed signs of life. Although the five Márquez Galindo brothers had revolted in the Sierra Norte de Puebla as early as December, a more important foray into the center of the state occurred in February. Tlaxcalan insurgent Juan Cuamatzi led a force into the cotton textile area near Atlixco, setting off a series of battles and strikes and embarrassing the government before returning to his redoubt on the Malinche volcano. At the same time, longtime cacique and ranchero Juan Francisco Lucas notified Maderista agents that henceforth he would take a neutral stance in the conflict, thus virtually ensuring a rebel victory in the strategic northern sierra. Also, that same month, Gabriel Tepepa, a hacienda foreman in Morelos, sacked Tepoztlán. In northern Guerrero, the Figueroa brothers rebelled in Huitzuco.[27]

The revolts of February produced a snowball effect that by April resulted in dozens of rebellions involving thousands of fighters. At first confined mainly to the center and northwest, the movements soon spilled over into other areas outside that of traditional Maderista strength, such as the Huasteca as well as other parts of Hidalgo and San Luis Potosí.[28] The rebellions were clearly rural in nature, located principally in areas of profound agrarian grievances (mainly, the loss of land and village autonomy). The insurgents' targets underline the character of their complaints—haciendas and their owners and administrators, caciques, *jefes políticos*, municipal presidents, and governmental offices containing land and tax records. Among the rural fighters (from peons to rancheros) were a small number of urban-based workers and middle-class radicals.[29]

Of all the groups to rebel in March and April, including the Mayo and Yaqui Indians of Sinaloa and Sonora, the most important was the Zapatistas. Named after their leader, Emiliano Zapata, a mule driver and stable manager from Anenecuilco, Morelos, the Zapatistas would soon extend their influence to several neighboring states. Like many early revolutionaries nominally fighting under the Maderista banner, they read into the movement's official program more than its leadership probably ever meant to imply, in this case still modest but nevertheless unacceptably radical land reform.[30]

Rebel forces rapidly proliferated during April and May, eventually appearing in nearly every state of the country. Even before the fall of Ciudad Juárez to Pascual Orozco on 10 May, there existed sure signs of a regime in rapid decline. As early as January, Díaz replaced Chihuahuan governor Alberto Terrazas, thus distancing himself from the Terrazas-Creel clan. In March other key governors followed Terrazas's fate, including the highly unpopular Mucio Martínez of Puebla.[31]

While Díaz changed governors and then cabinet members in an effort to shore up popular support, civilian and military authorities began to cut their losses. Newly appointed Puebla interim governor José Rafael Isunza and the local federal zone commander, General Luis Valle, for example, offered to surrender towns to the rebels in order to protect upper- and middle-class interests. They, too, slowly withdrew governmental forces from the countryside toward Puebla City. This tactic kept the state capital out of insurgent hands and allowed independent Porfiristas (those willing, like themselves, to come to terms with the Maderistas) and moderate Maderistas (those mainly urban elements who took little part in the fighting and, in general, condemned and feared the radical methods and politics of the rural fighters) to attempt to form a governing coalition upon Díaz's eventual overthrow.[32]

The capture of Ciudad Juárez proved to be the decisive blow to the Díaz regime. It not only demonstrated the vulnerability of the government to both national and international observers alike, but it also provided the Maderistas with a port of entry and a provisional capital. Nevertheless, it should not be overlooked that even as Juárez fell, thousands of rebels (augmented by urban rabble) were poised to attack and sack several major cities in the northwest and center of the country. Plans were even being made to march on the national capital when the Treaty of Ciudad Juárez was signed on 25 May 1911. Otherwise, Mexico City, defended by fewer than three thousand troops, would doubtless have fallen quickly; and this consideration must have been important in Díaz's decision to surrender. Madero also realized the threat to elite interests represented by the thousands of his radical lower-class followers ready to take over urban centers if the war continued; hence the revolutionary leader himself, like the opposition, had a vested interest in quickly signing the peace treaty.[33]

In Power

Madero came to power in late May 1911, buoyed by a large degree of popular support. Less than six months later, when he assumed the presidency in November 1911, this enthusiasm had largely dissipated. By the autumn of 1912, a year later, persistent rumors of an impending coup d'etat circulated widely. Madero was overthrown and murdered in February 1913.

The nature of the opposition to Madero and the reasons for his quick demise, only twenty-one months after defeating Díaz, are many and complex. First, the makeup of his movement must be understood, for its heterogeneous and unorganized nature contributed greatly to his downfall.

The Maderista revolution of November 1910 to May 1911 mobilized several thousands of mainly radical, rural, and lower-class fighters in many areas of the country, but nowhere as many and for as long as in the center and especially in the northwest. In most cases these rebels and their leaders had heard of Madero, but few had any clear idea of the contents of his program. Even those people who did know the principles and objectives of the movement often interpreted them more liberally than Madero had originally intended. The vast majority of the insurgents, however, merely took Madero's call to arms as an opportunity to seek redress of local and sometimes personal grievances, unaware or uncaring of Madero's pronouncements. Indeed, many who joined the movement, especially during the last weeks of fighting, could only loosely be called Maderistas and sometimes took actions contrary to the interests and goals of the movement's leadership. This large, dispersed, and heterogeneous group, then, wanted immediate satisfaction of its demands, even of those outside the scope of the revolutionary program, no matter how liberally one might interpret it. Madero, unable (and unwilling) to meet this radical agenda of his followers and with poor connections to and understanding of the countryside, failed therefore to maintain control in the rural areas.[34]

Second, Madero made a series of poor political decisions in the weeks following Díaz's surrender, decisions that would have an important impact regionally and quickly alienating his more radical adherents and giving his conservative opposition a chance to regroup. These events set the pattern for the breakdown of his loose coalition over the next several months.

Although professing nonintervention in state and local affairs as part of his democratization program (note his willingness to leave all the Porfirian era state legislatures intact), Madero did take part in the selection of governors during the interim. He was prompted to do so by popular pressure (Madero had already appointed several revolutionary governors during the fighting) and by the threat that the state congresses would name blatant conservatives to the posts. In the northwest, where Maderismo was most entrenched, governors with fairly substantial popular bases were named—Abraham González in Chihuahua, José María Maytorena in Sonora, and Venustiano Carranza in Coahuila.[35]

In the center, however, the results were mixed. In Tlaxcala, for example, the radical ex-factory worker Antonio Hidalgo gained the governorship only because a division within the local elites (in part, over Porfirian Governor Próspero Cahuantzi's effort to remain in office after May) opened the way for a truly popular candidate of the lower classes. In Puebla, a moderate lawyer who sat out the spring 1911 fighting, Rafael Cañete, got the nod from Madero. Juan Carreón, a banker and ally of the planter class, was first named governor in Morelos only to be replaced by Ambrosio Figueroa, the anti-Zapatista ranchero from neighboring Guerrero who was now cooperating with the hacendados.[36]

In no state, except Tlaxcala (Hidalgo was removed from office in 1912 by the hacendados with Madero's backing), did Madero allow the appointment of a governor who was truly from the masses who had fought and won the war against Díaz. Genuinely popular leaders were ignored (Pascual Orozco in Chihuahua) and even "eliminated" by those whom Madero helped put into power (Nicolás Torres in San Luis Potosí). Madero clearly demonstrated that he wanted and trusted power only in the hands of middle-aged, educated, and mainly urban-oriented elites.[37]

Another mistake on Madero's part, with repercussions at the regional level, was his decision to form a new political party, the Partido Constitucionalista Progresista (PCP) to replace the Anti-Reelectionist Party. Although most Maderistas went along with the change, a substantial minority balked. They felt that Madero was not only discarding an important symbol of the revolution (and perhaps also reneging on some of the revolution's principles), but also betraying a loyal supporter, Francisco Vázquez Gómez, whom Madero had replaced as his vice-presidential running mate with the Yucatecan José María Pino Suárez. Staunch Anti-Reelectionists, many of whom saw themselves as the true inheritors of the liberal tradition, remained critical of Madero and formed the backbone of a vocal but loyal opposition in states like Puebla.[38]

As Francisco Vázquez Gómez was being eased out of the picture, Madero also backed interim President Francisco León de la Barra's decision to fire Francisco's brother, Emilio, from the cabinet. Emilio, although an opportunist, had proven to be one of the strongest Maderistas in the federal government. He constantly defended the left wing of the movement, even interfering in states' affairs as secretary of *gobernación* to check the influence of the conservatives and to push for faster implementation of reform measures. His ouster provoked a near uprising among an important group of insurgent officers headed by Juan Andrew Almazán of Guerrero, Cándido Navarro of Guanajuato, and Gabriel Hernández of Hidalgo. Madero ordered the arrest of four of them, including Navarro.[39]

Maderista officers and troops were also angered over Madero's decision to license them and keep the Porfirian army as the only official force in the nation. Insurgent soldiers expected more than a handshake of thanks, a few pesos for turning in their weapons, and a safe pass home for the sacrifices they had made in bringing Madero to power. When they resisted demobilization and clashed with federal units (most notably in Puebla City in mid-July 1911), Madero resorted to the hated levy to build up the regular army and converted newly licensed insurgents into Rurales to fight their former colleagues. The disaffection of spurned Maderista fighters had an impact on all parts of rural Mexico, seriously undermined Madero's base of support, and led to rebellion.[40]

Finally, Madero proved slow to implement the reform program that he had promised. The federal government could and did undertake some measures, such as the creation of a labor department and the construction of schools. Nevertheless, Madero's belated assumption of the presidency, his general reluctance to interfere in nonfederal governmental affairs, and the fact that most reforms directly involved state and local levels of administration meant that Madero mostly had only an indirect say in what steps were taken.

In most places, the lack of resources and time, a divided leadership, conservative opposition, poor planning, the failure to meet the needs and desires of the people, and continuing violence resulted in little or no progress being made, even in such key and universally desired areas of change as land and water, labor, education, finances, and governmental personnel. In the northwest, the greater commitment to Maderismo among state officials seems to have made the reform effort more successful than in other areas. Nevertheless, even the positive steps taken in Chihuahua were seriously undermined by Madero. The reform program's main architect in the key northwestern state, Governor Abraham González, was recruited to Madero's cabinet only six months after taking office, thus allowing much of González's efforts in the state to deteriorate.[41]

As a result of the disillusionment of much of his left wing and the continued adamant opposition of the conservatives, joined in part by backsliding moderate Maderistas who feared the increasingly violent masses, Madero faced a series of rebellions, beginning in the summer of 1911. Most of these movements were localized affairs and posed no serious threat to the regime, although they drained its resources, both financially and politically, and disrupted the government's reform program. Among the more notable revolts were those of the Yaquis in Sonora, the Figueroa brothers in Guerrero, the Cedillo brothers in San Luis Potosí, Che Gómez in Oaxaca, and the patently conservative one of Félix Díaz in Veracruz.[42] They occurred both within and outside the central and northwestern regions. The two most important, however, the Zapatista and the Orozquista-Vazquista, took place within these two key regions, demonstrating once again that these areas of the country played a dominant role in the fate of the Maderista movement.

The first major rebellion to challenge the new regime came from the center of the country. There, the Zapatistas, based in Morelos but with followers in surrounding states, had joined the Madero revolution in March 1910. During the weeks after the fall of Díaz, they waited, with increasing impatience, for the government to begin to fulfill its promises, especially the restitution and protection of communal lands. This measure was the key to restoring village autonomy and local self-government. Zapata and his adherents became especially angered when the authorities demanded their demobilization and the surrender of their arms, the only guarantee they had that their demands would be met. Zapata tried to reason with Madero, but President León de la Barra, sensitive to any challenge to his authority, especially from what he considered rural bandits, sent General Victoriano Huerta into Morelos to force the Zapatistas' submission.

Thus provoked into rebellion in late August 1911, the Zapatistas quickly refurbished and expanded their regional connections of the previous spring and were soon operating over a wide area of south-central Mexico. In November 1911, they issued the Plan de Ayala, their formal declaration of rebellion against the government. It called for, among other things, the overthrow of Madero and the return, confiscation, and division of lands. It became the rallying call for land reform and peasant rights throughout the nation; it was a call that would last for decades.

Although never able (and perhaps unwilling) seriously to threaten the seat of national power in Mexico City during the Madero period, the Zapatistas did make life miserable for provincial authorities and elites, sapped the government's resources, and undermined its military and political credibility. Zapatistas panicked Cuernavaca and Puebla City on more than one occasion, and they even set up their own state government in southern Puebla. Attacks on haciendas, small towns, the railroad and telegraph systems, and other targets constantly disrupted the economy and society in many areas. Conditions by the spring of 1912 had deteriorated to the point that Madero was forced to suspend consitutional guarantees in Morelos, Guerrero, Tlaxcala, and parts of Puebla and the state of Mexico. Throughout 1912 and 1913 the Zapatista threat waxed and waned from place to place and time to time (in part because of the cycle of planting and harvesting crops), but it never went away. Madero was constantly kept on the defensive.[43]

The second major and even more threatening (at least in the short run) rebellion that occurred while Madero was in power took place in the northwest. In Chihuahua, the popular and ambitious Pascual Orozco, while serving as a state Rural commander, came under heavy pressure to lead a growing tide of disenchanted groups against the government. Most of these people, many of whom had fought for Madero during the revolution of the winter and spring of 1910–1911, now faulted the new administration for its failure to implement the provisions of the Plan de San Luis Potosí—freedom of expression; municipal autonomy; the end of the *jefe político*, the *tienda de raya*, and the *leva*; labor, land, and tax reform; and the Mexicanization of the railway, among others. Among those elements in contact with Orozco were the Vazquistas, followers of Emilio Vázquez Gómez, who had declared against the regime in November 1911.

Orozco finally rebelled in early March 1912, but not before he had made an alliance with conservatives in the state, including members of the Terrazas-Creel clan, for financial support. Quickly, Orozco gathered a force of several thousand men and began to push southward. His defeat of the federal army at Rellano on 23 March caused panic in the nation's capital and forced Madero to turn to Huerta to lead the government's counterattack. In the meantime, Orozco consolidated his hold on Chihuahua and parts of surrounding states, while his allies, the Vazquistas, raised revolts, for example, in San Luis Potosí and the Sierra de Puebla. Then, at the second battle of Rellano on 23 May, Huerta saved the regime by decisively routing Orozco and dispersing the bulk of the rebel army into the rugged mountains to the north and northwest, from where they originally came.[44]

Although the Orozco rebellion (and its Vazquista appendage) was defeated within a relatively short time, its repercussions were much more long lasting. Like the Zapatista and other insurgencies, it sapped the government's resources (although its demise did help briefly to restore some of Madero's military and political capital). The Orozquistas themselves remained in the mountains of the northwest, fighting the regime by using guerrilla tactics; this armed resistance led to official repression, thereby further undermining the administration's liberal credentials and adding to the alienation of people in the region. Finally, the Orozco movement forced Madero to increase the size of the army, thus not only requiring the transfer of monies from other pressing needs but also giving the military greater say in the civilian political sector. This process of militarization is, of course, best epitomized in the enhanced role given to General Victoriano Huerta, the man who successfully defended the government, and who, within a few months, would also bring it down.[45]

Conclusion

Francisco I. Madero was a man in the right place at the right time. He did not cause the revolution; he merely served as a rallying point around which hundreds of groups with different agendas coalesced to create "many movements" or "revolutions" that have conveniently and traditionally, and to a large extent inaccurately, been gathered together under his name.[46] Madero's catalytic role, in other words, did not create a truly integrated and centrally guided national revolution (not to be confused with putting someone into national office). This revolution was primarily a regional phenomenon in which the northwest and center of the country dominated the political and then the armed movements nominally led by Madero.

Indeed, the revolution(s) began decades before Madero entered the scene. Capitalistic penetration and political centralization, especially in the northwest and in the center, had a profoundly disruptive impact on traditional structures. The resultant underlying social discontent was then leavened at the regional levels by groups like the PLM and Protestants; politically conscious workers, peasants, and students; and skillful local leaders. Opportunity for political and then revolutionary action came when the façade of national control cracked under the pressure of economic depression and political infighting over Díaz's successor.

Once the dictatorship fell, Madero, as nominal head of the revolutionary movement, was not capable of controlling and molding his heterogeneous and geographically dispersed coalition into a solid national political base with a universally accepted common program. Madero's coalition, then, also soon fell prey to the "destructive" centrifugal forces of regionalism just as the old regime had. In Madero's case, however, a military coup d'etat headed off what probably would have been a continuation of rural insurgencies originating principally in one or both of Mexico's two most agitated regions, the northwest and the center. After all, the remainder of the revolutionary decade (1910–1920) was largely shaped by armed movements from these same two areas.

Notes

1. For the two best book-length studies of the causes of the Maderista revolution, both of which take into special consideration regional factors, see François-Xavier Guerra, *México: Del antiguo régimen a la revolución*, 2 vols. (Mexico City: Fondo de Cultura Económica, 1988); Alan Knight, *The Mexican Revolution*, 2 vols. (Cambridge: Cambridge University Press, 1986).

2. Barry Carr, *The Peculiarities of the Mexican North, 1880–1928: An Essay in Interpretation* (Institute of Latin American Studies, University of Glasgow, 1971), 1–21; Friedrich Katz, *La guerra secreta en México: Europa, Estados Unidos y la revolución mexicana*, 2 vols. (Mexico City: Ediciones ERA, 1982), 1:36–40.

3. Mark Wasserman, "The Social Origins of the 1910 Revolution in Chihuahua," *Latin American Research Review* 15:1(1980): 15–38; Wasserman, *Capitalists, Caciques, and the Revolution: The Native Elite and Foreign Enterprise in Chihuahua, Mexico, 1854–1911* (Chapel Hill: University of North Carolina Press, 1984), 43–147; Robert Sandels, "Antecedentes de la revolución en Chihuahua," *Historia Mexicana* 24:3(January-March 1975): 390–402; Harold D. Sims, "Espejo de caciques: Los Terrazas de Chihuahua," *Historia Mexicana* 18:3 (January-March 1969): 379–99; Friedrich Katz, "Labor Conditions on Haciendas in Porfirian Mexico: Some Trends and Tendencies," *Hispanic American Historical Review* 54:1 (February 1974): 35–36, 45–46; Ralph H. Vigil, "Revolution and Confusion: The Peculiar Case of José Inés Salazar," *New Mexico Historical Review* 53:2(April 1978): 146–48. For analysis of the impact of the railroad during the Porfiriato, see John H. Coatsworth, *El impacto económico de los ferrocarriles en el porfiriato*, 2 vols. (Mexico City: SepSetentas, 1976); Arthur Paul Schmidt, Jr., "The Social and Economic Effect of the Railroad in Puebla and Veracruz, Mexico, 1867–1911" (Ph.D. diss., Indiana University, Bloomington, 1974).

4. Héctor Aguilar Camín, *La frontera nómada: Sonora y la revolución mexicana* (Mexico City: Siglo XXI Editores, 1977), 19–261; Susan M. Deeds, "José María Maytorena and the Mexican Revolution in Sonora," *Arizona and the West* 18:1(Spring 1976): 21–40; Evelyn Hu-DeHart, "Sonora: Indians and Immigrants on a Developing Frontier," in *Other Mexicos: Essays on Regional Mexican History, 1876–1911*, ed. Thomas Benjamin and William McNellie (Albuquerque: University of New Mexico Press, 1984), 177–211.

5. Paul Eiser-Viafora, "Durango and the Mexican Revolution," *New Mexico Historical Review* 49:3(July 1974): 219–40.

6. Douglas W. Richmond, "Factional Political Strife in Coahuila, 1910–1920," *Hispanic American Historical Review* 60:1(February 1980): 50–51; Richmond, "Confrontation and Reconciliation: Mexicans and Spaniards during the Mexican Revolution, 1910–1920," *The Americas* 41:2(October 1984): 216–17; Richmond, *Venustiano Carranza's Nationalist Struggle, 1893–1920* (Lincoln: University of Nebraska Press, 1983), 20–21; Guerra, *México*, 2:166–68; Knight, *The Mexican Revolution*, 1:71.

7. William K. Meyers, "Politics, Vested Rights, and Economic Growth in Porfirian Mexico: The Company Tlahualilo in the Comarca Lagunera, 1885–1911," *Hispanic American Historical Review* 57:3(August 1977): 425–42; Meyers, "La Comarca Lagunera: Work, Protest, and Popular Mobilization in North Central Mexico," in *Other Mexicos* 244–68; Katz, *La guerra secreta*, 1:31–32.

8. Guerra, *México*, 2:160–63; Knight, *The Mexican Revolution*, 1:71.

9. Ian Jacobs, *Ranchero Revolt: The Mexican Revolution in Guerrero* (Austin: University of Texas Press, 1982): 19–27, 74–78.

10. John Womack, Jr., *Zapata and the Mexican Revolution* (New York: Vintage, 1968), 14–66; Arturo Warman, . . . *Y venimos a contradecir: Los campesinos de Morelos y el*

estado nacional (Mexico City: Casa Chata, 1976), 53–103; Guillermo de la Pena, *A Legacy of Promises; Agriculture, Politics, and Ritual in the Morelos Highlands of Mexico* (Austin: University of Texas Press, 1981), 54–62.

11. David G. LaFrance, *The Mexican Revolution in Puebla, 1908–1913: The Maderista Movement and the Failure of Liberal Reform* (Wilmington, Del.: Scholarly Resources, 1989), xxix–xxxiv; Jean Pierre Bastian, *Protestantismo y sociedad en México* (Mexico City: Casa Unida de Publicaciones, 1983), 69–118.

12. Raymond Th. J. Buve, "Protesta de obreros y campesinos durante el porfiriato: Unas consideraciones sobre su desarrollo e interrelaciones en el este de México central," *Boletín de Estudios Latinoamericanos*, no. 13 (December 1972): 8–14; Buve, "Peasant Movements, Caudillos and Land Reform during the Revolution (1910–1917) in Tlaxcala, Mexico," *Boletín de Estudios Latinoamericanos y del Caribe*, no. 18(June 1975): 117–24.

13. Guerra, *México*, 2:210–12; Knight, *The Mexican Revolution*, 1:133–39.

14. William H. Beezley, "Madero: The 'Unknown' President and His Political Failure to Organize Rural Mexico," in *Essays on the Mexican Revolution: Revisionist Views of the Leaders*, ed. George Wolfskill and Douglas W. Richmond (Austin: University of Texas Press, 1979), 10–11.

15. Carlos B. Gil, *Life in Provincial Mexico: National and Regional History Seen from Mascota, Jalisco, 1867–1972* (Los Angeles: Latin American Center, University of California, 1983), 103–4.

16. Ibid., 118.

17. Gilbert M. Joseph, *Revolution from Without: Yucatán, Mexico, and the United States, 1880–1924* (Cambridge: Cambridge University Press, 1982), 1–2, 83–88; Allen Wells, *Yucatán's Gilded Age: Haciendas, Henequen, and International Harvester, 1860–1915* (Albuquerque: University of New Mexico Press, 1985), 10–11, 61–88, 179–84; Luis Aboites, *La revolución en Espita, 1910–1940: Microhistoria de la formación del estado de la revolución* (Mexico City: Cuadernos de Casa Chata, 1982), 25–26, 46–51, 60.

18. Daniela Spenser, "Soconusco: The Formation of a Coffee Economy in Chiapas," in *Other Mexicos*, 137–139. Marcela Tostado Gutiérrez, *El Tabasco porfiriano* (Villahermosa: Gobierno del Estado, 1985), 141, 157; Knight, *The Mexican Revolution*, 1:88–89, 97.

19. Margarita Menegus Bornemann and Juan Felipe Leal, "Las haciendas de Mazaquiahuac y El Rosario en los albores de la revolución agraria, 1910–1914," *Historia Mexicana* 31:2(October-December 1981): 237.

20. Ronald Waterbury, "Non-revolutionary Peasants: Oaxaca Compared to Morelos in the Mexican Revolution," *Comparative Studies in Society and History* 17:4(October 1975): 418–28; Francie R. Chassen, "Los precursores de la revolución en Oaxaca," 40–41, 85–87, in *La revolución en Oaxaca, 1900–1930*, ed. Víctor Raúl Martínez Vásquez (Oaxaca: Instituto de Administración Pública de Oaxaca, 1985).

21. Ricardo Avila Palafox, ¿Revolución en el Estado de México? (Mexico City: INAH; Toluca: Gobierno del Estado, 1988), 207, 237–39.

22. Knight, The Mexican Revolution, 1:99; Beatriz Rojas, La destrucción de la hacienda en Aguascalientes, 1910–1931 (Zamora: El Colegio de Michoacán, 1981), 35–49.

23. John Tutino, From Insurrection to Revolution in Mexico: Social Bases of Agrarian Violence, 1750–1940 (Princeton: Princeton University Press, 1986).

24. Guerra, México, 2:266–68; Knight, The Mexican Revolution, 1:71, 75; LaFrance, The Mexican Revolution in Puebla, 34–35.

25. LaFrance, The Mexican Revolution in Puebla, 45–49.

26. Guerra, México, 2:281–85; Knight, The Mexican Revolution, 1:176–82.

27. Jacobs, Ranchero Revolt, 80–84; LaFrance, The Mexican Revolution in Puebla, 63–66; Womack, Zapata, 74.

28. Dudley Ankerson, Agrarian Warlord: Saturnino Cedillo and the Mexican Revolution in San Luis Potosí (DeKalb: Northern Illinois University Press, 1984), 20–29; Knight, The Mexican Revolution, 1:192–93, 200.

29. Knight does a good job in dealing with types of rural movements; see The Mexican Revolution, 1:78–127, 301–19, 333–82; "Peasant and Caudillo in Revolutionary Mexico, 1910–1917," in Caudillo and Peasant in the Mexican Revolution, ed. D.A. Brading (Cambridge: Cambridge University Press, 1980), 22–36.

30. Womack, Zapata, 67–158.

31. Guerra, México, 2:314–20; Knight, The Mexican Revolution, 1:201–2; LaFrance, The Mexican Revolution in Puebla, 66–68.

32. LaFrance, The Mexican Revolution in Puebla, 77–79.

33. Knight, The Mexican Revolution, 1:203–4; Jesús Luna, La carrera pública de Don Ramón Corral (Mexico City: SepSetentas, 1975), 160.

34. Beezley, "Madero," 1–24; Arnaldo Córdova, La ideología de la revolución mexicana: La formación del nuevo régimen (Mexico City: Ediciones ERA, 1973), 142–43.

35. Knight, The Mexican Revolution, 1:258.

36. Raymond Th. J. Buve, "Agricultores, dominación política y estructura agraria en la revolución mexicana: El caso de Tlaxcala, 1910–1918," in Haciendas in Central Mexico from Late Colonial Times to the Revolution, ed. Raymond Th. J. Buve (Amsterdam: CEDLA, 1984), 218–224; LaFrance, The Mexican Revolution in Puebla, 101–4; Womack, Zapata, 86–126.

37. Knight, The Mexican Revolution, 1:264; Romana Falcón, Revolución y caciquismo en San Luis Potosí, 1910–1938 (Mexico City: El Colegio de México, 1984), 53–54.

38. Charles C. Cumberland, Mexican Revolution: Genesis under Madero (Austin: University of Texas Press, 1952), 162–65; LaFrance, The Mexican Revolution in Puebla, 152–53.

39. Cumberland, Mexican Revolution, 159–160; Knight, The Mexican Revolution, 1:248–49.

40. LaFrance, The Mexican Revolution in Puebla, 109–14, 120–21.

41. William H. Beezley, Insurgent Governor: Abraham González and the Mexican Revolu-

tion in Chihuahua (Lincoln: University of Nebraska Press, 1973), 89–114, 149–51; Beezley, "Governor Carranza and the Revolution in Coahuila," *The Americas* 33:1 (July 1976): 53–59; Richmond, *Venustiano Carranza's Nationalist Struggle*, 22–40; Deeds, "José María Maytorena," 28–40; David G. LaFrance, "Failure of Reform: The Maderistas in Puebla, 1911–1913," *New World* 1:2(1986): 44–64.

42. For fuller treatment of these rebellions, see Evelyn Hu-DeHart, *Yaqui Resistance and Survival* (Madison: University of Wisconsin Press, 1984); Jacobs, *Ranchero Revolt*; Ankerson, *Agrarian Warlord*; Falcón, *Revolución y caciquismo*; Héctor Gerardo Martínez Medina, "Génesis y desarrollo del maderismo en Oaxaca, 1909–1912," in *La revolución in Oaxaca*; 88–158; Peter V. N. Henderson, *Félix Díaz, the Porfirians, and the Mexican Revolution* (Lincoln: University of Nebraska Press, 1981).

43. Córdova, *La ideología*, 144–55; LaFrance, *The Mexican Revolution in Puebla*, 178–79; Womack, *Zapata*, 86–144.

44. Knight, *The Mexican Revolution*, 1:339; LaFrance, *The Mexican Revolution in Puebla*, 179–80; Michael C. Meyer, *Mexican Rebel: Pascual Orozco and the Mexican Revolution, 1910–1915* (Lincoln: University of Nebraska Press, 1967), 36–77.

45. Knight, *The Mexican Revolution*, 1:329–30.

46. David C. Bailey, "Revisionism and the Recent Historiography of the Mexican Revolution," *Hispanic American Historical Review* 58:1 (February 1978): 73–74.

3

Revolutionary Confrontation, 1913–1917

Regional Factions, Class Conflicts, and the New National State

John Tutino

The social and political conflicts that drove the Mexican revolution had deep historical roots.[1] The endemic national instability that began in 1910 lasted decades.[2] But the fundamental revolutionary confrontation—the violent conflict over the structures of state and economy, fueled by the grievances of long subordinate peoples—was concentrated in the years from 1913 to 1917. The battle that followed the collapse of Francisco Madero's reformist presidency in February 1913 made the Mexican revolution a revolution—a violent process of fundamental social and political transformation.

Within the four years of the revolutionary confrontation, the first thirty months from February 1913 to July 1915 were decisive. During those two and a half years, no state effectively ruled in Mexico: there was no national monopoly of coercion, of justice, and of the rules of property. In the absence of a national state, factions with different regional and social bases, along with conflicting ideologies and programs, organized political–military forces to fight for the power to build the new Mexican state and to define the new rules of property and of justice that would order Mexico throught the coming decades. In the summer of 1915, the Constitutionalist faction led by Venustiano Carranza claimed military victory and thus the power to become the new state. The Constitution of 1917 was the first step in the long and often disputed process of consolidating the new state's power.

This essay probes the regional and social bases of the major revolutionary factions, their economic means, their ideological goals, and their political–military organizations. It goes on to explore the alliances and conflicts among the factions and their relations with outside powers—mostly in the United States—seeking to explain why the Constitutionalists won the battle for state power.

In 1910, Francisco Madero led an assault on the Díaz regime, raising the issues that would long dominate the Mexican revolution. Along with nationalist elites, Madero shared the goal of lessening foreign economic domination. Among the middle sectors, Madero raised hopes for a democracy of broad participation. And through vague statements about rural justice along with alliances with agrarian radicals such as Emiliano Zapata, Madero led many among the rural poor to expect the return of lost lands. But once in power in 1911, Madero retained the old Federal army and the political support of many established elites. Blatant contradictions plagued Madero's regime. The mere discussion of land reform alienated elite backers, while the lack of redistribution left agrarian rebels with a deep sense of betrayal. The result of Maderista rule from 1911 to 1913 was to polarize Mexican politics without making basic reforms.[3]

Complaining of Madero's failure to maintain order, conspirators representing powerful elite interests came together to oust the reformer in February 1913. Participating in the coup were: General Bernardo Reyes, who had long served Díaz in northern political posts and who had refused to lead the opposition to the aging patriarch when his regime began to unravel before 1910; Felix Díaz, the old ruler's nephew; General Victoriano Huerta, who had remained in the Federal army under Madero, but found the reformer too accommodating to demands from below; and Henry Lane Wilson, United States Ambassador and a Taft Republican with ties to the Guggenheim interests that nearly monopolized Mexican silver mining. After ten days of duplicity and violence upon the residents of the capital, Huerta dominated a new government.[4]

Huerta's regime aimed to limit the talk of democracy and to block the mounting expectations of land reform. Huerta sought and generally got support from established Mexican elites and foreign economic interests, most of whom had earlier backed Díaz. But in the face of rising discontent, the new conservative regime could not replicate the prerevolutionary system. Díaz had built an authoritarian regime backed by economic powerholders, while limiting the role of the military. Now, as revolutionary mobilizations escalated, Huerta worked to rebuild the power and the political role of the military and to bring it to the center of his regime. He aimed to block revolutionary agitation by using repression in the interests of established elites.[5] He succeeded only in stimulating opposition and escalating the revolutionary confrontation.

While in office, Huerta claimed to head a national state. But opposition to his rule developed so rapidly and across such wide areas that his government may be viewed more accurately as one among the several factions that emerged in 1913 to engage in revolutionary conflict. It was a faction that began with many advantages. It was organized around the national state bureaucracy, which Madero had preserved. It was backed by many of the most powerful economic interests in Mexico, both national and foreign. It had the Federal army to fight its battles. And early on, it was treated as the government of Mexico by Great Britain and the United States, though not formally recognized by the latter.

The Huerta regime primarily generated opposition. The overthrow and murder of Madero deeply alienated many upper- and middle-class reformers.[6] They were not merely angered by their leader's brutal death. Many also concluded that the democracy and accelerated economic development they sought could not be attained through Madero's chosen means of moderation and accommodation with the old regime and established economic interests. Growing numbers concluded that only the destruction of the existing state would allow the implementation of their vision. Madero's death brought many reformers to face the limits of reformism and to turn to the violent path of revolution.

Huerta's government also faced the staunch opposition of rural rebels from many regions. Madero might have made vague agrarian promises and delivered nothing. But Huerta blatantly backed local landed elites and colluded in their efforts to crush agrarian mobilizations. Agrarian grievances and uprisings spread and intensified in the face of Huerta's coup and reactionary regime.

Within six months of taking office, Huerta faced opposition so widespread that a military response was beyond the capacity of existing Federal forces. Rather than addressing the grievances that generated such opposition, Huerta turned to the task of increasing his military capacity. He attempted to build his armies by two means: conscription, and pressure on loyal landlords to arm their estate dependents as progovernment troops. Both programs brought only limited success, while creating new difficulties for the Huerta regime.

Conscripts were, at best, reluctant soldiers. Many peasants facing Huerta's draft quickly decided to join a local rebel band. At least then they fought under a local leader pursuing local interests, and avoided becoming foot soldiers in the army of a reactionary regime. And those who were successfully drafted had to be paid—the minimal price of minimal loyalty—which became increasingly difficult as Huerta's army grew while economic disruptions undermined tax collections.[7]

Unlike poor conscripts, landlords who admired and stood to benefit from Huerta's program of order and entrepreneurship might have been eager to field forces to defend their lands and the regime. But in the many regions where villagers were rising in violent agrarian protests, landlord activism invited retaliation. Few landlords proved ready to take that risk for Huerta. Only where revolutionary mobilization was minimal did landed elites field significant forces in defense of the regime.[8]

The Huerta government was also weakened by waning foreign support. Though Ambassador Henry Lane Wilson helped bring him to power, Huerta soon faced the uncertainties of newly inaugurated Woodrow Wilson. President Wilson worried about Huerta's nondemocratic route to power and about his friendship with important British interests. Never formally recognized by Washington, Huerta faced a chilling neutrality from Mexico's powerful northern neighbor from the summer of 1913—and then blunt opposition from early 1914. In February of that year, the United States opened its borders to legal arms sales to Mexican rebels. And in April, U.S. Marines occupied Veracruz, denying Huerta the customs revenues and shipping facilities of Mexico's primary Gulf port.[9]

General Huerta claimed to be president of Mexico from February 1913 until July 1914. More accurately, he was chief of the most reactionary, elite-led faction in a revolutionary confrontation. He faced the opposition of all the other major factions and of many smaller ones. Huerta fled Mexico in July 1914, his conservative coalition the first to be eliminated from the contest for national power.

Among the movements that fought against the Huerta government, the forces led by Emiliano Zapata deserve first discussion. In February 1913 they were Mexico's longest active insurgents with the clearest revolutionary program. And while the Zapatistas eventually faced defeat as a political movement, their adamant agrarian agenda long defined revolutionary social debates.[10]

The Zapatista movement was grounded in the peasant villages of central Mexico, primarily in the Morelos basin just south of Mexico City. Zapata rose to fame as leader of the village of Anenecuilco, fighting in the courts and in the fields for the villagers' claims to lands held by a neighboring sugar estate. In 1910, Madero's vague promises of agrarian justice were enough to link Zapata to the fight against Díaz. Once Madero was in power, Zapata demanded the immediate return of disputed lands to the Morelos villagers. Madero, son of a great landed family in the northern borderlands, balked, calling instead for caution and study. When the new regime they had helped install offered only rhetoric on land reform, Zapata and his peasant forces remained in arms. When Federal troops were sent to "pacify" them, the conflict escalated. Madero never began a land reform, and Zapata remained in rebellion—proclaiming in November of 1911 his fundamental goal of "land to the villagers" in the Plan of Ayala.

With the fall of Madero, Zapata, remained in opposition. Huerta had been one of the generals sent by Madero to subdue the Zapatistas. And Huerta's government quickly demonstrated its staunch opposition to the villagers' land claims. If Zapatistas saw Madero as deceitful, offering reform but not delivering it, they knew that Huerta and his allies bluntly opposed their peasant goals.

The Zapatistas were classic peasant revolutionaries. Their utopia was a world of villages with enough land for each family to raise its own maize and beans—and left alone by those claiming higher authority. Such a utopia of local autonomy had never existed in Morelos, of course. The history of the region, however, had revolved around centuries of conflict and cooperation between landed peasant villages and commercial sugar estates.

Through the centuries of Spanish colonial rule, most villages in Morelos and across the Mexican central highlands had retained lands that allowed most families there to raise much of their own food. Yet most had to supplement that subsistence cultivation with the wages of seasonal labor on nearby estates. The links thus forged between estates and villages were simultaneously symbiotic and exploitative. Estates needed seasonal workers from the villages to generate profits; the villagers needed the paltry earnings of seasonal field labor to sustain their families. Such relations between estates and villages were institutionally symbiotic; but they were socially exploitative. Landlords reaped profits while villagers gained but minimal wages. Yet social exploitation structured as institutional symbiosis proved stabilizing. For centuries, conflict between estates and villages remained local and limited.[11]

It was the breakdown of the structure of symbiotic exploitation during the nineteenth century that led the villagers of Morelos to revolutionary violence. Many of the leaders of independent Mexico professed a liberal ideology that saw only "privilege" and "stagnation" in the colonial structure of community landholding. Claiming national power in the 1850s, the liberals abolished community land rights in law—though in practice the transition occurred only slowly and incompletely during the next half-century. This was not a policy of expropriation; villagers would receive as private property lands they had long held as village properties. But the shift to private property left peasant plots newly susceptible to sale and foreclosure—and apparently also to theft. At the same time, the late nineteenth century brought a surge of population growth to the villages of central Mexico. The intersection of land privatization with population growth left central highland villagers less and less able to sustain themselves on their own lands as the nineteenth century progressed.

Then the coming of the railroads and the political peace of Porfirio Díaz in the 1880s forced the Morelos villagers to face more intense challenges. Sugar production expanded rapidly and Morelos estates grasped for additional land and especially water resources. They also demanded growing numbers of seasonal workers. By about 1900, there was no longer enough land held by villagers to sustain the population of seasonal workers sought by the estates. The estates, unable to profit without the inexpensive, seasonal work force sustained by subsistence production, stepped in and made estate lands not used for cane available to villagers for sharecropping maize. Morelos peasants could thus continue to combine subsistence production with seasonal labor to maintain their families. But now they would pay half their maize to the estate. And they had become dependent on the estates for both subsistence lands and seasonal wages. That newly entrenched dependence coupled with painful insecurities outraged the villagers of Morelos. When they had grown maize on their own or village lands, seasonal labor at the estates appeared as a beneficial supplement to family production. The new dependence on the haciendas for lands as well as wages, in contrast, created a more encompassing dependence that deepened the insecurities of peasant life. Climatic difficulties had long plagued peasant families. Now, a drop in the sugar market or even a personal conflict with an estate manager could bring both loss of lands and of wages to an extended family. Ever more irate with lives of deepening dependence and threatening insecurity, Morelos villagers became ready to protest and eventually to rebel after 1900. Their solution was the reconstitution of landholding villages—to recreate at least limited autonomy for their families. Emiliano Zapata would lead their efforts.

The Zapatista revolt began on a small scale before Madero's challenge to Díaz's rule. Joining Madero, however tenuously, broadened the movement and introduced it to the intrigues of national politics. Later, facing the Federal armies sent against them by Madero hardened the Zapatistas, deepened their ties to the Morelos villagers, and taught them guerrilla warfare. By early 1913, they were experienced agrarian guerrillas with clear goals and established leadership.

The great strength of the Zapatista movement was the coherence of its social and economic bases, its ideological program, and its political and military organization. All were grounded in the peasant communities of Morelos. There, the Zapatistas recruited fighters. It was villagers who maintained and then expanded subsistence production (as the conflict undermined the estate economy) to sustain themselves and to provision Zapata's troops. The ideology of the movement focused insistently on village rights to land for peasant production and on local political independence.[12] And Zapatista political organization built on the local tradition of village councils. Zapata had first held office as head of the council of Anenecuilco, and his revolutionary movement developed as a league of community governments. Until Zapata's death in 1919, leadership remained with men from the villages. Intellectuals with urban roots might join and serve the movement; they could not lead it.

That coherence rooted in Morelos communities made the Zapatistas long impregnable on their home ground. Opposing armies might march through and win battles, but the Zapatistas could fade into the hills and into the villages, to reappear as locally predominant once the troops left.

Such defensive strength, however, brought offensive weakness. Peasants quick to fight for their families, lands, and communities saw little reason to do battle outside their homelands. Peasant subsistence production easily fed guerrillas, but it generated little surplus to be taxed or sold to obtain arms and ammunition. Zapata's armies often were limited to the munitions they could steal or capture, severely restricting their offensive capacities. Zapata understood the difficulty. When he ruled uncontested in Morelos during 1914 and 1915, he watched the villagers reclaim lands and turn to subsistence production. He urged them to grow some cane, too, to generate revenues for the army. But Zapata also understood his political base. When the villagers showed little interest in cane and insistently raised maize and beans to feed their families, he acquiesced. He would not force his followers to commercialize for the sake of the movement. Zapata knew that alienating his peasant supporters to strengthen his armies would be counterproductive. He accepted peasant values and goals—and thus the political strengths and limitations they brought to his movement. [13]

Foreign assistance was precluded for the Zapatistas. Given the commercial interests inherent in United States and European diplomacy early in the twentieth century, the powers that mattered in Mexico saw Zapata and his peasant rebels as mere bandits. Isolated in an interior basin far from ports and borders, the Zapatistas had little chance to trade local produce for foreign supplies, even had the villagers been willing to do so. Zapata also understood this weakness. Late in 1913 and early in 1914 he sent emissaries seeking loans from the United States. They were rebuffed. [14] No government nor moneyed interest in the United States was about to fund "bandit" revolutionaries— that is, rebels who would take land from commercial estates and give it to peasant villagers.

The oft-noted inability of Zapata to project his movement beyond its regional base was not caused by ignorance or naivete. It revealed instead his fine understanding of the values and goals of the peasant villagers he led—and the inherent defensive strength and offensive weakness of a mobilized peasant society.

The Zapatistas were not the only peasant movement in the revolutionary confrontation from 1913 to 1915. In the central highlands, where the rural populace had long lived in peasant villages and recently had faced difficulties akin to those in Morelos, innumerable local bands rose to demand land and community rights. In Tlaxcala, for example, a region just east of the capital and at the fringe of the Zapatista domain, villagers demanding land and autonomy rose in 1910 in alliance with the Maderista movement. They, too, pressed land claims on Madero with little result. Thus, when in 1913 Huerta moved to back the landlord reaction in Tlaxcala, bands of agrarian rebels quickly fought back. Some allied with Zapata, others with the northern Constitutionalists, but all insisted on "lands to the villagers."[15] It was the combination of the closely organized and strategically located Zapatistas with other agrarian bands of less strength, but equal adamance, that made peasant goals the core social questions of the revolutionary confrontation in rural central Mexico.

The other major factions that developed in 1913 to oppose the Huerta regime all came from northern Mexico, especially the borderlands adjacent to the United States. The social and historical traditions of the north were radically different from those of the central highlands. The Mexican north was little settled by Europeans during the colonial era and long remained home to widely scattered indigenous peoples quick to defend their independence. Mining and grazing drew Mexicans northward but slowly, until the railroads of the Díaz era linked the borderlands to both central Mexico and the United States in the 1880s. Then the rush to develop silver and copper mines, cattle ranches, cotton estates, and other enterprises brought rapid settlement. Thousands of uprooted, mobile, and often entrepreneurial families migrated from older Mexican regions to the borderlands to join the boom.[16]

Politically, Díaz treated the borderlands like most other regions. Early in his regime, he consolidated provincial power in the hands of personally loyal dependents—and compensated regional elites with unprecedented economic opportunities. Provincially powerful clans such as the Maderos of Coahuila, the Terrazas of Chihuahua, and the Maytorenas of Sonora lost political power, but gained new wealth. Then around 1900, those stabilizing political relations began to change. A few provincially important clans, notably the Terrazas, were allowed to return to political power. Others, notably the Maytorenas and the Maderos, remained excluded. Political discontent escalated rapidly. In Chihuahua, both the middle sectors and the poor deeply resented the Terrazas' combination of political and economic dominance. In Coahuila and Sonora, the Maderos, Maytorenas, and others resented their continuing exclusion from political power, which denied them the benefits reaped by the highly visible Terrazas. [17]

Emerging political conflicts were deepened by the economic collapse that struck the borderlands after 1905. The shift to the gold standard that year, followed by the rapid impact in Mexico of the financial panic that began in the United States in 1907, brought shortages of capital and shrinking markets that undermined the borderlands boom. Northern elites, especially those politically excluded by Díaz, began to resent the regime that had tied them to the United States economy and for a time had brought them great riches—but that had also excluded them from office and now left them to pay the price of economic dependence on their powerful neighbor to the north. For many northern elites and families of the entrepreneurial middle sectors, political participation and economic nationalism would become key demands of revolutionary politics after 1910. [18]

The same cycle of economic boom and collapse that peaked the political discontent of borderlands elites brought acute social grievances to the region's working majority. The boom in economic development during the Díaz era led to widespread and deeply resented expropriations. Lands were taken from the Yaqui of Sonora and other native peoples, as well as from established Mexican settlers, by newcomers with the capital and the political backing to profit from the export boom. Simultaneously, migration brought growing numbers of working families to the borderlands, newcomers who lived dependent upon the newly developed and export-oriented mines, cattle ranches, and cotton estates. After 1905, thousands of recently uprooted families faced the sudden collapse of the boom that had drawn them north. Declining wages, unfavorable tenancies, and spreading unemployment afflicted growing numbers. The intersection of the grievances of established northerners expropriated by the boom with the outrage of the newcomers undermined by its collapse led to massive revolutionary mobilizations along the borderlands after 1910. [19]

It was a son of one of the borderlands' wealthiest families, Francisco Madero, who led the challenge to Porfirio Díaz in 1910 and 1911. Much of his support came from northern regions. With the overthrow and murder of Madero in early 1913, revolutionary opposition quickly mobilized there again. The uprisings to protest the death of Madero had three centers in the borderlands. Eventually they would realign into two major revolutionary factions. Where northern elites had opposed Díaz and backed Madero in 1910, as in Coahuila and Sonora, the risings of 1913 were led by established local leaders and they later coalesced into the Constitutionalist movement. In Chihuahua, in contrast, where the dominant Terrazas had backed Díaz against Madero, and where the Maderista governor, Abraham González, was murdered soon after Huerta's coup, the revolutionary mobilization was led by the upstart Pancho Villa and would evolve into an independent and more radical revolutionary faction.

Venustiano Carranza was a landowner who had remained at the fringes of Coahuila politics during the Díaz era. He was the Maderista governor of the state when Huerta so brutally claimed the presidency. Refusing to recognize the usurper, Carranza led the government of Madero's home state into rebellion. At the same time, the state government in Sonora also refused subordination to the new regime in Mexico City. The Constitutionalist faction that resulted from the eventual fusion of these rebellions was able to organize around important fragments of established state structures. Leadership came from established regional elites, along with ambitious men of middling origins. They sustained their political organizations and their armies by maintaining, even promoting, the borderlands export economy—and economy easy to tax to purchase arms from the United States.[20]

The ideological program of the Constitutionalists was liberal, statist, nationalist, and populist. It was liberal in promoting an entrepreneurial, capitalist vision of Mexico's future, insisting on private property, social individualism, and a limited role for the traditional church. It was statist in demanding a strong national state as the necessary means to promote liberal economic goals. It was nationalist, not by seeking to isolate Mexico from international influences, but by demanding more Mexican control over Mexican politics and Mexican involvement in the international economy. And it was populist in insisting that the state and economic elites would provide for the well-being of the masses.[21]

Organized as a rebellious state and based upon an export-oriented commercial economy, the Constitutionalists developed strengths and weaknesses almost exactly the opposite of those of the Zapatistas. The Constitutionalists were weakest in their relations with their social base, the poor majority of the northeast and northwest borderlands. They promised to help the poor, but organized the movement to all but preclude the participation of the poor in crucial decisions. Carranza insisted that his Plan of Guadalupe—the founding charter of Constitutionalism—make no mention of agrarian reform.[22] The poor thus participated in Constitutionalism primarily as taxpayers and as paid soldiers—hoping for the best, but powerless to work in their own interests.

The strength of the Constitutionalists lay in their ability to use the earnings of export production to maintain armies that could operate across Mexico. There were times in 1913 and 1914 when Carranza lost control of his home state of Coahuila, yet his armies fought on elsewhere. The Constitutionalists proved to be the revolutionary faction most able to utilize external resources. Their vocal nationalism was not pleasing to the United States and the British, but their deep devotion to capitalism made them preferable to peasant rebels such as the Zapatistas. Thus, while the Constitutionalists were limited in their ties to their social base, they were offensively strong militarily and most acceptable to the foreign investors and governments most involved in Mexican affairs. They would eventually triumph.

But that victory came only after long months of cooperation and conflict with the other major borderlands faction led by Pancho Villa. The Villista movement has long defied characterization. Assembling in 1913 and 1914 the largest armies of the revolutionary era in his Division of the North, Villa rapidly disappeared as a revolutionary contender after 1915. To some, he joins Zapata as a peasant leader.[23] From the United States, Villa often appears only as the bandit who raided Columbus, New Mexico, and then eluded the Pershing expedition sent to punish him in 1916.[24] At times Villa was a northern Zapata; at other times he was merely a bandit. But he was much more. He organized and led a very powerful revolutionary movement—a movement most effective in destroying the Huerta regime and the Federal army that sustained it. But Villa's faction also incorporated fundamental contradictions and eventually disintegrated.

Pancho Villa was like Zapata in insisting on agrarian change and in seeking both political support and military recruits among the rural poor. He found many of his most devoted followers among the expropriated rancheros of western Chihuahua, and among the struggling sharecroppers of the cotton-export regions of Coahuila and Durango known as the Laguna. Yet Villa's agrarian base was also different from Zapata's, reflecting the different traditions of the Mexican north. Villa's rural supporters were rarely villagers rooted in pre-Hispanic and colonial traditions of community property and cultural separatism. Rather, the rural poor of the borderlands lived in a world of private property and of more mobile—ultimately more Hispanic—individuals and families. Agrarian complaints emphasized the return of stolen lands and the creation of new small holdings—as private properties that would be used for both subsistence and commercial production. In addition, there were potential conflicts among Villa's agrarian backers. The lands that rancheros demanded returned as stolen had often been let in the meantime to immigrant sharecroppers, who might demand the same lands by right of possession and production. Doing justice in old land disputes could conflict with the distribution of lands to new revolutionary claimants.[25]

Villa's movement also differed from Zapata's in that it was never a singularly agrarian faction. Villa incorporated into his forces disgruntled members of the middle classes, as well as borderlands elites opposed to the Terrazas clan. He also cooperated with important foreign actors, including Hearst interests and the Guggenheims' American Smelting and Refining Company. These alliances have led to arguments that the social orientation of the Villistas was essentially the same as that of the Constitutionalists. Both factions did incorporate people of all classes.[26] But the Constitutionalists were led by established elites who controlled remnants of the old state and who had long refused to court agrarian demands. In contrast, the Villistas were led by men of plebian roots, who tolerated middle- and upper-class collaborators, while actively pursuing agrarian support.[27]

What Villa shared with the Constitutionalists was a model of economic and military organization for the pursuit of revolutionary victory. Villa, too, sustained his faction by the active promotion of commercial and export production. He organized a skeletal state and maintained a paid army with complex supply and medical support systems. Such commercial–state organization of Villa's faction reflected not only the historical tradition of the borderlands, but also his competition for regional hegemony and national power with Carranza. It reflected Villa's clearly military vision of the revolutionary confrontation. And it allowed him to build and maintain large and effective armies.[28]

But while Villa's chosen means of economic support and military organization brought military strength, they also deepened the social contradictions within his faction. To recruit tens of thousands of committed fighters, Villa promoted a vision of a radically changed rural Mexico. To earn the funds to pay those troops and maintain them in the field—even far from home—Villa had to preserve the existing economic structures in his borderlands base. And he had to win at least the collaboration of the Mexican and foreign elites who ruled that borderlands economy. In sum, Villa attempted to incorporate both the beneficiaries and the victims of Díaz's model of borderlands development into one faction. For a while he succeeded, focusing all on opposition to Huerta and successfully assembling the largest army in revolutionary Mexico.

In time, and in the face of military difficulties, however, internal contradictions would wrack the Villista movement. The weakness was evident early on in the absence of a clear Villista program. Yet Villa could not issue an unequivocal revolutionary ideology. To do so would inevitably alienate some segment of his coalition. So while Zapata fought staunchly for the reconstruction of landed peasant communities, and while Carranza pursued a very public vision of a more nationalist, capitalist Mexico, Villa appeared to hesitate. His sympathies for the poor majority were known; his programs for Mexico's future were not.

Villa repeatedly proclaimed his commitment to the rural poor. He often talked of a borderlands with no great estates, their lands divided into modest ranchos owned by families who worked them, and would have arms to defend them. But in 1914 and 1915, when he had the power to implement that vision, he did not. The immediate construction of Villa's ranchero utopia would have undermined his armies. Estate division and land redistribution would disrupt the commercial export economy that made his troops so effective even away from home. The mere beginnings of such a transformation would alienate the wealthy Mexicans and North Americans who ruled the borderlands economy. And the redistribution of land would give Villa's soldiers compelling reasons to return home to claim their ranchos and to stay to defend them. The immediate redistribution of land would have made Villa's movement much like Zapata's—strong locally and defensively. But Villa was locked into competition with the Constitutionalists to build and maintain mobile armies based on export production and to topple a regime in distant Mexico City. Villa needed offensive power, which precluded any revolutionary fulfillment of his commitments to the rural poor.

The best Villa could attempt was a compromise. His forces claimed the vast estates of the Terrazas clan and other elites who opposed the movement. But they held them intact as revolutionary properties, worked as large commercial operations, often for export, to maintain the troops. Working conditions surely improved under revolutionary administration. But the basic economic structure did not change. Villa promised that once his movement triumphed, the estates would be divided to provide lands for the veterans of his armies and for the widows and orphans of those who died in combat. To benefit from Villa's delayed agrarian reform, northerners had to join his armies. The goal was clearly to maximize military power in a region of deep agrarian grievances.[29]

But the compromise brought liabilities. Villa's opponents could challenge his agrarian commitment by pointing to the lack of structural change in the regions he ruled. And those who chose not to fight were excluded from Villa's land reform plans, thus weakening the ties between his armies and the population they claimed to serve. Should Villa's armies face defeat, there would be difficulties. No entrenched social gains would lead Villistas and their backers to fight on doggedly—as would the Zapatistas—after military triumph was out of reach. Pancho Villa built and led a revolutionary faction capable of operating large, mobile, and powerful armies, but one subject to rapid collapse in the face of adversity.

The Constitutionalists and Villistas were the most powerful, but not the only, revolutionary movements based in northern Mexico beginning in 1913. There were many smaller groups, often driven by local agrarian grievances. But their actions were constrained by the need to operate in a northern revolutionary context dominated by the competition between the two dominant factions. The Yaqui of Sonora had long defined themselves as a separate people, often working in the commercial economy and adopting Christianity, but fiercely resisting full cultural and political incorporation into the Hispanic world. The border-lands economic boom of the Díaz era led to the expropriation of much of the Yaqui's fine river valley land, setting off violent conflicts that brought brutal repression and the deportation of many Yaqui to distant Yucatán. In those wars, the Yaqui primarily faced hated federal troops. Thus, many were ready to join the Sonoran Constitutionalists against Huerta's Federals in 1913. Yaqui forces were crucial to early Constitutionalist victories in the northwest.

In return, they expected confirmation of their traditional claims to lands and local autonomy. But the Constitutionalist leaders in Sonora came from the favored classes who were the beneficiaries of Yaqui land losses. And the movement insisted on maintaining commercial and export production on those lands to support mobile armies. So like the Villistas, when the Sonora Constitutionalists confiscated estates, the lands were not redistributed. The Yaqui felt betrayed. Many refused to stay in the Constitutionalist armies as they marched south. They would remain in the homeland. Their deeply agrarian goals were incompatible with Constitutionalism. Yet the Constitutionalist domination of their homeland—and their deep hate for the Federals—precluded a shift to opposition. They could only stay home, often sympathizing with Villa who at least promised a future redistribution, frustrated that the movement they had helped to empower refused to address their demands.[30]

A different kind of northern agrarian movement developed in the eastern reaches of San Luis Potosí, led by Saturnino Cedillo and his brothers. The Cedillos were rancheros, modest property owners long in conflict with the great estates that dominated their home region both economically and politically. Their conflict with local elites led the Cedillos to pursue not only the interests of other landed rancheros, but also to defend the rights of estate dependents—especially of the large numbers of sharecroppers who dreamed of becoming propertied rancheros. They had backed Madero in 1910 and 1911—and had rebelled against the reformer in September of 1912 to protest the lack of land redistribution. Thus, the Cedillos and their agrarian allies were already in rebellion when the more general risings of 1913 began. They sacked local estates. When they could, they ousted the owners and allowed sharecroppers to cultivate on their own account. The Cedillistas produced first for subsistence, but they also continued the local production of ixtle fibers for export to purchase arms. They admired Zapata from a distance, but had to deal with the northern reality of Constitutionalist and Villista power. Early on, they called themselves Constitutionalists—as did Villa—but always kept Carranza at a distance. The Cedillos saw plainly that Carranza's closest local allies in San Luis Potosí were landlords such as the Barragán family. The Cedillos led a staunchly agrarian movement, demanding land redistribution and effecting as much as they could amidst the conflicts. They prevented Huerta from ever establishing effective power in rural San Luis Potosí. When later forced to choose, the Cedillos joined with Villa against the Constitutionalists.[31]

From early 1913 until the summer of 1914, revolutionary conflicts focused on ousting the Huerta regime. Constitutionalists, Villistas, Zapatistas, and many smaller factions fought to eliminate those who aimed to reimpose the Díaz system with a strong new dose of militarism. The opposition factions, however, did not always work in harmony. They worried about each others' conflicting plans for postrevolutionary reconstruction. But they kept their differences contained by focusing on the common enemy. Villa accepted the fiction of subordination to Carranza. All the northerners had questions about the distant Zapata, but they also knew that the Zapatista threat just south of the capital prevented a strong federal move against the borderlands.

Opposition movements proliferated, and Huerta's armies could not face them all. The turning point came with the several bloody battles fought between Federals and Villistas around Torreón in March and April 1914. Villa's victories ended Huerta's pretense of ruling the borderlands and opened the way for northern armies to march toward the capital.[32] Also in April 1914, United States marines captured Veracruz to express Woodrow Wilson's growing disapproval of Huerta—an intervention that denied the struggling regime control of the nation's leading port, but also handed Huerta the posture of wounded nationalism.[33]

Confronted by multiple revolutionary factions, innumerable local revolts, and United States opposition, Huerta was doomed. He resigned and fled Mexico in July 1914, leaving his subordinates to grapple with the revolutionary forces converging on the capital.

With Huerta eliminated and the old regime in retreat, the revolutionary confrontation did not end. It did change—radically. Now, factions with different regional bases, varying class interests, and conflicting programs began to jockey to become the new state. The ensuing conflict would last another year and caused as many as two hundred thousand additional casualties.[34]

At first, revolutionary maneuvering proceeded on two fronts: the factions negotiated while they simultaneously sought strategic military advantages.[35] In July, Villa and Alvaro Obregón, the leading Constitutionalist general from Sonora, met at Torreón to explore borderlands unity. Villa insisted on a commitment to land reform and that Carranza be named interim president— eliminating a subsequent full term. Obregón agreed at Torreón, but Carranza rejected the pact, refusing to recognize agrarian demands or limits on his political ambitions.[36]

Revolutionary unity among the two major borderlands factions, then, was nominal at best as they moved to occupy the capital in August. Villa's troops had been in the forefront of the often deadly campaigns to oust Huerta, but Carrancista loyalists beat him to Mexico City. In part, that Constitutionalist advantage resulted from Villa's concern to consolidate his borderlands bases. But Carranza and his allies also plotted to block Villa's route to the capital— while U.S. Customs officials at El Paso limited Villa's access to the coal needed to take his trains rapidly south. With Huerta's fall, conflict escalated between Villistas and Carrancistas—and an emerging United States preference for the Constitutionalists began to come into play.[37]

As the Constitutionalists approached Mexico City, they negotiated a most revealing agreement with the Federal forces holding the city. The remnants of Huerta's troops would fortify the southern flank of the capital to prevent a Zapatista occupation. Huertistas thus guaranteed that the Constitutionalists would be the faction to claim Mexico City.[38] Huertistas and Constitutionalists were ready to war over political power, but both movements were based in Mexico's upper and middle classes, and both were deeply opposed to the Zapatistas and their adamant agrarian demands. In September, Zapata would demand that Carranza recognize the Plan of Ayala as the basis of any revolutionary unity. Carranza refused, given the Zapatista plan's insistence on the immediate delivery of lands to Mexico's villagers; and the split between Constitutionalists and Zapatistas was complete.[39]

To attempt to resolve the conflicts among the factions—or perhaps only to clarify them before battle resumed—a convention of revolutionary leaders met at Aguascalientes in October 1914. Neither Carranza, Zapata, nor Villa participated personally, though Villa remained nearby with troops. Weeks of fiery rhetoric and backroom negotiations revealed that Villa and Zapata could move toward alliance. They shared broad agrarian commitments and lower-class bases. But they could not create an effective revolutionary government nor an unequivocal revolutionary program. The limitations of the Villista–Zapatista alliance in the Convention reflected the historically rooted differences in the agrarian demands of the central highland villagers and borderlands rancheros—as well as Villa's inclusion of more conservative interests in his faction. The conservatives, led by General Felipe Angeles, were prominent among the Villista delegates to the Convention. And in the fall of 1914, Villa would not risk alienating the latter's economic and military support for a closer relation with his own agrarian base and an effective alliance with the Zapatistas. Regional differences and the contradictions within Villismo precluded radical agrarian unity in 1914.

But even the limited alliance of Villa and Zapata, with their rhetorical calls for an agrarian transformation, was anathema to Carranza, whose leadership was also plainly unacceptable to the agrarians. Carranza provoked the final split by refusing to recognize the Convention government. And Obregón, after pressing Carranza to at least consider agrarian issues, joined Carranza once the split was final late in November. Obregón understood the political importance of agrarian demands, for he came from the heartland of the Yaqui conflicts. But he viewed agrarian leaders of lower-class origins, including Villa and Zapata, as mere bandits. For Obregón, agrarian demands might be addressed, but independent agrarian leaders could not be allowed to rule.[40]

The Convention of Aguascalientes brought revolutionary factions with different regional bases together to face what were also class conflicts. Constitutionalist collusion with Huertistas against Zapata was clearly a class action. The Zapatista–Villista alliance was a class alliance, with its weakness caused in large part by the regional diversity that separated the lower classes across Mexico. And as the major factions took sides for another military confrontation, smaller movements had to take sides. Most northerners with strong agrarian bases, like the Cedillos, declared for Villa and the Convention government. Central highlands rebels with peasant roots, such as Tlaxcala's Domingo Arenas, lined up with Zapata and the Convention. Meanwhile, Arenas's local rival, Máximo Rojas—with an agrarian following, but more clearly political ambitions—remained a Constitutionalist.[41]

In an exhaustive study of the revolutionary decade from 1910 to 1920, Alan Knight argues that these factions are best understood as movements divided by their leaders' ambitions and by differences in vision. In Knight's view, the Constitutionalist vision was national, while Villistas, Zapatistas, and others were limited by provincial perspectives.[42] Differences of class, however, lay directly behind conflicts played out by ambitious leaders and expressed as contrasting visions. The differing class constituencies of the regionally based factions have already been outlined, emphasizing that class relations are regional phenomena in a nation as diverse as Mexico. The conflicting class goals promoted by the factions' ideologies have also been noted. That the Carrancistas had a more national vision resulted from the upper-class and middle-sector interests represented by Constitutionalism. Zapatista vision was provincial because the lives of peasant villagers were historically limited to provincial domains, a class-based constriction. And Villista vision was contradictory—at times national and even international, but often provincial—because of the contradictory class composition of the movement.

Even apparently personal political conflicts had class dimensions. Carranza and Villa did detest each other, in part because of their very different personal class origins and in part because of the distinct class orientations of their movements. Repeatedly, their conflicts peaked over whether land redistribution would be a core revolutionary promise. Class was also obvious in Carranza and Obregón viewing Zapata as a rustic bandit—and what they resented most was his powerful insistence that peasant villagers immediately and independently implement land reform.

The revolutionary confrontation in Mexico cannot be explained as a conflict among two or three national classes.[43] Class relations varied regionally in Mexico in 1914, and thus class-based conflicts were played out by regionally constituted factions. That did not make class conflict less important in the Mexican revolution—only more complex.

By late 1914, class issues had come to the foreground in alignments soon to be tested on battlefields. During the next six months it became clear that the upper- and middle-class Constitutionalists could attain greater national unity as well as international backing, while the lower-class Zapatistas and the multi-class Villistas remained regionally divided and internationally isolated. Those historically rooted differences of class unity and external support would structure the outcome of the revolution.

The revolutionary confrontation moved into another phase in December 1914. The Constitutionalists evacuated Mexico City, allowing the agrarian alliance another important advantage. The radicals then held almost all of the interior highlands from the Zapatista heartland south of the capital to the staunchly Villista central borderlands. Villa and Zapata met at Xochimilco, outside the capital, early in December. They agreed on the need to break up the great estates, to eliminate Carranza, and thus to move jointly to the east and against the Constitutionalist forces barely clinging to Mexican soil along the Gulf at Veracruz.

But again, the alliance proved weak. Soon after agreeing to move east, on 10 December, Villa pulled his main forces back to the northwest, to the Bajío—apparently concerned first to consolidate his links with his borderlands home.

Zapata did send armies east and they captured Puebla on 16 December—already complaining of the limited assistance provided by Villa. Without Villista coordination and assistance, Zapata's weak offensive capacities made holding Puebla difficult. Movement further east against Carranza was impossible.[44] The tenuous agrarian alliance had reached its limit.

Why were the two factions most grounded in the concerns of the rural poor unable to forge a unity capable of attaining national power? Answers abound. Adolfo Gilly argues that peasants are structurally incapable of leading a national revolution to victory.[45] Alan Knight sees the agrarians crippled by provincial vision.[46] But the failure of agrarian unity was the result of neither class incapacity nor of restricted vision by agrarian leaders.

Real differences divided Villistas and Zapatistas—differences reflecting regional variations of class relations. Villa and Zapata each built movements grounded in the rural poor of their homelands. For Zapata, that meant seeking lands and autonomy for peasant villagers. For Villa, that meant demanding small private properties for ranchero families. And while Zapata built a guerrilla movement defensively anchored in Morelos villages, Villa organized mobile, offensive armies capable of fighting far beyond the borderlands. Zapata could thus effect land reform immediately; Villa had to insist on a delay. These movements were not different because of their leaders' limited visions. They differed because of Zapata's and Villa's clear grasp of the demands of their regional followings. Their abilities to respond to regional grievances gave their movements strength. The same clarity of perception limited the possibilities of effective alliance—an outcome further restricted by Villa's continuing inclusion of important conservative interests within his less cohesive faction.

Those differences surfaced quickly in early January 1915 as the Convention met again in Mexico City, now as a Villista–Zapatista congress. Zapatistas again insisted on immediate land redistribution, to be implemented by villagers. And they called for a national regime that was parliamentary and purposefully weak at the center. Villistas, in contrast, insisted on delayed and state-controlled land reform—for immediate redistribution would undermine Villa's armies and cost him important economic support. Villistas also insisted on a strong state to rule Mexico's future.[47] No unity was attained. In late January, as Constitutionalists again approached the capital, the Zapatistas retreated to Morelos, taking the Convention with them. Villa then named his own ministers of government, effectively renouncing the recognition of the Convention. Thus ended the attempt at agrarian unity.[48] Regional differences of agrarian class relations had prevailed.

That opened the way for a rapid Constitutionalist resurgence. Carranza, Obregón, and those they led were not without resources as 1915 began. Building upon the regional bases in Coahuila and Sonora, with Huerta gone they gained the allegiance of many members of the Mexican middle and upper classes, who found the Constitutionalist program of nationalist capitalism more acceptable than the radical, agrarian proposals of Villa and especially Zapata. Yet upper- and middle-class backing, even if unanimous (which it was not), could provide only a minority social base in a society of extreme inequalities and mass poverty.

International linkages, however, allowed the Constitutionalists to surmount the limitations of their social base within Mexico. Carranza proclaimed his nationalism vociferously. He publicly insisted that foreigners would not dictate Mexican political developments, while he demanded that Mexicans play a more powerful role in Mexico's deepening involvement in the international economy. Carranza's nationalism, however, did not limit his seeking arms and recognition from the United States. And Constitutionalist nationalism in no way opposed Mexico's continuing incorporation into the world capitalist economy. In fact, Carranza organized his revolutionary faction and later his regime to depend heavily on externally linked economic activities.

The United States occupation forces evacuated the crucial port of Veracruz to the Constitutionalists late in November 1914, just as Carranza broke with the Convention. John Hart has recently argued that the delivery of that port to the Constitutionalists was at the center of an ermerging campaign by the Wilson administration to support Carranza as the revolutionary leader most acceptable to North American economic interests in Mexico. Hart has also uncovered evidence that the United States not only gave the port to Carranza, but also left behind ample supplies of arms and ammunition—aiming to strengthen the Constitutionalists while simultaneously working to limit Villa's access to arms across the northern border.[49]

Control of Veracruz also gave the Constitutionalists a major point of access to world markets. From that base along the Gulf, they fought to take control of the revenues generated by two of Mexico's most valuable exports: petroleum and henequén. The Constitutionalists took control of Tampico, Mexico's primary oil port, in the fall of 1914 and defended it against Villista assault until securing a clear victory in March 1915. Meanwhile, nationalistic pronouncements about Mexico's rights to its oil helped to press foreign-owned oil companies for increased tax and royalty payments, while the great war in Europe drove up demand.[50]

Carranza also worked from late 1914 until March of 1915 to take control of Yucatán and to tax the henequén fiber exports also stimulated by wartime demand. In March 1915 Salvador Alvarado, another Sonoran, led a Constitutionalist force of six thousand men that made Yucatán part of Carranza's domains. In the absence of local agrarian mobilization, the revolution came to Yucatán via Constitutionalist armies. That export region thus served to provide revenues to expand and sustain Carrancista armies in the crucial battles fought in central and northern Mexico.[51]

With arms from the United States and revenues from export production, the Constitutionalists had the resources to begin to reassert their power. But they also needed to broaden their social base within Mexico. Foreign resources were important, but alone they could not bring the Constitutionalists to power. In search of new support, early in 1915 Carranza finally gave in to the advice of his leading general, Obregón, and his primary ideologue, Luis Cabrera—who insisted that the only way to compete with Villa and Zapata within Mexico was to offer a Constitutionalist social program with a strong agrarian slant. The result was a turn to populist politics, offering programs designed by the powerful to attract the political support of the poor.

For Carranza, even such a limited orientation toward the masses came reluctantly, and only from political necessity. As the Constitutionalists fought back toward the capital, their armies captured Tlaxcala on 1 January 1915 and Puebla on 5 January. They thus held strategic cities in regions where irate villagers ruled the countryside, and where agrarian demands infused all political discussion. Carranza could consolidate his power there only with an agrarian program. At that critical moment, on 6 January 1915, he issued decrees enabling Constitutionalist field commanders to return disputed lands to villagers—with final rights subject to approval by the national executive, Carranza. Of course, Carranza insisted that his reform be state controlled. His commanders, notably General Francisco Coss, set about winning local agrarian support in the Puebla–Tlaxcala region via an active land redistribution in January and February 1915.

The 6 January decrees were a politically astute maneuver aimed at winning immediate gains in a region of intense agrarian conflict, and attempting to attract to the Constitutionalist banner agrarian rebels elsewhere in Mexico. It was a classic populist strategy, with the powerful implementing limited reforms in order to control them and to prevent more radical changes that might be implemented by the revolutionary masses. As a strategy within Mexico's revolutionary confrontation, it was effective, allowing the Constitutionalists to consolidate their hold on the Puebla basin, and from there to retake Mexico City in February 1915.[52]

Once in the capital, Obregón led the Constitutionalists into another populist alliance. The Casa del Obrero Mundial—representing urban, organized labor—joined the Constitutionalist coalition, providing political support, fighting brigades, and an ideological claim to wider labor support. Why urban workers chose to back the Constitutionalists rather than the Villistas or Zapatistas is much debated. Yet the reasons are clear. Organized urban laborers lived in the rapidly commercializing, industrializing world that the constitutionalists represented—and promoted. The fundamental conflicts between that world and the agrarian utopia envisioned by rural radicals was made painfully plain in February 1915 when the Zapatistas cut the water supplies and restricted the provision of food to the capital. Mexico's rural peoples had long resented the extraction of the food they produced to sustain urban society—while they remained hungry. Organized labor was part of that urban society. And the conflicting economic interests that divided agrarian radicals and urban workers were compounded by cultural contradictions. City labor leaders were shocked by the deep religiosity of the Zapatistas who occupied Mexico City.

There was no natural alliance of urban labor and peasant revolutionaries. Meanwhile, Constitutionalist nationalism could attract many industrial workers whose complaints often focused on mistreatment at the hands of foreign capitalists and managers. Sharing a commitment to a commercializing, industrializing Mexico; sharing a nationalist perspective on that commitment; and sharing opposition to the agrarian radicals' anticommercial and religion-infused visions, labor leaders and Constitutionalists joined together in early 1915.[53]

As the Constitutionalists expanded their coalition and build their economic base, and as critical military tests loomed near, Villistas and Zapatistas remained divided. In March, Obregón again abandoned the capital to organize for battle, and the Convention government returned. Zapatistas and Villistas continued to debate whether land reform should be immediate or delayed, and how it should be organized. And each faction continued to complain, with justification, of a lack of assistance from the other.[54]

Meanwhile, the Constitutionalists contained the divisions that might develop from their new populist politics. Many of Carranza's backers from the upper and entrepreneurial classes worried about the new promises to the lower orders. In April 1915 Carranza addressed upper-class fears by proclaiming his staunch support for the rights of productive private property.[55] Within four short months, Carranza promised first to deliver lands to the peasants and then to protect existing property rights. These were political commitments—expedient positions more easily compromised than the deeper social obligations that guided the Zapatistas and, to a lesser degree, the Villistas. As the summer of

1915 approached, the Constitutionalists' populist political coalition held together, while regionally based social commitments kept agrarian revolutionaries divided.

Beginning in April, Obregón provoked a series of decisive battles against Villa in the Bajío, first at Celaya and later at León. Fighting at first with his armies still dispersed across the north, and always without Zapatista aid, Villa faced bloody stalemates and then deadly defeats. Amidst those battles, Villa finally grasped the need for an unequivocal agrarian program—promising small private properties to the poor—but it came too late.[56] Fighting alone against Obregón's armies—whose external linkages were symbolized by the adoption of trench-warfare techniques from the conflict raging in Europe—Villa's troops lost decisively in June outside León.[57] Divided popular factions proved no match for a united populist movement with ample arms and the revenues of a booming external economy. The regionally based divisions among the revolutionaries representing the rural poor allowed populists with foreign sources of wealth and arms to triumph in Mexico's revolutionary confrontation.

From the summer of 1915, the Constitutionalists moved to consolidate their victory on the battlefields of the Bajío and become the new Mexican state. The United States gave de-facto recognition to Carranza's regime in October. Villistas and Zapatistas were not eliminated, but they were reduced to the enclaves of regional resistance. Conflict was not over—violence would persist through the 1920s—but the basic question of the national state was settled. The battles to come would focus on how the new state would deal with those it had defeated, but not eliminated, and how it would implement the populist promises the Constitutionalists had made in order to become that state.

Following the battles of the Bajío, the major factions each took a close look at their programs. The Zapatistas changed little. Always staunch in defense of the goals of Morelos villagers, they persisted in demanding the immediate return of land to peasant cultivators. Villa continued the move toward his agrarian base begun in the heat of battle. He broke with many of the more conservative members of his coalition. Thus could the Zapatistas and the remaining Villistas move closer together. In October 1915 the remnant of the Convention government finally generated a common program. It demanded the return of lands to those who worked them, and allowed for both small private properties and community holdings. It called for a government based on autonomous municipalities, coordinated by a parliamentary regime responsive to local and regional interests. And an armed peasantry would replace the military—organized more to repel social exploitation than to deal with foreign threats.[58]

Agreement, however, came too late. Zapata and Villa were now isolated from each other in their distant homelands. Both now operated defensively as guerrillas, making coordinated offensive actions against the Constitutionalists' emerging state impossible. The adamant agrarians would fight on to pressure the new regime—to make it clear that victory was not the same as pacification, and that pacification would not come without an agrarian transformation. But there was no prospect of a radical agrarian victory after 1915. The unifying visions of that autumn would remain visions. Those who fought in the interests of the rural poor would not become the Mexican state.

With victory, the Constitutionalists also reassessed their priorities. The call for agrarian reform, so strong in January, began to fade. Carranza again assured landowners of his respect for property rights, and welcomed many into the leadership of the new regime—especially in the provinces. He proved his commitments to the propertied few by returning to them during late 1915 and 1916 most of the lands his troops had confiscated during the time of armed conflict. For example, in strategically important Tlaxcala, where land redistribution had been critical to the Constitutionalist triumph, Carranza long delayed final approval of the numerous grants made by his field commanders when the revolution hung in the balance early in 1915. For many, confirmation never came, or land areas were reduced to insignificance. For Carranza, agrarian reform began to have a new meaning, emphasizing increased production for urban consumption and export earnings. These were the strengths of the old landed elites.[59] Carranza's agrarian reform would address the interests of the entrepreneurial and urban sectors of society that he had long represented.

Carranza's relations with organized labor also changed with victory. He made it increasingly clear that he expected workers to back his regime and accept limited material benefits. He encouraged their involvement with mutual aid programs. But when labor organizations sought independence and made political demands, threatening and then staging economically disruptive strikes early in 1916, Carranza cracked down with force.[60] Carranza's populist state would offer limited reforms and brook no independent demands from below. Organized labor was quickly frustrated; but where could it turn once the revolutionary confrontation was concluded and Constitutionalist power entrenched in the state?

Not all Constitutionalist leaders backed Carranza's rapid retreat from populist commitments. Obregón recognized that the social promises necessary to his military victories in 1915 would remain central issues in the long process of regime consolidation. He was able to pursuade Carranza to allow some provision of lands among constitutionalist supporters in Sonora, Obregón's home state. But these were political concessions reluctantly granted.[61] In 1917, Obregón would leave the Carranza administration, mostly because of disagreement with the president's retreat from populist promises. Before leaving, however, Obregón worked to assure that the populist agenda was incorporated in the new Constitution of 1917.

Late in 1916, the Constitutionalists met in convention at Querétaro to write the new national charter that their name had promised. The resulting document incorporated all the contradictions inherent in the victorious faction. The charter defended the principle of private property, while promising land to peasant villagers, and left implementation in the hands of the executive. It promised wage and other benefits to organized labor, and left it subject to tight state control. It promised economic nationalism, and left Mexico tied to the externally driven capitalist economy.[62] The new constitution did not resolve the issues that had fueled the violent confrontation from 1913 to 1915. It simply made legal what was concluded on the battlefields of 1915. The Constitutionalists would rule an increasingly powerful state that would grapple with fundamental and still unresolved social questions.

During the decades after 1917, postrevolutionary governments worked to consolidate their power and to promote capitalist development, while regionally based popular movements demanded policies of land reform and labor rights. In that contest, populist promises became effective programs only when popular forces made it clear that land redistribution and commitments to workers' rights were the only means to pacification—thus contributing to regime stabilization. In 1917, Zapata, Villa, Cedillo, and many others remained in arms with staunch local followings. Obregón went home to Sonora to attend to his fortune and to his political future. Carrancistas assassinated Zapata in 1919. But when Carranza tried to block Obregón's accession to the presidency in 1920, the Sonora populist took power in alliance with agrarians such as Cedillo and surviving Zapatistas. Carranza was killed in flight.

Under Obregón, the early 1920s saw a more active populism. Land reform came quickly to states like Morelos and Tlaxcala, where redistribution was essential to pacification. Elsewhere, often where rural mobilizations had been limited before 1920, rural people organized, protested, and periodically rebelled, demanding that they too be pacified with land.[63] In 1923, facing a revolt led by General Adolfo de la Huerta and backed by elites and much of the army, Obregón relied on the armed beneficiaries of land reform to defeat his foes and to allow his chosen successor, fellow Sonoran Plutarco Elías Calles, to become president in 1924.

Calles would attempt to retreat from agrarian populism while he dominated Mexico from 1924 to 1934. But in facing the massive Cristero uprising from 1926 to 1929, he too had to rely on the armed recipients of land to support his army—again strengthening populist claims. Then the depression of the early 1930s weakened the commercial and export-oriented elites who backed the Constitutionalists and had worked to limit populist reforms.

In that context, Lázaro Cárdenas took power in 1934. It was Cárdenas who implemented the populist transformation promised by the Constitutionalist victory in the battles of 1915, and by the charter of 1917. He used a massive, state-directed land reform to undermine landed elites, to pacify long restive peasants and rural workers, and to make the recipients dependent on the state. Cárdenas support for strikes simultaneously benefited organized labor and left it dependent on the state. And the expropriation of foreign oil companies in 1938 loudly proclaimed Mexican nationalism and strengthened the state, without lessening Mexico's basic dependence on the international economy. Finally fulfilling populist promises, Cárdenas stabilized the postrevolutionary state. His national reconstruction helped to homogenize regional differences that had long fragmented Mexican society and political life. Cárdenas's state-directed, populist reforms laid the foundation for the political stability, capitalist growth, and social immiseration that would characterize Mexico through the half-century after 1940.

All the factions that rose in 1913 to oppose the Huerta regime began as regional movements. They had different social bases, economic organizations, and political agendas. It was the Constitutionalists, who moved beyond their regional base to address a national, upper- and middle-class, urban constituency and who effectively utilized international resources, who claimed the power to become the national state in 1915. Regional and agrarian forces were not then vanquished, but they were forced into a defensive posture. The dominance of a populist, nationalist state, addressing first the concerns of already favored sectors of society, while promoting international economic linkages—along with the subordination of regional factions more responsive to popular and agrarian demands—were the primary legacies of the revolutionary confrontation of 1913–1917. Twentieth-century Mexico was structured by that outcome.

Notes

1. For that background, this analysis depends heavily on John Tutino, *From Insurrection to Revolution in Mexico: Social Bases of Agrarian Violence, 1750–1940* (Princeton:

Princeton University Press, 1986). In completing this essay, I must thank the anonymous reader for the University of New Mexico Press and especially Friedrich Katz for helpful comments on an earlier draft.

2. See, Arnaldo Córdova, *La ideología de la Revolución Mexicana; La formación del nuevo régimen* (México: Ediciones Era, 1973); and Nora Hamilton, *The Limits of State Autonomy: Post-Revolutionary Mexico* (Princeton: Princeton University Press, 1982).

3. Córdova, *La ideolgía*, pp. 108–13.

4. On the coup, see Michael Meyer, *Huerta: A Political Portrait* (Lincoln: University of Nebraska Press, 1972), 45–63.

5. Friedrich Katz, *The Secret War in Mexico: Europe, The United States, and the Mexican Revolution* (Chicago: University of Chicago Press, 1981), 119; Alan Knight, *The Mexican Revolution*, 2 vols. (Cambridge: Cambridge University Press, 1986), 2:1, 18, 62–63. For regional perspectives on Huerta, see Raymond Buve, "Peasant Movements, Caudillos, and Land Reform during the Revolution (1910–1917) in Tlaxcala, Mexico," *Boletin de Estudios Latino-Americanos y del Caribe* 18 (June 1975): 133; Dudley Ankerson, *Agrarian Warlord: Saturnino Cedillo and the Mexican Revolution in San Luis Potosí* (DeKalb: Northern Illinois University Press, 1984), 61–62; and Romana Falcón, *Revolución y caciquismo: San Luis Potosí, 1910–1938* (México: El Colegio de México, 1984), 71.

6. On Madero's death, see Meyer, *Huerta*, 69–82.

7. Meyer, *Huerta*, 90–91; Knight, *Mexican Revolution*, II:45, 77–78, 129–36.

8. Knight, *Mexican Revolution*, 2:81–87.

9. Katz, *Secret War*, 156–202; Knight, *Mexican Revolution*, 2:31, 138.

10. On the Zapatistas, see John Womack, Jr., *Zapata and the Mexican Revolution* (New York: Alfred A. Knopf, 1969). This discussion is based on that classic, unless otherwise noted.

11. This interpretation is developed in Tutino, *From Insurrection*, 321–25; see also Arturo Warman, *Y venimos a contradecir: Los campesinos de Morelos y el estado nacional* (México: La Casa Chata, 1976); and Roberto Melville, *Crecimiento y rebelión: El desarrollo económico de las haciendas azucareras en Morelos, 1880–1910* (México: Nueva Imagen, 1979).

12. See Womack, *Zapata*; Córdova, *La ideología*, 144–55; and Arturo Warman, "The Political Project of Zapatismo," trans. Judith Brister, in *Riot, Rebellion, and Revolution: Rural Social Conflict in Mexico*, ed. Friedrich Katz (Princeton: Princeton University Press, 1988), 321–37.

13. Womack, *Zapata*, 235–36, 240–41.

14. Ibid., p. 184.

15. Buve, "Peasant Movements," 122–39; and Raymond Buve, "Neither Carranza nor Zapata: The Rise and Fall of a Peasant Movement that Tried to Challenge Both: Tlaxcala, 1910–1919," in *Riot, Rebellion, and Revolution*, 341–46.

16. For Díaz-era developments in the borderlands, see Mark Wasserman, *Capitalists,*

Caciques, and Revolution: The Native Elite and Foreign Enterprise in Chihuahua, Mexico, 1854–1911 (Chapel Hill: University of North Carolina Press, 1984).

17. See Ibid., as well as the essays in Thomas Benjamin and William McNellie, *Other Mexicos: Essays on Regional Mexican History, 1876–1911* (Albuquerque: University of New Mexico Press, 1984).

18. See Wasserman, *Capitalists, Caciques, and Revolution.*

19. Ibid.; see also William K. Meyers, "La Comarca Lagunera: Work, Protest, and Popular Mobilization in North Central Mexico," in *Other Mexicos*, 243–74; and Jane Dale Lloyd, "Rancheros y revoluciones en el noroeste de Chihuahua," in *Campesinos, terratenientes, y revolucionarios*, ed. Oscar Betanzos, vol. 3 of *Historia de la cuestión agrarian mexicana* (México: Siglo XXI, 1988), 78–106.

20. On Carranza, see Douglas Richmond, *Venustiano Carranza's Nationalist Struggle* (Lincoln: University of Nebraska Press, 1983); on Sonora and the use of state organization, see Hector Aguilar Camín, *La frontera nómada: Sonora y la revolución mexicana* (México: Siglo XXI, 1976).

21. See Richmond, *Venustiano Carranza's Nationalist Struggle*; and Córdova, *La ideología*, 188–218.

22. Richmond, *Venustiano Carranza's Nationalist Struggle*, 49–50; Córdova, *La ideología*, 195–96; Katz, *Secret War*, 128–31.

23. Adolfo Gilly, *La revolución interrumpida* (México: El Caballito, 1971).

24. For a more analytical view, see Friedrich Katz, "Pancho Villa and the Attack on Columbus, New Mexico," *American Historical Review*, 83:1 (February 1978):101–30.

25. See Wasserman, *Capitalists, Caciques, and Revolution*; Meyers, "La Comarca Lagunera;" and Lloyd, "Rancheros y revoluciones."

26. Knight, *Mexican Revolution*, 2:118–19, 270.

27. Ibid., 297.

28. Katz, *Secret War*, 136–52; Silvestre Terrazas, *El verdadero Pancho Villa* (México: Ediciones Era, 1981).

29. Friedrich Katz, "Agrarian changes in Northern Mexico in the Period of Villista Rule, 1913–1915," in *Contemporary Mexico*, ed. James Wilkie et al. (Berkeley: University of California Press, 1976), 259–73; see also, Katz, *Secret War*, 139–41; Knight, *Mexican Revolution*, 2:120–24; and Córdova, *La ideología*, 158–59.

30. On the Yaqui background, see Evelyn Hu-Dehart, *Yaqui Resistance and Survival* (Madison: University of Wisconsin Press, 1984); on the revolution, see Aguilar Camín, *La frontera nómada*, 334–37, 373–74, 378.

31. Knight, *Mexican Revolution*, 2:50–51, 188; Ankerson, *Agrarian Warlord*, 1–91; Falcón, *Revolución y caciquismo*, 21–96.

32. For the battles of Torreón, see John Reed, *Insurgent Mexico* (New York: International Publishers, 1969).

33. Katz, *Secret War*, 195–202; Robert Quirk, *An Affair of Honor* (Lexington: University of Kentucky Press, 1962).

34. Charles Cumberland, *Mexican Revolution: The Constitutionalist Years* (Austin: University of Texas Press, 1972), 209.

35. Ibid., 171; Linda Hall, *Alvaro Obregón: Power and Revolution in Mexico* (College Station: Texas A. and M. University Press, 1981), 76.

36. Robert Quirk, *The Mexican Revolution, 1914–1915: The Convention of Aguascalientes* (Bloomington: Indiana University Press, 1960), 41–43; Hall, *Alvaro Obregón*, 66–69; Knight, *Mexican Revolution*, 2:167.

37. Quirk, *Mexican Revolution*, 53–54; Knight, *Mexican Revolution*, 2:115, 169; John Mason Hart, *Revolutionary Mexico: The Coming and Process of the Mexican Revolution* (Berkeley: University of California Press, 1987), 152–53, 294.

38. Quirk, *Mexican Revolution*, 55–56.

39. Womack, *Zapata*, 206.

40. Quirk, *Mexican Revolution*, 101–31; Katz, *Secret War*, 274, 280–81; Knight, *Mexican Revolution*, 2:236, 251–63, 307–9; Hall, *Alvaro Obregón*, 93–97.

41. Ankerson, *Agrarian Warlord*, 73; Buve, "Peasant Movements," 136–38.

42. Knight, *Mexican Revolution*, 2:232, 239, 274, 283–85.

43. A tendency in Gilly, *La revolución interrumpida*.

44. Quirk, *Mexican Revolution*, 135–43; Cumberland, *Mexican Revolution*, 187; Womack, *Zapata*, 221–22; Knight, *Mexican Revolution*, 2:309–11.

45. *La revolución interrumpida*, 139–74.

46. See, n. 42.

47. Quirk, *Mexican Revolution*, 153–57; see, also, Warman, "Political Project."

48. Quirk, *Mexican Revolution*, 176–78.

49. Hart, *Revolutionary Mexico*, 276–303; see, also, Quirk, *Mexican Revolution*, 130–31; Cumberland, *Mexican Revolution*, 181; Hall, *Alvaro Obregón*, 99.

50. Katz, *Secret War*, 270; Lorenzo Meyer, *México y los Estados Unidos en el conflicto petrolero, 1917–1942* (México: El Colegio de México, 1972), 21, 91–99.

51. Katz, *Secret War*, 272; Knight, *Mexican Revolution*, 2:247–51; see, also, G. M. Joseph, *Revolution from Without: Yucatán, Mexico, and the United States, 1880–1924* (Cambridge: Cambridge University Press, 1982).

52. Quirk, *Mexican Revolution*, 152; Cumberland, *Mexican Revolution*, 187, 232–34; Córdova, *La ideología*, 202–4; Hall, *Alvaro Obregón*, 103, 107; Richmond, *Venustiano Carranza's Nationalist Struggle*, 68–69; Knight, *Mexican Revolution*, 2:313–14; Buve, "Peasant Movements," 140–41, 145, and "Neither Carranza nor Zapata."

53. Quirk, *Mexican Revolution*, 183–87; Barry Carr, *El movimiento obrero y la política en México, 1910–1929* (México: Ediciones Era, 1981), 62–67; Ramón Eduardo Ruíz, *La revolución mexicana y el movimiento obrero, 1911–1923* (México: Ediciones Era, 1978), 71–79; Hall, *Alvaro Obregón*, pp. 110–19; Richmond, *Venustiano Carranza's Nationalist Struggle*, 72–73.

54. Quirk, *Mexican Revolution*, 213–14; Hall, *Alvaro Obregón*, 114–19.

55. Cordova, *La ideología*, 212.

56. Ibid., 160–62; Katz, *Secret War*, 283–84.

57. Quirk, *Mexican Revolution*, 223; Hall, *Alvaro Obregón*, 132; Knight, *Mexican Revolution*, 2:321.

58. Córdova, *La ideología*, 166–72; Katz, *Secret War*, 283–85; Warman, "Political Project."

59. Katz, *Secret War*, 287–93; Richmond, *Venustiano Carranza's Nationalist Struggle*, 80–81, 114–18, 121–24; on Tlaxcala, see Buve, "Neither Carranza nor Zapata," 350–75; and on San Luis Potosí, see Falcón, *Revolución y caciquismo*, 96–97.

60. Ruíz, *Revolución mexicana*, 79–82; Carr, *El movimiento obrero*, 72–79; Richmond, *Venustiano Carranza's Nationalist Struggle*, 125–32.

61. Hall, *Alvaro Obregón*, 160–61.

62. See Córdova, *La ideología*, 214–21; Hall, *Alvaro Obregón*, 163–83.

63. See José Rivera Castro, "Política agraria, organizaciones, luchas y resistencias campesinas entre 1920 y 1928," in *Modernización, lucha agraria, y poder político, 1920–1934*, ed. Enrique Montalvo, vol. 4 of *Historia de la cuestión agraria mexicana* (México: Siglo XXI, 1988) 21–149.

64. On Cárdenas, see Hamilton, *Limits of State Autonomy*; Arnaldo Córdova, *La política de masas del cardenismo* (México: Ediciones Era, 1974); and Luis González, *Los días del presidente Cárdenas* (México: El Colegio de México, 1981).

4

Laboratories of the New State, 1920–1929

Regional Social Reform and Experiments in Mass Politics

Thomas Benjamin

The Mexican revolutions of 1910–1920 were national in name and (at times and in some places) in aspiration, but they were profoundly regional in their origins, courses, and outcomes. The weakening, disintegration, and destruction of the central state from 1910 to 1914 unleashed regional, centrifugal political forces which bedeviled revolutionary and postrevolutionary national governments from Madero to Cárdenas. During the 1920s, a period of weak national government, certain state governors had enough leeway to experiment with social reform; they controlled mass political mobilization and thereby expanded the popular base of government. What were called at the time "laboratories of the Revolution" were in fact laboratories of the new state; in time, a powerful state emerged composed of mass organizations capable of harnessing "the energy and grievances of the popular movement to antithetical ends—state-building and capitalist development."[1] Gradually but inexorably during the 1920s and 1930s the experimentation of state governments was curtailed by central governments that eventually applied many of the political techniques pioneered by the regional laboratories to consolidate power nationally.

The Framework of Agua Prieta

The Mexican revolutions of 1910–1920 resulted in "the partition of the country into fiefdoms belonging to warlords."[2] The government of President Venustiano Carranza (1917–1920), brought to power by the military forces of Sonora and Coahuila, attempted to govern a country not yet at peace with an army outside the president's control, an army composed of powerful chiefs who controlled some states and regions like oriental despots. The rebellion which overthrew Carranza and led to his death in 1920 began as yet another regional reaction to the challenge of the national government. Carranza compounded his error of choosing a civilian "nobody" as his successor by sending federal troops into Sonora, the home state of another and far more popular presidential candidate, Carranza's logical successor, Alvaro Obregón. In April 1920 the Sonorans proclaimed the Plan of Agua Prieta, which accused the national government of violating the sovereignty of the states and withdrew recognition from the government.[3] The Sonoran regionalist rebellion fused with Obregón's besieged presidential campaign, was rapidly backed by most of the army and anti-Carranza rebels, and easily overthrew Carranza and his supporters in the states.[4]

General Alvaro Obregón, popularly and overwhelmingly elected to a four-year term in 1920, became president of a country which did not want to be governed from Mexico City. As the most respected military leader of the triumphant Constitutionalist–Carrancista movement, Obregón had the support of most military chiefs, but he did not by any means control the army. Deals were made with existing regional strong men and with most anti-government regional guerrillas: Zapatistas, Villistas, Cedillistas, Pelaecistas, Mapaches, and so on.[5] Peace was purchased cheaply through what John Womack calls a "regionalized reconstruction."[6] Obregón came to office promising peace based on accommodation not centralization.[7]

The national political framework established by the Agua Prieta movement in 1920 was one of considerable toleration of regional caudillos and state governors. During the electoral campaign Obregón had voiced his support for local control of local affairs. "This policy of staying out of local politics," writes Linda B. Hall, "was one he would follow during his presidency, when he urged his Secretary and Under-Secretary of Government above all to avoid friction with the state governors."[8] He tolerated conservative, even reactionary caudillos and governors like Amado Azuara of Hidalgo, Ignacio Enriquez of Chihuahua, Cesar López de Lara of Tamaulipas, Tiburcio Fernandez Ruiz of Chiapas, and Ángel Flores in Sinaloa, finding "it convenient not to trifle with these subordinates."[9] He also tolerated progressive, even radical caudillos and governors. The conservative Mexico City daily *Excelsiór* complained that "in Veracruz the authorities and workers live outside the constitutional regime; their position is identical to that of a group of rebels having taken possession of a portion of Mexican territory where in they establish systems of government, laws and political principles which reject the supreme law of the land. Yet the President appears not to be aware of such grave irregularities since he always tolerates them and occasionally he even protects and stimulates them." To the editors the problem was clear: "General Obregón crosses his arms with alarming frequency. To him the sovereignty of the States is all; society is nothing."[10]

Obregón's accommodation of the forces of regional autonomy was based partly on a genuine respect for federalism and a realistic assessment of the limits of power of the national government and the dangers of rash political centralization. Further, writes Randal Hansis, "Obregón refused to allow his personal and Presidential prestige to become mired in local political morasses where he might suffer with the defeat of each partisan."[11] Coming to terms with regional caudillos, particularly those who had continued to fight the Carranza government, was a good way to begin the pacification of the country. The Obregón government, nevertheless, implemented a policy of cautious centralization by building tentative bases of support among organized workers and campesinos outside the control of the army and the regional caudillos. This policy complemented, and to some extent grew out of the government's toleration of "caciquismo revolucionario" (revolutionary bossism) and the political experimentation of the "official" radicals in the provinces.[12]

"Experimental Laboratories"

The Obregón government's acceptance of the regional revolutionaries was not simply a result of caution bred of weakness. By carefully lending support to young governors whose local power was based upon control of the bureaucracy of the state governments and the creation "from above" of labor unions and agrarian leagues, Obregón wanted to decrease his dependence upon the military chiefs whose power was based upon troop strength. The progressive and radical governors needed Obregón as much if not more than he needed them; therefore their loyalty was repaid with considerable freedom of action, while disloyalty or lack of cooperation was punished by withholding central government support. Within this political framework, the reformers and radicals used the power of state government to patronize (and in several states, to arm) labor and campesino organizations; employed reform to mobilize popular support; established mass-based political parties; and attempted to redress the social and economic injustices that persisted after ten years of intermittent social revolution and civil war. In 1923 Carleton Beals characterized these states as "experimental laboratories" where "for the first time in Mexican history, a fundamentally new method of social control has been evolved."[13] (See Table 4.1.)

With only a few exceptions, these progressives and radicals were more revolutionary in rhetoric than in action. Although they called themselves socialists, many simply were reformers who sought to balance the interests of capital and labor, and landowner and peasant. They accepted, Ernest Gruening

Table 4.1

Prominent Reformist Regimes during the Obregon–Calles Presidencies, 1920–1928

State	Governor	Period
Chiapas	Carlos Vidal	1925–1927
Jalisco	José Guadalupe Zuno	1922–1926
Michoacán	Francisco I. Múgica	1920–1922
San Luis Potosí	Aurelio Manrique	1923–1926
Tabasco	Tomás Garrido Canabal	1922–1926
Tamaulipas	Emilio Portes Gil	1925–1928
Veracruz	Adalberto Tejeda	1920–1924
Yucatán	Felipe Carrillo Puerto	1922–1924

observed in 1927, "notions of the superiority of collective to individual rights, vaguely denominated as Socialism."[14] Above all these governors were modern politicians, pioneers of mass politics—"*la política de masas.*" They were precursors of the "institutional revolution."

Several of the reformers and radicals came to power in their states as a direct result of the Agua Prieta rebellion. Colonel Adalberto Tejeda was elected governor of Veracruz with Obregón's backing in 1920. Because military power (and landowner support) in the state was monopolized by an ambitious and conservative officer (and friend of Obregón), General Guadalupe Sánchez, Governor Tejeda turned to the only other possible base of political power, workers and campesinos. Tejeda encouraged the organization of labor unions, agrarian groups, and socialist parties. Finding urban labor difficult to control, in 1923 he joined forces with Ursulo Galván of the Veracruz section of the Communist party to establish the League of Agrarian Communities and Peasant Syndicates of the State of Veracruz.[15] During the de la Huerta rebellion of 1923–1924, Tejeda and Galván mobilized agrarista guerrilla forces in defense of the Obregón regime, which assisted in the recapture of Veracruz, guaranteed the political rise of Tejeda, and propelled the agrarian reform program in the state.[16]

Because of the geographic and economic importance of the state, Tejeda's political alliance with agraristas was strongly condemned but also copied. The United States consul in Veracruz wrote to Washington in the fall of 1923: "The working classes have been allowed to dictate in every case that has arisen until there is at present no respect for law and order. The officials either are afraid of the populace or sympathize with them against the foreigner."[17] Nine months after the formation of the Veracruz agrarian league, Primo Tapia and Francisco Múgica organized the League of Agrarian Communities of Michoacán in December 1923. In 1924 and 1925 similar agrarian leagues were established in Aguascalientes, Chiapas, Puebla, San Luis Potosí, Tabasco, and Tamaulipas.[18] The Veracruz League also served as the nucleus from which the Liga Nacional Campesina was established in 1926, integrating eleven state leagues (Chihuahua, Durango, the Federal District, Jalisco, Michoacán, Morelos, Puebla, Querétaro, Sinaloa, Tlaxcala, and Veracruz) and representing over three hundred thousand campesinos.[19]

In the southeast, two radical governors came to power in the early 1920s and set about to revolutionize their states. Felipe Carrillo Puerto, perhaps the inventor of the regional agrarian leagues (*ligas de resistencia*, 1915–1919), first rose to prominence in his native Yucatán as an agrarian organizer under Governor Salvador Alvarado. In 1919 he was the first regional leader to declare for Obregón, and with subtle support from the center he won the governorship against Alvarado in 1922. Calling his administration "the first socialist government in the Americas," Carrillo set about to unionize agricultural workers, distribute ejidos to all communities, and establish a powerful regional political party based on mobilized campesinos. Yucatán's "red Caesar" pursued similar policies in neighboring Campeche through his "puppet" Partido Socialista Agrario "Pro-Campeche."[20] More than 470 local leagues were united in the Liga Central de Resistencia which supposively provided mass support for the Partido Socialista del Sureste and the state government.[21] "Yucátan came to be regarded by the rest of the Republic," writes Gilbert M. Joseph, "as a social laboratory for the Revolution, where exciting experiments in labor and educational reform and women's rights were carried out."[22] Carrillo's mobilization of a campesino base was faulty, however, dependent upon established local caciques who could not or would not defend the state government during the de la Huerta rebellion. As a result, Carrillo was captured by rebel troops and executed; the socialist revolution of Yucatán (and Campeche) died with Felipe Carrillo Puerto in early 1924.[23]

Tomás Garrido Canabal was elected governor of Tabasco with Obregón's support in 1922. Two years earlier Garrido had served as provisional governor of Yucatán and had been profoundly influenced by Carrillo Puerto and "*socialismo estilo yucateco*" (socialism Yucatecan style). Like Tejeda rather than Carrillo, however, Garrido's power in Tabasco was greatly enhanced by the de la Huerta rebellion. Garrido never hesitated in his support of the national government, while his regional rivals went with de la Huerta and were defeated militarily and politically. Following the model of his Yucatecan mentor and that of Tejeda in Veracruz, Garrido established a regional labor–campesino federation in 1924, the Liga Central de Resistencia, which provided a mass base for his Partido Socialista Radical Tabasqueño. As a result of this regional political machine, Garrido remained cacique of Tabasco for over a decade. As a reformer, Garrido deemphasized agrarian reform, which he considered economically destructive to the plantation economy of Tabasco, and instead favored the establishment of cooperatives and the increase in agricultural wages. Despite his admiration for Felipe Carrillo Puerto and Lenin (after whom he named his son), Garrido was no socialist. His radicalism was expressed as revolutionary puritanism and Jacobin anticlericalism. Garrido imposed tight regulations on the sale of alcoholic beverages, closed all churches in the state, required marriage of all priests, and prohibited the exhibition of all religious images and the practice of religious customs. Like Carrillo's Yucatán, Tabasco under Garrido was widely praised as the "laboratory of the Revolution."[24]

In the northeastern state of Tamaulipas, Emilio Portes Gil directed a regional "official revolution," an experience he later drew upon as provisional president of Mexico. Portes Gil's first (provisional) administration in 1920 was derailed when he supported a general strike in the important petroleum port of Tampico and came into direct conflict with the powerful caudillo of the Huasteca, Manuel Pelaez.[25] In 1924 he formed the Partido Socialista Fronterizo (based on a constituency of local agrarian leagues) in preparation for the election the following year, which he won. During the three years of his administration, Portes Gil implemented anticlerical and antisaloon laws, assisted in the establishment of workers' cooperatives, pursued a vigorous agrarian reform program, and formed the Liga de Comunidades Agrarias y Sindicatos Campesinos del Estado de Tamaulipas. His collaborator, Marte R. Gómez, later remarked that "his administration in the government of Tamaulipas was characterized by the energy with which he pursued the solution to the agrarian problem, and by the vigor with which he lent his sympathy to [the] organized worker movement of the State."[26] Portes Gil left Tamaulipas in 1928, with his influence and power in the state secure, to take the most important post in the federal cabinet, secretary of government. At the end of the year he was appointed by Congress as provisional president. Heather Fowler Salamini's essay in Part II of this volume closely examines how land reform was employed to build a new bureaucratic state apparatus in Tamaulipas.

The "socialist revolutions" in the provinces in the 1920s were fragile experiments despite the often successful efforts on the part of governors to build popular support through alliances with labor and campesino organizations. Caudillistic forms of campesino mobilization, according to Hans Werner Tobler, "permitted the rapid growth of peasant organizations, [but] it left them—especially in the case of withdrawal of government patronage—weak and unable to resist strong external pressures, such as the intervention of the army or federal authorities."[27] That is what José María Sánchez discovered in Puebla in 1921–1922 and José María Elizalde learned in Aguascalientes in 1924–1925.[28] (Conversely, presidential backing could sometimes sustain in office governors with a weak popular base, as Raymond Buve shows in his essay in Part II of this volume.) The bottom line, as an analyst for the U.S. War Department wrote in 1926, was loyalty. "A governor who wishes to retain his Governorship must be in accord, or pretend to be in accord, with the leaders who control the Federal Administration. If he is not, means are generally found to put him out and to replace him, eventually, by a person who will support the plans of those who rule."[29] Those provincial progressives and radicals who survived the dangerous 1920s with their local power intact, like Tejeda, Garrido, and Portes Gil, were adept at demonstrating their loyalty to Obregón and, later, President Plutarco Elías Calles (1924–1928). Those who were not so politically agile, by far the larger group, were deposed.

Francisco Múgica, who lost the gubernatorial election in Michoacán in 1920 but seized power anyway with the support of Gobernación Secretary Plutarco Elías Calles, was widely considered at the time one of the most advanced and militant revolutionaries in Mexico. As governor, Múgica closed several Catholic schools, enacted a radical labor law, was energetic in accelerating land distribution, and took the first steps to form a state agrarian league. His fatal mistake, as his biographer Armando de María y Campos notes, was that "he did not tolerate even the most insignificant meddling of the Central government in the internal affairs of his State."[30] The specific issue which undermined Mùgica's position in Mexico City was his opposition to Federal troops disarming local campesino civil-defense units. When the Federal garrison in Morelia rebelled against the state government in February 1922, President Obregón took no action to defend the constitutional government of the state. Múgica had little choice but to resign and remain "underground" during the remainder of the Obregón presidency.[31]

In neighboring Jalisco, Governor Basilio Vadillo, brought to power by the Agua Prieta revolt, attempted to consolidate his power in the state through land and labor reforms. Following a legislative coup d'etat which deposed Vadillo, José Guadalupe Zuno was "elected" governor in November 1922 and took power the following March. By all accounts, Zuno was a ruthless opportunist who built an impressive regional *cacicazgo* in Jalisco, Colima, and Nayarit.[32] While enriching himself and his friends by shady deals, Zuno also established an alliance with radical labor and campesino organizations which had first developed under Vadillo. In order to reduce labor support in Jalisco for union leader Luis Morones and Plutarco Elías Calles (and thereby increase his political power in the state), Zuno threw his support to communist labor leaders and assisted in the formation of the Confederación de Agrupaciones Obreras Libertarias de Jalisco in September 1924. With the protection of Zuno, the Confederación aggressively promoted unionization of industrial workers and miners.[33] Zuno also vigorously promoted agrarian reform, provisionally granting more land than any other Jalisciense governor prior to the Cardenas presidency.[34] Zuno's *"amplia base social"* (broad social base) was not sufficient to secure his power and the influence and independence of the regional labor movement against the determined opposition of President Calles and Morones. In May 1926 the Federal Senate declared Zuno "guilty of the violation of the general constitution of the Republic and federal laws," and ordered him deposed from office. Zuno remained politically marginalized until the Cárdenas presidency.[35]

In the state of San Luis Potosí, Aurelio Manrique was elected governor in 1923 and "came in to power as the avowed apostle of labor and the enemy of capital."[36] A friend of Tejeda, Manrique accelerated agrarian reform, prohibited the sale of alcoholic beverages, sponsored the creation of labor and renter's unions, and formed a state agrarian league. The U.S. consul in San Luis Potosí certainly was alarmed: "Considerable attention has been given to the Government of the State of San Luis Potosí as it proclaims itself strictly a labor Government bent on socializing the state, and its methods of allowing the organized labor to enforce its demands and bring about the first steps of confiscation have such a bearing on labor conditions."[37] Referring to Tejeda, Manrique, and Zuno, the U.S. Consul-General in Mexico City wrote that "these men are frank adherents of radical labor, with [an] equally frank belief in a definite alliance between government and syndicalism."[38] Unlike Tejeda, however, Manrique had a revolutionary rival in San Luis Potosí, the powerful agrarian caudillo Saturnino Cedillo. Manrique achieved office, thanks to Cedillo's support and protection, and he was unable to establish an independent base of agrarian support; agraristas were already mobilized by and loyal to Cedillo. Therefore, when Manrique and his radical policies alienated both Cedillo and President Calles by 1925, he became easily expendable. The Cedillo-controlled state legislature removed Manrique in early 1926, and Calles impassively looked on. "Manrique had sought to create a revolution in San Luis Potosí," writes Dudley Ankerson, "without the power base that any revolutionary needs if he is to be even partially successful."[39]

In the southeastern state of Chiapas, General Carlos Vidal was elected governor in a disputed contest in 1924 but, with the support of President Calles, took office in May 1925. Not unlike Tejeda, Vidal had established a political alliance with a local socialist, Ricardo Alfonso Paniagua, founder of the Partido Socialista Chiapaneco in 1920. Once in power, Vidal and Paniagua established an official labor federation which began to unionize agricultural workers, enacted and enforced an advanced labor law, and initiated the first real agrarian reform in Chiapas. In 1927 Vidal directed the presidential campaign of Francisco R. Serrano and joined Serrano's rebellion against the reelection of Obregón to the presidency. The rebellion was almost immediately repressed, Serrano and Vidal were executed, and the commander of the Federal garrison in Tuxtla Gutiérrez, the capital of Chiapas, received orders from Mexico City to seize control of the state government. General Manuel Alvarez rounded up the major officials of the state government—including Provisional Governor Luis Vidal and Partido Socialista chief Paniagua—and had them shot. Vidalistas throughout the state were either executed or jailed, putting an end to the "socialist experiment" in Chiapas.[40]

The official revolutionary caciques of the 1920s failed to radically transform the social fabric of their regions. Their power and autonomy was insufficient against the determined opposition of regional landowners, powerful traditional caudillos, and Federal army zone commanders, and the passivity or intervention of the central government. All the same, these governors introduced the social program of "The Revolution" to many localities which had experienced its civil wars but not its reforms. It is doubtful that the populist reforms of the Cárdenas presidency (1934–1940), meager as they may seem today, would have been implemented without the popular mobilizations which took place in the 1920s. More importantly, the generation of politicians who successfully fortified and consolidated the new state of the Mexican revolution during the 1930s learned their political lessons and obtained valuable political experience in the regional "experimental laboratories" of the 1920s.

Centralization and/or Accommodation

When Plutarco Elías Calles assumed the presidency in December 1924, the central government was considerably stronger than when Obregón had taken office in 1920. The government's repression of the de la Huerta rebellion earlier in the year constituted an important step in the consolidation of national power. When General Adolfo de la Huerta, the former provisional president and cabinet member, launched a revolt against Obregón's imposition of Calles as his successor in late 1923, more than fifty generals and about 60 percent of the federal army deserted the central government. Some of the most powerful military caudillos in Mexico, including generals Guadalupe

Sánchez of Veracruz, Enrique Estrada of Jalisco, Fortunato Maycotte of Puebla, and Rómulo Figueroa of Guerrero, joined the revolt. The successful military campaign of the central government was due in part to the loyalty of such provincial radicals as Adalberto Tejeda and Tomás Garrido Canabal as well as the more traditional regional caudillos like Saturnino Cedillo who organized agraristas in defense of the government. In central Mexico, approximately 120,000 agraristas defended the regime. The government's repression of the revolt decreased the power and independence of the Federal army and increased the power of the center in many states.[41]

Obregón's policy of using land reform to build political support, and establishing alliances with campesino and worker organizations, had paid off and it was continued, but modified under Calles.[42] During his presidency, Calles gave his full support to the national labor federation led by Luis Morones, the Confederación Regional Obrera Mexicana (CROM), and its efforts to control state labor organizations. The same cannot be said about Calles's toleration of the provincial agraristas. The position of progressive and radical agrarian governors and their "laboratories of the Revolution" had never been absolutely secure under Obregón, of course, as the examples of Emilio Portes Gil (in his provisional tenure as governor in 1920), Francisco Múgica, and even Felipe Carrillo Puerto demonstrated. During Calles's presidency, however, the central government made a much more determined effort to control state governments and remove dissident and independent regional leaders.[43] Those progressive and radical governors and agrarian leaders who were politically vulnerable—such as Aurelio Manrique in San Luis Potosí; Heriberto Jara in Veracruz; José Guadalupe Zuno in Jalisco; Carlos Vidal in Chiapas; Primo Tapia in Michoacán; Francisco J. Barbosa, Luis Rojas, and Manuel Montes in Puebla—were either deposed or killed.[44]

During the Calles period the government in Mexico City either initiated or permitted the ousting of over twenty-five governors in fifteen different states. To a considerable degree this federal intervention had as its objective the replacement of Obregonistas (who were often agraristas) with Callistas (who were generally laboristas, allied with the CROM) in the state palaces.[45] Governors who managed to resist Calles's political offensive, like Emilio Portes Gil in Tamaulipas, had to be in complete political control of their states and be allied to either the Obregonista or Callista faction in Mexico City and around the country. The powerful regional caudillos, like Saturnino Cedillo, also controlled their own military forces which the central government from time to time had to call on.

Increasingly during the 1920s, the central government found unconditional and opportunistic allies in the localities and regions throughout Mexico. The downfall of powerful regional caudillos and radical caciques facilitated the political careers of younger men who were willing and eager to trade their independence for backing from the center and, once in office, the freedom to get rich. A good example of this trend was Abelardo L. Rodríguez who, as governor of Baja California Norte from 1923 to 1929, acquired nine companies while loyally serving Obregón and Calles.[46] Factional conflict at the state level further increased the power and influence of the central government since the extension or withdrawal of support often determined which group obtained (and, just as importantly, retained) office. In an election in Guerrero in 1927, "the deciding element in the local political conflict was the federal executive."[47] In reference to Hidalgo, Frans J. Schryer argues, "most governors and state military authorities, clearly in league with the larger landowners, were allowed to terrorize and even assassinate local peasant leaders who were real agrarians."[48] Ernest Gruening, writing in 1927, was equally critical: "It is not possible, given existing conditions in Mexico, to elect an honest and conscientious state government without dishonesty and lack of conscience."[49]

It became increasingly difficult for idealistic progressives and radicals, men comparable to Múgica, Manrique, and Carrillo Puerto, to obtain state power in the latter half of the 1920s. The lessons of the "laboratories of the Revolution" were not entirely lost. Unfortunately, it was not the methods or objectives of reform but the populist techniques of political control which were learned. "The reformist forces, when not beaten," Gruening wisely noted, "are in danger of being polluted."[50] In the state of Tlaxcala, Governor Ignacio Mendoza, an agrarista elected in 1925, followed the example of Tomás Garrido Canabal in Tabasco and organized a government party, the Partido Socialista, which in some districts was supported by landowners. "Land reform fell drastically under Mendoza who only granted ejidos to 12 villages during the four years of his time (1925–29)," writes Raymond Buve.[51] "The governors of Tlaxcala, Mexico, and Durango, have made the ejido an instrument of politics," complained former Zapatista Díaz Soto y Gama on the floor of the Congress in 1925.[52] Regional political machines incorporating agrarian leagues and labor unions and controlled by governors, appeared in states like Guanajuato (the Confederación de Partidos Revolucionarios) while existing "revolutionary" parties—the Gran Partido Socialista de Yucatán, Partido Socialista Agrario de Campeche, and the Partido Socialista Chiapaneca are good examples—lost their original purpose and were converted into instruments of political control and pacification. Mobilization of workers and peasants by state governments from "above," as opposed to mobilization by the people themselves from "below," could be manipulated by politicians for purely political and even reactionary purposes.[53]

Two model revolutionary laboratories, each committed to community self-government, were completely unacceptable to the Sonorans and their radical provincial allies during the 1920s. The Zapatista "Morelos commune" of 1914–1915, as Adolfo Gilly calls it, "had entrenched itself on the land, created its own village authorities, forged a new, egalitarian social relationship, and entered a military organization that was half-army, half-militia."[54] To avoid any reappearance of this dangerous model, the Obregón and Calles regimes liquidated most *latifundios* in the state but subjected Morelos to central control until 1930, when a constitutional government was finally elected.[55] The "liberated territories" of the Cristero rebels (who had taken up arms against the anticlerical Calles regime) offered a similar model of village democracy in central-western Mexico. Democratically elected civilian municipal councils provided justice, ran schools, taxed commerce, and campaigned against private vices and public corruption, "solidly re-establishing the rural world on its family and religious bases." Between 1927 and 1929, writes Jean Meyer, "the rural inhabitants, for the only time in the history of Mexico, were left to themselves to organize the Mexico envisaged by [José María] Morelos—federation of national geographic regions, formed by theocratic village republics."[56] A negotiated truce between Cristeros and the national state, like the earlier Zapatista defeat, guaranteed the disappearance of the model of "power to the people" in order to build a state which organized the people to concentrate and centralize power.

Despite the stronger position of the central government following the repression of the de la Huerta rebellion, the Gómez–Serrano revolt of 1927, and the Cristero rebellion of 1926–1929, and despite the progress made during the Calles period in reducing and professionalizing the Federal army, Mexico City still did not dominate the provinces and their governments as much as Calles would have preferred by the end of his term. Jean Meyer writes of Calles's failure to gain control of the "Gulf Bloc Mafia", the governors of Tamaulipas (Portes Gil), Tabasco (Garrido Canabal), and Yucatán (José Iturralde). "The Center was left with no alternative but to accommodate itself to this ambiguous situation."[57] Cedillo in San Luis Potosí, Tejeda in Veracruz, and Saturnino Osornio in Querétaro, furthermore, were untouchable.[58] "The state organization continued to be dominated domestically by a fragile, personalistic alliance of regionally based military and civilian bosses."[59] Political regionalism was not yet tamed.

"When the Mexican revolutions became The Revolution"

In 1928 General Obregón stood for reelection to the presidency, and with the support of Calles, Congress, and the army, he won. "The Revolution has simply not produced another man," Calles explained to Ernest Gruening; another man who could govern Mexico.[60] Obregón's assassination only two weeks following his electoral victory, however, required the production of "another man," and that man would be Calles. The president had to proceed very carefully since an attempt to remain in office would almost certainly provoke a rebellion by Obregón's partisans. By accepting an Obregonista, Emilio Portes Gil, as provisional president until an election could be held to elect a president to finish Obregón's term, Calles bought himself some time.[61] In his last annual Informe in September 1928, Calles announced that he would leave the presidency at the end of his term (on 1 December) and never seek reelection. The crisis provoked by Obregón's assassination, he proposed, could be turned to the advantage of the country by abandoning the rule of caudillos and establishing the rule of institutions and of law.[62]

Later in the fall, Calles conceived the idea of a political party which would unify all "revolutionaries" and consolidate all of the ideological, regional, and factional Mexican revolutions. The immediate purpose of such a party would be the institutionalization of an alliance between Obregonistas and Callistas. On 1 December, the day Portes Gil took office, the Organizing Committee of the Partido Nacional Revolucionario (PNR) announced its formation and invited all political parties and groups of a "revolutionary tendency" to join forces. The Organizing Committee, which was chaired by Calles, later announced the meeting of the inaugural Convention of the PNR during which the participants would officially establish the party, approve its statutes, and select a presidential candidate.[63]

During the four months preceding the PNR Convention in March 1929, the Organizing Committee negotiated with state governors and regional political parties for their federation within the new party. Since most of the committee members had themselves headed state parties, they understood the importance of presenting the national party as a great alliance of revolutionary parties which promised the contradictory objectives of national unity and regional autonomy. Through the party, the informal ties and alliances between the central government and regional caudillos/state governors could begin to be institutionalized, at first respecting the autonomy of each party but over time increasing the authority of the national party at the expense of the regional parties. The party was a mechanism designed to adapt to the real disposition of political forces in the country, not to confront regional caudillos and parties, but first only to incorporate them and later to extend its control.[64]

Because Calles had not cultivated close ties with agraristas during his presidential term, and was forced by Obregonistas following the caudillo's assassination to end his support of CROM, the PNR was not organized as a party of peasants and workers. The major campesino and labor organizations remained outside the new party, and as far as their members were concerned "the PNR was nothing but the electoral instrument of the Callista oligarchy."[65] The experience of "mass politics" at the regional level during the 1920s was ignored during this first stage of political institutionalization.[66]

Despite the centralizing policies of "Jefe Máximo" Calles and his hand-picked presidents, Pascual Ortiz Rubio (1930–1932) and Abelardo L. Rodríguez (1932–1934), and their efforts to terminate the agrarian reform program, several regional "experimental laboratories" survived into the early and mid-1930s, the period known as the Maximato. (See Table 4.2) It soon became clear, however, that their days were numbered. In 1932–1933, the government in Mexico City began to disarm the agrarian militias and "guerrillas" of moderate and radical state governments. The disarmament of agrarista guerrillas in Veracruz was followed by political dismantling of the Tejedista movement in the state. Agrarista governors in Hidalgo, Michoacán, and Puebla, furthermore, were replaced through PNR-controlled elections by conservatives.[67]

In reaction to Calles's conservative offensive at both the state and national levels, a number of progressive politicians who had been schooled in the "laboratories" of the 1920s exploited the PNR's weak and narrow base in order to promote the presidential candidacy of one of their own, General Lázaro Cárdenas. State agrarian leagues, led by those of Tamaulipas and San Luis Potosí, united in the pro-Cárdenas Confederación Campesina Mexicana (CCM) in 1933. In the same year, Vicente Lombardo Toledano formed a "pure CROM"

Table 4.2
Prominent Reformist Regimes during the Maximato, 1928–1935

State	Governor	Period
Guanajuato	Agustín Arroyo Ch.	1927–1931
Hidalgo	Bartolome Vargas Lugo	1929–1933
Michoacán	Lázaro Cárdenas	1928–1932
Puebla	Leonides Andreu Almazan	1929–1933
Querétaro	Saturnino Osornio	1931–1935
San Luis Potosí	Saturnino Cedillo	1927–1931
Tabasco	Tomás Garrido Canabal	1930–1934
Veracruz	Adalberto Tejeda	1928–1932

(without Morones), the Confederación General de Obreros y Campesinos de México (CGOCM), which brought an important part of organized labor behind Cárdenas. Regional strongmen Saturnino Cedillo and Juan Andreu Almazán, as well as other generals of Division, also supported Cárdenas. As a result, according to Lombardo Toledano, "the left wing of the PNR nominated Cardenas with our help, that of the labor movement, and General Calles . . . had to accept Cárdenas."[68]

Cárdenas, utilizing "mass politics" to achieve the nomination of the PNR and to win the general election, followed the same course to liquidate the Maximato. "The Cárdenas regime was relatively weak at first because of disputes with the Callista wing [of the official party]," writes Hans Werner Tobler. "Much as in the early 1920s, political and social organizations were therefore created 'from above' in order to give the new government a firm power base."[69] As Cárdenas incorporated the organized "popular masses" into the PNR, he institutionalized the political power of the presidency and ended the reign of the Jefe Máximo. The official reorganization of the PNR into Partido de la Revolución Mexicana in 1938 ratified the incorporation of mass organizations in 1935 and 1936. Lombardo Toledano's CGOCM was transformed into the official party's labor sector, the Confederación de Trabajadores de México, which was, according to one scholar of the labor movement, "the organization that Cárdenas considered indispensable . . . and was the instrument through which the working masses would be mobilized in support of the decisions of the state and in defense of the established regime."[70] The agrarian leagues of the CCM were incorporated into the corporately restructured party of the state as the Confederación Nacional Campesina, transforming the organized *campesinado* into "an integral part of the revolutionary party, and converting it into the most secure support of the [political] system for years to come."[71]

Conclusion

"There is a great deal of discussion about when the Mexican revolutions became The Revolution," noted J. H. Plenn in 1939, "when the first foundations were really laid for today's political structure."[72] As a result of recent studies of state politics and regional reform during the postrevolutionary period, it is clear that the "revolutionary caciques" and the techniques of "mass politics" they pioneered in the regional "laboratories of the Revolution" of the 1920s contributed fundamentally to the shape and function of the postrevolutionary state. The consolidation and centralization of the national state during the 1930s and 1940s resulted in the elimination of the remaining regional caudillos and the conversion of state governments into dependencies of the central government and state parties into compliant regional offices of the national party. The direct alliance between the state and the masses, ironically, diminished the power and autonomy of popular movements and organizations, thereby finally transforming the Mexican revolutions into "La Revolución mexicana," a unifying idea and centralized state in place of the plural reality of Mexico since 1911.

Notes

1. Alan Knight, *The Mexican Revolution. Counter-revolution and reconstruction* (Cambridge: Cambridge University Press, 1986), 527.
2. Jean Meyer, *La revolución mejicana, 1910–1940* (Barcelona: Dopesa, 1973), 71. An excellent analysis of how this fragmentation occurred is given by Heather Fowler Salamini, "Caciquismo and the Mexican Revolution: The Case of Manuel Palaez" (paper presented at the 6th Conference of Mexican and United States Historians, Chicago, Ill., September 1981).
3. Linda B. Hall, "Álvaro Obregón and the Mexican Revolution 1912–1920: The Origins of Institutionalization" (Ph.D. diss., Columbia University, 1975), 398–99.
4. Provisional President Adolfo de la Huerta forced the resignation of Governor Esteban Cantú Jiménez ("el último carrancista") of the Federal territory of Baja California Norte. De la Huerta and the Senate named fourteen provisional governors in 1920. See Alvaro Matute, *La carrera del caudillo. Historia de la Revolución Mexicana, 1917–1924* (México: El Colegio de México, 1980), 137, 150–54.
5. "A solution giving each faction control of its own territory with a 'neutral' president with limited powers, acceptable to all of them and to the United States seemed a viable compromise to most of the factions." Friedrich Katz, *The Secret War in Mexico: Europe, The United States and the Mexican Revolution* (Chicago: University of Chicago Press, 1981), 532.
6. John Womack Jr., "The Mexican Revolution, 1910–1920," in *The Cambridge History of Latin America*, vol. 5: *c. 1870 to 1930*, ed. Leslie Bethell (Cambridge: Cambridge University Press, 1986), 153.
7. David C. Bailey, "Obregón: Mexico's Accommodating President," in George Wolfskill and Douglas W. Richmond, eds., *Essays on the Mexican Revolution: Revisionist Views of the Leaders* (Austin: University of Texas Press, 1979), 85.
8. Hall, "Álvaro Obregón and the Mexican Revolution," 407.
9. Ramón Eduardo Ruiz, *The Great Rebellion: Mexico, 1905–1924* (New York: W.W. Norton, 1980), 257.
10. *Excelsiór*, 24 August 1923.

11. Randal G. Hansis, "Álvaro Obregón, the Mexican Revolution and the Politics of Consolidation, 1920–1924" (Ph.D. diss., University of New Mexico, 1971), 55. Gobernación Secretary (1920–1923), Plutarco Elías Calles, on the other hand, was less restrained regarding state politics.

12. Carlos Martínez Assad, Mario Ramírez Rancano, and Ricardo Pozas Horcasitas, *Revolucionarios fueron todos* (México: SEP/80, 1982), 57–62.

13. Carleton Beals, *Mexico: An Interpretation* (New York: B. W. Huebsch, 1923), 74, 102.

14. Ernest Gruening, *Mexico and Its Heritage* (New York: D. Appleton-Century Co., 1928), 481.

15. Local agrarian leagues, often organized by agronomists of the National Agrarian Commission with the objective of petitioning for land grants and defending communities from landowner coercion, were first formed in Jalisco, Zacatecas, Puebla, Michoacán, and Guanajuato in 1921 and 1922. Jean Meyer, *Estado y sociedad con Calles. Historia de la revolución mexicana, 1924–1928* (México: El Colegio de México, 1977), 93.

16. Heather Fowler Salamini, *Agrarian Radicalism in Veracruz, 1920–38* (Lincoln: University of Nebraska Press, 1978), 34–45; and Fowler Salamini, "Revolutionary caudillos in the 1920s: Francisco Múgica and Adalberto Tejeda," in *Caudillo and Peasant in the Mexican Revolution*, ed. D. A. Brading (Cambridge: Cambridge University Press, 1980), 182–89.

17. John Q. Wilson, U.S. Consul, Veracruz, to Secretary of State, 16 October 1923, 812.504/517, U.S. Department of State, *Records of the Department of State Relating to the Internal Affairs of Mexico, 1910–29,* microcopy 274, Washington, D.C.: National Archives, 1959 (henceforth referred to as RDS).

18. Paul Friedrich, *Agrarian Revolt in a Mexican Village* (Englewood Cliffs, N.J.: Prentice-Hall, 1970), 94.

19. Moisés González Navarro, *La Confederación Nacional Campesina: Un grupo de presión de la reforma agraria mexicana* (México: Costa-Amic, 1968), 130–33; and Romana Falcón, *El agrarismo en Veracruz, la etapa radical 1920–1935* (México: El Colegio de México, 1977), 30–41.

20. Hansis, "Álvaro Obregón, the Mexican Revolution and the Politics of Consolidation, 1920–1924," 65.

21. G. M. Joseph, *Revolution from Without: Yucatán, Mexico, and the United States, 1880–1924* (Cambridge: Cambridge University Press, 1982), 219–20; see also Francisco J. Paoli and Enrique Montalvo, *El socialismo olvidado de Yucatán* (México: Siglo XXI, 1977), and John W. F. Dulles, *Yesterday in Mexico: A Chronicle of the Revolution, 1919–1936* (Austin: University of Texas Press, 1961), chapter 16, "Carrillo Puerto and the Ligas de Resistencia de Yucatan," 136–44.

22. Gilbert M. Joseph, "The Fragile Revolution: Cacique Politics and Revolutionary Process in Yucatán," *Latin American Research Review* 15:1(1980):47.

23. Joseph, *Revolution from Without*, 263–75.

24. Carlos Martínez Assad, *El laboratorio de la revolución: el Tabasco garridista* (México: Siglo XXI, 1979), pp. 152–68; Dulles, *Yesterday in Mexico*, chapter 69, "Garrido Canabal and Tabasco, 'Laboratory of the Revolution' ", 611–24.
25. Alvaro Matute, *La carrera del caudillo. Historia de la revolución mexicana, 1917–1924* (México: El Colegio de México, 1980), 167–69.
26. James W. Wilkie and Edna Monzón de Wilkie, *México visto en el siglo XX: Entrevistas de Historia Oral* (México: Instituto Mexicano de Investigaciones Económicas, 1969), capitulo secundo, "Marte R. Gomez, Agrarista," 125, and capitulo sexto, "Emilio Portes Gil, Ex Presidente de México," 449, 507–9.
27. Hans Werner Tobler, "Peasants and the Shaping of the Revolutionary State," in *Riot, Rebellion, and Revolution: Rural Social Conflict in Mexico* ed. Friedrich Katz (Princeton: Princeton University Press, 1988), 512.
28. Hansis, "Álvaro Obregón, the Mexican Revolution and the Politics of Consolidation, 1920–1924," 84–85; and Beatriz Rojas, *La destrucción de la hacienda en Aguascalientes, 1910–1931* (Zamora: El Colegio de Michoacán, 1981), 71–86.
29. "Local Political Conditions," 30 March 1926, U.S. National Archives, record group 165: Records of the War Department General and Special Staffs and the Military Intelligence Division.
30. Armando de María y Campos, *Múgica: crónica biografica* (México: Compañía de Ediciones Populares, 1939), 156.
31. Heather Fowler Salamini, "Revolutionary Caudillos in the 1920s," in *Caudillo and Peasant in the Mexican Revolution*, 177–81; and Ricardo Pérez Montfort, "Francisco José Múgica Velázquez," *Desdeldiez. Boletín del Centro de Estudios de la Revolución Mexicana "Lázaro Cárdenas"* (September 1984), 18.
32. Ernest Gruening has a chapter on Jalisco in *Mexico and Its Heritage*, 440–51.
33. Jaime Tamayo, "La confederación obrera de Jalisco: 1924–29," *Cuadernos Políticos* (abril-junio de 1985):93–102.
34. Ann L. Craig, *The First Agraristas: An Oral History of a Mexican Agrarian Reform Movement* (Berkeley: University of California Press, 1983), 59.
35. J. Lloyd Mecham, "Federal Intervention in Mexico," in *Hispanic American Essays*, ed. A. Curtis Wilgus (Chapel Hill: University of North Carolina Press, 1942); 277–78; Meyer, *Estado y sociedad con Calles*, 188–90.
36. Walter F. Boyle, U.S. Consul, San Luis Potosí, to Secretary of State, 24 March 1924, RDS 812.504/541.
37. "Labor Situation," Walter F. Boyle, 19 March 1924, RDS 812.504/850.4.
38. "Labor Situation," U.S. Consul-General, Mexico City, 5 April 1924, RDS 812.504/556.
39. Dudley Ankerson, *Agrarian Warlord: Saturnino Cedillo and the Mexican Revolution in San Luis Potosí* (DeKalb: Northern Illinois University Press, 1984), 119.
40. Thomas Benjamin, *A Rich Land, A Poor People: Politics and Society in Modern Chiapas* (Albuquerque: University of New Mexico Press, 1989): chapter 6: "In Defense of Class Interests."

41. Meyer, *La revolución mejicana*, 116–20.

42. The first Ligas de Comunidades Agrarias (in 1921) were formed under the patronage of Mendoza López, Secretary of the Comisión Nacional Agraria. Armando Bartra, *Los herederos de Zapata: Movimientos campesinos posrevolucionarios en México* (México: Ediciones Era, 1985), 32.

43. Victoria Lerner, "Los fundamentos socioeconómicos del cacicazgo en el México posrevolucionario. El caso de Saturnino Cedillo," *Historia Mexicana* 39 (enero-marzo 1980):436.

44. Enrique Krauze (with Jean Meyer and Cayetano Reyes), *La reconstrucción económica. Historia de la revolución mexicana, 1924–1928* (México: El Colegio de México, 1977), 127–30. As the Federal army became more conservative and composed of nouveau-riche businessmen and hacendados it became a powerful counterrevolutionary force. See Hans-Werner Tobler, "Las paradojas del ejército revolucionario: Su papel social en la reforma agraria mexicana, 1920–1935," *Historia Mexicana* 21 (julio-septiembre 1971):38–79.

45. Marjorie Ruth Clark, *Organized Labor in Mexico* (Chapel Hill: University of North Carolina Press, 1934), 122–31.

46. Martínez Assad, et. al., *Revolucionarios fueron todos*, chapter 7, "El imperio economico de Abelardo L. Rodríguez," 282–340.

47. Ian Jacobs, *Ranchero Revolt: The Mexican Revolution in Guerrero* (Austin: University of Texas Press, 1982), 127.

48. Frans J. Schryer, *The Rancheros of Pisaflores: The History of a Peasant Bourgeoisie in Twentieth-Century Mexico* (Toronto: University of Toronto Press, 1980), 83.

49. Ernest Gruening, *Mexico and Its Heritage*, p. 489.

50. Ibid., 487.

51. Raymond Buve, "State Governors and Peasant Mobilization in Tlaxcala," in *Caudillo and Peasant in the Mexican Revolution*, 232–33.

52. Krauze, *La reconstrucción económica*, 128.

53. Joseph makes this point in his analysis of Yucatán after Felipe Carrillo Puerto in *Revolution from Without*, 288–98. And Marjorie Ruth Clark writes: "There are many independent state leagues and unions of agricultural workers, all of them attempting to control the peasants for their own ends, or to serve a political faction." *Organized Labor in Mexico*, 160.

54. Adolfo Gilly, *The Mexican Revolution* (London: Verso, 1983), 252.

55. Mecham, "Federal Intervention in Mexico," 272–73.

56. Jean A. Meyer, *The Cristero Rebellion: The Mexican People between Church and State, 1926–1929* (Cambridge: Cambridge University Press, 1976), 143, 154.

57. Meyer, *Estado y sociedad con Calles*, 186.

58. See chapter 5, "La violencia en Querétaro y la consolidacion del Estado mexicano," in Martinez Assad et. al., *Revolucionarios fueron todos*, 216–34.

59. Richard Tardanico, "State, Dependency, and Nationalism: Revolutionary Mexico, 1924–1928," *Comparative Studies in Society and History* 24 (October 1982):419.

60. Gruening, *Mexico and Its Heritage*, 492n.
61. Calles also made every effort to conciliate Obregonistas by appointing Emilio Portes Gil as his secretary of government and ending government support and patronage of CROM. See Rafael Loyola Díaz, *La crisis obregón-calles y el estado mexicano* (México: Siglo XXI, 1980), 103–16.
62. "Informe presidencial del 1 de septiembre de 1928," *El Universal*, 2 September 1928.
63. Luis Javier Garrido, *El partido de la revolución institucionalizada (Medio siglo de poder político en México): La formación del nuevo estado (1928–1945)* (México: Siglo XXI, 1982), 69–78.
64. Lorenzo Meyer, Rafael Segovia, and Alejandra Lajous, *Los inicios de la institucionalización (La política del maximato). Historia de la revolución mexicana, 1928–1934* (México: El Colegio de México, 1978), 36–44.
65. Garrido, *El partido de la revolución institucionalizada*, 173.
66. Arnaldo Córdova, *En una época de crisis (1928–1934). La clase obrera en la historia de México* (México: Siglo XXI, 1980), 37.
67. Lorenzo Meyer, *El conflicto social y los gobiernos del maximato. Historia de la Revolución Mexicana, 1928–1934* (México: El Colegio de México, 1978), chapter 4: "La Periferia y el Centro," 253–319.
68. James W. Wilkie and Edna Monzon de Wilkie, *México visto en el siglo XX, entrevistas de historia oral* (México: Instituto Mexicano de Investigaciones Economicas, 1969), 309.
69. Tobler, "Peasants and the Shaping of the Revolutionary State, 1910–40," 517.
70. Arturo Anguiano, *El estado y la política obrera del cardenismo* (México: Ediciones Era, 1975), 58. See, also, Joe C. Ashby, *Organized Labor and the Mexican Revolution under Lazaro Cardenas* (Chapel Hill: University of North Carolina Press, 1963), 81.
71. Romana Falcón, "El surgimiento del agrarismo cardenista—Una revision de las tesis populistas," *Historia Mexicana* 27:3 (Enero-Marzo 1978):384.
72. J. H. Plenn, *Mexico Marches* (Indianapolis: Bobbs-Merrill Company, 1939), 112.

Part II

Regions in the Mexican Revolution

5

Yucatán

Elite Politics and Rural Insurgency

Gilbert M. Joseph and Allen Wells

Unquestionably, the recent surge in regional and local studies of the Mexican Revolution has provided a much-needed corrective to the worst excesses of a traditional *historiografía capitalina*. Inspired by the landmark studies of John Womack and Luis González, an entire generation of Mexicanists—well represented in this volume—has been swept up in what Don Luis aptly terms "the regional impulse of our times." Abandoning the perspective (and daily indignities) of the great metropolis for the view obtainable in more remote and tranquil *patrias chicas*, these young historians have carved out veritable academic *cacicazgos*, becoming intellectual versions of the caudillos and *cabecillas* they write about. Their accumulated efforts have produced a storehouse of empirical research, which is particularly abundant for several areas (for example, Chihuahua, Sonora, San Luis Potosí, Morelos, Tlaxcala and Yucatán).

Yet now, as Mexicanists begin to step back and assess this rich patchwork of regional and micro-studies, it appears that for all of its virtues, in certain important respects the new regional literature may be missing the forest for the trees. Several provocative new syntheses, while disagreeing on a number of substantive questions, have hinted at the failure of much regional work to fully explore the complex, interactive relationship between center and periphery.[1] Too often, otherwise reliable, detailed monographs of regions and localities are poorly integrated into larger national (and supranational) structures and processes, ultimately rendering them liable to the same charge of parochialism that was once leveled against an earlier generation of provincial amateur chroniclers.

Moreover, regional specialists must guard against the danger of their work becoming compartmentalized chronologically as well as spatially. Like their predecessors who wrote from the perspective of the capital, many regional revolutionary historians treat 1910 as a sacrosanct benchmark. One need not deny its conjunctural significance to appreciate larger continuities at work in regional historical development. Much of the new work on *"la bola,"* the vio-

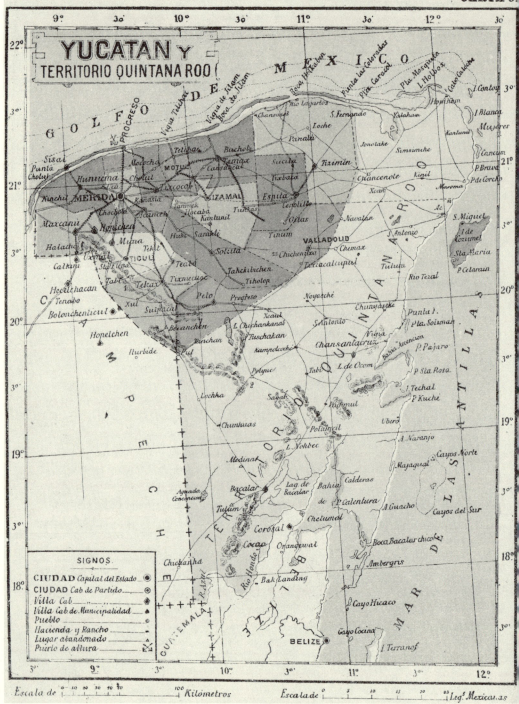

lent and chaotic first revolutionary decade, and particularly on Maderismo, would greatly benefit from a more comprehensive grounding in the history of the Porfiriato. Indeed, one of the most compelling tasks for revolutionary scholars is to analyze the larger period of transition joining the decline of the *ancien régime* and the emergence of the new revolutionary state. For many regions, certainly for Yucatán, one has little hope of understanding the melee that was Maderismo without a sure grasp of the contradictions embedded in the Porfiriato and the divergent mentalities that flowed from them.

The decline and fall of Porfirio Díaz removed many of the restraints that the Old Regime had imposed on popular movements, opening the floodgates of political competition among old-line Porfirian elites, members of Madero's largely urban, middle-class Anti-Reelectionist coalition, and incipient revolutionary chiefs who commanded powerful followings in the sierras, valleys, and pueblos of rural Mexico. Undoubtedly, the Mexican Revolution was never more "popular" than it was between 1910 and 1913. Yet as David LaFrance has shown in his essay on Maderismo in this volume, the popular drive was never translated into a coherent, successful revolutionary program, either nationwide or regionally. Surprisingly, little has been done to explain the mobilization of these Maderista-era movements or to examine their eventual fates.[2] Yet they are of great importance in understanding the character of the "epic revolution" (1910–1917) and the kind of revolutionary state that emerged from it.

The Yucatecan variant of this *"apertura maderista"* holds particular interest. Like other regions of Mexico during the period, Yucatán witnessed the opening of new political space, the movement of new actors and political alliances into this space, and in short order, a series of local revolts, some carefully orchestrated, others spontaneous and uncoordinated. However, whereas in much of the rest of Mexico these homegrown swells led inexorably to civil war and, ultimately, to the destruction of the traditional oligarchical order, in Yucatán it survived. Consequently, the revolution would have to fight its way in from without.

This essay seeks to understand why Yucatán failed to produce the kind of revolutionary momentum which engulfed much of the nation. We will argue that the most significant clues for understanding both the outbreak and limitations of the seasons of upheaval that gripped Yucatán intermittently during the Madero period lie in the history of the two preceding decades. Despite the fabulous wealth generated by the henequén or sisal fiber boom, the last years of the nineteenth century and the first decade of this century were a veritable "summer of discontent" for the vast majority of regional producers, merchants, workers, and campesinos, who found themselves subordinated in one way or another to the dominant oligarchical *camarilla* (faction) based on the *parentesco* of Olegario Molina and Avelino Montes. The mobilization of rival political groups led by contending factions of the regional elite, which began about 1909, was a highly complex affair, one that grew out of deepening (and interrelated) political, economic, and social contradictions in the late Porfirian oligarchical order.

Thus far, such a *radiografía* of the *ancien régime*—that is, an analysis that would articulate the economic, political, and social dimensions of this late Porfirian summer of discontent—has not been achieved, either for Yucatán or for Mexico's other regions. To date, studies of the late Porfiriato and outbreak of the Mexican Revolution have focused either on the political or economic history of regional elites or the social dynamics of incipient popular movements. Indeed, rarely have individual monographs attempted a systematic political economy of oligarchical power, exploring the linkage between elite politics and wealth, let alone analyzed the complex interaction of political factionalism and popular insurgency.[3] It is this crucial nexus, the dialectical relationship between changing configurations of Yucatecan elite politics and manifestations of rural protest during a pivotal juncture of transition, which most concerns us here.[4]

Political Contradictions

Porfirian Elite Politics: Defining the Rules of the Game (1876–1902)

Authoritarian rule at the regional and national level was never absolute during the Porfiriato. Even after Díaz reached the point of indefinite election in 1888, he still had to contend with power struggles in both the capital and periphery. It was Díaz's consummate skill as a politician that enabled him to set potential rivals against each other. Regional caudillos and powerful elite factions from Sonora to Yucatán were manipulated in a subtle game of *realpolitik* with Don Porfirio employing a classic strategy of divide and rule.

Díaz's efforts at political centralization were aided by the organization of political "parties,"[5] electoral campaigns, and limited criticism of state (but seldom of national) politics in the local press. Limited political participation thus became an effective tool of social control; the democratic facade which adorned Don Porfirio's authoritarian mansion served to mollify elite discontent in the provinces.[6]

The dictator's selection of governors also proved an effective method of curbing—but not eliminating—the incidence of violence which had always accompanied local elections in Yucatán and elsewhere during the Restoration. But embedded within this apparent strength of the Pax Porfiriana also lay its most glaring weakness. Power-seeking camarillas incessantly sought to focus the dictator's attention on their particular needs. For if an impatient opposition faction could demonstrate that the incumbent camarilla was unable to keep the peace, Díaz might be forced to intervene. Since regional power could not change hands without the consent of Mexico City, contending elites, were, in effect, compelled to promote unrest if they wished to regain political power.[7] If Don Porfirio felt a change was in order, he instructed the local federal garrison commander to temporarily seize, then redistribute, the reins of power. Invariably, the ousted incumbents would simply bide their time—sometimes not much time—then renew the intriguing and plotting that ultimately precipitated the next round of national intervention. Chronic unrest at the local level was accordingly built into the Porfirian system.

The system entailed certain risks for both the dictator and regional elites. Díaz had to ensure that these local camarillas were beholden unto him. As long as the factions accepted Don Porfirio's rule as the *sine qua non*, he would favor them with local power in due time. What had to be prevented at all costs was the emergence of a truly independent party, one that might question the legitimacy of Porfirian rule. Díaz managed to forestall this threat in the peninsula for thirty-two years. For their part, regional camarillas had to be careful that intraelite power struggles did not mushroom into a volatile situation in which the popular classes of regional society entered into the fray. This was of particular concern in Yucatán, where bitter memories of the apocalyptic nineteenth-century Caste War lingered in the minds of members of the planter elite.

Don Porfirio successfully alternated camarillas in Yucatán for over a quarter of a century. Yet the manipulation of the region's political carousel demanded the dictator's constant attention. Between 1882 and 1894, for example, Díaz sought to mitigate elite factional bickering by installing local military commanders—some of them outsiders—in the governor's palace. Yet while these Yucatecan and central Mexican *militares* did manage to curb overt violence and the worst excesses of factionalism, they themselves often could not escape the entanglements of elite political rivalry.

Nevertheless, in 1894, after more than a decade of rather peaceful military rule, Don Porfirio permitted the election of a civilian governor. During the regime of Carlos Peón Machado (1894–1897) political activity increased in Mérida and other towns, as members of the elite took advantage of the *apertura* to organize for future campaigns. By 1897, three rival camarillas were poised to contest the upcoming fall gubernatorial elections. The candidates included General Francisco "Pancho" Cantón, the "conservative" candidate and Caste War hero, and Olegario Molina, a rising henequén merchant who, though he realistically regarded himself a longshot in 1897, had his eyes set firmly on a future gubernatorial bid. Surprisingly, incumbent Governor Peón Machado also announced his intention to run, in defiance of the Porfirian ground rule that precluded succession. Dire consequences would attend Peón's refusal to follow the prearranged script, and the bitterly contested election is fraught with significance for understanding the subsequent political unrest on the eve and following the outbreak of the Mexican Revolution.

To begin with, the 1897 campaign sheds some light on one of the most overlooked facets of the political infighting which took place in Porfirian Mexico: the relationship among local camarillas, expatriate regional influence peddlers residing in the capital, and the select circle of counselors to the dictator. Many wealthy *yucatecos* lived in Mexico City and used their clientelist connections with Díaz's lieutenants to lobby regularly for favored regional candidates. The opinions of these expatriates were seriously considered by the influential *bloques del poder*[8] that surrounded Don Porfirio. Since the final choice of governor was ultimately made by the dictator and not the governors of Yucatán, it might be argued that these informal lobbies, which had familial ties to powerful *parentescos* in the peninsula, were of greater importance in determining the next governor of the state than the political preference of elites in Yucatán.[9]

Surrounding the dictator in the 1890s were two competing *bloques*.[10] One group, led by the Minister of Finance, José Yves Limantour, referred to as the *científicos*, was composed of bankers, prominent landowners, government officials, and technocrats. Its rival was a clique headed by military men, first by General Manuel González, and later by General Bernardo Reyes. This latter bloc, composed of traditional regional strongmen and some bureaucrats, was sharply critical of the increasing power and influence of the *científicos*. Given his military background and connections, Pancho Cantón was a natural choice for the Reyista clique, while Olegario Molina found favor with the increasingly more powerful *científicos*.[11]

On the other hand, Governor Peón's refusal to gracefully bow out of the campaign left him bereft of support in the national capital and vulnerable to attack at home. The results were predictable: the opposing "conservative" camarilla, postulating the candidacy of General Cantón, fabricated an incident in Mérida's central square on 11 August 1897, which left several dead and several more wounded. Díaz was forced to intervene, Carlos Peón was recalled to Mexico City, an interim "Cantonista" governor was named, and the "elections" proceeded apace that fall with victory assured for Pancho Cantón.[12]

The death of a few partisans that August night, while regrettable, was a small price for the Cantonistas to pay to force the dictator's hand. Although the official slogan of the Cantonistas during the 1897 election campaign had been the Porfirian *lema* of "no-reelection," there was much more at stake here than Peón Machado's right to succeed himself.

In Porfirian Mexico, the system of machine politics meant access to jobs as well as lucrative government contracts, railway concessions and land grants for those in power. The Cantonistas merely desired their own access to the till. After twelve relatively peaceful years of military rule, the consecutive elections of civilians Peón Machado and Cantón signaled to local elites that the gates of patronage were now open for those willing to organize their respective political machines. *Empleomanía*, the Mexican spoils system that was firmly rooted in Yucatán throughout the nineteenth century, would reach epic proportions during the administrations of Cantón (1897–1901) and his successor, Olegario Molina (1902–1906), as each camarilla enriched itself while in power.[13] What these factions could not foresee in 1897 was that the venerable mechanism of "divide and rule," which had maintained an uneasy peace among the alternating rival elites, would come to end in 1902.

The Olegariato: Breaking the Rules (1902–1909)

To a far greater extent than his more traditional predecessor, Pancho Cantón, Olegario Molina was driven with the desire to make Yucatán a dynamic participant in the modernization of Mexican society. He is best remembered by Yucatecans as *el constructor*—the "builder." The embodiment of nineteenth-century Mexican positivism, Yucatán's own *científico*, Don Olegario reasoned that, to the extent that he and his class prospered, so would Yucatán. For Molina, who secured degrees in topographical engineering and law, the future of Yucatán lay with its educated criollo elite, not the mass of illiterate Maya Indians who toiled on the henequén plantations. Although he is lionized in the region for the number of schools he built (most of which were constructed by his company, O. Molina y Compañía), Governor Molina's regard for Yucatán's working classes might be best described as paternalistic. While he inaugurated many more schoolhouses than his predecessors, raised teacher's salaries and pensions, and had the state overhaul Mérida's floundering public school system, the governor did little to introduce education to the tens of thousands of peons who lived on haciendas in the *zona henequenera*. Like other *científicos*, Don Olegario believed that, at least in the short run, the modernization of Yucatán and Mexico was dependent on the appropriation of foreign ideas, capital, and technology by an enterprising and educated native elite.

Perhaps Molina's greatest accomplishment as a modernizer, the paving and draining of Mérida's streets, was also the showpiece of his administration. Imitating the extensive pavement and drainage project recently undertaken by the national government in Mexico City, the governor levied a special tax on henequén to help defray the cost of public works. He then commissioned O. Molina y Compañía, in collaboration with foreign firms, to undertake the enormous task of constructing sewers, building sidewalks, and laying more than 350,000 square meters of asphalt, concrete, and brick in the downtown area. Ignoring cries of conflict of interest by his political enemies, Don Olegario spent more than five million pesos on paving and drainage, transforming Mérida into Mexico's most modern provincial capital.

Molina also coaxed wealthy *henequeneros* to supplement state funds by underwriting a spate of capital improvement projects in Mérida, including the O'Horan Hospital, the Juárez Penitentiary, the Ayala Asylum, and Mérida's grand boulevard, the Paseo de Montejo. To promote contributions and demonstrate civic spirit, Don Olegario himself contributed fifty thousand pesos each to the hospital and asylum funds (out of a total of over a million pesos raised from the community) and returned one year's pay from his governor's salary to the state treasury. In addition, he reorganized the state's registry of property to make tax collection more efficient. During his tenure, state revenues almost doubled and a surge in henequén prices enabled the state treasury to balance its books—a stunning accomplishment considering the sizable debt Molina had inherited from the Cantón administration. Somehow, he found time to rewrite the state constitution, reform the penal and civil codes, and reorganize both the state National Guard and the Mérida police force.[14]

While only a few bitter opponents dared to speak out against Molina's popular public works projects, critics lambasted the governor on a variety of fronts. Among the catalogue of charges, we find: his purported role in the loss of Quintana Roo to the federal government;[15] his numerous tax levies; his insatiable political ambitions (more specifically, his alleged yearning for the vice-presidency of the republic); the state's bureaucratic intrusion into the private lives and pastimes of ordinary citizens; his reorganization of the National Guard and the nefarious *leva*; and perhaps most gallingly, his questionable practice of handing out government positions, lucrative concessions, and contracts—such as the paving of the city—to business associates and family.[16] Opponents attacking Molina on the nepotism issue took great pains

Table 5.1
Nepotism during the Olegariato[18]

Relations	Name	Position
Brother	José Trinidad Molina Solís	President of the Board of the United Railways of Yucatán
Brother	Augusto Molina Solís	Director, School of Medicine, Deputy in State Congress
Brother	Manuel Molina Solís	Interim Governor
Son-in-Law	Rogelio Suárez*	Board director of Banco Yucateco, government concession for dynamite
Son-in-Law	Avelino Montes	Agent for International Harvester, on board of local banks, railways, head of binder twine factory, City Council
Son-in-Law	Carlos Casasus	Deputy to State Congress
Nephew	Ricardo Molina Hübbe	Owner of *Diario Yucateco*
Nephew	Trinidad Molina Ávila	Secretary and board director of Banco Peninsular
Nephew	Luis Demetrio Molina Cirerol	Jefe Político of Mérida, Deputy of State Congress
Nephew	Ignacio Molina Castilla	Director of Services to Hospital O'Horan
Nephew	Vicente Molina Castilla	Chief engineer of United Railways of Yucatán
Nephew	Manuel Molina Castilla	Justice of the Peace in Mérida

*It should be noted that Rogelio Suárez appeared to be the most independent of all the Molina relatives. This is borne out by his bankruptcy during the 1907–8 panic. To our knowledge he is the only Molina relation who succumbed to the hard times of the last years of the Porfiriato.
Source: *Yucatán Nuevo*, 6 November 1908, no. 8.

to print long lists of family members who had profited politically and economically from their association with the governor. Table 5.1 illustrates the validity of these charges.

What worried elite factional opponents most was Don Olegario's consuming ambition. Unlike his predecessor, Pancho Cantón, Governor Molina had little intention of stepping down at the end of his first term. In fact, Molina had the state constitution changed to permit a second term in 1906. The imminent prospect of "continuismo" aggravated and preoccupied his opponents. It was one thing to engage in patronage for his family and cronies, it was quite another to create a dynasty of privilege and wealth. How Molina dealt with his opponents to ensure his continued political control of the state is a textbook study in late Porfirian regional power politics.

First, the governor inhibited the political activities of his opponents by harassing the opposition press. Just as the pretense of open elections was maintained in Yucatán, so was the sham of a free press. No doubt taking his cue from President Díaz, Molina censored the press throughout his administration.[17] Reporters who raised substantive complaints about Don Olegario's rule found themselves languishing in Juárez Penitentiary; nettlesome editors had their newspapers shut down. Journalists were removed from circulation for months, even years at a time. Several came to know intimately the not-so-friendly confines of the state prison, nicknamed "Hotel Bolados," after the despised warden, Leonardo Bolados Garza.[19]

But press censorship was only part of the *"bola negra"* tactics of the Molina administration. During his first term, the governor not only reorganized the local constabulary, but brought in Spaniards and Cubans to direct a new state bureau of investigation with the foreboding name of "La Policía Secreta." The new agency was charged with ensuring the primacy of the Molinistas in local politics. The Cantonistas, now reorganized as La Unión Popular Anti-reeleccionista de Yucatán in order to offer *yucatecos* a choice in the upcoming 1905 elections, were a particular target of the Secret Police. At a political rally staged by La Unión in late November in Kanasín, a small town outside of Mérida, two Cantonistas were killed and five arrested; the president of La Unión, Manuel Meneses, was ushered into the "Hotel Bolados."[20]

While Molina used a heavy hand locally, he also made sure that his *científico* colleagues in Mexico City provided a positive image of his administration to President Díaz. Molina's public works projects were lauded in the Mexico City press, as *El Imparcial* regularly carried stories on the transformation of Mérida into the "Paris of Mexico."[21] These glowing reports, plus the influence and goodwill of the influential *científico* power bloc in the capital, persuaded the dictator that it now made good sense to alter the rules and permit the Yucatecan governor to run for a second term.[22] By the fall of 1905, with the state constitution amended by the Molinista legislature, Don Olegario's candidacy was declared; more importantly, it was also announced that the president of Mexico would come to Yucatán in early 1906 to inaugurate a variety of public works projects in Mérida.

In addition to legitimizing Molinista hegemony, Porfirio Díaz's trip to Yucatán was noteworthy for another reason: for the first time in history, a Mexican chief executive would visit the Yucatán peninsula. In a symbolic sense, Díaz's journey signaled the coming of age of the Yucatecan elite. Rather than engaging in the usual round of posturing that accompanied Porfirian elections, members of rival camarillas threw themselves into preparations for the presidential visit.[23] Díaz's trip confirmed that the region was no longer a provincial backwater, but an integral part of the rapidly modernizing Mexican nation. And if the Yucatecan elite had become a regional vanguard of the president's development plans, it was clear that Olegario Molina and his *camarilla* were among its chief architects.

For Don Olegario, the presidential visit brought a pleasant, if not unexpected bonus. Within a few months of the visit, Molina was offered and accepted the post of secretary of *fomento* (development) in Mexico City. Like his counterpart, Enrique C. Creel of Chihuahua,[24] Olegario Molina represented the best that the provinces had to offer, and his incorporation into the national superstructure illustrated the co-optative nature of Porfirian politics.

The departure of Molina, however, did not signal a change in local politics. Molina handpicked Enrique Múñoz Arístegui, a nondescript business associate with little to recommend him, to serve out his second term. The Molinista camarilla continued to dominate local politics from 1906 to 1910, although Múñoz Arístegui clearly lacked the political savvy of his *patrón*. By 1909, opposition to Múñoz began to coalesce behind two rival camarillas, the "Morenistas" and the "Pinistas." The Morenistas—or, more properly, the Centro Electoral Independiente (CEI)—were led by poet and journalist Delio Moreno Cantón, the nephew of Pancho Cantón. They represented the latest incarnation of what had originally been Don Pancho's Gran Club Liberal and, more recently, the short-lived La Unión Anti-reeleccionista of 1905. The Pinistas, or Partido Anti-reeleccionista (PA), were led by Tabascan-born journalist José María Pino Suárez. By 1909, both of these loosely organized, planter-financed parties were attempting to construct alliances reaching into the middle-class intelligentsia, the small urban working and artisan class, and the Maya *campesinado*. Increasingly, the Molinistas would find it more difficult to contain local protest and unrest.

Nevertheless, the Molinistas had broken the convention of "alternating," or sharing political power with competing camarillas. Their political dominance— underwritten, as we shall see, by their virtual control over the regional monocrop, henequén—effectively transformed the heretofore competitive nature of regional politics. Only by examining the economic contradictions of late Porfirian Yucatán can we appreciate how the political and economic power wielded by the Molinistas each served to reinforce the other, ultimately convincing "disenfranchised" local elites that the only way to combat such entrenched privilege was through the use of force.

Economic Contradictions

Oligarchical Control of the Spoils of Monoculture (1897–1909)

Yucatán's monocrop economy represented an untold bonanza for those elites savvy enough to understand how political influence and economic leverage over the burgeoning fiber trade might complement one another. The capacity of merchant and planter families to adapt to changes in the political arena amid the boom and bust shocks of the regional economy produced a tangled web of power relationships in the peninsula throughout the *auge henequenero* (henequén boom). Stepping back from the political–economic fluctuations of the period, we can construct a basic typology which links henequén export houses *(casas exportadoras)* to the personalistic political camarillas of the 1890s and 1900s. There were three political factions in late Porfirian Yucatán and each had the backing of at least one powerful export house.[25]

Escalante, Dondé, Ponce, Urcelay and Molina were all active family enterprises in the local agro-commercial bourgeoisie. While the henequén economy was the motor that drove their regional economic empires, these commercial houses did benefit at times from their political connections. A clear illustration of this phenomenon was found during the Cantón *cuatrenio*, when the general's political rise catapulted the fortunes of those loyal merchants who had supported him. As Table 5.2 demonstrates, Carlos Urcelay y Compañía saw its share of the fiber market soar during the Cantón years, from almost nothing in 1897 to a high of 17.3 percent in 1902.

If we combine the exports of Urcelay and Ponce, we see that in 1898 and 1899 (the first two years of the Cantón term) they had a greater share of the market than the perennially powerful Escalantes, who saw their own share dip to 17.4 percent and 16.7 percent, respectively—their lowest totals ever. Not coincidentally, the Escalantes's link to the state house was severed with the unceremonious dumping of Peón Machado in 1897. Conversely, the Urcelay and Ponce market share of 28 percent in 1898, the first year of the Cantón era, represented a whopping 21 percent increase over the year before Cantón assumed his duties. A year later, his business associates (taken together) were the second largest exporters in the state. While these statistics must be used

Fig. 5.1
Political Factions and Their Casas Exportadoras, 1890–1910

Peonistas	Cantonistas	Molinistas
E. Escalante e Hijo	Urcelay y Cía	Molina y Cía
Manuel Dondé y Cía	Ponce y Cía	

Table 5.2
Urcelay y Cía's and Ponce y Cía's Share of Henequén Exports to the
United States, 1897–1905

Year	Urcelay y Cía	Urcelay and Ponce
1897	0.0	7.0
1898	12.0	28.0
1899	15.2	21.1
1900	6.7	11.0
1901	14.8	15.3
1902	17.3	17.3*
1903	9.5	9.5*
1904	1.8	1.8*
1905	1.7	1.7*

*After 1902, José María Ponce y Cía exported so few bales of henequén that his name is not specifically listed with the leading exporters, but is instead lumped together with other sundry merchants. All the "other" producers combined accounted for a negligible percentage of exports, especially after 1903, when the henequén trade became increasingly monopolized by the Molina *casa*.
Source: Peabody Papers, H. L-1, 254–74; U.S. Congress, Senate, Committee on Agriculture and Forestry, *Importation of Sisal and Manila Hemp*, vol. 2 (Washington, D.C., 1916), 963; and Boletín de Estadística, 15 July 1905, no. 14, and 21 May 1906, no. 15.

with care since "nonpolitical" factors certainly influenced the fiber trade during these years, the meteoric rise of the Cantón-allied houses and their subsequent precipitous collapse after the general's *cuatrenio*, lead us to believe that political power and economic wealth went hand in hand in Porfirian Yucatán.

If the Cantonistas understood how patronage and profit complemented one another, the Molinistas would easily surpass them in siphoning off the growing wealth of the henequén boom. Although always a prosperous merchant prior to 1902, Molina, like General Cantón, saw his economic fortunes rise dramatically upon becoming governor. After assuming power in 1902, Olegario Molina became the most powerful economic force in the region. Unquestionably, he was aided by his business relationship with the International Harvester Company (IHC), but this collaboration, which was cemented during the first years of the century,[26] cannot be explained or evaluated without reference to Don Olegario's political power. By the end of the Porfiriato, Molina had become the largest single landowner in the state and cultivated more henequén on his haciendas than any other planter. As we have seen, numerous family members and business associates profited from his influence and stature. In short order, and aided by bright and able lieutenants, Olegario

Molina had created an economic empire within the boundaries of what was essentially his camarilla's political fief.[27]

Contemporary planters, merchants, politicians, and journalists openly discussed the impact of International Harvester's collaboration with the Molina–Montes *parentesco* on the regional economy. Harvester became a target in the regional press, especially after 1905 when the federal government began to take a decidedly more nationalistic posture vis-à-vis foreign investments in Mexico. Indeed, the perception of guilt seemed proof enough for many intellectuals and planters, who were disposed to saddle the collaborators with more blame than they probably deserved for the ills of an inherently unstable economy.

As the price of henequén plummeted from an artificaly high price of almost ten cents a pound in 1902 (inflated by the Spanish American War) to just under four cents a pound in 1911, the criticism of the "trust" became increasingly strident. Words were replaced with action in 1906–7 when disgruntled landowners and merchants formed a Cámara Agrícola to fight the power of the *casas exportadoras*. The Chamber spawned an activist group of hacendados determined to forge a more competitive balance in the henequén trade. They formed a Compañía Cooperativa de Hacendados Henequeneros and, late in 1907, secured a loan from the Banco Nacional's branch office in Mérida to enable producers to hold 16 percent of their fiber off the market and force a rise in the price.

Earlier attempts to withhold production and create a shortage of fiber on the market had failed miserably. Invariably, such agricultural societies had lacked the capital to compete with powerful *casas* with foreign backing such as Molina y Cía or Henry W. Peabody and Company. Capital-starved planters also had themselves to blame for the failures of these associations. A contentious lot even under favorable market conditions, the planters were hampered from the start by a lack of solidarity. An undercurrent of *disgusto*, setting family-based elites at odds throughout the Gilded Age, worked to inhibit these producer cooperatives. Generally speaking, cooperative societies only coalesced when the price of henequén dropped so low that it cut into the planter's considerable profits. This was precisely the worst time for such a maneuver to succeed, since money was stretched so thin when the price of henequén declined. In short, these *compañías, sindicatos,* or *sociedades*—the labels contemporaries gave to such planter cooperatives—had functioned as short-lived complaining confraternities, usually folding only months after their formation.

The *casas exportadoras*, however, did not take demonstrations of incipient planter solidarity lightly. Montes was particularly concerned about the formation of the Cámara Agrícola. According to some accounts, Montes and Molina (now in Díaz's cabinet as secretary of *fomento*), worked to undermine the cooperative. In 1908, the Banco Nacional's branch in Mérida, which held the stockpiled henequén as collateral on the loan, shocked the *henequeneros* by selling off the fiber at a low price. Critics of the Molina–Montes economic empire have pointed out that one of the principal board directors of the bank was Olegario Molina.

Whether such contemporary allegations of Molina's and Montes's complicity in the bank's "sell-off" were true will probably never be known. It is likely, however, that the Compañía Cooperativa's plan to withhold production would have failed on its own. In fact, the association could not have picked a worse time to get its cooperative venture off the ground. In 1907, a serious panic hit the financial markets of the United States and Europe, setting off a chain reaction that extended throughout Mexico.[28] Two of the oldest and most respected names in the financing and marketing of henequén, the New York-based Thebaud Brothers and Yucatán's Eusebio Escalante e Hijo, were both casualties of the crash.

Although the Compañía failed to end IHC–Molinista control of the market, at least one outspoken critic of the Molinista camarilla would later admit that the collapse of the valorization scheme was instrumental in reawakening the political consciousness of disgruntled hacendados who, whether rightly or wrongly, blamed Molina and Montes for the economic crisis gripping the peninsula.

The 1907 panic and traditionally loose credit practices also combined to contribute to the financial problems of the Escalante house. Although it could no longer lay claim to dominance in henequén sales, its investments in the Yucatecan economy were still considerable. Clearly, many stood to lose through association with this economic powerhouse.

In a desperate but futile attempt to avoid bankruptcy, Nicolás Escalante Peón went to Mexico City in May and June of 1907 to speak with Ministers Molina and Limantour. Yucatecan banks, especially the Escalante-controlled Banco Mercantil, were also in imminent danger of default. Secretary of *Hacienda* Limantour agreed to bail out the Yucatecan banks by authorizing the Banco Nacional to loan ten million pesos to the Banco Yucateco and the Banco Mercantil under certain unspecified conditions. Later in 1908, Limantour would agree to the fusion of the two weakened banks into one stronger institution, the Banco Peninsular Mexicano. While the federal government did intervene to prop up the banking industry during this financial crisis, it chose not to

rescue the ailing Escalante casa. Nicolás Escalante Peón and some of his cred-
itors would later suggest that Molina intentionally worked to subvert any
type of financial settlement that would save the Escalante house from failure.
Although we will probably never know if this is true, the Molinista faction
had little interest in propping up Escalante. As a direct result of the Escalante
failure in July 1907, Avelino Montes S. en C., the heir apparent to O. Molina
y Cía, would scuttle one of its principal rivals in the henequén trade, obtain
control of the Ferrocarriles Unidos de Yucatán and of the peninsular banks,
and then use its new clout to purchase a steamship line in 1908. Rarely has a
business profited so well from another's misfortune. Escalante's demise ensured
Molinista dominance over the key facets of the regional economy.

The failure precipitated the bankruptcies (*quiebras*) of several allied joint-
stock companies and prominent members of the Meridano elite, among them
the former governor, Carlos Peón Machado. Loan capital became even more
scarce as banks only provided funds to their most preferred customers. Private moneylenders offered capital at 2 to 3 percent interest a month to the
most desperate henequén growers.

The Escalante *quiebra* graphically demonstrated to many hacendados just
how little control they had over their own destinies and how unforgiving the
monocrop economy could be. A lack of solidarity and resolve by many planters in the face of powerful vested interests only contributed to the dire consequences of the financial crisis. But it was always easier to blame someone
else, and the Molina *parentesco* and the North American "trust" served as invit-
ing targets. A trail of circumstantial evidence which tied Molina, Montes,
and Harvester conspiratorially to the failure of the Escalante casa only provided more grist for the political opponents of the dominant oligarchical faction. The Escalante failure, and the collapse of the producers's cooperative before
it, crystallized the belief among most planters that, just as in the political
arena, the Molinista camarilla was unwilling to countenance any loss of economic control in the peninsula. Accommodation no longer seemed possible.
Political activity and, if necessary, violent rebellion increasingly were perceived as the only means to restore a more equitable reapportionment of the
spoils of the henequén economy.

Social Contradictions

The rise of henequén monoculture dramatically transformed the lives of
the tens of thousands of campesinos[29] who comprised the labor force. The
plantation devoured almost all the independent peasant villages in the north-

western quadrant of the peninsula (the *zona henequenera*), then began to encroach upon *comuneros* in transitional areas along the southeastern frontier. By the turn of the century, the great majority of the free Maya pueblos in the *zona* had lost their land base. Unable to hold off the expanding henequén plantations, Yucatán's campesinos were first pulled onto the estates and then isolated on them. Planters made sure that their work forces were heterogeneous groups, combining Maya campesinos with smaller numbers of ethnic and linguistic strangers: Yaqui deportees, indentured Asian immigrants, and central Mexican *enganchados*. Not only did peons have little contact with their fellow workers on other estates, but they were also isolated from potential allies in the urban areas. Yucatecan proprietors hoped that these precautions, coupled with a harsh labor regimen and a multitiered system of surveillance and repression—which included the state's national guard, federal and state battalions, private bounty hunters, and "La Policía Secreta"—would preclude another "Guerra de Castas." Still, the white masters (*dzules*) lived in constant fear of large-scale Maya uprisings.

The planters fears were justified. Although it served the propagandistic needs of both muckraking critics and *henequenero* apologists of the Old Regime to portray the Maya *campesinado* as a mass of passive, inert peons,[30] in reality there was a surprisingly high incidence of resistance to the *dzules'* brutal regime even prior to 1910. The Maya was no docile "sambo," meekly accepting his dependent status and extracting what meager morsels of benevolence the planter tossed in his direction. On the whole, workers rejected the weak paternalistic ethos of their masters, demonstrating their dissatisfaction in a variety of ways,[31] most commonly by running away, shirking, and chronic alcoholism, but to a lesser extent through suicide, the burning of henequén fields, and spontaneous, although ultimately futile, localized acts of violence.

One of the most poignant yet negative methods of resistance grew out of the worsening conditions for hacienda peons during the late Porfiriato. State judicial records document a frightening number of suicides, many induced by pellagra, a vitamin B deficiency which produces scaling, itching, and in some cases mental disorders.[32] When coupled with the alcoholism that was endemic in the *campo*, pellagra often led to tragic consequences. That so many peons hung themselves from trees or house beams, or threw themselves into wells, testifies to the poor diet, inadequate medical care, and feelings of desperation of many peons isolated on the henequén haciendas. One need not invoke the writings of the muckrakers to document the onerous plight of the resident workerse who cut fifteen hundred to two thousand spiny henequén leaves a day under relentless tropical sun, who existed in a perpetual state of indebtedness, and whose mobility was severely constrained by local authorities.

While pellagra plagued the *campesinado*, the planter elite was more concerned with acts of violence that periodically erupted on the estates. Invariably, the state would move quickly to isolate flare-ups, rushing a detachment of the national guard to the trouble spot. During the period 1907–1910, the region's newspapers featured a growing number of articles treating disputes over wages and labor conditions in the face of a continued decline in the price of fiber, protests by campesinos who refused to serve in the national guard, and conflicts between peasant villages and expanding plantations.[33] At first, these disputes appeared to be of minor consequence, yet their growing number and the campesinos' increasing recourse to violence soon suggested that active, often violent forms of protest were becoming the principal means of expression by Yucatán's *campesinado*. By 1910–1911, with a locust plague and steadily declining fiber quotations exacerbating rural conditions, every day brought new reports of violence, both in the henequén zone and on its southeastern periphery. Although, as we will see, many of the *cabecillas* and recruits of the popular rebellions that erupted during the era of Maderismo came from poor but "free" villages, they were often joined—sometimes willingly, but occasionally through coercion—by peons from nearby haciendas.

On the fringes of the *zona henequenera*, along the southern range of stunted hills known as the Puuc, and east of the prime henequén haciendas of Temax, independent smallholders stubbornly guarded their lands against the incursions of local hacendados. In some cases, these free peasants opted to fight local authorities rather than submit to the surveying of their traditional ejidal lands.[34] State authorities could not contain social unrest in these peripheral areas during the last years of the Porfiriato, since insurgents as well as cattle rustlers and bandits could easily slip off into the *monte* (bush). It was along the Puuc corridor running from Maxcanú to Muna, and in eastern *poblaciones* like Dzilám González, Temax, Yaxcabá and Chemax that the concept of "el hombre libre"—"a free and independent man"—became part of the daily lexicon.[35] Smallholders, often joined by petty merchants and artisans in these subregions, tenaciously resisted the incursions of powerful *henequeneros* like Alvino Manzanilla and the Regils in Temax, and Eusebio Escalante and Carlos Peón Machado in the Puuc, proprietors who coveted both their lands and labor. It is hardly surprising, then, that these fringe areas proved to be fertile recruiting grounds for the first rebellions of Maderismo.

A celebrated incident in 1908 outside the small town of Cepeda—located a short distance southwest of the Puuc—richly illustrates the nuances of the adversarial relationship between expansionist hacendados and a determined peasantry. An aged smallholder, Feliciano Chi, was brutally murdered while tending his *milpa* on his *paraje* (tract), San Francisco. Chi had been a spokesman for the nearby town of Halachó in its dispute over ejidal lands with the powerful hacendado, Arcadio Escobedo. The landowner (who would later become governor of the state under Huertismo) was in the midst of a protracted fourteen-year legal battle with both Halachó and Cepeda over some contested *baldíos*, or vacant lands. Escobedo hired one of the best trial lawyers in Mérida, Serapio Rendón,[36] to defend his overseer, who had been implicated in the crime, and later published a pamphlet, *En defensa de Faustino Méndez (El Crimen de Cepeda)*, to clear his own good name.[37]

In the trial, which was followed closely by the Mérida elite, the prosecution alleged that Escobedo's *encargado*, Faustino Méndez, had paid several servants from his estate, Dzidzibachí, the sum of eighty pesos to murder Chi. If convicted, the defendants stood to receive the death penalty under Molina's controversial new penal code. The prosecutor felt that the *encargado* was the chief architect of the crime, and in his brief commented on the intimidating relations of domination which overseers and landowners exercised over their peons.[38]

Cepeda was a new town, founded in 1876—named after the liberal hero of the peninsula who had defeated the Imperialists in 1867. Since Cepeda was created after the Reform Laws, it was not formally entitled to ejidal lands; it had to apply to the federal government for them. The courts reached a compromise ruling in 1894, asserting that the inhabitants of Cepeda ought to receive lands, which should come partly from Escobedo's *baldíos* and partly from the communal lands of Halachó. No one was pleased with the 1894 settlement: the villagers of Cepeda felt that they had not been given a large enough settlement; Escobedo was so upset he went back to the courts to win back his vacant public lands. Moreover, Serapio Rendón, the defense attorney, claimed that some of the townspeople of Cepeda, who worked as day laborers on Dzidzibachí and who allegedly had participated in the homicide, had been upset with Feliciano Chi, who, as a representative of Halachó, had helped work out the settlement. The prosecutor countered that Escobedo was enraged with the residents of Halachó for his ongoing difficulties: just months before the hacendado had lost another round in the seemingly endless judicial proceedings. It was that aggravation, the prosecutor contended, that eventually boiled over and led to the "Crimen de Cepeda."

The long litigious struggle and its violent denouement underscores the antagonistic relationship between hacendados and smallholding villagers in late Porfirian Yucatán. It also helps to explain why hacendados in subregions such as the Puuc became special targets for grassroots *cabecilla*-led bands during the first years of Maderismo. What was left of an independent peasantry found itself increasingly hemmed in by aggressive haciendas and a state which catered to their every need. As Alan Knight states: "It was not exploitation per se, but ostensibly new, arbitrary, unjustified exploitation which provoked resistance."[39] In Yucatán, that struggle played itself out, with few exceptions, in the pueblos and *montes* on the edges of henequén monoculture.

If the state was increasingly unable to contain unrest in these rural fringe areas, it was more successful in limiting protest and mobilization in urban areas, particularly in the service industries that were tied to the henequén industry. Dock workers, stevedores, carriage drivers, push-cart operators, printers, barbers, railway employees, binder-twine workers, carpenters, machinists, foundry smelters, and even secondary school teachers had begun to organize in Mérida and the principal port of Progreso during the late Porfiriato. And with good reason: management—labor relations in Yucatán in commerce and industry resembled those of the paternalistic world of the hacienda.[40] In fact, traditional mechanisms of social control were so ingrained in local labor practices that Yucatecan railway entrepreneurs utilized the institution of debt peonage to limit the mobility of their own labor force. Records of the Mérida—Peto railway reveal that *ferrocarrileros* accumulated substantial debts over a ten-year span (from 1899 to 1908).[41]

Although the limits of monoculture kept the peninsula's urban working classes smaller and weaker than in many areas of Mexico, nevertheless organizations such as the Sociedad de Trabajadores Marítimos and the Alianza Mutualista de la Compañía de Trabajadores Ferrocarrileros did attract the attention of state authorities.[42] Labor organizers such as Tomás Pérez Ponce and Gervasio Fuentes were harassed mercilessly by the "Policía Secreta." They were often packed off to the "Hotel Bolados" on trumped-up charges to keep them from organizing the workers; periodically, their union headquarters and print shops were raided.[43] Although urban workers seldom had contact with *cabecillas* in the peripheral pueblos, let alone peons on haciendas, they did represent an important, more "organized" constituency that was courted by both the Morenistas and the Pinistas after 1909.

The Molinista regime coupled its *"bola negra"* tactics with more subtle methods of social control. Again taking his cue from Mexico City, Don Olegario made a conscious effort to inject the new pristine morality of the "positivistic" state into the day-to-day lives of the laboring classes. In an effort to curb lower-class vices which, Yucatán's *científicos* believed, undercut labor productivity and efficiency, the Olegariato targeted alcoholism, vagrancy, gambling, pornography, and crime in urban and rural areas. From the closing of *cantinas* on Sundays and holidays to raids on bookstores that sold erotic poetry and picture post cards of French nudes,[44] the state extended its regulation into leisure pursuits which previously had afforded some measure of independence to the popular classes. Critics from opposition camarillas no doubt struck a common chord when they mocked the self-righteous morality of Yucatán's rulers.

As in other parts of Mexico, the key figure in the Porfirian state apparatus of social control was the district prefect or *jefe político*. William Beezley notes that "they could, and did, dictate social standards in the community."[45] In addition to political surveillance and keeping the peace, the *jefe* was oftentimes the town's chief moneylender, pawnbroker, real estate agent, merchant, and marriage broker.[46] *Jefes* also regulated the local economy by issuing permits for the sale of alcoholic beverages and by granting licenses to local stores and peddlers.[47]

Much has been made in the recent literature about the prefect's status as an "outsider," a functionary who was selected by, and answered to, federal officials and, hence, was perceived to be a threat by state authorities.[48] In Yucatán, this was clearly not the case. The *jefe* continued to be part and parcel of the lucrative state system of patronage. Each gubernatorial administration was empowered to clean house and appoint new prefects. Sometimes, as in the case of Luis Felipe de Regil, who was moved from one assignment (Progreso) to another (Valladolid), these *jefes* were merely rotated from *partido* to *partido*. Other times, prefects were permitted to establish virtual fiefdoms in their own communities—witness the case of Casimiro Montalvo Solís, who ruled Peto *partido* dictatorially from 1902 to 1911.

The hatred directed at *jefes* in Yucatán ran deep. Apart from the issues of imposition, arbitrary rule, and corruption, unquestionably the prefects were most despised for their implementation of the dreaded *leva*, or conscription into the state's National Guard. Villagers might serve in their hometowns, but they also might be shuttled to the southeastern frontier, to fight in state battalions based in God-forsaken places like Xocen, Yaxhacben and Chemax— the first line of defense against bands of rebel Maya who had never surrendered in the Caste War. Males between the ages of fifteen and sixty were required to serve in the Guard each year.[49] At fifty centavos a day, Guard pay offered little incentive, for it was roughly equivalent to the low wage a villager might earn from cutting henequén on a nearby plantation.

One need only read through the hundreds of petitions requesting exemption from Guard service to appreciate the overwhelming dissatisfaction with conscription in Yucatán. Case after case details military desertions, medical excuses, or the spectacle of *jefes políticos* dragging recalcitrant recruits from the countryside—thereby underscoring the great lengths to which *yucatecos* would go to avoid service. Interestingly, one of the first decrees promulgated by General Luis Curiel, sent by a desperate Díaz in March 1911 to bring some semblance of order to a rebellious state, was the elimination of the *leva* and the creation of a relatively well-paid volunteer army.[50]

Moreover, the cost of maintaining the social peace proved a considerable burden to the poor, as well as an irritant to the wealthy. The 1910 Yucatecan budget mandated 300,000 pesos (out of a total budget of just under 2 million; that is, 15 percent) for the state troops, National Guard, police constabulary, and the plainclothes detectives of the Secret Police. Costs for this varied peacekeeping apparatus were partially borne by special contributions, levied in the *partidos*, called *gastos extraordinarios*. They represented yet another state intrusion, and were collected by none other than the district prefects.[51]

Is it any surprise that the first target of Yucatán's insurgent bands from 1910 to 1912 was often the *jefe político*? Several of the *cabecillas* of Maderista-era rebellions had experienced firsthand *la mano dura* of the *jefes*. Pedro Crespo,[52] Juan Campos, José Loreto Baak, Manuel Fausto Robles, José Kantún, Maximiliano Bonilla, Miguel Ruz Ponce, and a young firebrand by the name of Felipe Carrillo Puerto—all ran afoul of local authorities and were jailed during the last years of the Porfiriato.

Given the suffocating controls imposed by a government bound and determined to protect the oligarchy's golden goose, the henequén economy, it is perfectly understandable why these *cabecillas*—typically smallholders, artisans, and petty traders from interior villages—would be receptive to an alliance with discontented urban groups. Joining together with disgruntled factions of the regional elite and modest groupings of middle-class intellectuals and urban workers, these incipient rural insurgents would form the first fragile coalitions of Maderismo.

The Crisis of an Oligarchical Regime (1909–1911)[53]

Although Molinista domination of late Porfirian Yucatán was qualitatively different than past rule by competing camarillas, rival elites still believed that the tactics which had worked so well in the past deserved to be tried again. For example, in 1908 and the first part of 1909, Morenistas (latter-day Cantonistas) began to employ the same strategy that they had used effectively in 1897. They plotted and intrigued and sought to draw national attention to themselves and the region in order to embarrass the local authorities and, ultimately, to force the federal government to intervene in local politics. The ploy had worked well enough twelve years before when Díaz sided with the Cantonistas and toppled the incumbent Peonista camarilla. The Morenistas reasoned that Don Porfirio would, as usual, play one faction against the other and that they would eventually emerge holding the reins of power. What they did not see at first was that the flexible system of power-sharing that had served Don Porfirio so well for three decades had become calcified by 1909; that too much lucrative peculation was now riding on the maintenance of the status quo. As John Womack has affirmed more generally for late Porfirian Mexico: "[P]olitics meant business. In maze upon maze of graft and collusion between politicians and businessmen . . . [change] meant renegotiation of a myriad of shady deals."[54]

The writing was on the wall; the Morenistas chose not to read it. Don Olegario's inclusion in the Porfirian team as secretary of *fomento* signaled the aging dictator's decision to stay with the Molinista incumbents during the last years of his rule. Yet it would be a costly mistake, one that soon revealed how badly the *científico* clique in Mexico City and Mérida had underestimated the determination and resilience of competing Yucatecan camarillas. When, late in 1909, in the wake of unceasing political harassment, the Morenistas came to realize that the old rules no longer applied and that power would have to be taken forcibly, they broadened their political organization and intensified their recruitment of peons and villagers in the outlying rural areas, and planned a wave of armed attacks on state authorities. Let us tease out the chronology of events that led inevitably to insurgency in order to better examine the responses of both elite factions and the popular classes.

Francisco Madero's visit to Yucatán late in June 1909 had encouraged elite opponents of the regime that change might still come by traditional political means. The Morenista Centro Electoral Independiente (CEI), the political heirs of Pancho Cantón, and the local chapter of Madero's Anti-Reelectionist Party (PA), led by Pino Suárez, had both formally been organized during the summer of 1910. While Madero was in Mérida he had urged the leaders of both parties, Pino and Delio Moreno Cantón, to patch up their differences and present a unified front against the incumbent, Múñoz Arísteguí.[55]

In class terms, there was little to choose between the rival elitist parties, either with respect to political platform or constituency. Beyond the heavy dose of anti-Molinista propaganda that saturated their broadsheets, both contenders were moderate, indeed ambiguous, in their political pronouncements. The Pinistas were perhaps a bit more specific with regard to the social question, but neither called for significant changes in the structure of regional monoculture.[56] Perhaps the chief difference between the two camarillas was rooted in their respective stances toward Díaz's national leadership. Always the opportunists, the Morenistas sought to work within the Porfirian system, at least until the system overtly turned against them. By far the more established of the two movements, they had the benefit of more than a decade of political organizing to draw upon, especially as they went about the task of forming political clubs in rural communities throughout the state. By contrast, the Pinistas were a component of Madero's new national movement, had only a small organizational base in Yucatán, and were determined (at least in principle) to peacefully oust the national dictatorship.

The Morenistas would show their true Porfirian colors in September 1909 when they sent a delegation to Mexico City—just as they had done in 1897—to seek the aging dictator's blessing in the upcoming elections. José Vales and Daniel Arjona carried three names with them as possible candidates for the CEI: Delio Moreno Cantón, José E. Castillo, and General Luis Curiel.[57] Díaz muttered that the military man, who had served in Yucatán during the 1890s, would make a fine candidate. Notwithstanding the counsel of the president, the CEI subsequently held a convention and nominated the nephew of Pancho Cantón for the governorship.[58]

What little trust had existed between the two rival parties began to dissipate as a result of the Morenista expedition to Mexico City. Madero, unhappy that the Morenistas had tried to accommodate themselves with the president, still realized that his organization in the state left something to be desired. Accordingly, he suggested that his followers tactically support Moreno Cantón for the governorship in return for a CEI promise to support Madero in the forthcoming presidential elections.[59] Even through Pino agreed not to run for governor, the coalition between Pinistas and Morenistas was never more than a fleeting marriage of convenience. Both parties mobilized followings in the cities and the countryside during the summer and early fall of 1909 and often stepped on each other's toes.

This *disgusto* is clearly demonstrated in a letter written in 1909 by Pino Suárez to Rigoberto Xiu, a twenty-year-old campesino and political organizer from Muna, a town on the fringes of the *zona henequenera*, about fifty kilometers south of Mérida. Xiu had a running feud with the local Molinista president of the Municipal Council, who made a practice of forcing campesinos to provide him with free labor. Xiu spoke out against such treatment and began to organize some townspeople during the summer of 1909. Initially, he had pledged his support for the Anti-Reelectionist cause, but his allegiance suddenly changed to Morenismo by the first week of September. Pino's letter to Xiu, written at a time when the two political parties were supposedly cooperating, implored the *cabecilla* to abandon the CEI. Ironically, Pino (himself a Tabascan) accused the Morenistas of trying to bring in an outsider for governor, General Curiel from Jalisco. He also attacked the Porfirian orientation of the CEI. "[T]hese Morenistas say they have the support of the President, but so do the supporters of the administration [Molinistas], which just goes to show that they are both deceivers, since the President cannot support both of them."[60]

While both parties worked at cross-purposes, state authorities knuckled down on CEI electioneering. In the pueblo of Chemax, just kilometers away from the Morenista stronghold of Valladolid, several members were arrested trying to organize a political club. The *jefe político* jailed the Morenistas, claiming he had it on good authority that they were "about to create a disturbance."[61] A spate of similar crackdowns throughout September amply convinced the president of the CEI, Alfonso Cámara y Cámara, that traditional political options "al estilo Porfiriano" had been exhausted.[62]

Cámara y Cámara, who had served as president of Pancho Cantón's Gran Club Liberal in 1897 and who had been a highly visible participant in the violent events of 11 August 1897, immediately began to arm his forces statewide to overthrow the Molinista government.[63] The *conjura*, or conspiracy, which came to be called "La Candelaria,"[64] included plans to capture the armories in Mérida, assault the electric plant, cut telegraph and telephone lines, and then storm the house of Avelino Montes to take money to pay for the expenses of the rebellion. More importantly, the *conjura* in Mérida, set for 14 October, would be joined by similar risings throughout the state, specifically in Kanasín, Valladolid, Peto, Muna, Tizimín, and Cuzamá. The Morenistas had key men in each of these *poblaciones* committed to the cause, all of whom had been laying in machetes and caches of small arms. Despite the uneasy pact between the two opposition parties, Pinista clubs in the interior had agreed to participate in the revolt. Cámara y Cámara was reported to have said in one meeting: "I have more faith in the people of the pueblos than I do in those of Mérida."[65]

All of Cámara y Cámara's preparations were for naught, however, as state authorities got wind of the conspiracy. On 9 October, warrants for the arrest of Moreno Cantón and Pino were issued and the offices of the Pinistas were searched. Although both opposition leaders went underground, a host of Pinista and Morenista partisans, including Cámara y Cámara, were rounded up and thrown in Juárez penitentiary. The opposition press was closed down and warrants were issued for the editors.[66]

Francisco Madero had suspected that dislodging the Molinista oligarchical faction would prove exceedingly difficult. He shrewdly advised Pino to sit tight, bide his time, and then pick up the pieces after the more visible Morenistas had faced the inevitable repression.[67]

In the short term, "La Candelaria" gave the regime some breathing space, but its real importance lay in the contacts the Morenistas—and to a lesser extent, the Pinistas—made in the countryside. The tenuous alliance between elite factions in the cities and smallholders, artisans, and petty merchants in the interior would continue to grow as the elites secured arms and cash, and local rural *cabecillas* recruited in their pueblos and on neighboring estates. Typically, Morenista and Pinista planters and middle-class intellectuals, based in Mérida, would plan a rising and then, through a network of intermediaries, would mobilize sympathetic elements (and often coerce less-than-sympathetic ones) in rural towns, villages, and haciendas.

What the elites could not foresee as they constructed these rudimentary insurgent networks was that the incipient rural rebels also had their own agendas, which were not congruent with the elite's own, rather limited political projects. From the aborted Candelaria *conjura*, through the failed rebellion in Valladolid during the spring of 1910,[68] to the more free-wheeling revolts that periodically rocked the state during 1911 and 1912, locally based popular mobilization and protest began to evolve a life of its own, one that took little heed of political posturings or fraudulent election returns. Yucatán's competing elites had opened a Pandora's box, and try as they might they could never successfully harness the rage that exploded in peripheral areas like the Puuc and the eastern *partidos* of Temax, Valladolid, and Sotuta.

Here, on the fringes of monoculture, haciendas were overrun by marauding bands who "liberated" peons and provisions alike. On some estates, jacqueries erupted from within. Rebels dynamited the houses and stores of local notables, attacked the barracks of National Guard detachments, and summarily "brought to justice" abusive *jefes*, municipal authorities, and hacienda personnel. Occasionally, they smashed henequén processing plants and tore up stretches of Decauville tram tracks in the best Luddite fashion. Indeed, such popular rebellion threatened to ignite the *zona henequenera* at times.[69]

Maderismo in Yucatán: A Porfirian Redux?

Given the small base of support which Maderismo enjoyed in Yucatán, it is perfectly understandable that first Pino Suárez and later his father-in-law and successor in the state house, Nicolás Cámara Vales, claimed few accomplishments during the two short years of Maderista rule. Even had the rhetoric of Maderismo been sincere, democratic reform would not have come overnight. Of course, the issue was compromised by the legacy of a cynical political process which promoted the enrichment of a few at the expense of the majority. Under these circumstances, it was inevitable that the popular classes would adopt a "wait-and-see" attitude toward their new governors. And since Madero's commitment was to democratization first and social change later, the patience of those who wanted land or an end to onerous state impositions was sorely tested.

Clearly, Madero's liberal movement was a bundle of contradictions, but the single largest cleavage, which precluded stability and crippled the Maderista project in Yucatán, was the marked difference in social outlook between contending urban elites, on the one hand, and the rural insurgents they had unleashed, on the other. Despite their bickering, Morenista and Pinista elites basically sought a return to the political liberalism of Juárez; by contrast, most rural insurgents struggled for vindication, greater dignity, and a way of life that afforded some measure of autonomy in their day-to-day existence. As Maderismo lingered on, this dissonance only grew louder, underscoring a distinct adversarial relationship between the new elite ruling group and the motley collection of rebels who continued to attack local symbols of power and prey on haciendas throughout the *campo*. With the Pinistas now cast in the role of the authorities, it was understandable that, unless they tangibly benefited from the change, mobilized rural bands would now perceive the new governors as their enemies.

In fact, in the area of social and economic reforms the Pinista record was uninspiring, to say the least. Shortly after being named interim governor in June 1911, Pino spoke of evolutionary change on the state's henequén haciendas. While gradual measures were undertaken, Pino counseled, workers should "remain in their present enslaved state to prevent brusque transitions that might injure their well-being."[70] He emphasized that emancipation of indebted peons was an issue that had to be resolved only after deliberate study. Similarly, no serious attempt was made to return ejidal lands to villagers who had been expropriated by hacendados during the Porfiriato. Pino's failure to expeditiously correct the most egregious wrongs of the past regime also alienated those progressive planters and intellectuals—albeit a minority—who were interested in improving working conditions and efficiency on the plantations.

Madero's cause was further undermined in the state because the political mechanisms employed by the new governors reminded locals of the recent past. From the outset, a series of interim governors were *imposed* on the state by Mexico City. In addition, Pino, the first of four interim governors in the second half of 1911, attempted to run Yucatán and run for the vice-presidency of the nation at the same time. His constant trips out of the state reminded locals of Olegario Molina's frequent absences and hampered any type of momentum the new regime could muster.

The Pinistas also proved themselves adept at the art of rigging elections. In September 1911, Pino handily won the governorship in an election as blatantly fraudulent as any held in Porfirian Yucatán. Madero, the erstwhile "democrat," had visited the state to personally campaign for Pino in early September. The irony was not lost on the followers of Moreno Cantón, who ran and lost the disputed election, despite a far stronger statewide organization.

To make matters worse, Porfirian-style nepotism reached into the upper echelons of the government. Pino's father-in-law and brother-in-law became governors of Yucatán and Quintana Roo territory, respectively, once Pino assumed the vice-presidency. For good measure, Nicolás Cámara Vales's son was named director of the United Railways of Yucatán.[71]

Additional abuses undercut Pinista legitimacy in the state. First, the *jefatura política*, that symbol of Porfirian malice, continued to exist, and Pinista prefects rode roughshod over political opponents in the *campo*. Of course, in order to secure stability and production of the monocrop, Maderista *jefes* had little recourse but to clamp down on the rural violence which wracked the state between 1911 and 1913. Nevertheless, the *apertura* had unleashed the popular classes and few could now respect the "rule of law" when it so clearly resembled the practices of the past. *Jefes políticos*, members of their staff, and imposed municipal authorities remained prize targets for rural insurgents throughout 1911 and 1912.

Even more difficult to swallow for many was the presence of a number of ex-Molinistas in important posts in the state bureaucracy.[72] Most egregious of all was the inclusion of Tomás Castellanos Acevedo, a Molinista politician said to be in the hip pocket of Avelino Montes, in Governor Cámara Vales's cabinet. When Castellanos was appointed to head the state's new henequén regulating agency, *yucatecos* sarcastically joked that Governor Cámara Vales had put the fox in charge of the hen house.[73]

Finally, *"bola negra"* tactics continued as the Pinista censored and harassed the local press after a brief summer of freedom in 1911. As the Morenistas whipped up anti-Maderista sentiment throughout the state, one of their chief weapons was a highly inflammatory press that regularly sensationalized and, on occasion, even invented unrest in the countryside to prove that the Pinistas were incapable of keeping the peace. Led by Carlos R. Menéndez's *Revista de Mérida* (later *La Revista de Yucatán*) and a host of ephemeral partisan newspapers and broadsheets, the Morenistas patently abused the newly won freedom of the press. Yet beneath the yellow journalism, there often lay an accurate critique of glaring abuses: Madero's imposed governors, rigged elections, nepotism, and abuses by *jefes políticos*. The Pinistas replied in Porfirian fashion, closing down papers, jailing editors (including Menéndez) for libel, and countering the bad press they received with their own self-serving newspapers.

All things considered, the political climate during the Madero years in Yucatán was somewhat reminiscent of Múñoz Arístegui's last year in office.[74] In fact, given the chaos and obstacles they inherited, the Maderistas had little choice but to rely on the tried and true strategies of their predecessors. Perceived as outsiders, they did not have a strong political base of support in the state to begin with—in contrast, say, to the Morenistas. Economically, their clout was also limited. The Molinista faction, despite its political defeat, still dominated the regional monocrop. While the Maderistas might try to undercut Montes and Harvester by creating a Comisión Reguladora del Mercado de Henequén, charged with maintaining a reasonable and remunerative price for the fiber, they never were able to achieve even this modest goal. Operating in an open market still controlled by Montes, whose collaboration with Harvester worked to depress the price, the state government lacked the requisite political leverage to ensure the success of the Reguladora.[75]

In Yucatán *la mano dura* lived on, and Maderista liberal reform was stillborn. Indeed, the state's "response to popular rebellion . . . implied a derogation of liberal principle, and a revival of both Porfirian methods and Porfirian interests."[76] Given the entrenched forces that opposed Pino and his successors and the host of political, economic, and social contradictions that bedeviled Yucatecan society, the results were sadly predictable. The assassinations of Madero and Pino were gleefully welcomed by rival Morenista and Molinista elites, who, by and large, approved of Huertismo's subsequent Porfirista solution to the problems of popular insurgency and chaos. Military governors chosen by the center were imposed on the state; deals were cut with the opponents of Maderismo, including several strategically placed rural cabecillas; and Huertista justice was meted out alternately with Porfirian shrewdness and verve. The executive and judiciary amnestied certain opponents and led others to the *paredón*. By mid-1913, the *campo* had effectively been demobilized.

Conclusions

General Huerta's imposition of authoritarian military rule institutional-ized a political stalemate among the three contending elite factions that com-pelled them to acquiesce to an *entente* that preserved the social peace. But the local elite's honeymoon with Huertismo would be a brief one. As taxes and forced loans escalated and federal military levees continued to erode their labor force, rival elites found Huertismo increasingly odious. In mid-1914, when Huerta was, in turn, defeated at the national level by a revolutionary coali-tion of Constitutionalists, Yucatán's uneasy alliance of elite camarillas con-tinued to resist the arrival of the Mexican Revolution. In January 1915, when bribes no longer served to keep the national movement at a distance, the old plantocracy buried its factional differences and mounted a last, futile rebel-lion to preserve the *ancien régime*. The organizers and financiers of this revolt, ostensibly to uphold "state sovereignty," were Olegario Molina, Avelino Mon-tes and other heavyweights in their camarilla.[77] Yucatán, it appeared, had come full circle.

Or had it? Certainly, the popular classes had been changed by their partic-ipation in the seasons of upheaval from 1909 to 1912. Certain *cabecillas,* like Pedro Crespo, Juan Campos, Loreto Baak, Elías Rivero, and, most impor-tantly, Felipe Carrillo Puerto, had built local clienteles that would later be consolidated into *cacicazgos* after the Mexican Revolution gained a foothold in Yucatán.[78] Even prior to Constitutionalist General Salvador Alvarado's inva-sion in March 1915, rural workers had utilized the political instability of the post-Díaz years to wring some concessions from the local authorities, most notably a 1914 decree that abolished debt peonage. Although it was never implemented and represented an expedient measure enabling the planter class to buy time, the reformist decree provided an important precedent upon which the later revolutionary governments of Alvarado and Carrillo Puerto, backed by substantial campesino support, would build.

And yet the oligarchical order had endured from 1910 to 1915. It would take Alvarado's eight thousand troops to neutralize its repressive power and usher in the revolutionary era. Ultimately, how do we account for the Yuca-tecan phenomenon of political conflict and insurgency that stopped short of a generalized rebellion?

The old order had certain "built-in" advantages in Yucatán that permit-ted it to contain festering discontent and ride out the initial challenges pre-sented by the Mexican Revolution. First, Yucatán's location on the far periphery impeded communication with revolutionary chiefs in Mexico's core and made coordination of joint campaigns virtually impossible. Secondly, Yucatán's local revolts were often poorly armed and logistically isolated. This was due in part to the inability of competing Morenista and Pinista elites to set aside their differences and unite against the ruling oligarchical faction. But it was also due to the coercive and highly regulated system of social control that landowners and the state had fashioned during the *auge*, which often worked to impede collaboration between villagers and peons. Thirdly, unlike the north, from which so many of the middle-class leaders of Mexico's new revolutionary state would eventually come, monocultural Yucatán had a small and weak middle class and did not generate insurgent coalitions led by middle-sector or petty bourgeois elements. This enhanced the prospect that contending elites might eventually patch up their differences and prevent a more generalized insurrection.

Finally, and perhaps most importantly, the haunting spectre of another Caste War gave Yucatecan elites second thoughts about a full-scale mobilization of railway and dock workers, let alone Maya villagers and peons. Although many Morenista and Pinista planters itched to defeat the Molinista camarilla in 1909, the majority feared that arming the rural masses would undermine the elaborate mechanisms of social control that had so successfully underwritten the *auge*. Now, if planter-supported mobilizations ignited a social revolution, Yucatán's contending elites might well lose their properties, their social world, and even their lives in another "Guerra de Castas." That certain elites would take such a chance and arm campesinos throughout the state demonstrates the divisiveness of the elite in late Porfirian Yucatán, as well as their sense of desperation. It was precisely this ambivalence that enabled the Molinista old guard—always dominant economically—to bide its time, ride out the turbulence of Maderismo, and eventually reassert its hegemony by late 1914. Thus, while Maderista-era insurgency sprang from within the region, the impetus for true revolutionary change ultimately had to be imposed from without.

Notes

The authors gratefully acknowledge support by the National Endowment for the Humanities, the American Philosophical Society, the University Research Committee of Appalachian State University, and the Institute of Latin American Studies of the University of North Carolina, Chapel Hill in the research and writing of this essay.

1. Alan Knight, *The Mexican Revolution* 2 vol. (Cambridge: Cambridge University Press, 1986); John Womack, "The Mexican Revolution, 1910–1920," *Cambridge*

History of Latin America vol. 5, (Cambridge: Cambridge University Press, 1986) 79–153; Friedrich Katz, *The Secret War in Mexico: Europe, the United States and the Mexican Revolution* (Chicago: University of Chicago Press, 1981); Ramón Eduardo Ruiz, *The Great Rebellion: Mexico, 1905–1924* (New York: W.W. Norton, 1980); and François-Javier Guerra, *Le Mexique: De l'Ancien Régime à la Révolution* 2 vol. (Paris; Edition L'Harmattan 1985).

2. Some studies which do emphasize popular movements during Maderismo are John Womack, *Zapata and the Mexican Revolution* (New York: Vintage Books, 1968); Raymond Th. Buve, "Peasant Movements, Caudillos and Land Reform during the Revolution (1910–1917) in Tlaxcala, Mexico," *Boletín de Estudios Latino-americanos y del Caribe* 18 (June 1975): 112–52; David LaFrance, "Failure of Reform: The Maderistas in Puebla, 1911–1913," *New World* 1:2 (1986): 44–64; LaFrance, "A People Betrayed: Francisco I. Madero and the Mexican Revolution in Puebla" (Ph.D. diss., Indiana University, 1984); Dudley Ankerson, *Agrarian Warlord: Saturnino Cedillo and the Mexican Revolution in San Luis Potosí* (DeKalb, Ill.: Northern Illinois University Press, 1984); and Romana Falcón, *Revolución y caciquismo: San Luis Potosí, 1910–1938* (México: El Colegio de México, 1985).

3. For a discussion of trends in the literature on this period of transition, see Gilbert M. Joseph and Allen Wells, "Summer of Discontent: Economic Rivalry among Elite Factions during the Late Porfiriato in Yucatán," *Journal of Latin American Studies* (hereafter cited as *JLAS*) 18:2 (1986): 255–82.

4. The penal records of the Ramo de Justicia of Yucatán's state archives, more than any other source, document the relationship between elite factionalism and rural insurgency. This essay represents a portion of an ongoing book-length study of politics and society in Yucatán, entitled *Summer of Discontent, Seasons of Upheaval: Elite Politics and Rural Rebellion in Yucatán, 1890–1915*.

5. It is important to note that these political clubs were not broad-based parties in the modern sense of the word. They were rather short-term associations, highly personalistic in nature, far more similar to extended family groups or *patrón*–client coalitions than to the political parties which were developing in Europe and the United States at the same time. See Friedrich Katz, "Mexico: Restored Republic and Porfiriato, 1867–1910," in *Cambridge History of Latin America*, vol. 5, 38.

6. Alan Knight characterizes Díaz's strategy as one based "on some lingering legitimacy, as well as on coercion, and the coercion was selective and limited, not indiscriminate." *The Mexican Revolution*, I:35.

7. Ibid., I:37–39.

8. The expression is borrowed from an insightful piece by Juan Felipe Leal, "El estado y el bloque en el poder en México, 1867–1914," *Historia Mexicana* 23:2 (1974): 700–21.

9. Cantón, who had spent the better part of fifteen years in the capital as a federal deputy, understood the nature of Porfirian politics. He relied heavily on his old lawyer friend and confidant, Tabascan Joaquín Baranda, who as Minister of

Justice and Public Instruction, had the ear of the president. This is not to say that local camarillas did not have some input in the decision-making process. Various delegations or commissions came to Mexico City in the months before the decision was made to meet personally with the president and argue their case for a particular candidate. As always, Don Porfirio listened attentively and said little. A good description of how Don Porfirio chose his governors is found in José C. Valadés, *El Porfirismo. Historia de un régimen* 3 vol. (Mexico City, 1941–1948), II:28–29.

10. For a discussion of these cliques see Katz, "Mexico: Restored Republic and Porfiriato," 38–39; and Leal, "El estado y el bloque en el poder."

11. When Olegario Molina saw which way the political winds were blowing in the capital, he threw his support to Pancho Cantón This, despite the fact that he and Cantón had a long history of political contratemps dating back to the empire, when Molina fought with the victorious liberals against Cantón and the Imperialists. Molina used his political connections with the *científicos* to weaken the bid of the incumbent governor, Peón Machado. The reasons for this were more economic than political. Peón married into the family of Eusebio Escalante e Hijo, one of Molina's chief competitors in the henequén trade. In 1897 the Peón–Escalante economic partnership was of greater concern to Olegario Molina and his young financial lieutenant, Spaniard Avelino Montes, than the political persuasion of the Cantonista conservatives.

12. Most accounts of the *tumulto* in the Plaza de las Armas are predisposed to castigate or exonerate one of the political groups in question. For the Cantonista account, see *La Revista de Mérida*, 15 August 1897, no. 3285. Peón Machado's position is brought out in some judicial documents found in the private collection of Hernán Menéndez: "Instancia del Lic. Alvino Manzanilla pidiendo que el Juzgado del Distrito se avoque el conocimiento de la causa que se sigue al Juez local por los sucesos del 11 de agosto en la plaza principal de Mérida," 1897; and "Escrito a la Suprema Corte de Justicia sobre el amparo que le dictó contra mi [Manzanilla] con motivo de los sucesos del 11 de agosto de 1897," 1898. The most dispassionate analysis comes from an eyewitness, Felipe Pérez Alcalá. "Los sucesos del 11 de agosto en Mérida," in Carlos R. Menéndez, *Noventa años de historia de Yucatán* (1821–1910) (Mérida, 1937), 539–44. The Cantonistas were very experienced in such political maneuvers. A nearly identical incident occurred in the same plaza in 1873, with similar tragic results. As we shall see, similar incidents were planned by the Cantonistas in 1909 to force Díaz to intervene once again in Yucatecan politics. See Urzáiz, *Del Imperio a la Revolución* (Mérida, 1971), 74–75; and Menéndez, *Noventa años*, p. 159.

13. A good description of *empleomanía* is found in Laurens Ballard Perry, *Juárez and Díaz; Machine Politics in Mexico* (DeKalb, Ill.: Northern Illinois University Press, 1978), 12.

14. This analysis of Molina's accomplishments is gleaned from largely apologistic

accounts of his first term. See Urzáiz, *Del Imperio a la Revolucíon,* 141–72; *Mensajes del (Gobernador Constitucional), C. Lic. Olegario Molina al Congreso de Yucatán, 1902–1906* (Mérida, 1906); *Yucatán 1902–1906,* purportedly written by José Inés Novelo, (Mérida, 1907); Francisco A. Casasús, "Ensayo biográfico del Licenciado Olegario Molina Solís," *Revista de la Universidad de Yucatán,* 14:81 (1972): 68–95; and Alberto María Carreno, *Licenciado Don Olegario Molina* (Mexico City, 1925).

15. The federal government in 1902 partitioned the state of Yucatán and created the territory of Quintana Roo. This is an inordinately complex issue which proved to be a divisive issue among the various camarillas of the local elite. Molina supported the partition, and for his efforts received 300,000 hectares of land in the jungles of Quintana Roo from the federal government. For a thorough discussion of the implications of the partition, see Wells, *Yucatán's Gilded Age: Haciendas, Henequén and International Harvester, 1860–1915* (Albuquerque: University of New Mexico Press, 1985), chapter 4.

16. A perfect example of the kind of criticism that opponents dished out to the Molina regime is found in *El Padre Clarencio* (hereinafter cited as *EPC*), 17 January 1904, no. 24.

17. Molina knew that political newspapers had served to ignite political passions in past electoral campaigns. The Cantonistas had published several ephemeral papers in 1897, and these publications proved indispensable in galvanizing support for their cause.

18. This brief list only takes into consideration the most obvious political linkages as reported by an ephemeral opposition newspaper, *Yucatán Nuevo.* Interestingly, this paper was published in Campeche, due to the incessant harassment of the press in Yucatán by the Molinista regime. For a fuller examination of the far-flung economic empire of Olegario Molina and his *parentesco,* see Wells, "Family Elites in a Boom and Bust Economy: The Molinas and Peóns of Porfirian Yucatán," *Hispanic American Historical Review* (hereinafter cited as *HAHR*), 62:2 (1982): 224–53.

19. *EPC,* 13 December 1903, no. 18. Carlos Escoffié, editor of *El Padre Clarencio,* was apparently arrested on fifty-one occasions by the Molinista administration. Interview with journalist Hernán Menéndez, 5 July 1987.

20. Ibid., 19 November 1905, no. 14 and 3 December 1905, no. 16; *El Ciudadano,* 8 April 1911, no. 25; and *Mensajes del . . . Olegario Molina,* 205. A good summation is found in Cosío Villegas, *Historia Moderna,* vol. 9, (México: Editorial Hermes, 1972), 461–67.

21. For example, *El Imparcial,* 18 January 1904, no. 2677, 25 May 1904, no. 2808, 18 April 1905, no. 3123; 2 May 1905, no. 3137; and 4 January 1906, no. 3383.

22. Díaz followed a similar strategy of forsaking alternation for "continuismo" in other states during the 1900s. See Katz, "Mexico: Restored Republic and Porfiriato," 56–59 and 62–63.

23. Preparations for the unique visit by the president were carried both in the local press and *El Imparcial*. For example, see *El Imparcial*, 2 November 1905, no. 3320 and 10 December 1905, no. 3358. A thorough description of Díaz's trip to Yucatán is found in Moisés González Navarro, *Raza y Tierra: La Guerra de Castas y el henequén* (Mexico: El Colegio de México, 1970), chapter 6.

24. Mark Wasserman, "Enrique C. Creel: Business and Politics in Mexico, 1880–1930," *Business History Review* 59:4 (1985): 645–62.

25. The only notable *casa* which managed to steer clear of regional politics during the 1890s and 1900s was Henry W. Peabody and Company. Represented locally by the British consul, Arturo Pierce, the Boston-based Peabody firm seems to have made a conscious decision to refrain from meddling in *la política*, in which, owing to its foreign status, it would be at a distinct disadvantage. Unlike the other Yucatecan houses, Peabody steered away from investments in regional railway companies, banks, and henequén's attendant service industries, which required more *palanca* (political clout). Thus, the Pierce–Peabody operation was the least horizontally integrated among the major henequén firms and had the least to gain from the concessions, contracts, and patronage that politicians had to offer. This astute, noninterventionist policy may also help explain Peabody's longevity in the henequén trade. By limiting its business investments to planter advances and the export of henequén, it insulated itself somewhat from the worst effects of the debilitating recessions which swept the peninsula.

26. A secret contract consummated between IHC and Molina y Cía, in October 1902, dramatically transformed the political economy of Yucatán by weeding out competitors and forcing down the price of fiber. See Gilbert M. Joseph and Allen Wells, "Corporate Control of a Monocrop Economy: International Harvester and Yucatán's Henequen Industry during the Porfiriato," *Latin American Research Review* (hereinafter cited as *LARR*), 17:1 (Spring 1982): 69–99.

27. The following discussion draws heavily on our article, "Summer of Discontent."

28. A healthy historiographical debate has developed over the relative importance of the 1907–8 panic on the formation of revolutionary coalitions in Mexico during the last years of the Porfiriato. Cf. Knight, *The Mexican Revolution*, I:64–65; Ruiz, *The Great Rebellion*, passim; and Katz, "Mexico: Restored Republic and Porfiriato," especially 62–68. Our own data corroborates the view that the panic had a substantive impact on the process of coalition-building in late Porfirian Yucatán.

29. We use the term *campesino* as a generic term. Although the majority of the workers on the henequén estates were peons tied by debt, some were villagers who hired themselves out on an irregular basis, had some mobility, and exercised a degree of choice.

30. Critics of the Old Regime like John Kenneth Turner, *Barbarous Mexico* (Chicago, 1910), put forth a rather static view of violent and unceasing oppression of the docile and faceless many by a greedy few. Planter apologists countered by paint-

ing labor conditions in aristocratically benign, almost consensual terms. For a critique of the contemporary polemic over the "labor question," see Wells, "Yucatán: Violence and Social Control on Henequen Plantations," in *Other Mexicos: Essays on Regional Mexican History, 1876–1911*, ed. Thomas Benjamin and William McNellie (Albuquerque: University of New Mexico Press, 1984), 59–81. A thorough review of the literature on debt peonage is found in Alan Knight, "Mexican Peonage: What Was It and Why Was It?" *JLAS* 18:1 (1986): 41–74.

31. For a seminal discussion of "everyday forms" of peasant resistance that is indebted to the rich comparative slavery literature on this theme, see James C. Scott, *Weapons of the Weak* (New Haven: Yale University Press, 1985).

32. For example, Archivo General del Estado de Yucatán (hereinafter cited as AGEY), Ramo de Justicia, "Diligencias en averiguación de la muerte de José María Eb, vecino que fué de la hacienda San José," 1912; "Diligéncias con motivo del suicidio de Candelario Cauich, sirviente de la finca Chunkanán," 1913. These are poignantly descriptive episodes, but multiple references from the Ramo de Justicia could be provided for any year in this study.

33. See Wells, "Yucatán: Violence and Social Control," 235–37, which contains references to these conflicts from *La Revista de Mérida, El Agricultor*, and other periodicals.

34. A perfect case in point was the southern pueblo of Santa Elena in the *partido* (district) of Ticul. This town had fought the incursion of local surveyors at the turn of the century and would become a prime staging area for revolutionary violence during Maderismo. See Wells, *Yucatán's Gilded Age*, 103–4. Hunucmá and Halachó provide similar agrarian pockets of resistance.

35. Interviews with Juan Campos Esquivel, 26 December 1986, 2 January 1987, and Melchor Zozaya Ruz, 31 December 1986 (for Dzilám González and Temax).

36. It is ironic that Rendón who for twenty years worked as a public defender for the indigent should so eloquently defend a powerful hacendado in this case. See Arturo Menéndez Paz, *Serapio Rendón (1867–1913) en la Revolución Mexicana* (Mérida, 1986).

37. (Mérida, 1908).

38. AGEY, Ramo de Justicia, "Primer cuaderno de prueba instrumental que ofrece el representante del Ministerio Público en la causa seguida a José Encarnación Huichim y socios por el delito de homicidio perpetrado a la persona Feliciano Chi," Caja 679, 1908.

39. Knight, *The Mexican Revolution*, I:166.

40. Beatriz González Padilla, "La dirigencia política en Yucatán, 1909–1925," 126–27, in Luis Millet Cámara, José Luis Sierra Villarreal, Blanca González Rodríguez and Beatriz González Padilla, *Hacienda y cambio social en Yucatán* (Mérida, 1984).

41. Wells, *Yucatán's Gilded Age*, 157, n. 17.

42. A cursory examination of early working class organizations is found in Fidelio Quintal Martín, "Breve historia de Yucatán durante la última década del Porfiriato

(1901–1910)," *Boletín de Ciencias Antropológicas de la Universidad de Yucatán*, 11:65 (1984): 43–62.

43. On Pérez Ponce, AGEY, Ramo de Justicia, "Toca a la causa seguida a Tomás Pérez Ponce por falsedad," Caja 676, 1908; and *EPC*, passim. On the jailing of Gervasio Fuentes, the founder and head of the Círculo General Obrero, see *EPC*, 25 March 1906, no. 32.

44. AGEY, Ramo de Justicia, "Causa seguida a Rufino Fernández y socio por ultrajes a la moral pública," Caja 668, 1908. A similar campaign against the vices of pornography had first been implemented by the governor of the Distrito Federal, Landa y Escandón.

45. William H. Beezley, "Madero: The 'Unknown' President and His Political Failure to Organize Rural Mexico," in *Essays on the Mexican Revolution: Revisionist Views of the Leaders*, ed. George Wolfskill and Douglass W. Richmond (Austin: University of Texas Press, 1979), 4–5.

46. Knight, *The Mexican Revolution*, I:26.

47. Beezley, "Madero," 5.

48. Both Beezley, "Madero," and Knight, *The Mexican Revolution*, II:25–26, emphasize that prefects were imposed from without by the federal government.

49. Exemptions could be secured in three ways: if the individual could pay a set fee or find a replacement to serve for him; if a peasant was classified as a permanent resident laborer attached (which came to mean "indebted") to a hacienda; or, if one had a debilitating illness. See Wells, *Yucatán's Gilded Age*, 159.

50. To entice would-be recruits Curiel paid a one-time enlistment bonus of twenty pesos, and a daily wage of a peso. *Diario Oficial*, 28 March 1911, no. 4092. For a comparative perspective on peasants's resistance to such levees, see Scott, *Weapons of the Weak*, especially chapter 2.

51. *Diario Oficial*, 20 October 1909, no. 3647. Data on the various extraordinary contributions levied against the poor are found in the *Diario Oficial*, passim.

52. A case study of a revolutionary *cabecilla* is presented in Joseph and Wells, "The Rough and Tumble Career of Pedro Crespo," in *The Human Tradition in Twentieth-Century Latin America*, ed. William Beezley and Judith Ewell (Wilmington, Del.: Scholarly Resources, 1987), 27–40.

53. Besides the works already cited, there are several other interesting accounts of this period. For example, see Enrique Múñoz Arístegui, *La situación política de Yucatán en 1909: Cartas del Gobernador D. Enrique Múñoz Arístegui* (Mérida, 1937); Miguel Civeira Taboada, "Francisco I. Madero contra Carlos R. Menéndez," unpublished ms., 1974; and David A. Franz, "Bullets and Bolshevists: A History of the Mexican Revolution in Yucatán, 1910–1924," (Ph.D. diss., University of New Mexico, 1973). The most lucid and dispassionate account of the period is Ramón D. Chacón, "Yucatán and the Mexican Revolution: The Pre-Constitutional Years, 1910–1918," (Ph.D. diss., Stanford University, 1982), especially chapters 1 and 2.

54. Womack, "The Mexican Revolution, 1910–1920," 82.
55. Civeira Taboada, "Francisco I. Madero," 57.
56. A good summation of the political platforms of the two parties is found in Chacón, "Yucatán and the Mexican Revolution," 83–85; also see Blanca González Rodríguez, "Cuatro proyectos de cambio en Yucatán," 80–83, in Cámara, et al., *Hacienda y cambio*.
57. Pinista broadsheet, part of *Periodista Libre*, n.d. 1911, Biblioteca "Carlos R. Menéndez," Mérida.
58. Franz, "Bullets and Bolshevists," 19.
59. Civeira Taboada, "Francisco I. Madero," 50; Franz, "Bullets and Bolshevists," 19–20.
60. AGEY, Ramo de Justicia, "Causa seguida a Rigoberto Xiu y socios por rebelión," 1909.
61. AGEY, Ramo de Justicia, "Acusación presentada por Cresencio Aguilar y socios contra el jefe político de Valladolid por abuso de autoridad," Caja 725, 1909.
62. Chacón, "Yucatán and the Mexican Revolution," 86, n. 126.
63. According to one witness who attended an important organizing session of the party leaders, Pancho Cantón, although present at the meeting, categorically refused to participate in any uprising against Porfirio Díaz. AGEY, Ramo de Justicia, "Causa seguida contra Alfonso Cámara y Cámara y socios por el delito de rebelión," 1909.
64. On 29 October, the house of Alfonso Cámara's mother, Candelaria, was searched as well as the nearby church of the Candelaria, a few blocks south of the center of the city, in a futile effort to find the ringleader of the conspiracy, Alfonso Cámara himself. Finally, two weeks later he was arrested, but the plot now had its name from the mother and the church of the same name.
65. AGEY, Ramo de Justicia, "Causa seguida contra Alfonso Cámara y Cámara."
66. Carlos R. Menéndez, the editor of *La Revista de Mérida*, managed to escape arrest by fleeing the state. Carlos Escoffié, who had moved to Campeche to continue his work with *El Padre Clarencio,* was not so lucky. Yucatecan authorities sent a telegram to the Campechano governor who arrested and held Escoffié until a group of soldiers from Yucatán could retrieve him to stand trial for libel in Mérida. AGEY, Ramo de Justicia, "Causa instruida a Carlos P. Escoffié por el delito de calumnia," Caja 730, 1909.
67. Civeira Taboada, "Francisco I. Madero," 58–59.
68. Although much of the literature on the outbreak of the Mexican Revolution in Yucatán has focused on the failed rebellion of Valladolid in 1910, we contend that the rising in the eastern portion of the state was just one example of the kind of revolts which surfaced during the last years of the Porfiriato. Since "La Candelaria" provided the spark which triggered the subsequent rebellions of 1910 and early 1911, we have chosen to emphasize its role here. Cf. Carlos R. Menéndez, *La primera chispa de la Revolución Mexicana: El movimiento de Valladolid en 1910*

(Mérida, 1919); and Antonio Betancourt Pérez, *La problemática social: ¿Primera chispa de la Revolución Mexicana?* (Mérida, 1983).

69. For example, see AGEY, Ramo de Justicia, "Causa seguida a Guillermo Canul y socios por los delitos de daño y destrucción de propiedad ajena," 1912; "Toca a la causa seguida a Pedro Chi por el delito de destrucción de propiedad ajena por incendio," 1912; "Causa seguida a Juan Jiménez y socios por el delito de provocación al delito de rebelión," 1913.

70. Quoted from Pino Suárez, "A Manifesto to the People of Yucatan," 14 June 1911. Cited in Chacón, "Yucatán and the Mexican Revolution," 116.

71. *El Ciudadano*, 24 January 1912, no. 28.

72. Ibid., 11 January 1912, no. 17.

73. *La Voz del Pueblo*, 21 December 1911, no. 6.

74. Chacón, "Yucatán and the Mexican Revolution," 115.

75. In fact, it is not even clear whether the Maderista governor in Yucatán was prepared to work against the Montes faction or whether he had been put on Montes's payroll. Some observers suggested that Madero's national government was opposed to the Reguladora and supported the attempts of Montes and Harvester to cut off loans to the new agency. See Joseph, *Revolution from Without: Yucatán, Mexico, and the United States* (Cambridge: Cambridge University Press, 1982), 137–38, n. 63.

76. Knight, *The Mexican Revolution,* I:333.

77. The separatist revolt and the conquest of Yucatán by Constitutionalist General Salvador Alvarado in March 1915 are detailed in Jopseh, *Revolution from Without*, prologue and chapter 4.

78. See, for example, Joseph and Wells, "The Rough and Tumble Career of Pedro Crespo."

SAN LUIS POTOSI

SIGNOS

CIUDAD *Capital de Estado* ⊙ Villa *Cab. de Municipalidad* ◉

CIUDAD *Cabecera de Partido* ⊛ Pueblo *» » »* ◎

Ciudad *Cab. de Municipalidad* • Pueblo •

Villa *Cab. de Distrito* ◉ Hacienda ▪

NUEVO LEON

TAMAULIPAS

VERACRUZ

ZACATECAS

JALISCO

GUANAJUATO

QUERETARO

S. Luis
El Salvado
S. Vicente
La Parrida
Vanegas
Cedral
MATEHUALA
Charco
Ancona
Guadalupe
Perezindo
Laguna Seca
Norias
Nuevas del Tonde
Arista
GUADALCAZAR
S. Isidro
EL MAIZ
Tlalitas
Cerritos
Carpazal
Picachos
Iturbide
Piedad
Zaragoza
S. Nicolas
R. Verde
Sta. Catarina
S. MARIA DEL RIO
Villela
Tierra Nueva
S. Bartolo
DOLORES HIDALGO
Reyes
Jaral
Arriaga
S. LUIS POTOSI
Tlaxcalilla
Ahualulco
Villa Garcia
Espiritu Santo
Boca
SALINAS
Ramos
Sta. Domingo
Concordia
VENADO
Mozquite
Cuautitlan
Pobloazon
Protillas
Cardenas
Alaquines
Lagunillas
VALLES
Tamuin
Tantajas
TANCANHUITZ
Coxcatlan
Aguasmon
Tampla
Tancaneluyub
Tamoyn
Tanquian
S. Martin
TAMAZUNCHALE
Xilitla
Axtla
Tanjanaleb
R. Sta. Maria
R. de Santa Maria
AGUASCALIENTES

6

San Luis Potosí

Confiscated Estates—Revolutionary Conquest or Spoils?

Romana Falcón

Among the central themes that were broached during the sessions of the Sovereign Revolutionary Convention—when the most popular factions of the Mexican Revolution came together to discuss the road they should follow—the destiny of the haciendas, ranches, and other properties that had passed into the hands of revolutionary forces during the struggle was of great concern.

José Nieto, a delegate from northern Mexico, sarcastically criticized what had been done by the revolution to that point with the confiscated estates:

I saw with my own eyes the result of these seizures, the estates had been left completely destroyed; the seeds, the pastures, the equipment had been taken; all had been taken, absolutely all, until they had become wasteland, deserts . . .

A veteran leader of the Casa del Obrero Mundial proposed a prompt punishment for those corrupt revolutionaries who were exploiting these lands to their own gain: the gallows. Antonio Díaz Soto y Gama, a spirited speaker and former member of the Mexican Liberal Party, now the distinguished ideologue of Zapatismo, also took part. Reaffirming his revolutionary and agrarian creed, he asked that panic not carry in the face of the ruin of the destructive period of the revolution, for they would then lose sight of the essential goal: justice. Wealth, said Soto y Gama, was neither in the plows nor in the crops, but in the land. When the reconstruction phase arrived, the land should produce more and better because it would be worked by free men, not farm laborers, poor farmhands that until then had survived almost without bread or clothes, "with nothing of anything."[1]

In the mind of the majority of Mexicans, and also traditionally in the academic world, the 1910 revolution has been considered a popular and nationalist movement with the struggle for land at its core.[2] During the 1970s historians devoted themselves to disrobing the revolution of some of its more attractive clothes. In light of this they attempted to find a more complex explanation, one that would accommodate the many shades and details that, with respect to the original idea of the revolution, had made academic production of recent years concerned with recreating in detail the ups and downs of this movement in the most diverse localities of the country. As a result of the new research and interpretations, doubt arose whether the revolution really was a movement originating from the bottom of society benefiting the dispossessed focused on agrarian reform. Revisionism even placed in doubt that the Mexican Revolution was a real revolution.[3] Paradoxically, in the last few years, new comprehensive interpretations have returned to argue on behalf of the validity of the revolution's heroic, pouplar, agrarian, and social justice image.[4] Thus, three-quarters of a century after Madero's call to arms, the struggle for land continues to be the essential variable in understanding and interpreting the Mexican Revolution.

Historians have explored the agrarian problem in various ways. Among these are research into the origins of the demands of campesinos; examination of the amount, vicissitudes, deficiencies, and failures of the ejidal program; and detailed analysis of the agrarian plans and accomplishments of the various armed factions. A less conventional but no less fruitful approach in determining the agrarian nature of the revolution involves analyzing the manner in which the different revolutionary groups subverted or conserved the established agrarian order in dealing with the estates, ranches, houses, and other properties that the confusion of armed struggle had placed in their hands. There were various responses to the sudden collapse of the legitimacy and authority of established dominant class and its agrarian structure. The possibility of transforming the fabric of society was presented to armed factions. What revolutionaries and campesinos did then, or were permitted to do, with the properties and their owners demonstrates their most intimate convictions with respect to the revolution and to the agrarian and social order that they sought.

This line of analysis is particularly promising if the period of greatest dispersion of power is chosen, that is, from 1913 to 1917, when none of the contending groups were able to impose its conditions on the others. It was in this moment of greatest freedom of political action, when revolutionary factions were most autonomous and protected by the absence of real central authority, that the most genuine and concrete plans of a multitude of leaders and small bands—many which are now nearly forgotten-flourished. Perhaps it is in these local efforts and attitudes arising from the bottom of society that we can best uncover what was the Revolution.

The object of this study is to examine the similarities and differences of some contending revolutionary groups with regard to their handling of seized estates. Given the magnitude of this theme, and the considerable difficulties in researching it, this chapter will focus primarily, but not exclusively, on those factions that operated in San Luis Potosí.

Differences throughout Mexico

Zapatismo, which has been considered the prototype of agrarian movements and the Mexican Revolution itself, was the faction that disposed of seized estates in the clearest manner by distributing land to landless campesinos. Such agrarian stand was implicit given the way that the sugar plantations had devoured Morelos' villages, and given the clear ideological and programmatic consistency which the movement demonstrated from beginning to end. The Plan de Ayala not only demanded the return of those fields which had been usurped to the villages, but also declared that lands possessed by "monopolists" and enemies of the revolution be expropriated. As soon as the Zapatistas controlled Morelos they elected provisional authorities and expropriated and nationalized the property of their enemies. Lands thus confiscated were turned over to the villages. Furthermore, they appropriated the sugar mills and distilleries in order to keep them working, not as private enterprises but as public services.[5]

But despite the efforts of the ranking commanders, some Zapatista generals did not resist the temptation to take advantage of the seized haciendas for personal gain. When this point was debated in the Sovereign Revolutionary Convention, Zapatista delegates displayed their callousness and conviction, insisting that "if all the generals of the Revolution steal, they be shot," and that in no way could "a single inch of land" be returned to hacendados. At the same time they recognized that, with some confiscated properties, they had committed

the greatest outrages, . . . not in favor of the people, but for our generals to steal haciendas, . . . This . . . happens in all the states, including Morelos. This morning I have been with the peons of Temixco hacienda and I asked them if they were running the rancheria, and they told me it is being run by Colonel X (applause).[6]

In Tlaxcala, when revolutionary general Máximo Rojas—whose movement had been criticized as "poorly disguised Zapatismo"—assumed the governorship in mid–1914 he immediately ordered the confiscation of the rural and urban properties of Huertistas and the principal landowners. He named supervisors (trustees?) for these estates and sent armed detachments to guarantee their production so that, eventually, this wealth would benefit the public good. These orderly and productive confiscations of Tlaxcalan haciendas stood side by side with the independent occupations made by some leaders, supported by the power of their arms and which, in general, acquired a predatory, destructive, and personally vengeful character. Finally, there were in Tlaxcala, as in Morelos, confiscations with a character of direct agrarian distribution. In effect, some independent armed groups and, paradoxically, some groups of ex-soldiers of the dissolved federal army directly took haciendas and effected the division of land. At the same time, certain revolutionary leaders encouraged or supported groups of campesinos to hang on to the seized estates.[7]

Agrarian distribution was not the only redistributive solution given to confiscated estates. The other great popular faction of the revolution, the Villistas, followed its own road. In 1913, while occupying the governorship of Chihuahua, Villa ordered the takeover of extensive properties of the most well-known landowners in order to deprive them of the resources to pursue their counterrevolutionary intentions. Chihuahua's history and social composition determined that the followers and supporters of Villismo were not strictly campesinos and that Villista mobilization was not based on agrarian reform. Realizing that if land was immediately redistributed a large number of his soldiers would demobilize to cultivate it, Villa postponed agrarian reform until the triumph of the revolution. On the other hand, the resources extracted from these seized estates were decisive in financing his large revolutionary armies. Therefore, Villismo had no incentive for proceeding with the immediate distribution of land, although it did distribute some of its fruits. For example, the sale of a part of the cattle of these haciendas at very low prices increased the level of meat consumption of his solders and of the people of Chihuahua in general. This kind of confiscatory action strengthened the popular base of Villismo.[8]

It is impossible to calculate with certainty the number and importance of the estates which revolutionaries seized throughout the country, but it cannot have been small.[9] Some officials responsible for the management of these properties concluded that, in certain regions, the bulk of the ranchos and *latifundios* had been seized. Such was the case in San Luis Potosí, where at the end of 1915 a knowledgeable functionary calculated that the confiscated estates were worth more than one hundred million pesos, the "equivalent in value (almost) of all the rural property in the state."[10]

When the revolutionary factions reached a certain military and political stability, one of their preoccupations was the regulation and administration of confiscated estates. This gave rise to a tangle of functions and directives, particularly during the first half of 1915, when Mexico was, in fact, administered by various governments. Thus, for example, immediately after the Sovereign Revolutionary Convention established its General Office of Confiscations, it entered into open conflict with its supposed ally, the Zapatista secretary of agriculture, Manuel Palafox, who created his own office with the same name. The Convention official supposedly in charge of the confiscated properties complained to the president because Palafox had made known that "he would recognize no orders from [this] office," giving rise to "a conflict of arrangements and agreements," and leaving his office "paralyzed by an absence of defined duties."[11]

One attitude that united the diverse revolutionary factions was their interest in keeping in operation those confiscated estates conspicious for their capital investment, productivity, or their social importance, for example as sources of employment. Therefore, inasmuch as the Villistas and Carrancistas went on occupying territories, they threatened with confiscation and exploitation those mines that were behind in the payment of taxes or those that they did not find in full production within one month. Frequently they carried out their threats, as happened in the case of the Cia. Carbonifera de Sabina in Tamaulipas which was run directly by the Carrancistas.[12]

When Carranza, the "First Chief," was in a position to initiate the construction of a regime of national reach, and had managed to reduce his principal opponents—the Villistas and Zapatistas—to mere guerrilla fighters, the new regime displayed a profoundly conservative character in agrarian matters. To the already slow and bureaucratic mechanism in charge of ejidal redistribution, new obstacles were put into place. As a result, at the beginning of 1916, Carranza sought to bring agrarian reform to a sharp halt by indicating to the Comisiones Agrarias Locales that "you should in no case proceed to redistribute [lands] because the absence of the enabling legislation which still has not been expedited, makes it inopportune." A little later, the *comisiones* were instructed that the lands of the confiscated estates were not among those subject to agrarian reform.[13]

Perhaps even more important than the preceding order was the Carrancista effort to restore economically and politically the old landowning elite. To that end, a massive return of the confiscated estates to the *latifundista* aristocracy of the *ancien regime* was ordered from the end of 1915. This counterrevolutionary process—which, to date, has received little attention from historians— was carried out across the length and breadth of the country, and constitutes a peculiar occurrence of the Mexican Revolution, distinguishing it from comparable social revolutions.[14] The Constitutionalists were not timid in assuring that "their revolution" had nothing to do with the "depredatory seizures" which were nothing but "violent seizures generated by judicial actions of the military or civil rule by Villistas, Convencionalistas, and Zapatistas."[15]

The diversity of viewpoints held by different revolutionary factions, including those within Carrancista ranks, is well exemplified by the fact that not all of the commanders loyal to the "First Chief" accepted this conservative policy for rural Mexico. Veracruz provided an example. Here, the División de Oriente by the order of Cándido Aguilar initiated the formal confiscation of haciendas the same month that Huerta left the country. The legitimacy of this action was supported with agrarista standards: that the landowners had obtained these lands by means of "a series of thefts supported by titles extracted by pressure and threats during the Porfirian epoch . . ." Certain Carrancistas, such as Colonel Adalberto Tejeda, sought in practice to impede the return of the old structure of landholding. Tejeda, who had already distinguished himself with his agrarista plans, managed to place a supporter as head of the Office of Confiscated Properties of Veracruz (Oficina de Bienes Intervenidos de Veracruz). Furthermore, he knew how to take advantage of the enormous legal, bureaucratic, and political confusion that prevailed, in order to sabotage the return of estates to the landowners of the *ancien regime.* Take the case of Ramón Riveroll, who usurped community lands during the Porfiriato in the Huasteca Veracruzana, and obtained in 1916 an order of devolution signed by Carranza himself. As proof of the enormous de facto autonomy enjoyed by local authorities—those in Veracruz as much as those of the Huasteca—they simply overlooked Carranza's orders of devolution, and returned Riveroll to the bureaucratic tangle where his demands remained bogged down.[16]

Carranza did not return absolutely everything. He confirmed the confiscation of the properties of enemies such as Huertistas, Villistas—like those of the Madero family in Coahuila—and the clergy. The Constitutionalist "oficinas interventoras" (supervisory offices) kept the option of directly exploiting or at least renting these properties. They even attempted to put back into operation certain enterprises that had been paralyzed, as occurred in the spring of 1916 with the paper mill San Rafael, which in spite of having been occupied by Zapatistas retained its machinery in perfect condition.[17]

A considerable number of the properties whose confiscation was upheld by Carranza were rented afterward to private citizens. This situation favored certain "arrangements" between officials and those interested in renting them. For example, in Mexico City complaints were voiced against those who prevented free access to the confiscated estates, "by reason of previous obligations with specified persons, contracted by the Secretaries of Hacienda and the Chief of the Department of Confiscated Properties in the Federal District."[18]

Given the lack of clear procedures to guide the new revolutionary administration, many cases were decided simply by individual criteria taking into account specific situations. For example, when the supervisory department of the capital city began its activities, it found that several military quarters had been set up in some confiscated houses. Generally, they did not pay anything to anybody, and some houses were left in such poor conditions that, in at least one case, cases of typhoid were present. Upon the return of this house to its owner, the government had to pay compensation for the vile condition in which it was found. In contrast, when confiscations were upheld, as occurred for several estates of Morelense landowner Manuel Araoz, they were treated as nationalized properties. One was handed over to a labor union, and in another an office of the Registro Civil was set up. Those who had made arrangements and deals with Carranza were treated with particular deference. The Casa del Obrero Mundial was even given the choice of which confiscated houses they preferred for their offices, and they chose the former Jockey Club.[19]

In summary, there were three principal positions that the revolutionaries assumed with respect to confiscated estates. Some factions—especially the Zapatistas—redistributed lands and other possessions among their followers and their bases of social support. This was the most revolutionary and popular approach, since they proposed to keep these properties in operation but under new forms of ownership and labor. Nevertheless, during the Mexican Revolution this position was more the exception than the rule.

A second and more common attitude toward the confiscated estates was running them, maintaining the previous structure as well as the same forms of operation. In these cases, the properties were conserved as productive units in order to benefit the revolutionaries, especially to finance the costs of war, as a source of income for the governments and, on many occasions, in order to personally benefit their leaders.

One intermediate and frequent approach was adopted by, among others, Villistas. In a certain sense, it was a variation of the redistributive approach, since even if the properties were not broken up and were maintained intact as productive units, it was promised that they would be redistributed in the future. At the same time that the landowners were expelled, these estates were worked for the benefit of the revolutionary armies, and certain products— such as meat—were distributed among the soldiers and the poor.

Finally, as is frequent in all revolutionary movements, the seizures were carried out in a predatory and destructive fashion, with interest basically in immediately disposing of all the possessions in reach, without any further interest in the estate and without concern for its destruction as an economic unit. Even when the destructive seizures were taken with a clear dose of class revenge, and served as booty for the revolutionary armies—thereby augmenting their resources and the loyalty to the leader—they did not usually result in more revolutionary forms, such as the distribution of land or, at least, the promise of distribution.

To different degrees, these three approaches were to be found in each one of the insurgent factions and even during each particular confiscation. The process was also modified according to the environment in which it took place. These various modalities are useful in defining specific differences and similarities among the revolutionary factions.

San Luis Potosí

The "Confiscations"

In San Luis Potosí, as generally throughout the republic, when revolutionaries entered some hacienda or rancho their actions were motivated by a clear intent of class vengance and, frequently, a manifest interest in improving the conditions of campesinos.

Some seizures turned out to be typically predatory, totally violent, as well as vengeful against hacendados and administrators. For example, the faction of Nicolás Torres, during the anti-Porfirista struggle, attacked haciendas in the western region of San Luis Potosí and carried out extremely disordered and destructive seizures; it acted with fury against landowners—several were placed before firing squads in order to better extract ransoms—and especially against Spanish employees, some of whom were executed. At the same time, during the seizures, this band also divided up the maize and other possessions, ordered and disposed at will, and gave free reign to their imagination at the expense of the goods and people of the hacienda. Also, at the beginning of the revolution the hacendados in the north of San Luis Potosí lived in fear of destruction by the faction of Lazaro Gómez which, even when it respected private property, executed administrators of the estates known for mistreatment of their peons.[20]

Even when the situation did not degenerate to these extremes, most revolutionaries entering an estate simply warned the owners and employees against mistreating "their supporters," or against attempting to recover what had been given to those who remained. In the case of the brothers Cleofas,

Magdaleno and Saturnino Cedillo—a lowerclass and popular faction of the Valle de Maíz—this turned out to be more than a threat. In the middle of 1913, some Cedillistas entered the hacienda La Concepción, of the Partido of Ciudad Maíz and property of United States citizens. According to the account of an hacendado, the rebels

went to kill him by order of . . . Magdaleno Cedillo, because he had heard that Mr. Cunningham (the owner) had said that the revolution would not triumph and that he had also received the complaint of the servant Inéz Rodríguez that Don Santiago Cunningham searched his home for items stolen during the night Cedillistas first arrived at this hacienda, having recovered nothing of his since Cedillo gave them to the peons.

Following several threats to hang Cunningham, even to the point of putting a rope around his neck, the rebels proposed to spare his life in exchange for two thousand pesos in cash. While they were involved in this negotiation, the twenty-first Cuerpo de Rurales—which had rebelled in favor of the "First Chief"—and commanded by General Jesus Agustín Castro immediately joined forces with the landowners and brought an end to the affair by shooting the Cedillista rebels.[21]

In the middle of 1914, when revolutionary forces including those of the Cedillos and their allies, the agraristas Alberto and Francisco Carrera Torres, occupied San Luis Potosí, various hacendados were jailed. Among these were found the brothers José and Javier Espinosa y Cuevas, owners of the largest Potosina hacienda, La Angostura, which adjoined Palomas, a *pequeña propiedad* (small property) that the Cedillos had acquired during the Porfiriato, and that they had to defend in a quarrel with the hacienda. This case not only had an economic overtone, but a political one as well. José Espinosa y Cuevas had been precisely the last Porfirian governor. In August 1914, when La Angostura had been seized, the Cedillos shot his brother Javier and, to further the humiliation, exhibited his body before all the peones of his own hacienda. This event disturbed all of San Luis. With the help of various revolutionaries and the foreign consuls, José was taken from prison and fled the country so that he would not meet the same fate.[22]

What we can call "popular" rebels—like the Cedillos, the Carreras, and those led by Isabél Robles or the Navarretes—were always clearly representatives of campesino unrest. Their seizures were a decided action against the rich, their employees, and the status quo. Their followers appropriated arms, money, horses, saddles, and often enough, women, sowing panic among the landowners, administrators, and frequently, among their workers themselves. Generally, these kind of leaders did not worry about drafting pronunciamentos and grandiloquent plans; for the most part they identified with the causes of popular discontent, demanded certain claims, and assumed a righteous character. During the seizures, they ordered an assembly of "their people," that is to say, the bulk of the estate workers, in order to distribute to them corn and footstuffs, to burn the account books and exempt the peones from their debts, to encourage them to keep whatever they wanted from the finca, and to invite them to join the revolution.

The response of the campesinos to the rebel seizures is of considerable importance in understanding the depth of the revolutionary process. From the limited information that exists, it is clear that their reactions varied considerably. At times, as happened in La Concepción when the Cedillos arrived, "the servants and other residents . . . dedicated themselves to looting," and some even joined the rebel ranks. But frequently revolutionaries ran up against a wall of indifference and rejection by campesinos, as much from fear of reprisals as from the intense ties of paternalism which bound them to the landowners. In San Diego hacienda, for example, although the leaders insisted to the workers that the land was theirs and invited them to take what they wished, nothing was touched, not even the food and clothing that had been left scattered; and they even burned and buried the silk rebozos and lanterns that the rebels had given them. Moreoever, as the campesinos themselves recognized, the handful of men that joined the revolutionaries were not so much motivated by ideological reasons as they were concerned not to lose the horses that the rebels had taken.[23] From this perspective, it was clear that the advance of the revolution still struggled against powerful psychological barriers and the habits of traditional authority.

There were occasions when, upon entering haciendas, the insurgents adopted a clear agrarista stance. Since their first action, the Cedillos read the campesinos the Plan de Ayala, which they said they followed. When Navarrette seized the rich huastecan hacienda of San Diego, in addition to burning the account books and distributing the food he insisted to the workers that the land was now theirs, thanks to the revolution. For his part, from the beginning of 1912, Elías Fortuna shook up Santa María del Rio—a town that from the Porfiriato had asked for the restitution of their lands—by declaring in front of the peones of the haciendas his intention to divide the largest properties.[24]

But in San Luis Potosí not all rebels were revolutionaries, and some, like the Barragáns (father and son), members of the old landowning aristocracy, were frankly conservative. Their different objectives and political culture translated into particular kinds of "seizures" and takeovers of haciendas. Certainly, many leaders of the anti-Porfirian struggle came from the middle class, especially rancheros of the fertile Huasteca zone—like the Lárraga brothers—and were accustomed to exercising a certain economic and political predominance in their localities. As a result, these leaders—particularly at the beginning of the movement—paid their armed followers from their own pocket and almost never permitted robbery or "forced loans," especially when, in many cases, they rebelled on their own estates, armed their workers, and then occupied the properties of relatives and friends. In the beginning they controlled and disciplined their followers well, and upon seizing an estate they manage to keep order and pay or give receipts—which occasionally they redeemed when they were Maderista officials—for the food, horses, forage, and other goods they took for the cause.[25]

One of the most conspicuous examples of a conservative leader is that of General Agustín Castro who, as already noted, ordered the shooting of the Cedillistas who entered La Concepción intending to assassinate the owner. Castro, who to the delight of landowners seemed "respectable in every way," escorted the owners of La Concepción to the state capital "with every kind of attention and trying to serve them as much as he was able." According to these hacendados, given that his soldiers obeyed him "blindly," during his takeovers there was "peace and tranquility, contrasting notably this order with . . . the night of the arrival . . . of Cedillo in which all was abuses, robbery, sacking and destruction." Castro even explained to "the servants" the differences that divided the revolution in San Luis Potosí between "honorable revolutionaries," like himself, and bandits and "Zapatistas hordes," like the Cedillos:

We are fighting to make sure that a man of good faith represents the legitimate rights of the people . . . but not taking from any other that which belongs to him, . . . we do not work this way nor will we tolerate anyone despoiling another of his possessions . . . [we] do not believe that . . . this government for which we work will attend to the needs of the poorest by giving them goods taken from those who have more . . . if you want to be revolutionaries don't be bandits, better that you should continue working at the side of your family, . . . your patron has told me that he is happy with your work and hopes that you continue as always, doing what you should.[26]

"De Viva Voz y de Cuerpo Presente"

In the middle of 1914, upon the collapse of the Huerta regime and the disbanding of the old federal army, revolutionaries took possession of the country. San Luis Potosí was occupied peacefully. Eulalio Gutiérrez—a former

miner from Coahuila, strongly influenced by the Partido Liberal Mexicano—
was installed as governor and military commander. To the horror of the "crème
de la crème" of the extremely closed Potosino society, they experienced now
an extraordinary mobility within their ranks. Workers and campesinos, overwhelmingly illiterate, took into their hands both formally and informally the
reins of power. Lives and properties were at the mercy of the particular will of
recently created generals. San Luis Potosí, and in large measure the entire
country, was governed "de viva voz y de cuerpo presente," in a military manner, regardless of bureaucratic or legal forms by the strong man in power.

In the countryside above all, the former rebels were transformed into lords
and masters of lives and goods in the districts that they controlled. These
men and their immediate followers became the real entities of power. The
territory of San Luis Potosí was divided into a mosaic of small *cacicazgos* where
justice was imparted, and immediate orders were given on all matters. On
occasion, these localities were treated by the revolutionaries with a highly
constructive attitude, as if they were sure they were building the bases of a
new society.

Upon occupying Ciudad del Maíz, landowners complained that the Cedillos
made themselves the "lords and masters of all these localities." The principal
latifundistas, like "the Moctezuma boys," were held under house arrest and
prevented from leaving without permission. By one account, Cedillo made
himself into

the owner of the town and chief of a gang of Indians which, like the Zapatista, exercised an unconscious reprisal. The few whites of the city were surrounded, beseiged
and at the mercy of impromptu soldiers; without trial or any civilized guarantee. It
was a return to the Indian cacicato.[27]

The takeovers, banditry, extreme insecurity on the roads, and the military
and economic disorder drove no few hacendados, administrators, and managers to abandon properties entirely. The war brought its inevitable share of
death and suffering. In 1913 as reported in Ciudad del Maíz—the Cedillista
zone of operations—"the poor swarm in the streets . . . and we still have no
maize to eat . . . [plus] all the haciendas have suspended work since small
groups of rebels constantly visit [them]."[28] Between 1915 and 1917 famines
and epidemics marked the Potosino map in a particularly dramatic manner.

Entire towns and communities came to abandon their houses and properties, as in the case of the six hundred North American families, which formed
Colonia Atascador in the settlement of Cocos, and who returned to their coun-

try because of the continuous robberies, assaults, and rapes perpetrated principally by the Lárraga brothers between 1912 and 1918. As the U.S. consul complained,

there was nothing left in the Colony, the inhabitants having fled for safety, their cattle slaughtered or stolen, their houses either burned or raided, their crops destroyed and their furniture and farming implements either destroyed or stolen.[29]

The abandonment of estates, on the one hand, and takeovers and seizures of estates, on the other, constituted two sides of the same coin. One of the most frequent causes for confiscating a hacienda, rancho, or enterprise was the flight of its proprietors and managers, which very often took place after rebels had taken over. A notable case was that of Mariano Arguinzoniz, one of the most conspicuous members of the Potosino landowning aristocracy, whose properties suffered a particularly severe destruction since many of his former *arrendatarios*—whom he had expelled from the hacienda at the turn of the century—marched in the revolutionary ranks. The Arguinzoniz completely abandoned their once prosperous estate, La Joya, after rebels occupied it and destroyed the machinery and structures, carried off the cattle and agricultural products, and burned the house. It was not long thereafter that La Joya was quietly taken over for months.[30]

Almost by necessity, a contradictory attitude possessed revolutionaries regarding confiscated rural estates. On the one hand, they intended to appropriate as many goods as possible in the shortest period of time. Looting, a reflection of implicit class struggle, was almost inevitable since it reinforced the legitimacy of the rebels in the eyes of their troops and campesinos, and because, furthermore, it expressed old personal hatreds. But at the same time, and mixed up with a predatory attitude, revolutionary groups needed the estates to sustain their bands, the movement, and their government. If rebels considered staying for a while in the same zone of operations, it was indispensable to ensure that the estate did not suffer too many disturbances so that it could continue working. This necessity was especially important during the first years of struggle, when the absence of a real rebel army with a centralized command from which flowed funds, soldiers, and arms made the seized haciendas the principal support of the war.

On occasion, there was a fine line separating the exploitation of an estate to sustain revolutionaries from merely predatory destruction. A case in point was the hacienda Ganahl, property of the Tampico Navigation Company, and occupied repeatedly by different Constitutionalist leaders from 1913.

Money, contributions for "protection"—around two thousand pesos monthly, according to a receipt drawn up "on account of the monthly payments that have been assigned to the said hacienda"—arms, munitions, cattle, horses, food for officers and men, merchandise, medicine, and even hospital attention was extracted from Ganahl. The Constitutionalists also constantly utilized the steamers of the enterprise to transport troops and equipment through the system of rivers that cut through the Huasteca and its petroleum region, which was therefore turned into a strategic base of primary importance. No one better than the manager of the company could explain the situation:

They have made threats upon my life several times. Our mechanics have been compelled to work for them repairing arms, making bombs, cannons, etc. Employees and laborers, generally have been threatened in every way, and our whole organization is, due to these causes, absolutely demoralized and it is impossible . . . to carry on business. The rebel forces have used the steamers of the company to transport their troops, and I and my staff have been practically prisoners . . . for the last three months. Rebels have forced us on the point of their guns, to accept rebel money. . . . I and several members of my staff have been prisoners for several hours for having dispatched a steamer without permit . . .

The company finally decided to shut down when, in one of the takeovers, the rebels provoked a great fire which destroyed nearly all of the distillery, storage tanks, and furniture.[31]

In the end, and in spite of all the variations, the seizure of haciendas, ranchos, and houses in San Luis Potosí basically had, during the bloodiest years of civil strife, a military objective: to sustain the armed bands and the revolution. The distribution of confiscated lands was, most of the time, an entirely secondary objective in comparison to the more important one of preserving the estate as an economic unit. In any case, the immediately fundamental change consisted in the fact that the profits and the production remained at the disposition of the revolutionaries. By the same token, it was common that the conditions in which the workers lived in the confiscated estates did not depart too radically from tradition. Often enough, the same administrators and campesinos continued working and relating to one another as they always had. In many cases, the changes were noticed, above all among "the better sort."

In order to make efficient use of the resources available on a confiscated property, the revolutionaries created a careful and sophisticated organization. This was more a rule than an exception, even with those bands of popular origin, like those of the Cedillos. Thus, it was common that these rebels left on the estates those "in charge of revolutionary services" who remained responsible for the principal tasks: to get the greatest production and profits, recruiting new followers, and ensuring that social relations with the estate did not deteriorate to the disadvantage of the revolution, taking care, for example, that owners and administrators did not make reprisals against their sympathizers.

A notable case was the prosperous Huasteca hacienda El Jabalí, formerly the property of Pablo Escandón, the rich governor of Morelos on the eve of the revolution. El Jabalí came under Cedillista authority in the second half of 1914. Their control was so strict that the administrator saw the necessity of obtaining written permission from the revolutionaries before even permitting social activities as minor as circus performances. The rebels even managed to place some of their own men within the administration. These appointments were complemented with even more important ones, such as that of the military commander of the Río Verde region. All of this gave the rebels—at least for a time—extensive control over the estate: its production and marketing as well as part of the internal social relations. On fine paper with the letterhead "Brigada de Oriente de San Luis Potosí al mando de los hermanos Cedillo" (The Brigade of East San Luis Potosí under the command of the Cedillo Brothers), which displayed a beautiful watermark with the national symbol, the rebel band organized the principal functions relative to the supervision of El Jabalí. By this route, generously and without obstacles, flowed loads of maize, sugar loafs, fodder, cattle, yokes, clothes, and other requirements that, as the Cedillos declared, they needed "with urgency for the maintenance of the Constitutionalist forces."[32]

Another estate that repeatedly provided resources to the revolutionaries was the hacienda and sugar mill of La Concepción, which consisted of fifteen hundred hectares and produced sugar and alcohol, possessing at least two thousand head of cattle and horses. In June 1913 the Cedillistas took over this hacienda, carrying away maize, sugar, mules, and horses. This was the first of a long series of occupations. Between July and September of that same year they returned twelve more times. According to the owner, in November 1915, when Convencionista–Villista forces occupied San Luis Potosí, the Carreras and Cedillos came to expel the manager of the mill for getting involved in political activities, giving him seventy-two hours to leave Convencionista territory. Thereafter, it was even easier to extract resources since the entire enterprise was supervised in a stable manner. The insurgents then took all of the cattle and horses, the agricultural equipment, and maize, and sold 127 tons of sugar which reportedly earned more than one hundred thousand pesos.

During 1916, still under the direct orders of the Cedillos, the hacienda continued functioning, and all the profits from the cane milled and sold was turned over to the revolutionaries.[33]

The contrast with the Zapatista approach was clear: the central objective of the confiscations in San Luis Potosí was not the distribution of land for campesinos. One impressive proof of the relative social superficiality that these seizures sometimes possessed was that many campesinos had no memory of them. This did not prevent various kinds of direct contact between revolutionaries and workers. Félix Guerrero, for example, one of the few campesinos of San Diego who remembered when the hacienda was seized, recalls that despite the fact that he was charged with providing a large number of cattle to the soldiers, they continually stole from him spurs, horses, reins, foodstuffs, and other goods—abuses which were stopped only when a general granted him safe conduct. This case illustrates why safe conduct passes were so highly estimated and why leaders like the Cedillos strengthened their social grasp by extending them to their sympathizers. A typical one was granted by the Cedillos during their occupation of El Jabalí to Marcos Aguilar and

to his possesssions . . . pleading . . . to all the chiefs of the Constitutionalist army . . . that they provide him all the guarantees which are within their power . . . [given that they are] one of the most devoted persons to the cause for which we are now fighting.[34]

One decisive fact demonstrated the longing and limits of the Potosino popular revolution: despite its historical roots and agrarian tone, very little land came to be distributed. There were more than enough reasons: the prevailing insecurity, the military failure suffered by the most popular factions of the revolution from the second half of 1915—which wore down the Cedillistas, Carrancistas, and other groups—the fear that carrying out agrarian distribution would immobilize and disband the soldiers; and that, without the confiscated haciendas, there would no longer be resources for the war. As important as the reasons cited above were the many psychological barriers and traditional political culture.

Even though some Cedillistas fighters did receive land during the peak of civil strife, this was done in an informal way and temporarily. It is very difficult to confirm, but it seems that these revolutionary soldiers occupied vacant plots instead of receiving lands belonging to confiscated haciendas and ranches which were primarily exploited for the maintenance of war. These agrarian distributions did not appear to have been frequent, in spite of the repeated adherence of the Cedillos to the Zapatista plan and to the Ley Ejecutiva del Reparto de Tierras (Enabling Law of Land Distribution) of Carrera Torres which, from March 1913, mandated the return of lands stolen from pueblos and requested by the residents of any pueblo, hacienda, or rancho which was organized to deliver immediately ten hectares of land to each head of family. During those times when the Carreras and Cedillos controlled their territories with some autonomy, they began to put into practice something of the spirit which guided this agrarian law, as well as certain communal principles. According to the memories of one Cedillista rebel, "at the beginning of . . . 1914, lands were distributed to us, by the Plan de la Maradilla de Carrestoliendas and other woods [*montes*] of considerable importance were distributed for all, and the pastures were distributed to the soldiers." Furthermore, the first agrarian committee was formed, and it was intended that the soliders would be kept firmly integrated in their pueblos. Instead of receiving payment, they were provided without cost that which was elemental: shoes, sheets and blankets, hats, rebozos, and even foodstuffs. They even opened schools and began the construction of bridges.[35]

The Revolution In Power

The Convencionista government of Eulalio Gutiérrez (July to September 1914) and that of Villista Emiliano Saravia (February to July 1915) deepened the social course of the revolution in San Luis Potosí, forcing it to be prosecuted on behalf of the disinherited or, as Saravia put it, "to the end that the inhabitants of the state readily see the fruit of the efforts undertaken and of the rights won."

The Convencionista and the Villista governorships legalized the confiscated estates, giving a formal legitimacy by a constituted government to the encumbrance of private property. Guitiérrez created the Junta Calificadora de Fincas Rústicas y Urbanas (the Authorized Committee of Rural and Urban Estates), with branch offices in the municipalities, which would elaborate meticulous inventories of the confiscations in order to take the responsibility of managing them as a public trust. The Villista government created the Junta de Confiscaciones y Restituciones (the Committee of Confiscations and Restitutions), turning over to the supervisors (*interventores*) the responsibility of managing these properties. It is also important to notice that these decrees promoted a decentralizing impulse that granted to the state government, not to the federal authorities, both the capacity to decide about new confiscations as well as the final destiny of the estates. Even with this law, the possible restitution of haciendas and houses, or else their definite expropriation—a very radical position in Mexico at that time—came to depend upon the "political antecedents" of the owners. These criteria had a clear class content, since, as one of those who were affected complained, the local government "simply given the fact that we are hacendados consigns us as enemies."[36]

The Villista governor approved the first Potosino law for the modification of land tenure. According to this law, the government held the authority to acquire properties which, along with available national lands, would be divided and sold in small plots to the largest possible number of landless campesinos. Saravia ordered that the reform not simply remain on paper: he issued a notice "exclusively for the poor" to initiate the distribution of a recently acquired hacienda. The confiscated rural and urban estates also were kept in one piece in this redistributive and popular legislation. The object was "to provide work for the rural proletariat and to prevent the scarcity of grain"; the method was to promote the immediate utilization of the confiscated lands by means of sharecropping contracts. Saravia also ordered implemented in San Luis Potosí the dispositions relative to the confiscated properties that Villa had put into practice in Chihuahua, and which had considerably increased his popular support.[37]

Gabriel Gavira, the first Carrancista governor, continued this effort in favor of the masses. He carried out an action of enormous transcendance: he initiated the Constitutionalist agrarian reform in San Luis by restoring the community lands of Villa de Reyes, which had been lost centuries earlier. Given Gavira's extremist demeanor, his autonomy regarding the conservative policies of the "First Chief", his seizure of a large number of clerical estates as well as those of "científicos and their sympathizers," and his initiation of a study that would determine the ultimate disposition of the confiscated estates, within less than three months of becoming governor, in October of 1915, he was replaced by a more docile and moderate soldier. Immediately, the new governor General Vicente Dávila created a "Junta Dictaminadora" which, considering "their political antecedents and the conduct observed by the landowners" pronounced the restoration or retention of their estates.[38]

During the revolutionary regimes that controlled San Luis between the middle of 1914 until the fall and assassination of Carranza in May 1920, the management of confiscated estates, their rental, and the payment of contributions were an important source of income for the government: between August 1914 and June 1915 alone, they yielded 260,000 pesos. Furthermore, they continued to support the armies which remained active.[39] The supervisory offices and their municipal branches directly worked several haciendas, ranches, and factories, or else they rented them out. These offices were also authorized to control the removal and auction of all kinds of items from these properties: machinery, agricultural products, cattle, automobiles, and other things. Occasionally, the Juntas Dictaminadoras also took charge of compensating certain landowners for the damages to their estates during the period of occupation.[40]

But perhaps the most notable characteristic of the Carrancista revolutionaries in San Luis Potosí, while they were in power, was that they nearly brought to an end the early social generosity which certain rebel and more popular bands demonstrated with the confiscated haciendas, ranches, and houses they held. By the same token, this tendency turned the confiscated properties into something very similar to private property benefiting military chiefs and their followers.

Most of the urban properties that were confiscated were occupied by the revolutionaries on a personal basis or as government offices. Also a large number of houses in the capital city were used as barracks. Some of the houses that were seized included such magnificent ones as that of Javier Espinosa y Cuevas, where Eulalio Gutiérrez settled when he was governor—which was occupied when the assassination of the owner took place—or the superb Palacio Episcopal where the offices of the *ayuntamiento* were located, and from which even the pictures of a very valuable collection of European works were removed "in order to sell them to the gringos." Most of the time the occupants did not even pay rent and carried away everything they could, leaving the properties in terrible condition. The same General Dávila rented to some relatives of Barragán a house for some high officials who after a little while, according to the owners, not only refused to pay rent but also treated the owners "as annoyances." In spite of the fact that the administration of Gavira seems to have been relatively honest in the management of such properties, Barragán (the senior) was astonished by the fact that "even my General Gavira took Bohemian crystal lamps from the house of Javier Espinosa y Cuevas . . . and gave them to his mistress which scandalized all of society . . ."[41]

More substantial than what was taken from the houses was the destruction by those in charge of caring for—by not very transparent methods—the haciendas and ranchos seized. From the largest *latifundistas* came torrents of complaints against the supervisory functionaries, because they continued "taking everything within reach that they find in the haciendas," and because instead of "limiting themselves to watching, regulating and overseeing the acts of the employees and rendering accounts, they have been dedicated to destruction, to exploiting for their own account and handing over nothing to the government . . . destroying the national wealth, . . . and the state treasury fails to collect important sums."[42] Juan F. Barragán, the person who most intimately understood the situation of these estates in San Luis concluded that "the looting of country estates in the States is no less than 10 million pesos, yet the Constitutionalist Revolution only profits here in San Luis 100 and some thousands of pesos . . ."[43]

This utilization of power for private purposes was shared by all of the factions. During the government of Gutiérrez and that of Gavira, a couple of merchants close to the highest levels of power made themselves "scandalously rich" by monopolizing the production of the seized haciendas, principally articles of the greatest necessity, raising and lowering prices according to their interests.[44] Carranza himself complained that his subordinates, instead of "granting guarantees to the inhabitants and the owners" of the estates under the control of the government, only dedicated themselves to committing "damage" and "many abuses." In 1916 the supervisor of El Venado was jailed for embezzlement, having disposed of animals valued at 150,000 pesos. In that same *municipio* it was discovered, when Laguna Seca was restored to its owner, that Luis Gutiérrez, the brother of Governor Eulalio Gutiérrez, had been disposing of its *guayule*; while a Lieutenant Ramos was working El Salado "as if it had been his for a long time," carrying off animals, tools, furniture and several automobiles. When the Barragáns wanted to purchase some of the confiscated estates they found that these had already been rented out "in a financial deal with a well known Constitutionalist chief."[45]

The same revolutionaries recognized in the debates of the Sovereign Revolutionary Convention that in San Luis Potosí the confiscations had not supplied,

a single piece of land in the hands of the people, nor has it benefited at all the proletariat. . . . It causes shame and dishonor to say it . . . the confiscations have come to place diamonds in the hands of those in charge; have given wealth to those who before joining the Revolution did not possess even one cent.[46]

The Restoration Of The Landed Aristocracy

At the time of the triumph of Constitutionalism, before it fragmented into Conventionalistas, Villistas, and Carrancistas, the return to the confiscated estates to their former owners was a process whose results were insignificant. In those days landowners were still judged very severely; thus, Carranza was not able to impose all of his conservative standards, and many military chiefs—the principal beneficiaries of the seizures—were opposed tenaciously to giving up these rich resources. Many of the roads then taken by Potosino landowners to recover their estates resulted in dead ends. For example, in August 1914 the chief of the Oficina de Propiedades Confiscadas (Office of Confiscated Properties), a Major Escobar, presented to Carranza a categorically negative opinion regarding the restoration of the hacienda El Peñasco. His reasoning was based upon clear class considerations:

> The Espinosa y Parra are part of a group of hacendados from San Luis Potosí whose fortunes cannot be considered legitimately acquired capital, . . . it cannot be considered capital resulting from legitimate profit which the hacendados acquired after having paid their workers just salaries, but on the contrary the fortune of these individuals as that of the majority of the hacendados . . . is in my humble opinion nothing but the salary that these same hacendados should have paid their workers. It is these workers who produced the merchandise which has made the hacendados rich and which has allowed them to have palaces . . . while the humble workers on their haciendas . . . don't even have pants to cover their nakedness nor do they have shoes to wear and they are the main producers of national wealth.[47]

During that period prior to the factional struggle among Constitutionalistas, and frequently by mediation of the Barragán brothers and even Carranza himself, various distinguished Potosino landowners obtained orders of restoration. But the disorganization of the country was such that even these orders remained unenforced. At the beginning of 1915, for example, while the Potosino government remained acephalous, simply no attention was paid to an order given by Carranza for the devolution of the Barrenechea estates. A more direct route, but not always more effective, was negotiation with the chiefs of the supervisory committees. A case in point was the Soberón family, who in September 1914 tried negotiating in order to "handle the form in which the stated Sres. want to settle the referred interests, and we are now quite encouraged because they told us that by means of a sum that we are to pay in cash they will return everything to us." In the end, however, the deal remained without effect since only governor Gutiérrez could "fix the sum" required and, after being named provisional president by the Convention, he never returned as head of San Luis Potosí.[48]

The situation turned around by the fall of 1915, when a conservative and centralizing Carrancismo consolidated its power in San Luis, and Carranza and the Barragáns ordered fundamental directives to be implemented. In accord with the practice imposed all over Mexico, ejidal distribution in San Luis practically was brought to a halt. Not only was change blocked, but an attempt was made to restore the changes that the revolutionary process had imposed by that point in the rural structure, order the massive and expedited return to the confiscated houses and haciendas to their former owners. The objective of this very conservative process was clear: to restore politically and economically the former landowning aristocracy.[49]

San Luis remained under the aegis of General Juan Barragán and his father. The young Barragán was very close to the "First Chief," and became the dominant figure within San Luis and governor of the state from June 1917. Barragán senior, a member of one of the most illustrious families of the former landowning aristocracy and relative and friend of many distinguished *latifundistas*, did not wait—according to his own phrase—"to force" the restoration of the former landowning structure throughout San Luis. By the time he took charge of the Jefatura of the Secretaría de Hacienda in San Luis Potosí, now the sole office responsible for the confiscated estates, only the properties of the very powerful and deceased Encarnación Ypiña had been given back to his family, and that because he had helped the Maderista revolution and had occupied, briefly, the governorship at the time of Díaz's fall. In only four months, Barragán returned at least 240 houses and 72 haciendas to the most prominent members of the old regime. This amounted to more than one hundred million pesos which, he declared, is "the value of the property in the State." Among the haciendas that were put again in possession of its previous owners, La Angostura had special relevance not only because it was the largest in all San Luis Potosí, but also because of its symbolic force. It had been precisely here where, only a few months before, the Cedillistas had assassinated one of its owners, the brother of the last Porfirian governor.[50] Restoring legitimacy and property to the landed aristocracy, the Carrancista administration in San Luis Potosí attempted to turn back the clock and reestablish significant parts of the former rural order.

This restorative process was handled, furthermore, in a way that notably increased political centralization, strengthening the new regime in Mexico City. The "First Chief" instituted a Dirección General de Bienes Intervenidos at the national level, headed by Pascual Ortíz Rubio, the future president, who established that the long bureaucratic process of the devolution of estates should be confirmed by his own signature. In this way, he ensured the loyalty to the landowning elite toward the federal government. Within San Luis, the enormous power of deciding which properties would be returned and which ones would remain confiscated was taken away from the state committees and their branch offices and given to the Jefatura of the Secretaría de Hacienda headed by Barragán senior. As expected, the centralist tendency became a source of conflict with the local supervisors who did not easily give up their prerogatives or their power. The situation was so tense that there were even judicial proceedings brought against some of them.

But in spite of the fact that Carranza attempted to determine from the center of the country the process of restoration, given the weakness that still permeated the government apparatus, much still depended upon the informal arrangements with the officials in San Luis and its regions. In order to judge those who were "enemies of the Constitutionalist cause," there were created "boards of public health," "adjudication committees," and the Departamento de Verificación de la Propiedad (the Department of Property Verification). In exchange for the return of their properties, those so favored had to formally renounce "every kind of claim which [they could] put forward for damages and injury to their estates, during the time that they were confiscated." The order of confiscation was confirmed for only a few estates: this occurred basically to well-known Huertistas like Mariano Arguinzoniz and Pablo Escandón, to the clerics like Montes de Oca, and also on occasion to those who had abandoned their estates, for example, the owners of the hacienda San Diego in Cerritos.[51]

In this State in formation, an enormous legal, bureaucratic, and political confusion obstructed the management of all government affairs, including the working and return of the confiscated estates. One case among many— that of Laguna Seca—is revealing. In 1915, this hacienda, together with its mescal distillery, had been rented to Captain Rafael Cardenas by the Supervisory Committee of Confiscated Estates of San Luis Potosí. At the end of the year, when Carranza ordered that all of the confiscated properties be turned over to the Secretaría de Hacienda, the new officials seized, together with the real property, ixtle and cattle that Cárdenas claimed as his own. Since the supervisor of confiscated properties of this municipality had just been thrown in jail, Cárdenas obtained an order of restoration from the local subordinate supervisor. But Barragán blocked this order, alleging that Cárdenas still owed money to the supervisory office and that, while he had worked the estate, he had not even paid salaries to the peons. Cárdenas handled this matter directly with the "First Chief." But when Carranza again turned the matter over to Barragán, Cárdenas simply went to Laguna Seca and carried off the animals. In the middle of 1916, Ortíz Rubio, the head of the national Departamento de Bienes Intervenidos, ordered that they return to Cárdenas the rest of his possessions, but Barragán succeeded in nullifying the order by dealing directly with Carranza. The dispute seemed to go on indefinitely, given the conflict of interests and prerogatives among the various local, state, and federal officials. These were the natural ambiguities of a national regime in the process of being formed.[52]

The bureaucratic tangle that surrounded the return of the confiscated estates allowed an even greater spreading of the prevailing corruption. A notable example was that of Felipe Leija, who could be seen daily with Governor Dávila "drinking in the different establishments of the city," and acting "as an agent or an influence close to the government." According to the Barragáns, Leija took advantage of the "weak character" of Dávila in order to make repeated and substantial charges for obtaining the restoration of estates. Thus, for example, the Elioro family gave him ten thousand pesos for this service. Even more important, given its great symbolic value, was the charge he imposed on the owner of Gogorrón, for arranging the return of the lands which Gavira had just restituted to the ejido of Villa de Reyes, the first agrarian distribution of Carrancismo in San Luis Potosí. At the same time, some relatives of Dávila made "good deals" regarding the restoration of estates in the Río Verde region. Rafael Nieto, undersecretary of Hacienda and also very close to Carranza, as well as the future governor, was accused of involvement in the same kinds of practices; in particular, of arranging the restoration of the hacienda El Jabalí, long occupied by the Cedillo brothers, a deal that supposedly cost Pablo Escandón twenty thousand pesos.[53]

During the heyday of conservative Carrancismo, the principal beneficiaries of these kinds of deals were precisely the Barragáns. A conspicious example was that of the powerful *latifundista* Mariano Arguinzoniz whose estates had not been restored by Carranza, given his close attachment to the Huertista cause. Furthermore, the "First Chief" himself had asked Gavira to judge him "as a criminal or expel him from the country as a 'pernicious foreigner.' " From that time on he lived in exile with his family in the United States. In February 1916, while beginning the massive return of confiscated estates, Carranza again confirmed the confiscation of Arguinzoniz's properties. This valuable opportunity was not lost. Immediately, Barragán senior sugested his son to "pressure" the "First Chief" to return the houses to Arguinzoniz, for

after all Don Mariano has millions and so he can respond to all charges which result. For the restoration . . . if it occurs, it could be delayed so that this old miser would let go of at least about one hundred thousand or two hundred thousand pesos or about ten thousand dollars. Get the authorization to handle this matter with him, but I am going to San Antonio. Here it is known that there are many interested parties in favor of dealing with Don Mariano, not out of affection but out of greed . . .[54]

Accordingly, it seems Barragán rapidly reached an understanding with Arguinzoniz, because on 16 February he wrote the *latifundista* at San Antonio, Texas, where he lived in exile, notifying him of the restoration of his properties in the Valle de Maíz and in the state capital and again offering him his help so that he could return to Mexico and "settle the charges made against you." In fact, only the estates of his wife and sons had been restored, most of which had now been left useless. An interesting case was his hacienda El Salado, which, by "special order" of Carranza on 14 February—that is, two days before Barragán's letter—remained confiscated. On this same date, Barragán, as chief of the hacienda in San Luis, accepted a contract to work El Salado's *guayule*, from which he hoped to get a million pesos. Furthermore, the state government agreed to pay for a permanent armed force, supervisor, and an estate manager for this hacienda. It was not until 1918, after the Barragáns had attempted to charge Arguinzoniz for other favors and after his death, that his estates were restored and that finally Carranza permitted the return of this widow and children to the country.[55]

In conclusion, just as Juan F. Barragán confided to this son, the knowledge he possessed regarding the handling of confiscated estates "has given me the opportunity to know many important things that have been done, but this is not something I should talk about let alone spread around. Dirty clothing is washed in the house and in the house there is a lot of dirty clothes . . ."[56]

The confiscated estates came to an end almost at the same time that the Carranza regime was overthrown. In June 1920, when the triumph of the Agua Prieta revolt was not yet a month old, the federal government ordered "the restoration of all the properties that are now being held." Most of the guidelines established by the "First Chief" were followed: only the confiscated properties of notorious enemies—Victoriano Huerta, Félix Díaz, Francisco Villa and José Maria Mayorena—together with those estates that were not reclaimed by their previous owners, remained in possession of the Departamento de Bienes Nacionales. But there was an exception to this rule that clearly demonstrated the considerable sensibility acquired by the new government in contending with promises that the revolution had made to the campesinos. In accordance with the agrarian program, those rural estates that had been confiscated and were already "attached" to an ejido were not given back.[57]

So it was that an aspect of revolutionary Mexico came to an end, one that gave particular evidence to its uncertainties and contradictions. The fate of the confiscated estates demonstrated, on the one hand, the clear limits that limited the actions of the popular classes; but, at the same time, it revealed some of the most profound feelings of justice and generosity which, on occasion, resulted from this social struggle of the Mexican people.

Notes

This essay was translated from Spanish by Thomas Benjamin.

1. Luis Fernando Amaya, *La Soberana Convención Revolucionaria, 1914–1916* (México: Ed. Trillas, 1975), 214.

2. "The motivating drive," Tannenbaum argues, "has come from the inhabitants of little scattered villages, small population groups, with simple ideas and simple attitudes toward the world, . . . the elemental cry was land and water." Frank Tannenbaum, *Peace by Revolution: Mexico After 1910* (New York: Columbia University Press, 1968), 127; Jesús Silva Herzog, *El agrarismo mexicano y la reforma agraria. Exposición y crítica* (México: Fondo de Cultura Económica, 1959), 160.

3. Among the principal revisionists are Ramón Eduardo Ruiz, *The Great Rebellion: Mexico, 1905–1924* (New York: W. W. Norton, 1980); G. M. Joseph, *Revolution from Without: Mexico, the United States, and Yucatan, 1880–1923* (Cambridge: Cambridge University Press, 1982).

4. Alan Knight, *The Mexican Revolution* 2 vols. (Cambridge: Cambridge University Press, 1986).

5. John Womack, *Emiliano Zapata y la revolución mexicana* (México: Siglo XXI, 1969), 221.

6. A document signed in Huitzilac, Morelos, attempting to prevent these abuses, 31 October 1915, Archivo General de la Nación (AGN), Fondo Gobernación, Ramo Revolución (hereafter cited as FG-R) Caja (c)3; and *Crónicas y debates de la Soberana Convención Revolucionaria*, 3 vols. (México: Biblioteca del Instituto Nacional de Estudios Históricos de la Revolución Mexicana, 1965), II: 161–66.

7. Juan Felipe Leal and Margarita Menegus, "La violencia armada y su impacto en la economia agrícola del Estado de Tlaxcala, 1915–1920," *Historia Mexicana*, 26:4 (April–June 1987): 595–643; Raymond Buve, "Agricultores, dominación política y estructura agraria en la revolución mexicana: el caso de Tlaxcala, 1910–1918," in *Haciendas in Central Mexico from Late Colonial Times to the Revolution* (Amsterdam: CEDLA, 1984), 226.

8. Friedrich Katz, "Villa, Reform Governor of Chihuahua," in *Essays on the Mexican Revolution: Revisionist Views of the Leaders,* ed. George Wolfskill and Douglas Richmond (Austin: University of Texas Press, 1979), 35; Silvestre Terrazas, *El verdadero Pancho Villa* (México: Editorial Era, 1984).

9. Taking into account only those citizens from the United States who presented claims to their government concerning the confiscation of their estates throughout Mexico, one can find data of the number of confiscations per year that is relatively certain and constant. According to these claims, in 1914 there were 93 estates confiscated; during 1915, 22 estates; during 1916, 87; the next year, 23; during 1918, 23 estates, and in 1920, 20 estates. Sheffield to Secretary of State, 24 December, 1926, from United States National Archives, Washing-

ton, (hereafter cited as NAW), Record Group (hereafter cited as RG) 59, 312.11/9180.

10. Juan F. Barragán to Mariano Arguinzoniz, 16 February 1916, Archivo Juan Barragán (hereafter cited as AJB), CXVIII/14/ff.34–35.

11. Jefe de Oficina General de Confiscaciones to Presidente Soberana Convención Revolucionaria, 28 May 1915, AGN, FG-R, c8, e3.

12. Cia. Carbonífera de Sabina to Carranza, 27 November 1915, and Viceconsul of Spain to Carranza, Centro de Estudios de Historia de México, Condumex (hereafter cited as CEHMC), Fondo (F)XXI (Venustiano Carranza) Leg. 6867; Bryan to Spring Rice, 23 March 1914, NAW, RG 59, 312.41/205 3 May 1915; Department of State to British Embassy, 10 April 1914, NAW, RG 59, 312.41/212.

13. "Circular del Gobierno de la República Mexicana," 7 May 1916, AGN, FG-R, c161, e111; the order to not proceed with redistribution of land can be found in Venustiano Carranza, *Plan de Guadalupe. Decretos y acuerdos 1913–1917* (México: Secretaría de Gobernación, 1981), 51.

14. Friedrich Katz provides a brief and brilliant pioneering study of the massive return of these estates in *The Secret War in Mexico: Europe, the United States, and the Mexican Revolution* (Chicago: University of Chicago Press, 1981), 287 and ff.

15. Declaración of Departamento de Verificación de la Propiedad, 1916, AGN, FG-R, c167, e2, and e3.

16. Romana Falcón, *La semilla en el surco. Adalberto Tejeda y el radicalismo en Veracruz, 1883–1960* (México: El Colegio de México, 1986), 89–93.

17. Proyecto de un antiguo empleado de la fábrica, 7 April 1916, AGN, FG-R, c6, e5.

18. Queja sobre la Dirección de Bienes Intervenidos, June 1916, AGN, FG-R, c7, e21.

19. Concerning the confiscated house given to the Casa del Obrero Mundial, 19 October 1915, AGN, FG-R, c17, e14; January 1917, Ibid., c61, e31 and 32, January 1917; Lists of seized houses in the Federal District, January 1916, Ibid, c162, e8.

20. Romana Falcón, "Los orígenes populares de la revolución mexicana de 1910? El caso de San Luis Potosí," *Historia Mexicana* 29:3 (1978): 222–227; Archivo Histórico, Secretaría de la Defensa Nacional (hereafter cited as AHSDN), índice elaborado por Luis Muro, 6 May 1911, expediente (e)XI-481.5/249, ff.1–7; 26 May 1911, Ibid., ff. 39–42; Rafael Cepeda, "Copias de documentos de mi archivo personal sacados por mi secretario particular el culto escritor potosino Don Juan del Tejo en el año de 1917." AJB, cV/12/ff.68–111 (123.3).

21. "Actas levantadas por el juez auxiliar de la hacienda de La Concepción," 3, 6, 12 June 1913, anexas a reporte de Wilson a Stronge, 16 July 1913, British Public Record Office, London (hereafter cited as PRO), Foreign Office (hereafter cited as FO) 204, volume (hereafter cited as v.) 211, 271/13; Marijose Amerlink, "From hacienda to ejido: the San Diego de Rio Verde Case" (Ph.D. diss. State University of New York, Stony Brook, 1980), 238 ff.

22. 9 September 1914, AGN, FG-R, c23, e80, f6; Nolan to Foreign Office, 24

August 1914, PRO, F0204, v.444, number (hereafter cited as n.) 492; Jesús Silva Herzog, *Comprehensión y crítica de la historia* (México: Colección Cuadernos Americanos/Nueva Imagen, 1982), 369; José Vasconcelos, *La tormenta* (México: Editorial Jus, 1958), 277.

23. "Actas levantadas . . ." PRO, F0204, v.221, 271/13; for San Diego, interview with Juan Hernández and Vega en Amerlinck, "Diario de campo", Amerlinck, "From hacienda . . ." 238; these were kindly made available to me by the author.

24. Romana Falcón, *Revolución y caciquismo. San Luis Potosí, 1910–1938* (México: El Colegio de México, 1984), 62.

25. Falcón, "Los orígenes . . ." 216 ff.

26. "Actas levantadas . . ." PRO, F0204 v.221/13; Rafael Montejano y Aguinaga, *El Valle del Maíz* (San Luis Potosí: Imprenta Evolución, 1967), 351. A general discussion of the different kinds of revolutionaries to be found in San Luis Potosí can be seen in Romana Falcón, "Charismo, Tradition and Caciquismo: Revolution in San Luis Potosí," in *Riot, Rebellion and Revolution: Rural Social Conflict in Mexico*, ed. Friedrich Katz (Princeton: Princeton University Press, 1988). 376–417.

27. Vasconcelos, *La tormenta*, 282; AJB, cV/21/ff50–55 (132), Comas to Barragán.

28. Sánchez to Departamento de Trabajo, 20 August 1914, AGN, Ramo Trabajo (RT): c54, e42, f.2. Concerning hunger, see Falcón, *Revolución y caciquismo*, 103–16, 135–37, 153–56.

29. Claim vs. Mexico of Mr. Duff, 9 February 1931, NAW, RG 59: 312.11, D871.

30. Papers related to the restoration of Arguinzoniz's estate: AGN, FG-R, c5, e18; Govea to Carranza, December 1914, Ibid, c77, e58; Ernesto Hocker to Carranza, 1 December 1914, CEHMC, Fondo XXI, Venustiano Carranza, leg. 6863.

31. Watt to General Manager, 17 April 1914, NAW, RG 59: annex to 412.11, T15/92; Tampico Navigation Co. Claim vs. Mexico, 26 April 1912, Ibid, T15/87; 4 May 1912 and 16 February 1914, Ibid., T15/89.

32. A typical request of the Cedillista Jefe de Armas in the region to the administrator of the hacienda ordered him that "as soon as you can forward to me . . . 2000 hectolitros of maize making use for that, of all the carts and wagons that there are in the zone." Week after week, these demands were repeated. Between May and August 1914 only, the Cedillos took 6000 hectolitros of maize, 400 loads of sugar loaf, eight teams of oxen, five cattle, 52 mules, five "fattened cattle," and beans. For various documents regarding the supervision of this hacienda, see AGN, FG-R, c6, e72.

33. Cunningham Investment Co. 58, Draft of Cunningham Investment Co. before the Special Claims Commission, United States of America and United States of Mexico, NAW, RG 59:412.11. D.537.

34. Safe conduct pass of 10 July 1914, AGN, FG-R, c6, e72, fs62; Interview of Amerlinck with Félix Guerrero, in Amerlinck, "Diario de . . .", Amerlinck, "From hacienda . . ." 243.

35. Luis Martínez García (a soldier that fought with Ildefonso Turrubiartes, a close

associate of Cedillo), "Recuerdos de la Rebolución [*sic*] Mexicana," generously provided by Gerardo Velázquez Turrubiartes; Alberto Alcocer Andalón, *El general y profesor Alberto Carrera Torres* (San Luis Potosí: Academia de Historia Potosina, 1975), 67 and 35; Primo Feliciano Velázquez, *Historia de San Luis Potosí. Tomo IV. De como vino la revolución* (México: Sociedad Mexicana de Geografía y Estadística, 1946), 235.

36. *Periódico Oficial*, 11 March 1915; Juan F. Barragán, *Informe rendido por el C. Juan F. Barragán a la Secretariía de Hacienda y Crédito Público sobre la intervención de la propiedad raiz en la Estado de San Luis Potosí* (San Luis Potosí: Esquivel e Hijos, Febrero 1916); the accusation of the hacendado in Espinosa y Parra to Carranza, 9 September 1914, AGN, FG-R, c23, e8.

37. *Periódico Oficial*, 27 March 1915; Falcón, *Revolución y caciquismo*, 134.

38. *Periódico Oficial*, 15 September and 15 November 1915.

39. It is impossible to know the exact number of confiscated haciendas in San Luis Potosí. Judging by the cases that Uniited States citizens reported to their government, 1916 was the year in which most confiscations took place. For 1914 they listed Espíritu Santo, San Dieguito Colony, and a property of Mrs. Sierra; in 1915 no confiscations were reported; in 1916 there were Cunningham Investment Co., Mexican Crude Rubber Co. in Cedral, Mexican Import and Export in Matehuala, Rascón Manufacturing and Developing Co., and San Dieguito Colony; in 1917 Mexican Crude Rubber Co., and Kennedy; in 1918 El Capulín, and in 1920 a property in Cerritos. Sheffield to Secretary of State, 24 December 1926, NAW, RG 59:312.11/9180.

40. Falcón, *Revolución y caciquismo*, 95–120; Departamento de Bienes Intervenidos to Jefe de Hacienda in San Luis Potosí, 13 April 1918, AJB, cVI/25/ff.44–103 (399); Cárdenas to Secretario de. Gobernación, 11 March 1916, AGN, FG-R, c6, e72. The supervisory office compensated Mesón del Toro for two hundred pesos for damages caused during the Constitutionalist occupation. 28 December 1915, CEHMC, fXXI, c64, leg. 7083.

41. Juan F. Barragán to Barragán, 5 February and 5, 30, 31 March 1916, AJB, cV/0/ff.1–90 (47); Juan F. Barragán to Mariano Arguinzoniz, 16 February 1916, AJB, cXVIII/14/f.34–35; and Severino Martínez to Juan Barragán, 1 June 1918, AJB, cVI/25/ff.44–103; Carranza to Dávila, 17 November 1915, CEHMC, FXXI.4; Silva Herzog, *Comprensión y crítica*, 366 ff.

42. One complaint among many was that of the Toranzo Hernández Soberón family, who swore that the supervisor of one of his estates took ten thousand pesos in cattle and machinery. Luis Hernández Toranzo to Barragán, AJB, cVI/15/f.44–45 (316).

43. Juan F. Barragán to Barragán, 6 February 1916, AJB, cV/9/ff.1–90; Apoderado de Pedro Barrenechea to Barragán, 6 January 1915, AJB, cVI/8/ff.43–48 (261); Apoderado de Díez Gutiérrez to Barragán, 23 October 1914, AJB, cV/21/ff.50–55 (132).

44. The Villista Tomás Urbina confiscated all of their merchandise and imposed on these merchants a forced loan of ten thousand pesos, but these did not prevent them from returning soon afterward and "monopolizing all of the articles of greatest necessity." Nava to Carranza, 7 December 1915, CEHMC, fXXI, c62, leg. 6897.

45. Juan F. Barragán to Barragán, 30 March 1916, and 17 March 1916, AJB, cV/9/ff. 1–90 (47); Barragán to Carranza, 14 February 1916, AJB, cXVIII/14/f.7 (27–33); Carranza to Lárraga, 7 January 1915, CEHMC, FXXI, c64; Carranza to Dávila, 29 December 1915, CEHMC, FXXI, c63; Franco Verástequi to Barragán, March 1917, cVII/27/f.3 (34–36).

46. *Crónicas y debates*, Tf, II, 178 ff.

47. Escobar to Carranza, 13 August 1914, quoted in Katz, *The Secret War in Mexico*, 289.

48. Apoderado de Soberón to Barragán, 28 September 1914, and correspondence regarding the restoration of the estates of Díez Gutiérrez, 1914–1915, AJB, cV/21/f.50–55 (132).

49. Falcón, *Revolución y caciquismo*, 140 ff; also, vid. supra, 10.

50. Juan Barragán, *Informe rendido*; Carranza to Juan Barragán, 13 January 1916, AJB, cV/16/f.5; Juan F. Barragán to M. Arguinzoniz, 16 February 1916, AJB, cXVIII/14/f.34–35; Nava to Carranza, 7 December 1915, CEHMC, FXXI, c62, leg.6894.

51. Juan F. Barragán, *Informe rendido*; Secretaría de Hacienda to Juan F. Barragán, 22 April 1916, AGN, FG-R, c6, e81; Solicitud de Desintervención de Montezuma, 25 April 1916, and of Pablo Escandón, 22 July 1916, AGN, FG-R, c6, e72; papers relating to the restoration of Presbítero Abraham Cantu's estates, April–July 1917, AGN, FG-R, c298, e6; Carranza to Barragán, 25 January 1916, CEHMC, FXXI; regarding San Diego, Schoenfeld to Secretary of State, 7 June 1927, NAW, RG59 312.11/9219.

52. Falcón, *Revolución y caciquismo*, 121–22.

53. Nava to Carranza, 1 December 1915, CEHMC, fXXI, c62, leg. 6867; Juan F. Barragán to Barragán, 5, 30, 31 March 1916, AJB, cV/9/ff. 1–90 (47).

54. Juan F. Barragán to Barragán, 6 February 1916, AJB, cV/9/f. 1–90 (47); Carranza to Gaviera, 26 August 1915, CEHMC, FXXI, quoted in Falcón, *Revolución y caciquismo*, 119; Expediente sobre la disintervención de las tierras de Arguinzoniz 1916–1918, AGN, FG-R, c5, ff.28 (283).

55. Juan F. Barragán, 30 March 1916, AJB, cV/9/f. 1–90 (47). For a more detailed review of the Arguinzoniz case, see Falcón, *Revolución y caciquismo*, 119–20.

56. Juan F. Barragán to Barragán, 30 March 1916, AJB, cV/9/ff. 1–90 (47), quoted in Falcón, *Revolución y caciquismo*, 118.

57. Poder Ejecutivo, *Circular relativa a la desintervención de bienes incautados*, 12 June 1920. A copy of this document is found in NAW, RG 59: 312.1151, 19 October 1921.

7

Oaxaca

The Rise and Fall of State Sovereignty

Paul Garner

Recent conflicting interpretations of Mexico's history from 1910 to 1920 have highlighted many questions about the essential character of the Revolution. With the so-called revisionist orthodoxy of recent decades now challenged by an eloquent and sustained attempt to restore the popular revolution to the forefront of the debate, the historiographical wheel appears to have come full circle.[1]

The absence of interpretative consensus is particularly noteworthy given that we now have access to a considerable amount of detail of revolutionary activity throughout the Republic, which has highlighted the extent of Mexico's regional (and sub-regional) diversity. In recent decades, regional studies have undoubtedly made the most significant contribution thus far to our understanding of the Revolution. The detailed reconstruction of regional dynamics from Chihuahua to Chiapas has demonstrated that those groups throughout the Republic that rose up in arms to overthrow the dictatorship of Porfirio Díaz in 1910 and 1911 did so for very different reasons and in very diverse environments. Above all, regional perspectives have demonstrated that the form and content of Revolution in Mexico were neither homogeneous nor universal; instead, they have emphasised that the regional response to the Revolution was a reflection of the disparity of regional development during the latter half of the nineteenth century.

The case of Oaxaca certainly highlights that disparity. Precisely because only a limited (and short-lived) political challenge to the Díaz regime emerged from the dictator's native state in 1911, I believe that the best way to analyze Oaxaca's participation in the Revolution is to view local developments as a response to the catalyst of national political crisis—a response necessarily conditioned by Oaxaca's recent history and its social composition in 1910. The broad framework for the analysis of the political conflicts—both within Oaxaca and between Oaxaca and the national Revolution—is provided by the Oaxaca Sovereignty Movement (1915–20), a vehicle for a broad spectrum of both

OAXACA

SIGNOS

CIUDAD Cap. de Estado
CIUDAD Cab. de Distrito
Pueblo, " "
Villa Cab. de Distrito
Villa Cab. de Municip.
Pueblo, " " "
Pueblo
Hacienda
Puerto de Altura
F.C. líneas en estudio

popular and provincial opposition to the form of political centralization that Constitutionalism attempted to impose upon the state after 1915.

As I shall argue, the roster of militants and apologists within the Sovereignty Movement included groups holding contradictory views. It encompassed both those who opposed Constitutionalism because they were conservative "reactionaries" as well as those whose affiliation to the Revolution—as was the case with many so-called major or minor Revolutionary movements in Mexico—was founded upon the protection and promotion of local, community, and regional autonomy, threatened by the imposition of an encroaching, alien, and central authority.[2] The constituency and social base of the Sovereignty Movement was the indigenous peasantry of the Sierra Mixteca and the Sierra de Juárez in central Oaxaca, and its leadership and military organization was based upon peasant mobilization through the mechanisms of classic nineteenth century *caudillismo*—kinship, patronage, and clientelism.

Because popular support for the Sovereignty Movement was rooted in the history and character of *sierra* society, in this essay I shall concentrate on the dynamics of the Revolution in the *sierras* of Oaxaca (and the relationship between the *sierras* and the state capital) rather than on the details of revolutionary activities in the other geo-political regions within the state (the Central valleys, the Pacific Coast, and the Isthmus of Tehuantepec). Each of these regions produced significant revolutionary mobilizations, especially in 1911–12, but I would argue that they were peripheral to the central issue of valley/*sierra* conflict at the core of the Sovereignty Movement.[3]

It is important, therefore, to emphasize the extent to which the Sovereignty Movement followed clearly established nineteenth century precedents: first, the staunch defense of federalism by the political elite—Oaxaca's sovereignty had been proclaimed on three previous occasions (1823, 1858, and 1871); and second, the influential role of *caudillos* from the Sierra Juárez to the northeast of the state capital, particularly since the 1850s.[4]

In this essay I shall concentrate on the circumstances that determined the resurgence of these political forces and the ultimate fate of the Sovereignty Movement's principles and protagonists during the Revolution. I argue these points: (a) that the political tensions generated throughout Mexico as a result of the impact of the social and economic transformations of the last decades of the Porfiriato were present in Oaxaca, but that they were insufficient to undermine the authority or unity of the provincial political elite (except for a brief period in 1911–12); (b) that the Sovereignty Movement was the manifestation in Oaxaca of a political process initiated throughout Mexico by the collapse of the Porfirian regime in 1911, which resulted in emasculation of central political authority and in turn stimulated regional and provincial autonomy; (c) that Constitutionalism, the faction which emerged triumphant in the civil war after 1914, had not only found few converts in Oaxaca before 1920, but had proved largely impotent; and (d) that despite the conspicuous failure of Constitutionalism, the Sovereignty Movement could hardly be said to have achieved a resounding victory in 1920.

Oaxaca in 1910

On the eve of the Madero Revolution in 1910, Oaxaca appears at first glance to have been a provincial sanctuary of the *pax porfiriana*. Superficially, very little appeared to have changed during the course of the nineteenth century. An overall picture of the structure of provincial society is elusive, in view of the extensive subregional variations (whether in terms of climate, demography, or history), and the lack of solid historiography.

At the risk of generalization, it appears that the limited commercialization of agriculatural production had meant only a limited evolution (still less destruction) of systems of land tenure and peasant production prior to the Revolution. As a consequence, the agrarian conflicts between *hacienda* and *pueblo* to be found in neighboring Morelos were largely, although not entirely, absent.[5] Agrarian tensions certainly existed throughout the state and gave rise to agrarian movements, particularly in the region of Tuxtepec/Ojitlán and Jamiltepec, on the geographical periphery of the state. Yet most conflicts centered upon atavistic rivalries between *pueblos* over long-standing territorial disputes, which in themselves were insufficient to generate (and, indeed, incapable of generating) a sustained agrarian movement.[6] In other words, despite the alliance with Emiliano Zapata in 1915, and despite the importance to the Sovereignty Movement of pueblo-based peasant militias, the *soberanistas* were not, for the most part, at least, *zapatistas* motivated principally by agrarian demands.[7]

Similarly, because of the low levels of capital investment, and the slow and, above all, uneven pace of urbanization and industrialization in the state, only a limited urban middle class existed (and even less of an urban proletariat), which might collectively have sought broader access to political participation denied by the Porfirian regime (as has been suggested as an important factor in revolutionary/*maderista* mobilization and leadership in Sonora.[8] This may well explain why there were few Constitutionalist sympathizers in Oaxaca. However, we must be wary of perpetuating the traditional image of Oaxaca on the eve of the Revolution as a stagnant, provincial, backward state, a society characterized exclusively by low levels of population density, literacy, and life expectancy, and high levels of ethnicity, poverty, and subsistence, unaffected by and resistant to Porfirian development. Recent research has confirmed that there had been substantial growth in the mining industry and the commercial exploitation of coffee, cotton, and tobacco in Oaxaca in the period 1890–1907.[9] But we now know that growth had occurred mostly on the geographical fringes of the state, especially the northeast on the border with Veracruz, on the Pacific Coast, and particularly on the Isthmus of Tehuantepec.[10] In these regions, the response to the Madero Revolution in Oaxaca was most vociferous.

Elsewhere in Oaxaca, most significantly in the central sierras and the city of Oaxaca, the economic opportunities provided by the stimulus of the Porfiriato had been actively pursued, and substantial profits, particularly in mining, had been made. But this economic change does not appear to have made a profound impact on the structure and organization of provincial society.[11] If we accept that a correlation existed between profound economic/social transformation and support for the Madero Revolution in 1911, we can perhaps begin to explain why support for Madero in these areas of Oaxaca was less than enthusiastic.

In the absence of clear evidence (we await the microhistory of the Porfiriato in Oaxaca), we can at this stage only identify the obvious paradox of a state that was an active participant in and enthusiastic apologist for the Porfirian regime, but which appears not to have suffered the political consequences of the limitd impact of Porfirian modernization.

An examination of what we know so far about the composition of the local elite may provide a clue. Although recent evidence has identified the growth in Oaxaca of export-oriented development, especially during the last decade of the Porfiriato, this appears not to have fragmented the unity of the political elite in the city of Oaxaca. If anything, the development seems to have consolidated and confirmed its identification with the Díaz regime. There is evidence, for example, that the post-colonial distinction between the *hacendados* in the Central valleys, hardly a "rural elite" given the notorious weakness of the hacienda in Oaxaca, and the capital's political classes, the miners, merchants, and professionals who had persisted throughout the nineteenth century, had been reduced as a result of the speculative opportunities presented by the Reforma and by the investment opportunities—albeit limited—provided by the Porfiriato. On the eve of the Revolution, prominent miners and merchants had certainly considered rural property worthy of investment.[12]

The members of this provincial oligarchy (the *vallistocracia* as they are referred to in Oaxaca) had thus been the promoters and beneficiaries of the limited export-oriented expansion during the last decade of the nineteenth century, which was symbolized by the arrival of the Puebla-Oaxaca railway (Ferrocarril Mexicano del Sur) in 1892 and had thereby strengthened their identification with the Díaz regime. Evidence of this high degree of compatibility or identification comes from the correspondence between Díaz and members of the provincial eilte, who sought and often received extensive favors and patronage.[13] In return, Díaz maintained a particularly keen interest in, and tight control over, all political appointments in Oaxaca, and he frequently used loyal *oaxaqueños* at all levels of the Porfirian bureaucracy throughout the Republic.[14]

As Madero discovered for himself when he visited Oaxaca on the presidential campaign trail in December 1909, despite a nucleus of political opponents organized in the Asociación Juárez since 1901, Oaxaca was hardly seething with vocal opposition seeking the violent overthrow of the dictatorship. A degree of political disaffection, and, consequently, of opposition activity did indeed exist, but was directed exclusively against state governor Emilio Pimentel rather than against the Díaz regime. And Díaz himself, who was, of course, a native *oaxaqueno* was rarely, if at all, the focus of discontent. Expressions of this personal loyalty to Díaz could assume some rather confused forms, and often clearly misunderstood the political realignments and conflicts taking place outside the confines of Oaxaca. In April 1911 a collective tirade from irate *oaxaqueños* against the state governor finished with the following exhortation: "¡Viva Oaxaca! ¡Viva Madero! ¡Viva Porfiro Díaz! ¡No Reelección!"[15].

Despite this high degree of loyalty to Díaz, the response to the national political crisis of 1911 was profound throughout the state. Moreover, it is conclusive proof that, contrary to previously received wisdom, Oaxaca witnessed a considerable amount of heterogenous revolutionary activity in 1911–12. When reviewing this phase of the Revolution in Oaxaca, a clear distinction must be made between the reaction on the geographical fringes of the state and the response of the central valleys and sierras. While violence erupted in the geographically peripheral areas, the state capital and the sierras remained relatively calm.

The Erosion of Constitutional Authority (1911–15)

Two themes dominate the history of the Revolution in Oaxaca before the Declaration of Sovereignty in June 1915. On the one hand, the progressive erosion of the political legitimacy of the constitutional authorities within the state, and, on the other, the deterioration of the relationship between the authorities in Oaxaca and the various regimes in Mexico City—whether *maderista, huertista,* or *carrancista.*

The speed with which the regime collapsed was a profound shock for the *porfiristas* who dominated state politics in 1910. None the less, every attempt was made to maintain the appearance of constitutional normalcy. It is indicative of the dynastic political traditions of provincial politics in Mexico, and perhaps of the weakness of *maderista* political forces in Oaxaca, that the two candidates postulated for the governorship in response to the political crisis of 1911 should be members of the most powerful family dynasties in Oaxaca—Juárez's son Benito Juárez Maza and don Porfirio's nephew Félix.

The machinations surrounding the gubernatorial contest of 1911 were largely insignificant. By May 1911 the political initiative in Oaxaca had clearly passed into the hands of those leaders (*cabecillas*) who had instigated armed uprisings throughout rural Oaxaca. Such activities were widespread, and after 1911 a series of local revolts took advantage of the politiical crisis to settle local grievances, which were either agrarian, personal, or political (or combination of all three).[16] The kaleidoscope of rural responses corresponded to the diversity of environments, and although the roots of each uprising were not unique to Oaxaca, each retained a predominantly local character. As elsewhere in Mexico, the circumstances in which the uprisings took place immediately converted these heterogeneous *cabecillas* into *jefes revolucionarios*. It was precisely the pressure brought to bear by the most cohesive of these rebel militias—the faction led by Ángel Barrios and Sebastián Ortíz from Cuitcatlán and Ojitlán—that led directly to the replacement of the state authorities with pro-maderista sympathizers in 1911, then to the period referred to as the "danza de los gobernadores," and, ultimately, to the short-lived governorship of Benito Juárez Maza (1911–12).

Without dwelling on the narrative of the complex machinations of *oaxaqueño* politics of this period, it must be emphasised that it was to prove impossible for any of the so-called constitutional governors of Oaxaca between 1911–14 to restore political authority. This failure prompted a resurgence of the political forces that had played a secondary role during the years of *maderista* hegemony (1911–12): first, the rump of the *porfirista* elite, who of course had everything to lose from the Revolution and who were given a tremendous boost by the national counter-Revolution led by General Victoriano Huerta in 1913; and second, the resurgence of *caudillismo* in the Sierra Juárez, which led in 1914 to the first serious mobilization of *serrano* militias in Oaxaca since 1876. In July 1914, as had happened in 1876, *serrano* militias overthrew a powerless state governor during a national political crisis and established *serrano caudillos* as the arbiters of the political destiny of the state.

The Ixtlán/*serrano* rebellion of July 1914 has frequently been misunderstood and its importance overlooked. The most common misconceptions involve the attempt to attribute the rebellion to ideological or factional affiliation (*porfirista, huertista, felicista*) with groups outside Oaxaca. But as with so many examples within the revolutionary decade, the adoption of the nomenclature of national movements disguised the true local character of the rebellion. It was, as Francisco Ramírez suggests, a rebellion that was "*localista* in both its inspiration and purpose"[17] Within the Sierra Juárez itself, the rebellion centered on Ixtlán, Lachatao, and their satellite pueblos, whose militias had recently been successfully involved with the suppression of the revolt of their *serrano* neighbors (and bitter rivals) Ixtepeji, which had threatened the state capital more than once during 1912.[18] This intervention enhanced both the cohesion, confidence, and prestige of the *serranos* and elevated their leaders Isaac Ibarra and Onofre Jiménez as defenders of the internal security of the state—a role that would be played more fully within the Sovereignty Movement.

Of more immediate concern in 1914 were the grievances that pushed the Ixtlán *serranos* into rebellion. These included the raising of taxes, the imposition of emergency war contributions by the administration of Governor Miguel Bolaños Cacho (1912–14), supposedly to repel the Yankee invaders in Veracruz. He also threatened to requisition the jealously guarded weapons the *serranos* had been allowed to maintain throughout the Porfiriato as a reward for their loyal service to Díaz since 1876.[19] The acute sense of grievance felt by the inhabitants of the Sierra was also compounded by widespread shortages and a growing famine, which had begun to affect the whole of the state in 1914.[20] It was, in short, a clear re-affirmation of *serrano* autonomy.

Discontent in the Sierra Juárez was mirrored by the disaffection of the *vallistocracia* in the state capital with the Bolaños Cacho administration and, of course, with the Revolution itself. Here the increased taxation was also resented, not to mention the proposed 25 percent reduction in bureaucratic salaries. In addition political complaints increased over corruption, nepotism, and Bolaños Cacho's unconstitutional decision to extend his term of office for two years. Furthermore, the arrests of leading *oaxaqueño porfiristas*, who were now, in the context of national politics of 1913, supporters of Félix Díaz (among whom were the President of the Club Felicista in Oaxaca and later author of the Declaration of Sovereignty José Inés Dávila) and former *serrano caudillos* Fidencio Hernández and Guillermo Meixueiro.[21]

As a representative of both the Sierra Juárez and of the Porfirian political elite, Meixueiro was the ideal conciliator between the *serranos* and the *vallistocracia*, and consequently, a natural figurehead for the rebellion. In early 1914 a representative of the *ixtlaneros* visited Meixueiro in Mexico City and informed him of the decision to rebel. Meixueiro accepted this implicit (rather than explicit) invitation, which allowed him to restore his personal authority and prestige in his native Sierra, which had been damaged as a result of his support for Felix Díaz in the governorship elections of 1911, when community leaders in the Sierra Juárez had made clear their support for Benito Juárez Maza.[22]

The rebellion of 1914, like its successor the Sovereignty Movement, was a coalition of disparate forces and interests representing both the valley aristocracy and the *pueblos* of the *sierras*. The important point to emphasize is that the *serrano* rebellion was certainly not dependent upon the leadership of Meixueiro, and it was only a fragile alliance of convenience. But it would be disingenuous to deny the influence that the old *caudillo* still maintained in the city of Oaxaca, which was a vital factor in the success of the rebellion.

The success of the *Ixtlán serrano* rebellion in 1914, which deposed Bolaños Cacho only days before Victoriano Huerta himself resigned, demonstrated the extent of the damage inflicted in Oaxaca on the fragile structure of Porfirian political centralization by the centrifugal forces unleashed by the Madero Revolution. This was, of course, a national patter. As the central state collapsed, and as civil war intensified after 1914, it became apparent that regional political autonomy had been re-established throughout the country. Once again in the history of nineteenth century Mexico, regional autonomy—or, to give it constitutional dignity, federalism—had re-asserted itself over central authority. This was a principle the Sovereignty Movement was determined to defend and the Constitutionalists equally determined to crush.

Sovereignty vs. Constitutionalism (1915–20)

Historical precedent, the composition of the provincial political elite, *serrano* rebellion, and the centrifugal dynamic of the Revolution made the Declaration of Sovereignty in June 1915 inevitable.[23] Equally inevitable was the clash between the *soberanistas* of Oaxaca and the political and military strategy pursued by the Constitutionalists under Venustiano Carranza. On a national level, Carrancisita strategy after the defeat of Huerta required, and actively pursued, the re-establishment and re-centralization of political control.

With specific regard to the southeast of Mexico, the strategy first required military occupation and the demobilization of rebel troops. These steps were a prelude to the establishment of administrations loyal to the hybrid ideology of Constitutionalism and loyal to the personal authority of Carranza himself. Consequently, young *norteño* revolutionaries who had risen through the ranks of the Constitutionalist army were despatched to Yucatán, Tabasco, Chiapas, Campeche, and Quintana Roo to supervise the creation of pro-Constitutionalist regimes, and the consequent centralization of both political and economic control.[24]

As a result, General Jesús Agustín Castro, who today would be described as an upwardly mobile ex-tram driver from Durango, was appointed *Commandante Militar* and Pre-Constitutional Governor of Chipas in September 1914. Castro introduced to the people of Chiapas a prototype of the program of social and economic reform that would be imposed unsuccessfully in Oaxaca between 1916 and 1920. He established complete control over the executive, legislative, and judicial functions of local government and imposed government by decree.[25] These politico-military missions undertaken by the Constitutionalists after 1914 were strongly resented. Instead of achieving the submission and integration of the southeastern states into the Constitutionalist fold, they provoked intense and prolonged resistance throughout the region.

Already before 1915, and especially in Chiapas, Carranza's strategy in the southeast had been challenged. The Declaration of Sovereignty in Oaxaca not only continued the trend, it constituted the most serious challenge yet mounted in the region, as Carranza himself demonstrated through his early determination to occupy the state and to crush the rebels in Oaxaca.[26] The open military conflict between Constitutionalism and the Sovereignty Movement, through its loosely coordinated militia under the title of *Fuerzas Defensoras del Estado* (State Defense Forces), lasted from August 1915 until the occupation of the city of Oaxaca in March 1916. It is here that most general histories of the Revolution finish with Oaxaca in the belief that resistance had been crushed.[27] The evacuation of the state capital was obviously a severe setback to the fortunes of the *soberanistas*, but it by no means meant the end of the Movement, which survived for several reasons. The first was the failure of the military authorities to establish effective jurisdiction, which in itself was a reflection of the limited resources at their disposal. And the second reason the Movement persisted was its strength and internal resistance, which were given added impetus by the harsh experience of military occupation.

In short, the five-year period of Constitutionalist rule in Oaxaca after 1915 was a conspicuous failure. By 1920 the Constitutionalist authorities controlled only the Central valleys, the Isthmus of Tehuantepec, and the northern part of the Sierra Mixteca in the northwest of the state. Their limited power is evident in the data on the establishment of *municipio*-based property registers: they existed in less than one-third of the 463 *municipios* in Oaxaca by 1920.[28] There is, in addition, evidence which clearly suggests the overall impotence of the military regime. It was reported in late 1919, for example, that the only reason the rebel *serrano* forces had not occupied the city of Oaxaca was because *serrano* leaders were anxious not to prejudice the outcome of the peace negotiations.[29]

The arrival in Oaxaca of the Constitutionalists (known there, as elsewhere, as *con-sus-unas-listas*) in fact heralded a period of political schism and economic depression not witnessed since the wars of the Reforma and Intervention. The evidence from Oaxaca certainly challenges the assertion of Venustiano Carranza's most recent biographer that the regime "resurrected a shattered economy."[30] The report presented to the British Legation in Mexico City in 1919 declared that "the state is in a very bad condition. Cattle have been destroyed, hardly any decent houses are to be seen except those stolen by the Carrancistas: crops have been ruined, farmhouses burnt down, and mines closed . . . even if order were restored now it would take many years before anything approaching former prosperity could be reached." The correspondent's stark conclusion was that the local economy was "hopelessly ruined."[31] As indicated earlier, the establishment of pre-Constitutional government in Oaxaca also had coincided with serious famines and shortages throughout the state, most acutely in 1915 and 1916. Memoirs and contemporary accounts tell a similar story in which the consequences of armed conflict were aggravated by drought, epidemics of typhoid and smallpox, poor harvests, and the refusal of local traders or merchants to accept Constitutionalist paper currency.

Although shortages persisted, the famines of the early years were not repeated. Moreover, it appears that the general economic depression that characterized the Constitutionalist occupation of Oaxaca gave a renewed impetus to economic autarky throughout the state, thus reversing the growth, admittedly weak and uneven, of inter-regional and export trade, which had begun to appear in Oaxaca during the last decade of the Porfiriato. It appears, in fact, that throughout the state peasant producers demonstrated their resilience to civil disturbance between 1915 and 1920 in the same way they had responded to the upheavals of the nineteenth century—they returned to a barter and subsistence economy.

This hypothesis is supported by evidence from the Sierra Juárez, and the Sierra Mixteca, particularly with regard to self-sufficiency in agricultural production. The military authorities assumed that the rebel forces would be starved out once they had taken to their respective hills in 1916; their assumption proved to be mistaken. The sporadic nature of the conflict after 1916 meant that the rank and file of the *serrano* militias returned to their *pueblos* when not on active service. When local production fell short of requirements, other locally produced commodities, particularly ore and livestock, could be exchanged for necessary supplies and equipment. This self-sufficiency and resourcefulness clearly contributed to the internal strength of the Sovereignty Movement and made *serrano* resistance very difficult to eradicate.

The disruption to commerce inevitably meant that special crops geared to the export market, which had been introduced into certain regions during the Porfiriato, declined in sales. Evidence from the coffee plantations on the geographical fringes of the state suggest that commercial exploitation on a larger scale suffered considerably. Even areas where coffee was not cultivated on large plantations but on small family plots, such as certain regions of the sierra where production for the market had not fundamentally altered the pattern of subsistence agriculture, also suffered severe disruption during the upheaval of the revolutionary years.[32]

Economic depression after 1915 also had a detrimental effect upon more traditional industries within the state. The mining industry had been particularly subject to the cyclical depressions of the local economy during the nineteenth century, but by 1900 mining had proved to be the principle beneficiary of the Porfirian boom. The number of registered mining properties in Oaxaca rose sixfold between 1898 and 1909. Although the decline in mining production remains unquantifiable, by 1922 the number of properties registered had fallen by over one-quarter. It must be said that while the decline of mining in Oaxaca had begun before the Constitutionalist years, no evidence exists of a revival before 1920, in contrast to the experience of other regions.[33]

The military authorities gave little stimulus for economic development. An invitation was issued to all "honorable capitalists" in February 1916 to invest in commercial and industrial enterprises in Oaxaca. But the invitation was never accompanied by legislative incentives or initiatives. Apart from the harsh economic realities of the period, Carranza's determination to establish central control over the exploitation of the nation's resources restricted the role the state administration might have played in promoting regional development. Carranza's decree of August 1916 prohibited state governments from issuing laws concerning the regulation of commerce, mining, banking, public lands, *ejidos*, or the exploitation of subsoil deposits. A further drain on local resouces was the progressive rise in the proportion of state taxes that went directly to the central government, from 25 percent in 1915 to 60 percent in 1918. This revenue shift to the central government is an early example of the process by which individual states would become progressively subject to the centralization of economic resources in the post-revolutionary era.[34] The absense of precise information regarding levels of production makes it difficult to quantify the extent to which the local economy had been devastated by 1920; however, it is clear that the damage was extensive. The available evidence certainly indicates that the "great work of reconstruction" promised in the Constitutionalist Manifesto to the Oaxacan People in 1915 was far from complete.[35]

Nevertheless, the initial commitment of individual military commanders to the hybrid ideology of Constitutionalism cannot be questioned. As elsewhere in Mexico, enthusiastic *carrancistas* in Oaxaca in 1915 independently implemented the spirit of revolutionary justice—the establishment of schools, the closure of churches, and the distribution of land. But the populist rhetoric of 1915 and 1916 slowly but perceptibly transformed into a grim authoritarianism once the scale of the task and the strength of resistance were recognized. After 1917 no more revolutionary proclamations were issued by the military authorities in Oaxaca: persuasion was replaced by coercion; spontaneous radicalism by bureaucracy; and idealism by frustration and cynicism. By 1920 the military authorities were in disarray, and the depleted garrisons of Constitutionalist troops were proving unable to stem the resurgence of armed resistance from a heterogeneous collection of rebel groups throughout the state, only loosely united under the banner of state sovereignty.

Paradoxically, therefore, Constitutionalist rule in Oaxaca was both authoritarian and impotent. Not only was the jurisdiction of the Constitutionalist authorities limited and the prevailing circumstances inimical to the implementation of the ambitious program of regeneration envisaged by Agustín Castro, but hostility from all levels of *oaxaqueño* society had been apparent from the first arrival of the División "Veintiuno" in 1915. Apart from the tenacity of the *serrano* resistance, Constitutionalists in Oaxaca complained to Carranza that the attitude of all levels of Oaxacan society to their presence in the state was one of "un desprecio insolente" (an insolent disdain).[36]

This initial hostility was very clearly exacerbated by the rapacity of Constitutionalist military occupation—clearly an important factor in the survival of the Sovereignty Movement. From a purely military point of view, after the initial and intense period of military activity in 1915 and 1916, guerrilla resistance intensified and resources available to the Constitutionalist authorities became scarce, and the conflict deteriorated into an uneasy stalemate punctuated by periodic raids on both sides.[37]

As a result, by early 1917 it was clear that the negotiations and political alliances made by the leaders of the Sovereignty Movement with national political factions held the key to both the character and the survival of the Movement.

This necessarily leads us to an examination of the ideology of the Sovereignty Movement, a question that hitherto often indicated more about the ideological or factional bias of the historian than that of the Movement itself. The ideological foundations of *soberanismo* have always been subject to intensely partisan speculation. Most historians have concluded that the Movement's prime concern was "the re-establishment of the Porfirian order." Accordingly, they have emphasised the personal association of the Movement's original political leaders with Félix Díaz and the Díaz establishment.[38] Only the protagonists of the Movement have sought to establish revolutionary legitimacy by emphasizing that the Sovereignty Movement established alliances not only with Félix Díaz, but with both *zapatista* and *villista* representatives—in 1915 and 1916 respectively.[39]

There can be little doubt, however, that each of these actions—including the alliance with Félix Díaz—were primarily for convenience. As such they had potential (rather than actual) strategic and political advantages and therefore do not represent ideological affiliation. The logic of these alliances was one of unification against the centripetal forces of a common enemy—Constitutionalism. The notion of an ideological affiliation, therefore, obscures both the internal dynamics of the Movement from 1915 to 1920 and, in particular, masks the internal divisions. The latter were present from its inception, but they became more intense after 1916 and the occupation of the city of Oaxaca by the Constitutionalist forces.

The first significant repercussion of the evacuation of the city of Oaxaca was to weaken the influence of the *vallistocracia* over the destiny of the Movement. Thus after 1916 the Sovereignty Movement was more identified with *serrano* interests than had been the case in 1915. Second, the evacuation of the state capital in 1916 had led to the establishment of two centers of authority within the Movement, one in the Sierra Mixteca with the administrative "capital" in Tlaxiaco, and the other in the Sierra Juárez with military "headquarters" in Ixtlán. This geographical separation reflected a growing political schism, which became more acute during the course of the conflict. Third, geographical divisions accentuated the ideological division between the two wings of the Movement as well as within its leadership. The issue that most clearly defines these divisions is the attempt to find a *modus vivendi* with Constitutionalism after 1917.

The leadership of the Sovereignty Movement in the Sierra Mixteca remained resolutely opposed to negotiations with the Carranza regime, and they were consistent in their loyalty to the political ambitions of Félix Díaz. In the Sierra Juárez, the leadership was always more conscious of linking the cause of Sovereignty to the national wave of anti-Carrancismo, which had been manifest in the Convention of Agauscalientes in 1914.

Although negotiations had been proposed in 1917 by the *serrano* leadership in the Sierra Juárez, it was the failure of these negotiations that frustrated and angered the new generation of *serrano* leaders, whose authority within the *serrano* community had developed since the political crisis of 1911 and particularly during the resistance to Constitutionalist military occupation. These aspiring *caudillos*, in particular Isaac Ibarra and Onofre Jiménez, openly claimed an ideological affinity with Constitutionalism. But although this spirit of fraternity and compromise with their former enemy in large part resulted from the recognition of the growing national legitimacy of Constitutionalism after 1917, it is arguable that the origins, aspirations, and political vision of Ibarra and Jiménez made their alliance with Constitutionalism in 1920 not only expedient, but logical.

From the pages of his memoirs, Ibarra emerges as a "self-made man," an entrepreneur with no formal professional qualifications and few kinship ties with the *serrano* elite. He had left his native Lachatao in the Sierra Juárez to seek his fortune in Mexico City just two years before the outbreak of the Revolution in 1910. This background placed him more in line as a *carrancista* than as a *serrano* rebel.[40] Whether Ibarra has distorted his personal history for the sake of claiming revolutionary legitimacy must be open to question, but it is interesting to note that in his memoirs he omits mention of the letter he and Jiménez wrote to Carranza in April 1917 in which a clear attempt was made to emphasise the uniformity of interest and aims that both Constitutionalism and the *serrano* resistance shared. They pointed out that, among other things, both movements respected the 1857 Constitution and condemned its abuses, and they desired to return to constitutional order "so that the people can begin to savour the fruits of the Revolution."[41]

The simmering conflicts and tensions within the leadership of the *serranos* (and of the Sovereignty Movement as a whole) were brought to a head in 1919: Meixueiro was removed as commander of the Sierra Juárez Division and replaced by Ibarra. It was Ibarra who signed the treaty of San Agustín Yataraní in May 1920 that brought the Sovereignty Movement to an end. The terms of the treaty appeared to be extremely favorable to the *serranos* and a vindication of the principles of the Sovereignty Movement. The local military authorities, who had recently supported Álvaro Obregón's coup against Carranza, declared that "they recognize the movement that the Sierra Juárez has sustained until today, and as such they are prepared to allow the forces of the Sierra to control the politics of the state." This triumph appeared to have been confirmed by the declaration by the provisional state legislature that Oaxaca "will be ruled by the Political Constitution of 1857." However, as a result of pressure from President Obregón, a decree was issued less than three weeks later recognizing the Constitution of 1917.[42]

This apparent betrayal of the constitutional principles of the Sovereignty Movement was symptomatic of the long-term political prospects of both the Movement and its protagonists. Although *serrano* leaders such as Ibarra and Jiménez may arguably be included in the new generation of revolutionary *caudillos* broadly sympathetic to the social and economic goals of the triumphant revolution, and although they were to enjoy presidential patronage after 1920, it became clear that the resumption of regional autonomy manifest in Oaxaca through the restored hegemony of *caudillismo serrano* would eventually be consumed by post-revolutionary political and economic centralization.

The Fate of the Sovereignty Movement

The survival of the Sovereignty Movement between 1915 and 1920 should not be misinterpreted as a victory. In spite of the maintenance of a constitutional federalism as a fundamental principle of the post-revolutionary political system, the centralist tendencies in political organization and party structure slowly, but inexorably, eroded the regional autonomy that flourished in various forms throughout the Republic between 1910 and 1930. Because of the institutional weakness of the presidency in the period 1920–30, both Obregón and his successor Calles were forced to rely upon, and to foster, alliances with a heterogeneous group of regional *caudillos*. As a result, the *caudillo revolucionario* dominated the politics of the era. But from 1929 onward with the foundation of the Partido Nacional Revolucionario, regional political movements began to be incorporated into a national party.

This national pattern was reflected in Oaxaca. Obregón was careful to cultivate the support of the new *caudillos serranos* who had emerged during the course of the revolution to control the state. This arrangement was mutually beneficial: it allowed the state's political leaders to consolidate their political power and economic interests; it also secured the loyalty of Oaxaca to the Obregón and Calles administrations, which were faced with open rebellion throughout the 1920s.[43]

Direct *serrano* control over the governorship came to an end before 1930, but the influence of *caudillismo* in the Sierra Juárez continued for at least another decade. By the mid 1940s, however, the basis upon which *caudillismo* had flourished within the region since the 1870s had been seriously and irrevocably undermined. Ironically, it was the new generation of *serrano caudillos* who were partly responsible for implementing policies that not only restructured social relations within the village but also destroyed the political autonomy and the former prosperity of the region.[44]

In the Sierra Juárez and throughout Mexico in this period, the central government established local committees of the central party of the state, federalized municipal schools, and extended centralization of fiscal control. There were three basic purposes for these reforms. First, the political purpose was to subvert the authority of regional *caudillos* (and their subordinate *caciques*) by establishing political office within the party apparatus as the seat of political power.[45] Second, the rural school program was designed to educate, secularize and generally "modernize" life within the serrano communities as a means of undermining traditional deference to the village elders, the local priest, and the *caudillo*. This would also undermine such community institutions as the *tequio*, (the obligation of each member of the community to provide reciprocal and communal labor) and thus provide a more mobile labor force. Finally, in terms of fiscal policy, the resources available to the individual states within the federation would clearly be reduced by the increased proportion of revenue that would go directly to the central government rather than to the state treasury.

To judge from the limited evidence available from the specific region of the Sierra Juárez, political integration into the national party apparatus, and greater economic integration into domestic and international markets after the recovery of world commodity prices toward the end of the 1930s, dealt a severe blow to community cohesion and resistance as well as precipitating migration on a large scale. As a result, the complex infrastructure of kinship, commerce, and patronage, which was a prerequisite of the development and maintenance of *caudillismo serrano* prior to the revolution, became fragmented.

In recent decades the Sierra Juárez has been effectively excluded from either state or federal development policies and investment; in fact, much the same could be said for Oaxaca within the context of Mexico. Contemporary statistics indicate that relative to the rest of the Republic, Oaxaca has received only limited benefits from the post-revolutionary economic boom. Quantitative analysis of federal expenditure and social change and the creation of "poverty indices" based upon levels of illiteracy, sanitation, diet, urbanization, and acculturation have highlighted Oaxaca's contemporary plight. For example, per capita expenditure on the inhabitants of the Federal District (Mexico City) during the 1970s was nineteen times the amount spent on the average *oaxaqueño*.[46]

Some of those oaxaqueños who have survived the decade 1910–20 have concluded, somewhat bitterly, that the state has been punished for its support of what has been perceived as the wrong side in the revolution.[47] Given the process of political and economic centralization since the revolution, the advocates of regional autonomy were perhaps bound to be heard as voices in the provincial wilderness. Thus the roots from which the Sovereignty Movement had grown—the political equilibrium between individual states and the federation and the hegemony of the *caudillo serrano* within state politics—were slowly but inexorably eradicated. Far from being isolated from the upheaval of the period 1910–20, the revolution in Oaxaca had a profound and conspicuous impact. It must also be emphasised that the process of transformation had barely begun before 1920.

NOTES

1. I refer, of course, to Alan Knight's *The Mexican Revolution*, vols 2 (Cambridge 1986).
2. See Knight, especially vol. 1, pp. 115–27, for a discussion of the role of *serrano* movements within the revolution, many of whose characteristics were shared by the Sovereignty Movement.
3. For details of this heterogeneous revolutionary activity in Oaxaca in 1911–12, see Francisco Alfonso Ramírez, *Historia de la Revolución Mexicana en Oaxaca* (Instituto Nacionaal de Estudios Históricos de la Revolución Mexicana, 1970); Victor Raul Martínez Vasquez, ed., *La Revolución en Oaxaca 1900–30* (Instituto de Administración Pública de Oaxaca, 1985), especially the chapter "Génesis y Desarrollo del Maderismo en Oaxaca (1909–12)," by Héctor Martínez Medina; Francisco José Ruiz Cervantes, *La Revolución en Oaxaca: El Movimiento de la Soberanía (1915–20)* (Fondo de Cultura Económica, 1986); and P. Garner, *La Revolución en la Provincia: Soberanía Estatal y Caudillismo en la Montañas de Oaxaca* (Fondo de Cultura Económica, 1988), especially chapter 2, "La Revólución de Madero 1910–11."
4. The nature of *caudillismo* in the Sierra Juárez and its influence on nineteenth-century politics in Oaxaca is discussed in Garner, "Federalism and Caudillismo in the Mexican Revolution: The Genesis of the Oaxaca Sovereignty Movement," *Journal of Latin American Studies* 17:1 (1985): 111–33.
5. Ronald Waterbury, "Non-revolutionary Peasants: Oaxaca Compared to Morelos in the Mexican Revolution," *Comparative Studies in Society and History* 17:4 (1975): 410–42.
6. See, for example, the request from the pueblos of Itundujia and San Andrés Cabacera Nueva, in the Sierra Mixteca, to Porfirio Díaz in January 1911 for a solution to

"cuestiones limitrofes de terrenos" with Yosondua and Santa María Yolotepec. Colección Porfirio Díaz (hereafter cited as CPD) Legajo XXXVI, doc. 1195.

7. Here, too, there were exceptions: Gaspar Allende Avellanes, a militant in both the *maqonista* Partido Liberal and the Sovereignty Movement, declared that many *soberanistas* in Oaxaca sympathized with Zapata's *agrarismo*; quoted in Ramírez, op. cit., 190.

8. Héctor Aguilar Camín, "The Relevant Tradition: Sonoran Leaders in the Revolution," in *Caudillo and Peasant in the Mexican Revolution*, ed. D. Brading (Cambridge, 1980), 92–94. The evidence indicates that any political protest generated among the small urban middle classs in Oaxaca during the latter years of the dictatorship was reformist, dilatory, belated, and, most significantly, never critical of Díaz himself; Martínez Medina, op. cit, 157. Whether this constitutes a "precursor" movement in Oaxaca must remain open to question.

9. See F. Chasen, "*Oaxaca: Del Porfiriato a la Revolución 1902–11*" (Ph.D. diss. Universidad Nacional Autónoma de México, 1986).

10. The Isthmus port of Salina Cruz was second only to the Sonoran mining town of Cananea as the fastest-growing urban center in Mexico on the eve of the revolution; Chassen, op. cit., chapters 2 and 4.

11. This is the thesis argued by T. Cassidy, in "Haciendas and Pueblos in Nineteenth-Century Oaxaca" (Ph.D. diss. University of Cambridge, 1981).

12. See ibid., "Conclusions."

13. In response to a request in 1910, for example, Díaz found employment for the great-grandson of his original political mentor in Oaxaca, the Serrano lawyer Marcos Pérez, who had provided Díaz with his first political appointment (as subprefect of Ixtlán in 1858); CPD XXXVI, 1544. There are many other examples.

14. Of the 227 federal deputies in the National Congress in 1886, for example, no fewer than 62 were from Oaxaca; see Chassen, op. cit, chapter 6, "La Organización del Poder Político," 262–334.

15. CPD, XXXVI, 5828.

16. Details of the extent of rebel activities in 1911 can be found in the Archivo Histórico de la Defensas Nacional (hereafter cited as AHDN), XI/481.5/206.

17. Ramírez, op. cit. 157.

18. The details of the Ixtepeji Revolt of 1912, and an explanation of the territorial and political disputes betewen Ixtlán and Ixtepeji can be found in Amado Pérez, *Apuntes Sobre la Revuelta Orozquista-Serrana-Ixtepejana de 1912*, (Ixtlán, 1975); and M. Kearney *The Winds of Ixtepeji: World View and Society in a Zapotec Town* (New York, 1972).

19. R. Pérez García, *La Sierra Juárez*, 2 vols, Mexico, 1956, 2:90–91.

20. Evidence for the hardships suffered by the pueblos of the Sierra Mixteca can be found in AHDN 210; Saul, *Sucesos Históricos de la Mixteca* (México, 1972), 250–58; and for the Sierra Juárez, Isaac Ibarra, *Memorias* (Mexico, 1975), 105.

21. The full text of the Plan de la Sierra can be found in L. Liceaga, *Félix Díaz*

(México, 1958), 342–44. For the careers of Meixueiro and Hernández, see Garner, "Federalism and Caudillismo," 121–27.

22. Ibarra, *Memorias*, 29–30.

23. The text of the Declaration of Sovereignty can be found in Garner, *La Revolución*, appendix 2, 213–16.

24. See Knight, vol. 2, 240–51, for an explanation of Carrancista–Constitutionalist strategy in the Southeast after 1914.

25. Constitutionalist legislation was dutifully published every week in the *Periódico Oficial del Gobierno Pre-Constitutional*, in Salina Cruz (1915 and 1916), and in the city of Oaxaca (1916–20); but its implementation was, at best, only partial.

26. Agustín Castro received orders to establish military headquarters in the Isthmus the day after the Declaration of Sovereignty: J. Márquez, *El Veintiuno: Hombres de la Revolución y sus Hechos* (México, 1916), 88.

27. "Late in 1916 . . . it was clear that oaxaqueño separatism had gone down to defeat"; Knight, vol. 2, 244.

28. The evidence for this comes from the *Periódico Oficial*. A more detailed discussion of the period of pre-Constitutional government in Oaxaca can be found in Garner, "Autoritarismo Revolucionario en el México Provincial: El Carrancismo y el Gobierno Pre-Constitucional en Oaxaca, 1915–20," *Historia Mexicana* 134 (1984): 238–99.

29. The Jefe de Operaciones in Oaxaca, General Gustavo Elisondo, apparently had less than six hundred troops at his disposal; Public Record Office (London), Foreign Office Papers (hereafter cited as FO) 204:532, File "Oaxaca 1919."

30. D. Richmond, "The First Chief and Revolutionary Mexico: The Presidency of Venustiano Carranza" (Ph.D. diss., University of Washington, 1976), 27.

31. FO 204:532 "Oaxaca 1919."

32. For details from the Sierra Juárez, see Kate Young "The Social Setting of Migration: Factors Affecting Migration from a Sierra Zapotec Village in Oaxaca, Mexico" (Ph.D. diss., University of London, 1976), 240–70; for the fate of coffee plantations and *fincas* in Cuicatlán, Teotitlán, Tuxtepec and Pochutla, see *Periódico Oficial del Gobierno Provisional del Estado Libre y Soberano de Oaxaca*, vol. 1, no. 4 (3/6/1920).

33. *Mexican Year Book*, Los Angeles (1920–21), 277–78.

34. *PO* (Oaxaca) vol. 7, no. 9 (26/2/1920).

35. *Manifesto al Pueblo Oaxaqueño PO* (Salina Cruz) vol. 1, no. 1 (16/9/1915).

36. Governor Juan Jiménez Méndez (Castro's successor) complained to Carranza about the numerous obstacles placed in the path of the military authorities by Oaxaqueño society. AHDN 213:ff. 42–8.

37. Details of the conflict after 1915 can be found in Garner, *La Revolución*, chapter 7.

38. José Valadés, *Historia General de la Revolución Mexicana*, vol. 5, 270. This is a view shared by Ruiz Cervantes (1986), 132.

39. Ibarra, *Memorias*, 199; Leovigildo Vásquez Cruz, *La Soberanía de Oaxaca en la Revolución* (Mexico, 1959), 560.

40. Knight, vol 2, 231, highlights the contrasts between the "nationalist, urban, literate, secular, bureaucratic, achievement-oriented" *weltanschauung* of the typical Constitutionalist, and the "Parochial, rural, illiterate, Catholic, personalist and ascriptive" spirit of the typical agrarian or Serrano rebel.

41. Ibarra and Jiménez to Carranza, 18/4/1917 AHDN 212 ff.61–2.

42. Ibarra claims that he had to ask President Obregón which constitution was in force; *Memorias*, 281.

43. Ibarra, *Memorias*, 308–33; Basilio Rojas, *Un Gran Rebelde: Manuel García Vigíl* (México, 1965), 548–645.

44. K. Young, "The Social Setting of Migration," 240–70.

45. An examination of this process at the local level is Antonio Ugalde, "Contemporary Mexico: From hacienda to PRI, Political Leadership in a Zapotec Village," in R. Kern and R. Dolkart, eds., *The Caciques: Oligarchical Politics and Systems of Caciquismo in The Luso-Hispanic World* (New Mexico, 1973), 119–35.

46. J. Wilkie, *The Mexican Revolution: Federal Expenditure and Social Change Since 1910* (Berkeley, 1970), 248–49.

47. Jorge Tamayo, *Oaxaca en el Siglo XX* (México, 1956).

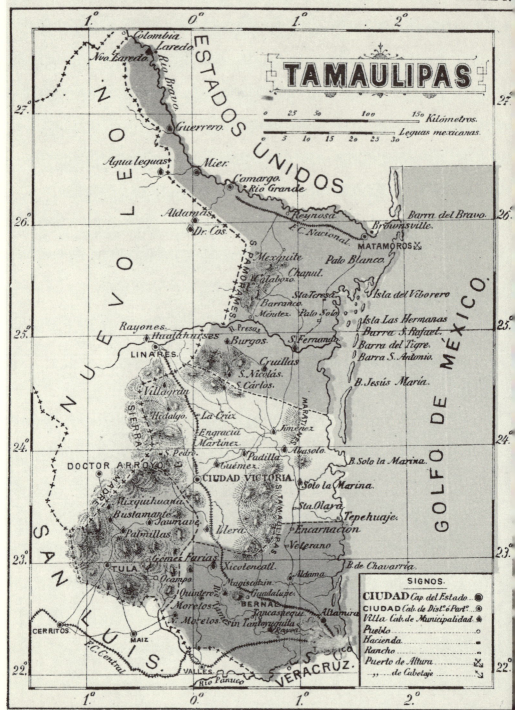

TAMAULIPAS

SIGNOS.

CIUDAD Cap. del Estado .... ◉
CIUDAD Cab. de Dist.º ó Part.º .... ◎
Villa Cab. de Municipalidad .... ◈
Pueblo .... ○
Hacienda ....
Rancho ....
Puerto de Altura ....
   ,,   ,,   de Cabotaje ....

8

Tamulipas

Land Reform and the State

Heather Fowler Salamini

The outbreak of the Mexican Revolution in 1910 not only brought the over-throw of the dictator Porfirio Díaz, but also more importantly initiated the collapse of the central state.[1] By 1914 the governmental apparatus and the army of the Old Regime had been effectively dismantled by the revolutionary armies of Emiliano Zapata, Francisco Villa, and Venustiano Carranza and replaced by regional military rule. The absence of a strong central authority created the conditions for the emergence of regional military *caudillos*, who cemented ties with commercial, landowning, and popular classes to build personal power bases.[2] As products of the revolutionary strife, some of these new caudillos launched programs of social reforms to gain popular support among their own troops as well as the civilian population.

The ascendance to power in the 1920s of the Sonoran popular military lead-ers, General Álvaro Obregón and Plutarco E. Calles, begins the process of the creation of a more centralized and activist state. They would reform the state apparatus so as to consolidate their own political position and under-mine the power of their former commanders, who had become powerful regional military *caudillos*. Since the central state was still relatively weak in the early 1920s, Obregón employed a strategy which has been described as a "balancing act" to play off regional *caudillos* against each other to postpone or avert out-right counterrevolutionary rebellions.[3] In addition, he strengthened his own position of power within the new state by coopting his former military lead-ers as well as oppositional leaders into government service. Raymond Buve, in Chapter 10, has clearly described this strategy in Tlaxcala.

Another political strategy of the Sonoran leaders to counterbalance unco-operative military leaders was the patronization of a new type of regional leader, the civilian *caudillo*. These politicians could challenge the regional political and economic power bases of military commanders. They began to serve as political brokers between the weak central government and the still-armed and partially mobilized peasant forces, newly organized labor organizations, and reemerging commercial and business classes. This new type of regional political broker was usually an urban-oriented, civilian, populist reformer of middle-class origin. Whether we are speaking of Ignacio Mendoza and Rafael Apango in Tlaxcala, Felipe Carrillo Puerto in Yucatán, Francisco Mújica in Michoacán, Adalberto Tejeda in Veracruz, Aurelio Manrique in San Luis Potosí, José G. Zuno in Jalisco, or Emilio Portes Gil in Tamaulipas, they all in some form organized new regional political movements and implemented educational, labor, and agrarian reforms through newly formed state governmental agencies. In addition, they catered to commercial and industrial groups by stimulating capitalist transformation.[4] Thus, they created new regional power bases built upon political patronage of lower- and middle-class groups, and they gradually decreased their reliance on the troops commanded by the military *caudillos*.

First, we will argue that between 1914 and 1934, before the central state was totally reconsolidated, there was a transitionary phase when military and civilian *caudillos* were able to exercise a considerable amount of political autonomy. In states where popular mobilization had not been strong between 1910 and 1920, *caudillos* were able to create embryonic bureaucratic institutions to stimulate a form of state populism and state capitalism. By fostering the formation of popular organizations such as peasant leagues and labor unions and by formulating public policies to encourage agricultural commercialization, industrialization, and foreign investment, *caudillos* manipulated state powers with the goal of consolidating new power bases.

Second, we will argue that military and civilian *caudillismo* must be linked to the transitional role played by state governments in the consolidation of the central state and the emergence of the postrevolutionary elite. For when these *caudillos* lost power, they were "assimilated into the bureaucratic apparatus which they themselves had created."[5] This critical interrelationship between the reconstruction of the central state and regional *caudillismo* develops in the particular context of the postrevolutionary era and effects the institutionalization of the Mexican Revolution. The central state in formation in a country undergoing revolution will be viewed here as the consolidation of the political—military organization by the monopolization of decision-making authority. In a manner of speaking, revolutions are not consolidated until new or tranformed state administrative or coercive organizations are securely established in the place of the Old Regime. Consequently, political leadership and party changes that consolidate revolutionized state organizations may play a central role in revolutionary processes.[6]

This study will analyze how three governors in the northeastern state of

Tamaulipas, César López de Lara, Candelario Garza, and Emilio Portes Gil, built new regional power bases between 1920 and 1928. They constructed bureaucratic mechanisms and fashioned public policies to win the support of lower-, middle-, and upper-class interest groups. Since it is impossible within the limits of this chapter to discuss all their activities, we will concentrate on the governors' agrarian policies. We will also discuss their relations with the central state. It will be shown that Obregón and Calles tolerated activist Tamaulipecan governments, whether reformist or antireformist, within certain prescribed limits as long as the governors remained politically loyal to the regime. Through this "balancing act," the Sonoran leadership impreceptively coopted these *caudillos* into what has come to be termed the postrevolutionary state.

In the first section we will outline how the revolution broke out in Tamaulipas. It destroyed the political apparatus, but it did not ostensibly alter the economic structure of the state. Between 1910 and 1920 attempts to reestablish state powers were fitful, and land reform was all but nonexistent. The second section will demonstrate how two governors in the early 1920s began to construct state mechanisms to implement social and economic policies on their own initiative. First, the Carrancista general, López de Lara, assumed the governorship in 1921 and developed an agricultural program favoring large-scale commercial agriculture while totally ignoring land distribution. After the revolt of 1923, a loyal Obregonist, Professor Candelario Garza, assumed power and reversed the *larista* agrarian policies and proceeded to implement quite rapidly a land reform program without any federal interference. The third section will analyze the rise of another political figure, Lic. Emilio Portes Gil, who launched what appeared to be an ambitious land reform program, beginning in 1925. Within one year the program was dramatically cut back, primarily because of pressure from the Calles administration. The fourth and final section will show how Portes Gil shifted his energies away from the highly controversial issue of land reform to the political mobilization of land reform beneficiaries. Thus, three state leaders constructed bureaucratic mechanisms and political institutions to develop strong agrarian political bases in the 1920s. Their accomplishments would indirectly assist in the consolidation of the postrevolutionary state and their incorporation into the political elite.

The Dismantlement of the Old Regime and the Emergence of the New State in Tamaulipas

Revolution came to Tamaulipas from without, unlike most other northern states states.[7] Major social, economic, and political tensions had not developed to the same degree as in the northern states of Coahuila, Chihuahua, Durango, and Sonora during the regime of Porfirio Díaz. When the wealthy Coahuilan landowner, Francisco I. Madero, publicly announced in the spring of 1910, his intention to run for the presidency with Dr. Francisco Vázquez Gómez of Tula as his running mate, enthusiasm for his candidacy surfaced in Tamaulipas only among certain segments of the Tampico working class, the professional middle class and a few disenchanted members of the landowning class.[8]

When Madero finally launched an armed revolt against President Díaz, revolutionary bands were slow to emerge. It was only in May 1911 that anti-Díaz rebels appeared outside the cities of Tampico, Nuevo Laredo, and Matamoros; but they hesitated to attack as long as there was some chance of a negotiated settlement. Although the workers in Tampico were restless, only in the southwest district of Tula did revolutionary unrest surface. Here, the poor sierra land was highly concentrated in the hands of such well-known *latifundistas* as the Zorrilla and Montemayor families, who were notorious for the exploitation of their peons on the *lechuguilla* plantations. A young rural school teacher, Alberto Carrera Torres, appalled by the manner in which a Spanish administrator maltreated his mestizo peons, was one of the first to join the anti-Díaz opposition as early as 1907. He began to organize armed peasants to rebel against their landlords soon after Madero issued his call to arms. His forces were too weak to launch any major offensive in the region during the Maderista rebellion. However on 21 May 1911, the day Díaz agreed to resign, Carrera Torres swept out of the mountains with his Ejército Libertador de Tamaulipas and seized Tula. He set fire to the public records and then supported the coming to power of an elected municipal government.[9]

The overthrow of Díaz and the triumph of the Maderista Revolution in May 1911 brought little dramatic change to the political system or the economic structure at the state level in Tamaulipas. With the resignation of Governor Juan Castelló, the uncle of Doña Carmen, the state legislature dutifully proceeded to elect a Tula landowner as his successor, who was the personal choice of Vázquez Gómez, Madero's new provisional secretary of foreign relations. Unfortunately, the upper classes never displayed any genuine enthusiasm for Madero, while the workers of Tampico and the small urban middle class were not sufficiently organized to provide him with a political base. As a consequence, when Vázquez Gómez broke openly with the Maderos, the Tamaulipecan elites forced the Maderista governor to resign and chose a well-known Porfirista to replace him.[10]

General Huerta's violent overthrow of the Madero regime in February 1913 likewise caused few dramatic reverberations in Tamaulipas because of the continued domination of landowning and commercial elites. Only Carrera Torres immediately issued a call for an armed revolt against Huerta and the immediate solution of the agrarian problem in March 1913. His agrarian plan demanded the immediate expropriation of the properties of Porfirio Díaz, Félix Díaz, Bernardo Reyes, Iñigo Noriega, and the Terrazas family by military commanders who were to divide them into 10 hectare parcels to be given provisionally to the families of their soldiers.[11] Although Carrera Torres established a grass-roots guerrilla movement composed of rancheros—that is, small and medium landowners, ex-peons, and sharecroppers—he had no time to implement his agrarian law, for he was kept busy with his military activities dislodging the Federalists from the Fourth District.

The Huertista governor, General Antonio Rábago, governed with an iron hand and executed without compunction any enemies of the state. Throughout 1913 the central government was able to retain administrative control of the state through the occupation of the major cities of Tampico, Ciudad Victoria, and Nuevo Laredo; however, President Huerta's control over the countryside was soon to be contested. The most immediate cause for rebellion in Tamaulipas was Rábago's dictatorial rule, which brought about the unification of all anti-Huertista forces in the spring and summer of 1913. Luis Caballero, a prominent landowner from Jiménez and former Maderista Rurales commander, was one of the first to organize volunteer forces.[12]

In April, Carranza appointed General Lucio Blanco military commander of Nuevo León and Tamaulipas and ordered him, with the assistance of Caballero's forces, to attack the strategic border town of Matamoros. Five months after its capture, Blanco, with his young chief of staff, Major Francisco J. Mújica, distributed the first land parcels in Tamaulipas "to representatives of the proletariat and individuals who had been dispossessed of their lands" on the intervened hacienda, Los Borregos, formerly owned by Iñigo Noriega. The second attempt by military leaders to initiate land reform in the state seem to have been primarily politically motivated to win popular support for the Constitutionalists.[13] Carranza immediately forced Blanco to rescind the order and transferred him out of the state for issuing orders without his authorization. When Carranza finally formalized his military organization by creating the Northeast Army under the command of General Pablo González, the Tamaulipan volunteer forces passed under his command. Within months the Constitutionalists forced Rábago to evacuate Ciudad Victoria, upon which Carranza named Caballero provitional governor and military commander of the state.[14]

Caballero set about to reconstitute the state powers at the end of 1914.

Since he was a wealthy landowner, he used his newiy acquired authority to fill political positions with his moderate supporters and he did little to promote actively social reform. Much like other military governors, he was most concerned with the immediate problems of financing his continued military operations and consolidating his own personal political power. He called on the bankers and merchants of Ciudad Victoria to make forced loans to support his troops and authorized the printing of money. He issued decrees to abolish debt peonage and to establish a Maderista type of agrarian commission to revise land titles, divide vacant lands, encourage irrigation, and study the creation of the state credit agency. However, these actions were aimed at countering the more radical agrarian plan of Carrera Torres rather than implementing any comprehensive land reform program. Once the Villistas had been forced to abandon the state after the exhausting seventy-two day battle of El Ebano, Caballero concentrated his efforts on crushing the Carrera Torres movement by capturing its popular agrarian leader. Finally, exhausted and sick from an old festering wound, the guerrilla leader gave himself up to the Constitutionalists only to be ignominiously executed by Caballero in February 1917.[15]

When President Carranza ordered gubernatorial elections in Tamaulipas for the spring of 1917, he had anticipated reestablishing control over local politics from the center. The president was not in the least interested in upholding his often praised principle of state sovereignty. His personal choice for the governorship was General César López de Lara, who had served him faithfully in the Isthmus of Tehuantepec and as governor of the Federal District. Born in Matamoros, López de Lara had first expressed his discontent with the Díaz administration as a journalist for *México Nuevo*. He had embraced the Maderista Revolution in 1910 and then enlisted with Lucio Blanco in 1913 to fight under Caballero. Many ex-Maderista *normalistas*, including Candelario Garza and Emilio Portes Gil as well as labor lawyer Federico Martínez Rojas, regarded him as the strong candidate to challenge the entrenched landowning interests in the state. They reorganized the Democratic Party into the party of social, economic, and political reform and won the support of urban middle-class groups of organized workers in Tampico, Nuevo Laredo, Matamoros, and Ciudad Victoria; and of Francisco Carrera Torres, who could not forgive Caballero for executing his brother.[16]

Caballero was in no way willing to relinquish the governorship to one of his former subordinates. Caballero had an even more distinguished military record than López de Lara, as a staunch Carrancista who had fought against both Huerto and Villa. His popularity in the state extended to the old Porfirian elites, the landowners, municipal officials, as well as to many members of the federal and state military. For his electoral campaign he enlisted the backing of the Liberal Party, the Porfirian party of the landowning elite, and the new anti-Carrancista party, the Liberal Constitutionalist Party (PLC),[17]

After a long and bitterly fought campaign, the election was at last held in February 1918 despite political conditions verging on open civil strife. From all indications, Caballero seemed to have captured the popular vote. To prevent the Caballeristas from coming to power, however, Carranza ordered the legislative chamber sealed, while the Senate dissolved state powers and appointed a provisional governor, Antonio Osuña, to restore order.[18] The president had effectively shown that the central government could prevent the election of an anti-Carrancista governor by resorting to the use of force. Even a native son of Tamaulipas with a strong political base composed of the landowning elite and local military supporters did not have the political and military strength to confront the central state. With the dissolution of state powers, it was clear that the Caballeristas had been unable to create a sufficiently strong or broad regional base of support. Part of his failure might be attributable to his unwillingness to implement any social reforms. The only two attempts to launch land reforms by revolutionary generals between 1910 and 1920 had been effectively blocked by the Carrancista leadership. Not until new political forces emerged at the national and regional level would the balance of power in the state begin to shift toward the new urban, reform-based sectors.

The Role of the State in the Land Reform Process under Alvaro Obregón

The consolidation of the central state began to gain momentum in the 1920s after the Sonoran triumvirate had overthrown the autocratic Carranza regime. In order not to alienate the still influential landowning classes, President Obregón had to continually uphold the right of private property. Simultaneously, he needed to weaken the power bases of regional military *caudillos* so as to subordinate or coopt them into the political system. Thirdly, his strong peasant following, which was still in arms in many states, had to be in some way rewarded for its participation in the revolution. How could he satisfy these conflicting interest groups without alienating any of them? Obregón's public statements, made before he assumed office, tried to satisfy all three groups. On the one hand, he explicitly reiterated, when addressing landowner groups, that breaking up the *latifundio* would be a blunder; no good would come of it. In fact, the *latifundio* would need to be preserved to keep agricultural production high. In the same breath, he added that the government must encourage small-scale farming, but not at the expense of the "illogical division of properties." Small-scale farming, he argued, had not yet shown its potential to replace the *latifundio*. Peasant villages must naturally be granted their ejidos in accordance with the principles of the revolution. But what was left unsaid was that he regarded land reform as only one part of a much more comprehensive strategy to modernize and commercialize agriculture through the active intervention of the state.[19]

Although a number of different interpretations of President Obregón's land reform policy have been advanced,[20] Hans Werner Tobler's application of the Gramscian concept of "catastrophic equilibrium" and "harmony" between capital and labor appears most convincing. When Obregón spoke of the "social equilibrium" and "harmony" between capital and labor, this was a manner of saying, argues Tobler, that the less social conflict the greater the possibility for consolidation of the bourgeois state and the growth of capitalism. According to this view, Obregón used land reform as a political tool primarily in regions where agrarian rebellion had broken out between 1910 and 1920. In other regions, where the population was still 70 percent illiterate and the rural bourgeoisie was still weak, he curried the support of the landowning classes. Thus Obregón took pains neither to speak of a break with the past nor to make use of a radical interpretation of Article 27 of the Constitution. The traditional peasant institution, the ejido, would be recreated, but it would coexist alongside the private farm. Only in the Zapatista and Villista strongholds and in Yucatán and Veracruz, where agrarista governors had taken the initiative to implement their own land reform programs, did the Obregón administration grudgingly accept major land distribution, although roadblocks were constantly placed in the governors' way. On the other hand, in the northern states of Sinaloa, Sonora, Coahuila, Nuevo León, and Tamaulipas, where any form of communal ownership was viewed as anathema, land distribution was negligible.[21]

Tobler's approach can also shed light on the interrelatonship between the federal and state bureaucracy in the land reform process. He has contended that, by the 1920's, the army more often acted as a counterrevolutionary force reenforcing land tenure patterns rather than as a revolutionary force. There can be no doubt that many military *caudillos* did not desire to carry out land reform primarily because it would have endangered their own land acquisitions. For example, Obregón did little or nothing to challenge the antireformist positions of Generals Enrique Estrada, Guadalupe Sánchez, and César Lopez de Lara in Michoacán, Veracruz, and Tamaulipas, respectively, or to discourage their close ties with landowner groups. Obregón intervened very little in regional affairs in the area of land reform as long as the governor or military commander remained loyal to the administration; but when the president did intervene it was as often on the side of the landowner or the foreigner as on the side of the peasant. His ultimate objective was to balance the various contending regional *caudillos* who were still powerful enough to challenge his authority while at the same time upholding large-scale agriculture.[22]

If Obregón permitted state authorities to interpret the need to distribute land according to their own political wishes, how did governors manipulate state powers in the 1920s to implement their land reform program? What organs of the state government did they establish and employ for the implementation of their policies? Were these organs different from those used by the central government, and if so, how did the latter respond to their programs? What new political organizations did they create to mobilize a peasant base of support? Did tension arise between the central and state governments over the independent stance of the latter, and how was it resolved? Let us turn back to the state of Tamaulipas.

By the spring of 1920 General López de Lara astutely realized that President Carranza's policies of *continuismo* in the upcoming presidential elections were not viable, given the widespread popularity of Alvaro Obregón. As a consequence, when Obregón launched the Agua Prieta revolt against Carranza, López de Lara quickly joined the rebellion, more out of political expediency then ideological conviction. In this manner, he secured for himself once and for all the governorship of Tamaulipas, which had eluded him for four long frustrating years. In the gubernatorial elections of February 1921 he ran for all intents and purposes unopposed because he was supported by the Obregonistas. Once he was installed as constitutional governor, he began to consolidate his own regional political base built on the support of state bureaucrats, business and commercial leaders, landowners, and certain key segments of the Tampico working class.

López de Lara's primary political objective was to cement an alliance with the traditional landowning groups and emerging commercial interests to build a strong rural and urban political constituency. He also repeatedly turned to local civilian and military authorities to prevent the emergence of any popular political rival, in particular his former supporters Emilio Portes Gil and Candelario Garza. At the same time, he displayed a singular lack of moral integrity in awarding licenses for gambling houses to his close personal associates. He thus assured himself a strong clientele among the commercial classes in the border towns and in Tampico. In addition, he continued to protect and defend the moderate but extremely powerful stevedore union, the *Gremio de Alijadores*, by providing them with funds to buy out the American firm, E. M. Rowley, which had exercised a monopolistic control for many years over

stevedore contracting. However, he was unable to extend his political patronage to the Tampico oil workers, who resented his refusal to permit them
to organize independent unions.[23]

General López de Lara's views on agrarian problems were rooted in the
Liberal ideology of the Porfiriato. He believed there was no need to attack
the institution of *latifundismo* in Tamaulipas because of the scarcity of population. Since the rural population only numbered 150,000, and the density
of the population was no more than two persons per square kilometer, he
argued that "no agrarian problem exists in the state." Adhering to the Liberal tradition, he promoted the creation of small properties through the state's
purchase of private property, the distribution of federal lands, and the encour-
agement of colonization projects.[24]

The governor blatantly refused to attack the *latifundio* system, in a state
where 552 or 1.7 percent of the landowners still owned 51 percent of all
private land. Almost three-quarters of the rural populations still lived on haciendas, according to Frank Tannenbaum. Thus, he collaborated closely with
the landowning classes in his quest to foster commercial agriculture. In particular, he cultivated good relations with the Manuel González family, the
scions of the state, which owned over 400,000 hectares of land. In 1921, the
state signed a contract with Guadalupe Fernández de González, wife of the
ex-president, to rent fifty irrigated hectares of her Hacienda Tamatán, lying
outside Ciudad Victoria, for eight thousand pesos annually to build a state
agricultural school. A year later he purchased the entire hacienda for 138,377
pesos, including its electrical plant which furnished power for the capital. In
Aldama, the state purchased 11,400 hectares of the huge El Cojo Hacienda to
divide up into 150 lots for agricultural colonists. He also encouraged the
Gonzálezes to enter into a lucrative agreement with U.S. investors to sell plots
to American colonists. Señora González was also awarded a state contract to
rebuild another electrical plant at Estación González for the use of the town.
Another example of state financing of small, expensive colonization projects
was the 200,000 peso loan extended to Lic. Miguel Cárdenas, director of the
Companía de Luz, Fuerza, y Tracción de Tampico, to irrigate and divide one
thousand hectares into two hundred five-hectare lots for colonization. The
governor justified his land reform policy by arguing that it was not in violation of the ejidal law but a rather different interpretation of its provisions,
whereby the state government instead of the federal government would be
the land purchaser.[25]

López de Lara employed state funds to stimulate agricultural production so
as to cement his ties with small and medium landowners. He directed the

Department of Development within the Agriculture Department to encourage municipalities to create agricultural committees of "small" farmers to petition for financial aid from the state. The Matamoros committee was singled out for special praise; this was a region where large landowners totally dominated the economy and politics. In the war-ravaged fourth district of Tula, where agricultural and cattle production had not recovered from twelve years of agrarian unrest, the governor tapped the former revolutionary leader, General Francisco Carrera Torres, rather than a landowner to head the new agricultural committee. The general had already distributed land to his soldiers in the form of military colonies after the triumph of Obregón in 1920. López de Lara now offered 100,000 pesos in state loans to landowners and a four-year exemption from rural and urban property taxes to stimulate agricultural production in the region. Clearly, the governor was attempting to woo the state's most powerful cacique into his political camp. Carrera Torres was soon to join the ranks of the wealthy rural bourgeoisie. He became, along with Saturnino Cedillo in San Luis Potosí, the chief monopolist of *ixtle* production under the protection of the postrevolutionary state.[26]

López de Lara's land reform policies seemed on the surface to be in conflict with those of the Obregón administration, for he continually interpreted Article 27 from a states' rights position. He admitted Article 27 did call for the division of *latifundia* and the restitution or granting of ejidos. Yet the right of restitution and the granting of lands were powers invested in the state governments, he argued. What is more, local congresses, he maintained, were responsible for the drawing up of laws to divide *latifundia* and to create small properties because the variations in the quality of the land throughout the republic would make any federal law unjust. He appears to have based his states' rights position on the National Agrarian Commission circular issued in July 1920, which had temporarily given state governments once again the authority to issue provisional land distribution resolutions. It should be noted that his political position was not entirely dissimilar from that espoused by reformist Governors Francisco J. Mújica in Michoacán and Adalberto Tejeda in Veracruz, who both defended their right to carry out progressive land reform programs without interference from the central state.[27]

The governor took other measures which showed his opposition to land reform. He quietly dissolved the Local Agrarian Commission (CLA) within a few months of assuming office, even though the 1921 state budget had allocated ten thousand pesos for its expenses. The explanation he gave for not refunding the CLA was rather comical. The law did not permit any of its members to own more than fifty hectares, and everyone in Tamaulipas is a landowner, he retorted. When he was finally pressured into reestablishing the CLA, he appointed his own lawyer, Lic. Lizardi, and a landowner, Jacobo Martínez, to serve as members. Its only meetings were convened in Lizardi's house. What is more, the governor consistently expelled from the state CNA delegates sent to Ciudad Victoria to initiate the agrarian reform process. The governor refused to allow CLA even to consider the petition of Reynosa residents for lands belonging to the two-million-hectare property of La Sauteña Corporation.[28]

The governor's refusal to implement federal agrarian legislation and his support of only isolated colonization projecs brought him under fire in the Chamber of Deputies in December 1922. Tamaulipan deputies Candelario Garza and Emilio Portes Gil publicly accused him of violation of the agrarian laws, and Secretary of Agriculture Ramón de Negri supported their claims. The most outspoken members of the National Agrarian Commission (CNA), Manuel Mendoza López Schwartzfeger and Tamaulipan representative Ing. Marte R. Gómez joined Antonio Díaz Soto de Gama, the prominent leader of the National Agrarista Party (PNA), in roundly condemning him for obstructing the land reform process. Two congressional commissions had been sent to investigate the governor's agrarian policies, and they had both concluded he had not issued a single agrarian resolution since assuming office. Petitions for land had not been acted upon within the legal time limit; thus, the commissions concluded that the CLA was operating in violation o f Article 3 of the 1921 Agrarian Law. De Negri now called for the Senate to formally censure the governor of Tamaulipas for violation of the laws of 28 December 1920 and 10 December 1921. Although the CNA recommendation to censure López de Lara and other antiagrarista governors was supported by the Agrarian Commission of the Chamber, the motion was withdrawn when Obregón directly intervened. He was acutely aware that he could not alienate the northern governors over the issue of land reform.[29]

The resolve of López de Lara to oppose the distribution of land, to discourage the mobilization of the peasantry, and to continue thwarting the policies of the Department of Agriculture can be dramatically illustrated by events which occurred in the municipality of Hidalgo. Situated just thirty kilometers northwest of Ciudad Victoria, Hidalgo had prospered during the Porfiriato when the building of the Tampico–Monterrey railroad line gave it access to new markets. Its corn haciendas were expanded with the construction of extensive landholdings in the state. During the revolution, Hidalgo landowners, including the Manuel González family, protected their estates by permitting Huertistas and, later, Constitutionalists to quarter their troops on their properties. Despite the relative prosperity of the region, the peasants who worked as sharecroppers or day laborers on the Santa Engracia, San Francisco, La Cruz, Santa Gertrudis, La Diana, and Guadalupe haciendas had experienced no significant change in their material conditions by 1920. In particular, wages were lower than most other parts of the state, averaging between fifty and seventy-five centavos a day.

As we find in many parts of Mexico in the 1920s, the stimulus for mobilization of the rural workers seems to have originated from outside middle-class organizers. In the comunity of Estación de la Cruz, a doctor most probably with links to the Regional Confederation of Mexican Workers (CROM), Luis E. C. Garza; a merchant, Wistario Medina; a schoolteacher, Olivia Ramírez; and others organized two hundred "free" peasants who were *journaleros* and *medieros* working on the surrounding haciendas to form the Mutual Agrarian Union of Estación Cruz, *Union Mutualista Agraria de Estación Cruz*, in 1921. By 1923 the union had affiliated itself with the CROM, which claimed to have organized over a million peasants. The union's goals called for the elimination of the *tienda de raya*, the abolition of onerous labor contracts, espousal of mutualist and cooperativist principles, establishment of colonies, and land distribution. It also advocated the creation of a broad multiclass coalition of peons, farmers, merchants, and professionals to work for these goals.[30]

The efforts of the union to petition for lands of the Hacienda La Cruz, owned by the American Land and Cattle Co., and Hacienda San Francisco, owned by Juan Filasola, as well as the right to farm lands in the Federal Zone of the Río Purificación were continually met with fierce resistance by local and state authorities until well into 1923. Likewise, union efforts to establish other CROM-affiliated local committees composed of small farmers and sharecroppers throughout central Tamaulipas met with armed repression by state authorities. Hacienda administrators refused to employ or rent land to union members, while the rural police, with the active support of the Larista municipal president, arrested its officers. The union was even forced to move its records to Nuevo León for safekeeping. In desperation, Dr. Garza wrote to Deputy Lic. Emilio Portes Gil and President Obregón seeking their assistance against what they termed the obstructionism of López de lara.[31]

When these letters brought no results, union officers traveled to Mexico City in the spring of 1923 to voice their grievances personally to Obregón. Both Portes Gil and the CROM urged the president to uphold the rights of the union and to protest the arbitrariness of the governor. The president felt compelled to take action, despite his reluctance to intervene in the politics of a state where the governor had been his loyal supporter. However, this was a blatant case of disregard of the law. Obregón reprimanded López de Lara for allowing the rural police and the municipal president to carry out such flagrant abuses and called on the governor and the chief of military operations, General Arnulfo Gómez, to provide adequate guarantees. López de Lara impudently replied that the leaders of the union, Luis E. C. Garza and Lt. Col. José Silva Sánchez, were not legitimate peasant representatives but merely agitators. When gentle proddings met with little success, the president dispatched army and CNA investigators to Tamaulipas to check out the union's charges. Once they had been substantiated, Obregón urged De Negri to give Estación Cruz a political category as a congregation so that it could legally petition for a grant of thirteen hundred hectares. Despite the presidential ruling, the community did not receive a political category immediately because of a land conflict with the neighboring community of Ollama. The CLA did not even begin working on the resolution while López de Lara remained in office.[32]

The decision by López de Lara to support the revolt of Adolfo de la Huerta in December 1923 resulted in his ultimate demise. General elation swept the state when he fled the capital, for he had employed military and political oppression to prevent land distribution, squelch labor and peasant mobilization, and repress all political opposition. The political environment changed dramatically when the Permanent Committee of the Chamber of Deputies, presided over by Deputy Portes Gil, appointed Professor Candelario Garza provisional governor. Garza and Portes Gil had turned against the governor when he began to employ autocratic practices and conservative agrarian policies. Although Garza was to play only a transitional role in state politics, serving as a bridge between a repressive and a relatively participatory regime, he set the stage for what was to come. He also initiated the first land reform program within the state.

When Candelario Garza assumed the governorship in February 1924, he immediately took steps to use the executive branch to initiate land reform. First, he exercised his gubernatorial powers to urge the state legislature to raise four unincorporated villages, including Estación Cruz, to the political category of community in order to entitle them to land restitution or grants. In July 1924 a provisional resolution was issued for Estación Cruz, not because of Obregón's intervention in the case but as a result of changes in gubernatorial policies. In addition, Garza actively encouraged agrarian communities to begin petitioning for lands, despite the continued presence of small bands of Delahuertista rebels throughout the state. The former U.S. community of Columbus (Altamira), renamed Cuauhtémoc, submitted the first petition to be officially registered on 17 February, but it was closely followed by thirty-six more within the space of nine months.

Among Garza's priorities was the establishment of a bona fide state agency for the distribution of lands. The CLA was reorganized in April and began surveying lands and distributing them within a month. In June, Columbus received a provisional land grant of 1,508 hectares from the holdings of the American International Fuel and Petroleum Company, despite the company's appeals to the president, who refused to become involved in the decision. Unfortunately, in the case of Columbus, land titles had been researched too rapidly and the provisional resolution affected certain small properties. What is more, although the resolution had granted the minimum five hectares of irrigated land to each beneficiary, it had not set aside any land for housing, a *fundo legal*. As a consequence, the definite resolution handed down by the CNA had to revise the original resolution in terms of the number of properties affected and the amount of land granted.[33]

Another controversial CLA ruling was the case of the community of Santa Engracia located on the Hacienda Santa Engracia in the municipality of Hidalgo. Although Santa Engracia had not been raised to a political category, day workers and tenant farmers had organized a CROM-affiliated Agrarian Union in 1923. Soon after it petitioned for land in the spring of 1924, its owner, Jacobo Martínez, and his friend, Portes Gil, urged the president of the CLA to drop the case and allow Martínez to sell lots of the hacienda to sharecroppers and renters farming his properties. This was not legally permitted. No decision was taken by Garza before the October gubernatorial elections.[34]

During Garza's ten months in office, thirteen favorable provisional resolutions were issued which granted 19,277 hectares (see Table 8.1). However, land distibution was carried out in a rather unprofessional and sometimes extralegal fashion, with the entire administrative process taking sometimes no more than a month. This was not uncommon when the land reform process was first initiated throughout the republic. Thus, the CNA found itself saddled with more controversial resolutions from Tamaulipas which had to be revised or reversed. Yet Obregón seems to have made no effort to intervene or to slow down the land reform process. Governor Garza's reasons for carrying out such rapid reform in the space of a few months seem to have been partially politically motivated. By the spring of 1924 his friend and colleague, Portes Gil, had publicly declared his intention to run against him in the upcoming gubernatorial elections. Garza's desire to build his own independent popular base as rapidly as possible appears to have been the most immediate reason why he pushed for land distribution. However, Garza soon found himself on a collision course with his erstwhile friend, who had already strong labor and middle-class support. Meanwhile, Portes Gil had also won the critical backing of the Orbregón regime's presidential candidate, Plutarco Calles.

The Role of the Stae in the Land Reform Process under Plutarco E. Calles

When General Plutarco E. Calles assumed the presidency in December 1924, he ushered in a second stage in the centralization of the state. His policies were characterized by more stringent efforts to rein in state governors and concerted efforts to institutionalize the popular organizations they had created and patronized. While Calles came to power with support of the reformist Gulf governors and politicians, Emilio Portes Gil, Adalberto Tejeda, Tomás Garrido Canabal, Saturnino Cedillo, and Felipe Carrillo Puerto as well as the most important national peasant and labor organizations, the PNA and CROM, Calles soon began to curtail the power of precisely these populist governors and these social organizations. Calles brought Tejeda into his cabinet, which had the result of neutralizing some of his influence in Veracruz. Portes Gil was to be more peacefully coopted into the Callista machine, since he was of a more cooperative and compliant nature. Without discounting the critical role played by military figures in the Calles regime, Portes Gil would gradually emerge as one of Calles's new civilian advisors, along with Luis León, Dr. J. M. Puig Causaranc, Marte R. Gómez, Luis Morones, and Adalberto Tejeda.[35]

Although President Calles actively pushed for the distribution of over 3 million hectares of land in the first years of his administration, his views on land tenure were even more conservative than those of Obregón. Since his days as governor of Sonora, he had considered Mexico's primary need to be creation of small private properties. He even believed that the division of properties should not only be carried out by the state but also by landowners themselves. For him, the ejido should not even be a permanent institution, but a transitional stage to serve as a training ground for the private property holder. Needless to say, he was adamantly opposed to communal work on the ejido, which he viewed as inefficient. To deemphasize the land reform process, he reorganized the CNA to weaken its autonomy and placed it under his secretary of agriculture, Luis León. The Callista Law of Ejidal Patrimony of 1927, in particular, modified existing agrarian legislation by calling for the replacement of communally farmed ejidal plots with individually farmed ejidal plots. Although he created the National Bank of Agricultural Credit and the Ejidal Bank to provide credit for private property owners and ejidatarios, most of the money was loaned to a mere thousand large landowners, whom the

Calles administration felt could more profitably promote commercial agriculture.[36] Did this shift away from land distribution toward the commercialization
of private agriculture have any impact at the state level? We have shown how
Obregón permitted considerable freedom to governors in their land reform
policies because the central state was still weak. Did the same kind of
relationship exist between Calles and the governors? Let us turn once again to
Tamaulipas to see how his loyal henchman, Porte Gil, implemented agrarian
reform policies.

Portes Gil had come to know Obregón and Calles in 1916 when he served
as a Constitutionalist judge of the Supreme Court in Sonora, soon after he
had joined the Constitutionalists. He had subsequently returned to Tamaulipas
to set up law practice with his chiapaneco law school classmate, Federico
Martínez Rojas in Tampico. Like many lawyers in the booming port, they
began to assist workers in their litigations against the oil companies. His
defense of the stevedores and the petroleum workers helped him to secure a
congressional seat in 1917 for the Tampico district. When Carranza proved
reluctant to pass any labor reforms, Portes Gil joined the more pro-labor
Obregónistas. With the overthrow of Carranza, he was rewarded for his loyalty with the provisional governorship of his native state. However, certain
military leaders, who were eager to retain their lucrative business dealings in
the state, cut short his term in office. This did not perturb the rising
Obregónista who returned to the Chamber of Deputies in 1920, where he
quickly rose to the presidency of the National Cooperatist Party with the
blessing of its strong man, Jorge Prieto Laurens. When Prieto Laurens
spurred the majority of the self-serving Cooperatistas to challenge President
Obregón's choice for the presidency, General Plutarco E. Calles, Portes
Gil resigned from the party to join the Callistas. By the time the ill-fated
Delahuertista revolt broke out in December 1923, Portes Gil had secured
for himself the key post of president of the Standing Committee of the
Chamber of Deputies. In this capacity, he was instrumental in securing the
appointment of his colleague, Deputy Garza, as provisional governor of
Tamaulipas. In the spring of 1924 he formally launched his own political
campaign for the governorship with the creation of the urban, middle-class
reformist political party, *Partido Socialista Fronterizo*, the Socialist Party of
the Frontier (PSF).[37] This party provided him with the political machine to
organize an extensive campaign and to upset Governor Garza in a very controversial election. Upon assuming office in February 1925, he began to mold
a state bureaucracy capable of carrying out his reform programs staffed with
loyal PSF members. It was abundantly clear that Portes Gil had received a

clear mandate from the new president, Calles, who saw in him a loyal and faithful lieutenant.

Porte Gil has placed himself in his voluminous writings alongside the most important social reformers of the 1920s. As a supporter of the urban worker and the peasant he compares his governorship with that of Adalberto Tejeda in Veracruz, Felipe Carrillo Puerto in Yucatán, and Aurelio Manrique in San Luis Potosí. Eyler Simpson referred to him as the governor who pushed agrarian reform farther than in any other state in the republic with the exception of Morelos. In later years, Portes Gil placed himself above all other governors in the state, claiming that he had distributed during his administration all the land that the peasants needed.[38] Are these assessments correct? If so, what was the nature of his agrarian ideology? What kind of postrevolutionary agricultural unit did he favor and how did he intend to mobilize the peasantry? In what manner did he implement land reform in Tamaulipas between 1925 and 1928? What state agencies did he employ to distribte land and encourage agricultural development? Finally, were his policies at variance with those of President Calles? If not, can we find any instances of collaboration between the president and the governor?

Portes Gil was first and foremost a politician rather than a social reformer. Every policy he advocated had a political objective. He can be considered the example par excellence of the new civilian postrevolutionary politician, who emerged in the 1920s by building a political base on patron–client relationship rather than on military ties. Much like Obregón, he espoused "socialist" principles, but he associated them with social harmony among the classes rather than any conception of a socialist economy. He was a fine model of the modern pragmatic politician, who worked within the established rules of Mexican politics, allying himself with such regional strong men as Saturnino Cedillo and Francisco Carrera Torres to achieve political ascendence. In simple terms, agrarian reform was merely one strategy to use state powers to stimulate rural capitalism in order to consolidate his own political position within the new postrevolutionary ruling elite. It is within this context that one must view his agrarismo.[39] (See Table 8.1.)

If one examines Portes Gil's record in the early 1920s before he assumed the governorship, one finds neither a clearly articulated agrarian ideology nor a determination to spur actively agrarian reform policy. His major concern seems to have been to promote the formation of a small farmer class by encouraging rural education, to cater to a few CROM-affiliated peasant groups, and to assist landlords confronting peasant groups, and to assist landlords confronting peasant agitation. He had taken great interest in attacking his polit-

Table 8.1
Land Distribution in Tamaulipas in the 1920s

State Administrations	Petitions	Provisional Resolutions	Provisional Grants (Hectares)	Irrigated Land	Temporal Land	Pasture & Woodland	Beneficiaries	Definitive Grants (Hectares)
César López de Lara								
1921								
1922	1							
1923								
Candelario Garza								
1924	29	13	19,277					
Emilio Portes Gil								
1925	36	34	57,706					5,359
1926	16	17	23,409	1,478	1,215	20,176		17,574
1927	21	19	16,025	869	2,073	13,952		22,713
1928 (Aug.)		30	27,520	939	666	25,915		10,012
Portes Gil Total	73	100	124,660	3,286	3,954	60,043	6,000	55,658

Sources: *Informes*, 1925–28; Emilio Portes Gil, *Raigambre*, 178–94.

ical rival, Governor López de Lara, and publicly accused him of collaboration with *latifundistas* and the upholding of the peonage system. But he had only intervened in a handful of cases when it was in his personal interest. As we have noted, when his friend, Jacobo Martínez, had contacted him for assistance against the agraristas on his Santa Engracia Hacienda, Portes Gil had asked the secretary of agriculture to desist in expropriation proceedings. Martínez had always been "so kind" to his workers and wished to divide up his lands himself and to sell them individual lots.[40] The Agrarian Union of Estación Cruz had won his attention in its efforts to gain the release of its imprisioned leaders. In another instance, an agricultural cooperative pleaded for his cooperation in getting one one of his landowning friends to respect their provisional grant.[41]

Once Portes Gil took office in January 1925, his northern agrarian ideology became more manifest. In his 1926 annual message, Governor Portes Gil declared that the agrarian reform problem could be solved by ensuring agricultural progress of the state and peace of the nation.[42] It was not the monopolization of land by the rural oligarchy which was his chief concern, but rather economic progress and the end of political unrest. Much as the Sonoran leadership, his primary concern was the protection and the promotion of private property. He had no intention of destroying the landowning class or of dismantling the *latifundio* as an economic institution. On the contrary, his interest was in preserving this institution, for he was convinced that large-scale export agriculture was a prerequisite for increased agricultural production. Increased agricultural and livestock production was the key to the state's development, but to his mind, this could only be accomplished if the state collaborated with the landowning classes.

Thus, agrarian reform was limited, selective, and carefully calculated to obtain the most political benefit. What is more he developed a policy of negotiation rather than confrontation with the landowners, which won him high marks among the upper classes. Only certain landowners were directly affected by expropriation, while others were not affected in the least. In addition, a good part of the land distributed during his administration was located in a half-dozen municipalities, so that the largest estates were left in tact. He continually supported the creation of the ejido, but he viewed the institution as a transitory one to be eventually replaced by private property. Let us examine the bases of Portes Gil's agrarian ideology and the reasons why he only implemented land reform in certain parts of the state.

Portes Gil's agrarian ideology was essentially based upon the ideas of his friend and fellow Tamaulipecan, Ing. Marte R. Gómez, who emerged as the theoretician of *agrarismo* in the state of Tamaulipas. As an agronomy student, Gómez had gained firsthand experience in distributing lands while working on the Zapatista Agrarian Commission of the South in Morelos in 1913. Under Obregón, he had been active in the PNA and had served as the Tamaulipan representative on the CNA. Gómez's frustrating experiences on the CNA, when it tried unsuccessfully to exert pressure on the recalcitrant López de Lara, might have influenced him to believe that state governments could more effectively implement land reform than the federal government.

Gómez's views on agrarian reform were best developed in a speech he presented to the Second Convention of the League of Agrarian Communities in 1927. He began by comparing the Mexican Revolution to the Russian Revolution, but he cautioned that Mexico should not follow the Russian model of wide-scale nationalization imposed from above. Despite our long armed struggle, he argued, no true revolutionary leaders had emerged and no revolutionary laws had been issued to spur agrarian reform in Mexico. The central state had not yet carried out sufficient agrarian reform, and this had resulted in growing agrarian unrest. It must be carried out slowly and not hastily by a local reform agency which was not subject to favoritism or corruption. For Gómez, agrarian reform was an integral process which needed to be initiated by an activist state. It involved not only the distribution of land, but also the distribution of tools and credit, the creation of cooperatives, and the building of rural schools to spur the development of a prosperous class of small and medium landowners.[43]

Portes Gil set about reshaping the state organs and state agrarian laws to implement this northern style of integral agrarian reform. The CLA budget was increased to thirty-one pesos in 1926, although this was a small percentage of the state's 2.8 million peso budget. He appointed Gómez to the two positions of president of the CLA and chief of the Department of Development in the Ministry of Agriculture. He justified the decision to combine these two jobs on the basis of budget limitations and the lack of qualified technicians. One can also discern here a clear ideological inclination to view land reform and agricultural production as intimately related. Although Portes Gil did not draw up any comprehensive state legislation to modify or supplement federal legislation as other state governors, he proposed two important changes in land tenancy which tended to ease land pressures and shift attention away from the large *latifundia*. Due to the large number of peasants still living on haciendas who were being subjected to antiquated provisions of the Porfirian law of Agricultural Rental, the governor introduced certain revisions and additions to the labor law covering rental and sharecropping contracts. The law stipulated that rental contracts had to be honored, and when they expired they had to be renewed. The second piece of legislation, the Law of the Division of Rural Communities, called for the division of all communally owned properties with three or more co-owners within six months. Portes Gil also created regional minimum salary commissions which represented worker, business, and government interests. During his administration the minimum wage for agricultural workers on haciendas rose to 1.50 pesos.[44] These measures can be viewed as part of an integral agrarian reform program, but their long-term consequences were to promote and protect private property. Let us now turn and examine Portes Gil's record on land distribution.

As we have seen while Portes Gil was federal deputy before 1925, he gave only token support to *agraristas* petitioning for land. As soon as he assumed the governorship he worked hard to modify his image by portraying himself as an active *agrarista*. The day after he assumed office, on 5 February, he traveled to the Hacienda Santa Engracia, thirty kilometers to the north of Ciudad Victoria, to give personally provisional possession of the properties originally owned by his grandfather and now in the hands of his friends, the Martínez brothers. Ing. Gómez, president of the CLA, and Ing. Jorge Prieto of the CNA accompanied him to this ceremony where land was expropriated under the State Law of Forced Expropriation of 15 December, 1922, which gave the state the power to expropriate lands for the improvement and expansion of cities and for the creation of new centers of population with full or partial compensation in cash over five years. In his memoirs, Portes Gil claims this was the first dotation of an ejido in the state, and it was done in the spirit of social harmony with the cooperation of the landlord himself. Both of these statements are not entirely accurate. Garza had, in fact, distributed the first lands during 1924. What is more, the provisional resolution for Santa Engracia had been written by Ing. Gómez in December 1924, even before Portes Gil had assumed office. The Martínez brothers had finally agreed to the expropriation only after the state generously offered them 89,000 pesos for 690 hectares.[45]

Land was distributed with incredible rapidity during the thirteen months that Marte Gómez was president of the CLA. thirty-four villages received 57,706 hectares (see Table 8.1). What is even more remarkable, however, is the rapidity with which he executed the provisional possessions. Many ejidal lands in the center of the state were given out within a week of the decision. Portes Gil employed land distribution as a propaganda tool to project his image as a revolutionary governor. He traveled to as many villages as possible with representatives of the CNA and the CLA and the president of the Liga to grant provisional possessions. Newspaper reporters were carefully included in the entourage, so they could meticulously describe all the activities, including the fiesta which always followed the act of provisional possession.[46]

In February 1926 Gómez resigned his post in the CLA to assume the subdirectorship of the newly formed National Bank of Agricultural Credit (BNCA). With the departure of Gómez, the rate of land distribution fell precipitously to 23,409 hectares in 1926, 16,025 in 1927, and 27,520 in 1928. The number of petitions dropped by 50 percent (see Table 8.1). Portes Gil attributed this drop in land distribution to the inability of the CLA to process petitions until the new implementing law for the Law of Dotation and Restitution was ratified on 23 April, 1927.[47] The geographical location, type of land, and size of holdings affected by the Portes Gil land reform also explains much about the nature of his program. If one groups the agrarian resolutions by municipality, it immediately becomes apparent that more land was distributed in some regions than in others. A number of explanations for this uneven distribution can be found. Most importantly, peasant mobilization had primarily occurred in the municipality of Hidalgo by 1924. Its proximity to the capital made it ideal for a model agrarian reform project, where it could be closely monitored and controlled. The *agraristas* had been active here since 1921, and they had found both Portes Gil and Gómez sympathetic listeners to their petitions. In addition, the landholdings were not so large nor the owners so well entrenched in this municipality to represent a threat to the governor's program. These factors seem to explain why more provisional grants of lands occurred in Hidalgo than in any other municipality in the state.

On the other hand, land distribution was all but nonexistent in the north and south. This was partially the consequence of the strength of the hacienda system, for the majority of the rural population still lived in villages on haciendas. According to Frank Tannenbaum, only 5.5 percent of the rural villages in Tamaulipas were classified as free villages in 1921, the second lowest in the nation. Peasant mobilization was much more difficult under these conditions, for resident peons had little hope of obtaining lands, while the tenants farmers and sharecroppers were economically dependent on the landowner for their livelihood. What is more, in the north and the south the CLA ran into stiff resistance from the landowning elites and was unable to implement its resolutions at all. For instance, when a petition called for the expropriation oflands belonging to the Hacienda de las Rusias in Matamoras, the local Agricultural and Commercial Chamber acted as a powerful lobby in support of the landowner. The Chamber bought 1,153 hectares of less valuable land to give to the petitioners in lieu of the ejidal grant. At first, the CLA and the governor rejected the offer as an evasion of the law. The landowners refused to be intimidated and began to wantonly kill rural workers in 1926 and 1927. The matter was finally resolved when Portes Gil relented and accepted the 1,100 hectare donation for the ejido.[48]

The southwestern Fourth District was the other region where land distribution was effectively blocked by the cacique Carrera Torres and the large landowners. When Ing. Fernández of the CLA summarized the agrarian reform program in 1926, he failed to even mention the region of Tula. Although the towns of Jaumave and Bustamente won the restitution of municipal lands lost in the 1890s, Bernardo Zorrilla won *amparos* which suspended attempts to affect his large landholdings. Carrera Torres had no intention of allowing the state to woo his loyal military colonists by offering them ejidal lands. In 1926 Portes Gil commissioned his friend, Lt. Col. José Dolores Alvarez, to organize peasants to petition for lands in Tula and to wrest control of the Council of Civil Adminstration in Bustamente away from Carrera Torres. The cacique simply ordered his military colonists to kill him. In desperation, Portes Gil pressured President Calles to transfer Carrera Torres to another military district, but this action did not appreciably diminish his power in Tula. For the most part, Portes Gil was obliged to collaborate with the Tulan leader.[49]

If we compare Portes Gil's distribution of land as governor with the *agrarista* governors of the 1920s, he pales beside them. The 125,000 hectares distributed under Portes Gil were surpassed by the governors of Yucatán, Chihuahua, San Luis Potosí, Guanajuato, Jalisco, Zacatecas, Querétaro, and Veracruz during the Calles presidency. Both Adalberto Tejeda and Lázaro Cárdenas distributed close to 400,000 hectares each between 1928 and 1932.[50] To some degree, Portes Gil appears to have fabricated his *agrarista* image in his voluminous writings and speeches throughout his long and controversial political career.

From Land Reform to Peasant Mobilization

The dramatic downswing in Portes Gil's land reform after 1925 cannot solely be attributed to changes in agrarian legislation or to the lack of peasant desire for land. At least four other factors might account for his shift in agrarian policies.

Foreign opposition to the Tamaulipan agrarian reform program began to surface by 1925. U.S. citizens controlled over 900,000 hectares, approximately one-eighth of all the landholdings in 1923, including the 315,000 hectare José de las Rusias hacienda in Soto de la Marina owned by O.W. Brickson. In the summer of 1925 the Chargé d'Affaires Arthur Schoenfield approached the Calles government specifically about American properties affected in Tamaulipas by the agrarian reform program. The president assured Schoenfeld that he had ordered a special federal investigation of the agrarian reform process and had plans to "federalize" the entire procedure. Among American properties affected were powerful oil companies such as the American International Fuel and Petroleum Company and the American Land and Cattle Co. Yet U.S. properties were not specially targeted by the Portes Gil administration. On the contrary, they seem to have been left largely untouched. The San José de la Rusias Hacienda was only affected by one petition during Portes Gil's term.[51]

Second, we know that Portes Gil's own fervor for land reform began to cool after 1925. A number of signs reflect this change in perspective. For one thing, after the departure of Gómez the CLA was not headed by an experienced reform-minded technocrat. For the remainder of 1926 the presidency of the CLA was not filled, and a PSF functionary, Arsenio Saeb, occupied the post in a provisional capacity. The impression one receives is that land reform became a secondary priority for the governor after the first year of his administration, as seen by his disinterest in placing a strong administrator in this position. What is more, when the position was finally filled in March 1927, it was given to the politician Portes Gil was grooming to be his successor.[52] The position of president of the CLA had passed from being a state office wielding considerable power in the implementation of social reform to a political patronage position for Portes Gil's party machine.

Third, Portes Gil's own views toward land reform seem to have become more closely aligned with those of President Calles and his minister of agriculture, Luis León. It appears that both Gómez and Portes Gil collaborated in the drafting of the Ejidal Law of Patrimony, which strengthened the role of the central government in the administering of ejidos and thereby weakening its local autonomy. The local administrative committees which had autonomously governed ejidos were replaced by ejidal commissariats, directly under the supervision of the Department of Agriculture. The ejido was becoming more and more a political creation of the government.[53]

Fourth, by the spring of 1926 Portes Gil had discovered that his efforts to distribute land to win the political support of the peasantry had not been entirely successful. Unlike other reformist governors such as Tejeda, Mújica and Carrillo Puerto, he had displayed little or no interest in organizing a peasant league. Most probably, Portes Gil had believed he could attract the peasantry through his urban-based political party, the PSF. To be sure, little grass-roots peasant mobilization existed. Yet since 1921 many local peasant unions, leagues, and other groups had been organized throughout the country. Nevertheless, into this unmobilized state swept the militant Veracruz peasant leaders, Ursulo Galván and Carolino Anaya in April 1926, men intent on organizing a state league in affiliation with the radical Veracruz league. They began their organizing activities in the one region where peasants had been previously organized, Hidalgo. In Santa Engracia they founded a state league composed of ten ejidos headed by Guillermo Zuñiga, the radical peasant leader of Santa Engracia.[54] To counter these organization efforts originating from outside the state, Portes Gil convoked a peasant convention in September 1926 to form a Portesgilista league. The governor enlisted Gómez, who was still working at the Agricultural Bank, to draft the statutes of the new organization and to supervise its creation.

The formation of the League of Agrarian Communities and Peasant Syndicates of the State of Tamaulipas was orchestrated by the state officials, who provided the financing, convoked its first convention, and elaborated the goals and objectives of the league. Gómez, who was the intellectual inspiration for the league, admitted that the state government even paid the expenses of the 128 delegates representing the 60 ejidos who attended.[55] The predominance of the Hidalgo ejidos, fifteen in all, is not remarkable given the selective way that land distribution had occurred. What is more, Luis E. C. Garza, served as one of the convention organizers. As a loyal Portesgilista, he had been collaborating with Portes Gil since 1920. The governor's presence at the convention made it evident that he had personally played a role in the selection of the president of the league, Miguel Martínez Rojo, a rural school teacher from the Ciudad Victoria region. Portes Gil would mold the league into a personal political machine, controlling its leadership and its policies until well into the 1930s. The Portesgilista league was to play a key role in the formation of the Cardenista Mexican Peasant Confederation in 1933.

The goals of the league were clearly aimed at the promotion of small-scale commercial farming rather than the breakup of the *latifundio* through land distribution. Its primary objectives were to spur better utilization of ejidal land, to form producer cooperatives, to build schools, and to establish ties with other peasant organizations, so as "to raise the economic, intellectual and moral level of its members."[56] These moderate goals, which stressed increased agricultural production rather than land reform, echoed the agrarian policies of the Calles regime. They were in marked contrast to the more radical goals of leagues formed in 1922 and 1923 in Veracruz and Michoacán where social justice, more equitable distribution of land, and social strugggle against the oppressive landowning classes were major goals.[57] Gone were the local initiatives for land distribution in Tamaulipas. By 1926 Portesgilismo had become almost synonymous with Callismo. The governor had been successfully co-opted into the politicial leadership, and he had foresaken any principles of revolutionary ideology that he might have espoused to share the fruits of political power.

Conclusions

One of the consequences of the disintegration of the Díaz political appartus was the emergence of strong regional *caudillos* who filled the political vacuum left by the Porfirian administration. These *caudillos* had to confront a new political environment in which large segments of the population had been mobilized to participate in armed combat. New mechanisms of control had to be fashioned to satisfy the needs and desires of emerging social groups. Since the revolution lacked any strong ideological blueprint, regional *caudillos* exploited revolutionary ideals, such as land reform, for their own political purposes. Thus, the 1920s reveal many variations in the land reform programs carried out by state governors in their drive to consolidate their own political bases. As the case of Tamaulipas demonstrates, López de Lara had little inclination to divide land or distribute water, but he launched state programs to finance colonization projects and to provide credit to private-property owners. The *larista* Department of Agriculture promoted commercial agriculture, colonization projects, and the creation of a state agricultural school. On the other hand, Governors Garza and Portes Gil saw the political advantages of a state-initiated land reform program tied to a federally sponsored credit program to spur commercial agriculture and the importance of peasant organization.

The interaction between federal and state governments was also critical in the 1920s in the formation of state structures and regional political elites which could be coopted into the postrevolutionary state. As Skocpol and Trimberger have emphasized, revolutions from above or below are not consolidated until new or transformed state mechanisms are established. In Mexico, one of the ways in which the central state reconstituted itself was through the subordination of regionally created social and political institutions. Thus, the state agencies, the political parties, and the popular organizations created principally by regional *caudillos* to build regional power bases were gradually merged into the federal bureaucracy. The creation of bureaucratic agencies such as the CLA as well as sociopolitical institutions such as the peasant league helped the Tamaulipecan governors to implement land reforms programs and to win rural bases of support. By the end of the Calles era, however, these institutions and their leaders had been incorporated into the postrevolutionary state. In particular, Portes Gil, who had carefully constructed a regional political base, found it politically expedient to collaborate with the Callista regime. By the end of the 1920s regional *caudillos* were finding it increasingly difficult to work outside of the Callista state without facing political marginalization.

Notes

1. The research for this article was partially funded by a Fulbright-Hayes Research Grant in 1983–84, and a NEH Grant for College Teachers at the University of Chicago in 1985. I would like to thank Alicia Hernández, and Ramón Jrade for their comments on an earlier draft of this chapter.
2. Alicia Hernández Chávez, "Militares y negocios en la revolución mexicana," *Historia Mexicana* 34:2 (October–December 1984): 181–212.
3. Hans Werner Tobler, "Las paradojas del ejército revolucionario: su papel social en la reforma agraria mexicana, 1920–1935," in *Historia Mexicana* 21 (July–September 1971): 44 n.7; "Alvaro Obregón und die Anfänge der mexicanischen Agrarreform: Agrarpolitik und Agrarkonflikt, 1921–24," in *Jahrbuch für Geschichte von Staat, Wirtschaft und Gesellschaft Lateinamerikas* (Koln, 1971), 321–22; "Peasants and the Shaping of the Revolutionary State, 1910–40," in *Riot, Rebellion and Revolution: Rural Social Conflict in Mexico* (ed.) Friedrich Katz (Princeton University Press, 1988) 487–518.
4. Arnaldo Córdova, *La ideología de la Revolución Mexicana* (México: Ediciones Era, 1973), 23, 23–29; Francisco Gómez Jara, *El movimiento campesino en México* (México: Editorial Campesina, 1970), 30–33, 49–50; Gil Joseph, *Revolution from Without. Yucatán, Mexico and the United States, 1880–1924* (Cambridge: Cambridge University Press, 1982); Gil Joseph, "Caciquismo and the Revolution: Carrillo Puerto in Yucatán," and Heather Fowler Salamini, "Revolutionary Caudillos in the 1920s: Francisco Mújica and Adalberto Tejeda, in *Caudillo and Peasant in the Mexican Revolution*, ed. by David A. Brading (Cambridge: Cambridge University Press: 1980) 169–192, 193–221; Raymond Th. J. Buve, "State Governors and Peasant Mobilization in Tlaxcala," in Brading, and see chapter 11; Dudley Ankerson, *Agrarian Warlord: Saturnino Cedillo and the Mexican Revolution in San Luis Potosí* (DeKalb, Il: Northern Illinois University Press, 1984).
5. Gómez Jara, 33, 49–50; See Hans Werner Tobler's discussion of the role of the *caudillo* in the consolidation of the state in "Conclusion: Peasant Mobilization and the Revolution," in Brading, 245.

Some social scientists working on the rise of the modern state have tended to view *caudillismo* as an obstacle to the concentration of power, which is misleading. See, for example, Nora Hamilton, *The Limits of State Autonomy* (Princeton: Princeton University Press, 1982), 197; Richard Tardanico, "Revolutionary Nationalism and State Building in Mexico, 1917–1924," in *Politics and Society* 10:1(1980): 72; see Ankerson, 197.

6. Theda Skocpol and Ellen Kay Trimberger, "Revolutions and the World Historical Development of Capitalism," in *Social Change in the Capitalist World Economy*, ed. by Barbara Hockey Kaplan (Beverly Hills: Sage Publications, 1978), 129; see also Tardanico, 61.

7. On the case of the Yucatán, see, in particular, Joseph, *Revolution From Without*. For the northern states, see Friedrich Katz, *The Secret War: Europe, The United States and the Mexican Revolution* (Chicago: Univerisity of Chicago Press, 1981); Hector Aguilar Camín, *La frontera nómada; Sonora y la revolución mexicana* (México: Siglo XXI, 1977); Douglas Richmond, *Venustiano Carranza's Nationalist Struggle, 1893–1920* (Lincoln: University of Nebraska Press, 1984).

8. Charles C. Cumberland, *Mexican Revolution: Genesis under Madero* (Austin, Tex.: Univeristy of Texas Press, 1952), 73–74, 106; Emilio Portes Gil, *Raigambre de la revolución en Tamaulipas: autobiografía en acción* (México: Fersa, 1972), 46; Francisco Vázquez Gómez, *Memorias políticas* (México: Imprente Mundial, 1933), 14, 23–24; Ciro R. de la Garza Treviño, *La revolución mexicana en el estado de Tamaulipas*, vol. I, 1883–1973 (México: Librería de Manuel Porrúa, 1975), 57.

9. U.S. consuls in Tampico, Nuevo Laredo, and Matamoros kept predicting imminent attacks by revolutionary bands in May 1911, but the attacks were postponed by the signing of the Treaty of Juárez. See Records of the Department of State Relating to the Internal Affairs of Mexico, 1910–1929, Record Group 59 (microcopy 264), 812.00/486,950, 1675, 1812, 1821, 1859, 1989 (hereafter cited as SD.) Alan Knight, *The Mexican Revolution*, vol. I, *Porfirians, Liberals and Peasants* (Cambridge: Cambridge Univeristy Press, 1986), 216–17, 405, 424–25.

   Alberto Alcocer Andalón, "El General y Profesor Alberto Carrera Torres," in *Archivos de Historia Potosina*, I:1 (July–September 1969): 32–33; Beatriz Rojas, *La pequeña guerra: Los Carrera Torres y los Cedillos* (Zamora: El Colegio de Michoacán, 1983), 20–22; Gabriel Saldívar, *Historia comprendida de Tamaulipas* (México: 1945), 279–80; Garza Treviño, 1:65

10. Vázquez Gómez, 191; U.S. Consul Tampico, Clarence Miller, to Secretary of State, 21 November, 1911, 23 February, 1912, SD, 812.00/2558, 2995; Garza Treviño, I, 73–74, 89, 96, 99, 103–4; Lief Adleson, "Historia social de los obreros industrales de Tampico, 1906–1919" (Ph.D. diss., El Colegio de México, 1982), 57–58; Saldívar, 281.

11. "Ley Agraria del Professor y General Alberto Carrera Torres, del 4 de marzo de 1913," in Garza Treviño, I:386–90.

12. Garza Treviño, I:161, 163, 167–68, 183; Saldívar, 323.

13. "Ley Agraria," in Garza Treviño, I:425; Saldívar, 204; Knight, II:49.

14. Garza Treviño, I:201, 224, 226–27; Saldívar, 324; Charles C. Cumberland *The Mexican Revolution: The Constitutionalist Years* (Austin: University of Texas Press, 1974), 73.

15. Garza Treviño, II:79, 87, 100, 109; Saldívar, 288, 290; Rojas, 37–40; Cumberland, *Constitutionalism*, 77–78.

16. Garza Treviño, II:166, 243–44; Cumberland, *Constitutionalism, 371;* Douglas W. Richmond, *Carranza,* 79; *Diccionario Porrúa*; Portes Gil, *Raigambre,* 61, 63; Ankerson, 75.

17. Cumberland, *Constitutionalism,* 145, 361, 368–69; See Linda Hall, "Alvaro Obregón y el partido único mexicano," in *Historia Mexicana,* 29 (July-September 1979); 607–9 for the formation of the PLC.

18. Garza Treviño, II:258–60, 263–65; Cumberland, *Constitutionalism,* 369–70; Portes Gil, *Raigambre,* 64–69. There are slight discrepancies between Garza Treviño and Portes Gil's accounts of the rebellion. See, also, Portes Gil, *Autobiografía de la revolución mexicana* (México: Instituto Mexicano de Cultura, 1964), 248; Knight, II:484.

19. Jesús Silva Herzog, *El agrarismo mexicano y la reforma agraria* (México: Fondo de Cultura Económica, 1959), 27, 273–75; Eyler Simpson, *The Ejido: Mexico's Way Out* (Chapel Hill: Univeristy of North Carolina Press, 1937), 87–88; Narciso Bassols Batalla, *El Pensamiento político de Alvaro Obregón,* 2d ed. (México: Ediciones El Caballito, 1970), 136; see Linda Hall's fine discussion in "Alvaro Obregón and the Agrarian Movement, 1912–20"; Brading, 132–138.

20. President Obregón's agrarian policy has been characterized as "contradictory" and lacking in a clear conceptual framework by Jesús Silva Herzog, who argued that the revolutionary leadership had not yet formulated a coherent agrarian policy by the 1920s. Linda Hall focused on how Obregón implemented the revolutionary goal of land reform for political purposes. To pacify the countryside and achieve national reconstruction, he used land reform when and where he saw fit. He also had no intention of seizing productive lands or of alienating foreign landowners. Obregón employed a selective land reform program in which ejidal lands were granted in the Zapatista and Villista strongholds: Puebla, Tlaxcala, Morelos, Hidalgo, and Guerrero in the south, and Durango and Chihuahua in the north in the early years. After the revolt of 1923 Delahuertistas strongholds such as Veracruz, San Luis Potosí, and Jalisco received special consideration. Silva Herzog, 276, 343; Hall, "Alvaro Obregón and the Politics of Land Reform, 1920–24," in *Hispanic American Historical Review* 50: 2 (1980): 214–30.

21. Tobler, "Alvaro Obregón," 320–26. See Córdova's treatment of Obregón's agrarian ideology, 276–87; and Arturo Warman, . . . *Y venimos a contradecir* (México: Siglo XXI, 1976), 148–158.

22. Tobler, "El ejército," 39 ff; Hall, 217, 232, n. 238; Fowler Salamini, 38–40.

23. *Informe rendido por el Gral. César López de Lara en la apertura del primero período de sessiones ordinarias del XXVIII H. Congreso del estado, el I de enero de 1923* (Ciudad

Victoria: Imprenta Oficial, 1923), 28; Lief Adleson, "Coyunctura y conciencia: factores convergentes en la fundación de los sindicatos petroleros de Tampico durante la década de 1920," in *El trabajo y los trabajadores en la historia de México*, ed. Elsa Cecilia Frost, Michael C. Meyer, and Josefina Zoraida Vázquez (México: El Colegio de México and Tucson: University of Arizona Press, 1979), 646–53.

24. *Informe de 1923*, 65; *El Universal*, 22 November, 1922, quoted in Tobler, "Obregón," 336, n.55.

25. Frank Tannenbaum, *The Agrarian Revolution* (Washington, D.C.: Brookings Institution, 1930), 351. *Informe leído por el C. General César López de Lara en la apertura del segundo período de sessiones ordinarias del XXVII Congreso, 1 de enero de 1922* (Ciudad Victoria: Imprenta del Gobierno, 1922), 34; *Informe, 1923*, 41–42, 47, 66–67, 96, 108; *Periódico oficial*, XI, VII:1 4 January, 1922), 3; SD 812.52/1443 and G58 on colonization of Hacienda Cojo; *Periódico oficial*, 47:4 (24 May, 1922).

26. *Informe, 1923*, 9–10; Ankerson, pp. 135–36.

27. *Informe, 1923*, 41–43; see Fowler Salamini, "Revolutionary Caudillos in the 1920s," in Brading, 169–221.

28. *Informe, 1923*, 41–43; "Presupuesto de Egresos," in *Periódico oficial*, 46:36 (4 May, 1921).

29. Congreso, Cámara de Diputados, *Diarios de los debates de la Cámara de Diputados del Congreso de los Estados Unidos de México*, 7 December, 1922 (México: Imprenta de la Cámara de Diputados, 19220, 7–21 (hereafter cited as DDd); M. Mendoza Schwartzfeger to Portes Gil, 12 October, 1922, Caja 12, Carpeta 1. Personal Archives of Emilio Portes Gil, Archivo General de la Nación (hereafter cited as AGN/EPG); Simpson, 82.

30. "Estatutos," in Caja 12bis, Expediente 5, AGN/EPG; see Luis Garza (Union) to State Supreme Court, 26 June, 1924, in Expediente Estación de la Cruz, no. 8, in Archive of Comisión Agraria Mixta, Cuidad Victoria (hereafter cited as CAM); Artura Alvarado, "Portesgilismo" (Ph.D. diss., draft, El Colegio de México, 1987).

31. C. Valenzuela (Union) to Obregón, 23 July, 1923, Caja 12, Carpeta J; Union to EPG, 22 January, 1923, Caja 2, Carpeta 288; 3 May, 1923, Caja 4, Carpeta sn.; 15 June, 1923, Caja 5, Carpeta 401, AGN/EPG; Luis Garza (Union) to State Supreme Court, 26 June, 1924, Estación de la Cruz, Expediente no. 8, CAM.

32. AGN/OC 818-E-11, cited in Hall, "Politics of Land Reform," 231–32; López de Lara to Obregón, 7 August, 1923, 243-T2-F-1, AGN/OC; see also Estación de la Cruz, no. 8, CAM., Subsecretary of Government to Union, 22 July, 1923, Caja 7, Carpeta s.n. and EPG to Silva Garza (Union), 20 December, 1923, Caja 7, Carpeta 393, AGN/EPG.

33. See Cuauhtémoc, Expediente no. 1, and Estación de la Cruz, no. 8, in CAM; Periódico Oficial, 49:62 (August 1924); Garza Treviño, II:386, 390, 397; Hall, "Politics of Land Reform," 237.

34. Expediente Santa Engracia, no. 10, CAM.
35. Jean Meyer, *Estado y sociedad con Calles. 1924–28 Historia de la Revolución, 11* (México, El Colegio de México, 1977), p. 115; John W. F. Dulles, *Yesterday in Mexico* (Austin: University of Texas Press, 1961), 290–5.
36. Luis L. León, *Crónica del poder en los recuerdos de un político en el México revolucionario* (México: Fondo de Cultura Económica, 1987), 193–94; Arthur Schoenfeld to DS, 7 January, 1925, SD 812.522/1259; Meyer, 83–88; Silva Herzog, 321–29; Aguilar Camín, p. 101; Simpson, 88–97, 322, 383–93.
37. Portes Gil, in *México visto en el siglo XX*, ed. James W. Wilkie and Edna Monzón de Wilkie (México: Instituto Mexicano de Investigaciones Económicas, 1969), 493–95, 549; *Raigambre*, 55–58; *Autobiografía*, 353; EPG to Calles (secretario de gobierno), 12 January, 1921, in EPG legajo, personal archives of Plutarco E. Calles.
38. Portes Gil, in Wilkie, 497, 549; Simpson, 109; Ernest Gruening, *Mexico and Its Heritage* (New York: 1928), 161–62.
39. See Shulgovsky's treatment of Portes Gil, 110–11; Córdova, 29–30; Gómez Jara, 56–58.
40. EPG to Daniel González (Unión Agraria de Santa Engracia), 19 May, 1923; EPG to Obregón, 8 June, 1923, Caja 5, Carpeta 441; EPG to Luis E. G. Garza, 18 April, 1923, Caja 4, Carpeta s.n.; Antonio López Colonia Agrícola de Obreros to EPG, 22 March, 1923, Caja 12, Carpeta. s.n.; F. Luna (Cooperativa Alfa) to EPG, 17 September, 1924, Caja 11, Carpeta 355, AGN/EPG.
41. M. González-Salinas to EPG, March 13, 1924, Caja 2, Carpeta 3; Jacobo Martínez to EPG, 4 August, 1924 and EPG to Ramón de Negri, 9 September, 1924, Caja 2, Expediente 156, AGN/EPG.
42. *Informe que rinde el C. Gobernador Constitucioal del Estado, Lic. Emilio Portes Gil ante el XXIX H. Congreso del mismo, el día 1 de enero de 1926* (Ciudad Victoria, Talleres Linográficos del Gobierno del Estado, 1927) 33.
43. Portes Gil, in Wilkie, 507; EPG, *Raigambre*, 194–95; *Segunda convención de la Liga de Comunidades Agrarias y Sindicatos Campesinos del Estado de Tamaulipas*, Recopilación del Ing. Marte R. Gómez (México, 1927), 300–305; see Gómez to De Negri, 22 October, 1925, in Marte R. Gómez, *Vida política contemporanea. Cartas de Marte R. Gómez* (México: Fondo de Cultura Económica, 1978), I:83–84.
44. "Ley de presupuestos," *Periódico oficial*, 50:9 (30 January, 1925), and 51 (2 January, 1926); *Informe 1927*, 30–31; *Periódico oficial*, 50:3 (13 March, 1926), and 53:44 (2 June, 1928); Portes Gil, *Raigambre*, 329.
45. EPG, in Wilkie, 495; Estación Santa Engracia, no. 10, CAM: *Periódico oficial*, 50:11 (7 February, 1925), 50:55 (11 July, 1925), 51:53 (3 July, 1926).
46. See Appendices of the *Tercera convención de la Liga . . .* Recopilación del Ing. Marte R. Gómez, en cumplimiento del acuerdo dicto por el Sr. Lic. Emilio Portes Gil, Presidente Constitucional Interino del los Estados Unidos Mexicanos (México:

Cultura, 1930). These figures are slightly lower than those given in the *Informes*. *El Mundo*, 20 January, 1925, 7–8 March, 1927.

47. *Informe que rinde el C. Gobernador Constitucional del Estado, Lic. Emilio Portes Gil ante el XXX Congreso del mismo, el dia 1 de enero de 1928* (Tampico: Talleres Linotipográficos de la Rosa, 1928), 67–68; EPG, *Raigambre*, 178–79, 182, 186.

48. Tannenbaum, 56; *El Mundo*, 24 January, 15 March, 16 October, and 12 and 14 December; *Informe, 1927*, 51–52; *Informe, 1928*, 68; *Segunda Convención de la Liga*, 103–4; EPG, *Raigambre*, 177.

49. *Primera Convención de la Liga, 1926*, 197–204; *El Mundo*, 11 April and 12 August, 1927; Garza Treviño, II: 413–14.

50. México, Departamento Agrario, *Memoria, 1945–6* (México: 1946); Fowler Salamini, 99.

51. Drew Linard to Secretary of State, 27 August, 1924, SD 812.00/27343; Schoenfeld to Secretary of State, 3 and 4 September, 1925, 812.00/27598, 812.52/1341,1488; Dwight Morrow to Secretary of State, 21 September, 1928, 812.00/29321; Tannenbaum, 362,512. See *Periódico Oficial*, 1925–28.

52. See *Periódico Oficial*, 1925–28.

53. Dulles, 291; Simpson, 322; Warman, 147–48.

54. Liga de Comunidades Agrarias del Estado de Tamaulipas, *La organización del movimiento campesino en Tamaulipas. Conmemoración de los 50 años de la Liga de Comunidades Agrarias y Sindicatos Campesinos* (Ciudad de Victoria: 28 de Septiembre de 1976), 60–61, 68; Secretary of Government to EPG, 9 July, 1926, Expediente Estación Santa Engracia, no. 10, CAM; Interview with Simón Torres de la Garza, 19 October, 1983.

55. Marte R. Gómez to Ramón P. de Negri, 28 September, 1927; Gómez I: 167.

56. *Primera Convención de la Liga, 1926*, 276–80.

57. For example, see Arnulfo Embriz Osorio y Ricardo León García, *Documentos para la historia del agrarismo en Michoacán* (México: Centro de Estudios Históricos del Agrarismo en México, 1982), 75; Fowler Salamini, *Agrarian Radicalism*, 51–53; Fowler, "Los origenes de las organizaciones campesinas en Veracruz: raíces políticas y sociales," in Historia Mexicana, 22:1 (July-September 1972), 52–76.

CHIHUAHUA

Chihuahua

Politics in an Era of Transition

Mark Wasserman

Three concurrent struggles dominated politics in Chihuahua during the 1920s. The first struggle was at the state level, between bitterly competing factions rallying around a charismatic leader or a powerful family seeking to capture the state government. The second struggle took place at the local level, where municipal political bosses or influential families combated the efforts of state governments to exert control over their bailiwicks. The third and most important struggle involved the unceasing efforts of the national government to extend its hegemony over the state and the efforts of state political elites to prevent these incursions. Underlying these struggles to establish a new political regime were the state's depressed economic condition, especially in agriculture; the increasing efforts of campesinos and workers to organize; and the search of the prerevolutionary elite for its place in the new order. This chapter will focus on the first and third struggles. It will identify the key contestants and will determine why one group or another gained the upper hand at various times. The 1920s were an era of transition, probing, and conflict that laid the basis for Mexico's subsequent political development. Although not all battles were won or lost during these times, much was set in place.

Two ongoing problems delimited and perplexed Chihuahuan politics: almost continuous economic depression and recurrent violence. The Mexican Revolution had inflicted enormous suffering on Chihuahua. Like Morelos, the state endured ten years of continuous fighting and its accompanying destruction. While the combat had ended in much of the nation by 1917, with the constitutionalists in control, it continued in Chihuahua until Pancho Villa retired from the field in 1920. The damage was monstrous. The state's transportation and communications were near ruin. Its major economic activities, livestock, agriculture, commerce, and mining were badly disrupted.

More than a million head of cattle had grazed Chihuahua's ranges in 1910. Perhaps one-tenth of that number remained in 1920. By 1930 the state had 685,000 head, a remarkable recovery, but not much more than 50 percent of the prerevolutionary figure.[1] To make matters worse, severe drought and lost harvests struck the region in 1920, 1921, 1922, and 1929. Although harvests improved in the middle of the decade, there was only one year when all three staple crops—corn, wheat, and beans—were sufficient.[2] In that year, 1926, crops were so plentiful that commodity prices plunged, still leaving farmers in bad straits.[3]

With the exception of mining, business was generally depressed throughout the 1920s. The retail trade never recovered its prerevolutionary vitality. Money was often scarce and credit usually tight. The major Mexican-owned banks in the state failed.[4] Two of the biggest stores in the region, Krakauer, Zork and Ketelsen and Degetau operated on the brink of bankruptcy.[5] Because of the poor economic conditions, the state government never had enough revenue. It was always behind in paying its employees.[6] Mining was the one strong sector, for it had recovered by 1918, surpassing 1910 production (in United States dollars) the next year. More ore was extracted and treated in Chihuahua in 1921 than at any time in its history. Mineral production stagnated the next year and then began a sharp rise of 400 percent from 1923 to 1926. Although production stayed at a substantially higher level, the industry endured depression from the end of 1929 until 1934. At the height of the boom, mining employed 20,000 in the state.[7]

The condition of agriculture and mining created crucial political issues. Disastrously erratic staple-crop harvests forced the state and national governments to seek a delicate balance between promised, hard-fought-for land reform—and the inevitable dislocations it would bring—and the desperate need for increased food production. Mining presented two interrelated problems. Since the industry was the driving force in the economy, the government had to juggle the needs of mine owners with the demands of emerging workers organizations for better wages, working conditions, and job security. Mining was, moreover, increasingly concentrated in the hands of large, foreign-owned corporations, most importantly the American Smelting and Refining Company (Asarco).[8] This had important consequences. The companies had enormous leverage in dealing with governments and labor unions, for they could use the threat of shutting down their operations—an action that would be ruinous to the state's economy—to negotiate. Furthermore, concentration in a few foreign companies and the almost total demise of small producers limited the benefits from the industry to the local economy. Mineral production was also concentrated in only four subregions of the state, Santa Eulalia, Santa Bárbara, Parral, and Cusihuiriachic.[9] Mining elsewhere was in ruins. Linkages from mining were thus restricted.

Militarily, Chihuahua was in constant upheaval. The decade began with the overthrow of Venustiano Carranza by Alvaro Obregón (the Plan de Agua Prieta). The following year, an uprising of three hundred Indians in the southwestern district of Andres del Rio took place which was put down by the local militia (*defensas sociales*). [10] Early in 1922, a rebel band led by Nicolás Rodríguez in the north was dispersed by federal troops. Rosalio Hernández led another group in Santa Rosalia. [11] Later, yet another rebel, Captain Valverde, with 150 men, briefly took Ciudad Juárez. [12] Adolfo de la Huerta led a nationwide rebellion in December 1923 that drew several ex-Villista leaders, such as Hípolito Villa, Nicolás Fernández, and Manuel Chao. The de la huertistas remained in the field in Chihuahua through the spring of 1924. [13] In June, after being deposed by the state legislature, the radical mayor of Santa Bárbara, Ricardo Cruz, armed twenty followers and took over the municipal government, only to be overrun by federal soldiers. [14] Nicolás Fernández revolted again in mid-July 1925. He stayed in the field well into 1927. [15] After the coup that ousted Governor Jesús Antonio Almeida in 1927, his supporters led a short-lived rebellion which the state militia ended in June. [16] In 1928 rebels operated with some success, at one time four hundred strong, in southwestern districts of the state, but they too were defeated by summer. [17] Finally, Marcelo Caraveo went over to the rebellion of General Gonzálo Escobar against Calles in March 1929. But by the end of June there was "not a rebel in the region." [18] Moreover, banditry was endemic throughout the decade. Until he was assassinated in 1923, Pancho Villa was a constant source of apprehension. What this all added up to was a continuous condition of disruption and uncertainty, considerable destruction, and an impossible climate for any kind of business.

The decade divides into political stages identified by their dominant figure. Ignacio C. Enríquez governed in close cooperation with President Alvaro Obregón in the first era from 1920 to 1924. From 1924 until he was ousted by a coup in 1927, Jesús Antonio Almeida ruled Chihuahua. Almeida was one of the strong men who arose during the 1920s in several Mexican states, and who tried to construct independent political bases. Marcelo Caraveo overthrew Almeida and took power until 1929, when he joined the doomed Escobar rebellion. The decade ended as it had begun, in chaos, with interim governors Luis L. León and Francisco R. Almada. The national government imposed order only with the return of General Rodrigo Quevedo to Chihuahua as governor in 1932.

Throughout the 1920s there was a dichotomy in Chihuahuan politics between the radical peasantry and proletariat and the state's political leadership, whose economic background and aspirations were essentially capitalist and relatively conservative. For much of the period, the conservatives held the upper hand. The most striking exceptions took place during the governorships of Ignacio C. Enriíquez and Luis L. León, when national political considerations more than personal conviction or ideology required substantial land reforms.

The election of General Ignacio C. Enriíquez as governor in 1920 marked the return of constitutional rule in Chihuahua for the first time since the assassination of Abraham González seven years earlier. It was also the fourth time he had occupied the office, having been previously the first Constitutionalist governor in 1916 and twice serving for short terms in 1918. Enríquez was the son of a hacendado and long-time *jefe político* during the Porfiriato. He had joined the revolution late, tending to his family's estate until the overthrow of Madero. As a soldier he was a loyal Carrancista and fought variously under the command of Alvaro Obregón and Pablo González, working his way up to the rank of brigadier general. He returned to Chihuahua in 1918 and subsequently served as interim governor and, then, as commander of the irregular, auxiliary troops known as the *defensas sociales*, which were used to fight the Villistas. After backing Obregón in 1920, he was elected governor.[19]

Enríquez had the difficult task of consolidating the regime in Chihuahua at a time when Obregón's hold on power was precarious nationally and the state was staggering from the burden of political tumult, drought, and economic depression. In late 1923 and 1924 he had to return to military duty to defeat the de la huertistas. During his term, the Chihuahuan state government adopted important new agrarian and labor laws, distributed considerable amounts of land to ejidos and agricultural colonies (*colonias agrícolas*), and began construction of an important irrigation system in the southern section of the state.[20] These years also brought the initiation of labor union and campesino organizations.

His record on land reform was mixed. Despite the fact that Chihuahuans obtained more redistributed land than residents of any other states except Yucatán and San Luis Potosí, numerous complaints arose from agrarians about the "systematic obstruction of rural forces and municipal guards against people who chose to pursue their recognized rights to solicit restitution of *ejidos*."[21] One official of the Partido Nacional Agrarista alleged that there was an "immoral government in the state" and hoped that the governor would be retired.[22] More indicative of both Enríquez and Obregón's attitudes and the dilemmas in reform was the unsuccessful attempt to sell the entire estate of Luis Terrazas to an American entrepreneur Arthur J. McQuatters. The governor, with the initial approval of the president, signed the contract and campaigned vigorously for its approval, believing it to be an important step in solving the state's perennial agricultural crisis. The agreement called for McQuatters to purchase fourteen haciendas, five million acres owned by General Luis Terrazas. He would improve this land and then sell it off in small parcels. Popular objections led first the state legislature and then the president to reject the proposal. Ultimately, the federal government purchased the properties from the Terrazas estate.[25] Enríquez and Obregón preferred small-scale private farming, but public pressures caused them to change their policies. In many instances, the pueblos that received lands through the land reform laws had been originators of the revolution in 1910 and 1911. Moreover, the number of restitutions (*restituciones*) and grants (*dotaciones*) increased notably with the threat of the de la Huerta rebellion in 1923.[24] The government was particularly careful with the Villistas. The national government bought the hacienda El Pueblito in 1923 to divide among the Division of the North.[25] Political expediency governed land reform.

The governor walked a similar tightrope in dealing with labor and mining. The state legislature passed a radical labor law in 1922. Enríquez, however, "tempered enforcement by good sense," in order to maintain the industry's recovery.[26] He also had to mediate a strike at Asarco in Santa Eulalia, the first against the company in five years. Enríquez sent in troops to protect property, but settled the conflict (though no one was pleased by his actions).[27]

After spending the winter of 1923–24 away from his post by fighting the de la huertistas, Enríquez resigned, leaving under a cloud of suspicion of having enriched himself from the state treasury.[28] Reinaldo Talavera acted as governor to the end of the term. Talavera was a ranch owner from Aldama, a former city council member in Ciudad Chihuahua, and legislator.[29] He also had to deal with a bitter strike in Santa Eulalia against the large American companies, sending in soldiers. There was bloodshed before the governor could supervise a settlement. During another strike in Santa Bárbara, rural guards allegedly shot workers "like dogs."[30]

Enríquez showed no inclination to establish an independent power base in Chihuahua, for he was loyal to Obregón. To the contrary, his successor, Jesús Antonio Almeida, set out to build an empire for himself and his family. The Almeidas were small landowners and merchants in western Chihuahua before the revolution. Jesús Antonio flirted briefly with the Orozquistas in 1912. He obtained prominence in 1917 when he joined the *defensas sociales* to fight the Villistas. In 1920 he sided with Obregón against Carranza. During the governorship of Enríquez, he rose through the ranks to head the *defensas sociales*.

Almeida used this as a springboard to run, with the backing of Enríquez, for governor in 1924.[31]

As governor, Jesús Antonio displayed two notable tendencies: a decided sympathy toward the old Porfirian elite and a driving ambition to acquire a fortune. He married a daughter of the Becerra family, the long-time political bosses of Urique in southwest Andres del Río district, and was enthusiastically engaged in the local social life of the Porfirian old guard.[32] While governor, Almeida founded an extensive economic empire. In partnership with Luis Esther Estrada, Juan F. Trevino, and brother Esteban, the governor bought the timberlands of the Chihuahua Lumber Company. Another brother, Casímiro, acquired the property of the Cargill Lumber Company.[33] The American managers of both firms accused Almeida of using the state's agrarian laws to force them to sell the properties.[34] They also claimed that he had stolen timber from their lands before purchasing them. The United States consul in Chihuahua maintained that when Almeida had taken office he was a man of modest means, but had accumulated enough money not only to obtain these two lumber operations for 300,000 dollars (U.S. currency) but a fine house in Ciudad Chihuahua for 25,000 (US) dollars. The funds reportedly derived from his rake-off from gambling in Ciudad Juárez and from protecting ore thieves.[35] After his ouster in 1927, his critics accused him of stealing from the state treasury as well. All of this led the U.S. consul to conclude that Almeida was a man of "rather unsavory reputation" and that Chihuahua was generally "in the hands of dishonest officials."[36] The family eventually became important ranchers.

Governor Almeida showed little sympathy toward land reform or labor. Little redistribution took place during his term. Moreover, little was done to distribute the Terrazas estate. In fact, the Terrazas managed to repurchase part of it.[37] He also showed no sympathy toward workers, refusing to implement labor reforms passed by the state legislature and actively intervening in labor-management disputes in order to prevent strikes. The head of the Confederación Obrera de Chihuahua accused Almeida of violating the state's labor law and trying to divide workers and campesinos. The governor feared that the radical new laws and strikes would jeopardize the recovery of mining.[38] The industry boomed during his term.

Jesús Antonio stridently tried to construct a political dynasty, installing a brother as municipal president (*presidente municipal*) of Ciudad Juárez and a brother-in-law as municipal president in Ciudad Chihuahua. He also initially had strong support in the western part of the state.[39] His marriage and efforts to accommodate the Porifirian elite were other important parts of his strategy.

Unfortunately for him, Almeida made enemies, organized into the Partido Liberal Progresista Chihuahense, led by Fernándo Orozco E., a local cattle agent. The governor complained as early as November 1925 that his opponents were trying to undermine his relations with the central government.[40] Orozco allied with the new chief of military operations (Jefe de Operaciones Militares) in Chihuahua, General Marcelo Caraveo; and with the help of PLPC members of the state legislature, Almeida was overthrown on 15 April 1927. Jesús Antonio barely escaped with his life, entering exile in El Paso, Texas.[41]

Almeida fell because he had no strong base either among the peasantry, like Saturnino Cedillo in San Luis Potosí; or among the labor unions, like Adalberto Tejeda in Veracruz.[42] The strong backing he once enjoyed in western Chihuahua among small landowners dissipated in the agricultural depression of 1926. As an emerging estate owner and cattleman, he had little in common with, or attraction for, peasants. As an industrialist, he exhibited no rapport with labor. The secretary general of the Confederacion Obreros de Chihuahua declared that "Almeida had lost all popularity," because of "an inexpert, weak government, dominated by a *camarilla*."[43] Reflecting growing sentiment, *El Correo de Chihuahua* judged Almeida's first year as the "political disaster of *almeidismo*."[44] Like many of the northern middle-class revolutionaries, Almeida had more sympathy with the ideas and goals of the Porfirian elite than with the peasants or workers. The governor also lost regional backing so important in Chihuahuan politics. We have already seen how support dissipated in western districts. His other bases, Ciudad Juárez and Ciudad Chihuahua, proved unstable. His brother Alberto was popular in Juárez, but the situation there was highly competitive and treacherous. More importantly, the garrison commander there was an ally of Caraveo. Brother-in-law Socorro García proved an unpopular municipal president, because he was imposed from the outside.[45] Without grass-roots underpinning, Almeida was extremely vulnerable to any loss of confidence by the central government.

There is some considerable debate over the role played by President Calles in the overthrow of Almeida. the U.S. embassy believed that Calles opposed the coup.[46] Ernest Gruening reported that the president found it "extremely distressing."[47] Mexico City newspapers considered the ouster a defeat for Calles, perhaps, the first blow of an anti-Obregón campaign.[48] A few days after the coup, the president publicly continued to believe that Almeida was a personal friend.[49] The *El Paso Times* maintained that the central governemnt had not precipitated the coup, but it had resulted from the feud between Almeida and jefe de operaciones militar Caraveo.[50] To add credibility to this view, Calles refused to recognize the rebels' choice for governor, Manuel

Mascareñas, Jr.[51] On the other side, the day before the coup a close associate of Calles, Senator Nicolás Pérez, had flown into Chihuahua, allegedly to give the go-ahead. Almeida himself blamed Pérez for his demise.[52] If the incident is placed in national context, the hand of Calles is seen more clearly, for in 1925, 1926, and 1927 no less than twenty-five governors were deposed.[53] Whichever the case, however, the central government could not or did not want to reinstate Almeida. The legislature named Fernándo Orozco E. to the office in May.

Almeida's fall marked the end of two important trends. He was the last independent political boss in Chihuahua. Caraveo, who might have established an autonomous, popular base, revolted after only six months in office. The others that followed, like Luis L. León and General Rodrigo Quevedo during the 1930s, had close ties to the national government. It was Almeida's independence that may have led Calles to support his overthrow. Almeida, in addition, represented the last gasp of western Chihuahua in state politics. Thereafter, the center of political power shifted, once and for all, to Cuidad Juárez and Ciudad Chihuahua.

The state legislature installed Manuel Mascareñas, Jr., as governor, but the national government refused to recognize him, because as customs collector at Ciudad Juárez he was a federal employee and, as such, was not eligible to hold state office. Consequently, Fernándo Orozco E. took over until October 1928, when Caraveo assumed the governorship. According to one American consul, Orozco gave the state its "best administration in many years," spending considerable sums on school and public works construction, although there was some question regarding the misappropriation of 200,000 pesos during his term.[54]

Marcelo Caraveo was one of the enigmas of the revolution. Born in western Chihuahua in 1884, he joined the revolt at its beginning in 1910. He fought under Pascual Orozco against Porfirio Díaz. Caraveo was thereafter successively a Huertista, Zapatista, Felicista, Pelaecista, and Obregonista, emerging as a brigadier general in 1920. He served in various military posts until transferred to Chihuahua in 1925 as chief of military operations in Chihuahua and Durango.[55] After helping to overthrow Almeida, he was elected governor in 1928. The U.S. Consul considered Caraveo a "high type," but did not extend the kind words to the rest of his administration.[56] He had not served six months when he joined the Plan de Hermosillo revolt against President Portes Gil in March 1929. After the defeat of the so-called Escobar or Renevador rebellion, Caraveo went into exile in El Paso, where he lived modestly. A self-professed man of principle, Caraveo believed that Calles and his puppets had betrayed the revolution.[57] Caraveo and Almeida, though opposed, were the last of the homegrown, independent revolutionary governors of Chihuahua.

After Caraveo went over to the rebellion, the regime sent trusted agent Luis L. León to Chihuahua as governor. León was a founder and the first president of the Comisión Nacional de Irrigación; founder and first president of the Comisión Nacional Agraria; and founder of the Banco de México and the Banco Nacional de Crédito Agrícola y Ganadero. Beginning in 1918, he served several terms in the national congress. In 1923 he was Subsecretario de Hacienda y Crédito Público. Calles named him Ministerio de Agricultura in 1928.[58] León made state politics more responsive to the national government and more radical by advocating land reform. León became the virtual boss of the state's agrarian organizations. In June 1929 he oversaw the creation of the Partido Revolucionario Chihuahuense.[59] León declared at its first convention that the principles of the revolution had not triumphed. The rural population had not received proper assistance, nor had workers obtained all of their rights. He maintained that previous governors had ruled in the name of the revolution but did nothing for the benefit of peasants and workers, while respecting the rights of the reactionaries. The governor condemned large landowners for their past influence on governors that prevented land reform. He also advocated free municipal elections to get rid of the old bosses. León had to rebuild a political base from chaos. He brought together divided campesino groups and began to reorganize labor. He treated the rebels of 1929 with magnanimity.[60]

Despite his advocacy of land reform, León did not favor collectivism, which he considered a foreign method unsuited for Mexico. In fact, he was a champion of small holders, whose rights he fought to protect against the onslaught of agrarians. As a large landowner himself, León espoused private property.[61]

Unfortunately for the political stability of Chihuahua, León spent much time out of state, spearheading the campaign of Pascual Ortiz Rubio for president in the North.[62] During his long absences, Francisco R. Almada served as interim governor.

Almada's career differed considerably from the other governors, for he was neither a military leader nor an agent of the central government. Originally a schoolteacher in western Chihuahua, in 1918 he had been appointed by the governor at age twenty-two as municipal president of Chínipas. He was subsequently elected to two consecutive terms in that post. In 1922, Almada was elected to the state legislature. From 1924 to 1926, he was elected deputy in the national congress. He returned to the state legislature in 1928. It was as a legislator that he was named interim governor for two periods, through most of 1929 and 1930. He faithfully carried on León's reform program, instituting a new Ley de Medidas y Enagenación de Terrenos Municipales that imposed high taxes on undeveloped city land and strongly warned local authorities not to side with large landowners.[63]

Through the efforts of León and Almada (added to those earlier of Ignacio C. Enríquez), Chihuahua had distributed more land than any other state by 1933—more than 2.5 million acres. Although landownership remained highly concentrated—in 1930, 3.5 percent of the landholdings owned 85.7 percent of the farm land—León and Almada oversaw much progress.[64]

The decade ended as it had begun, in tumult. Almada became embroiled in a dispute with the state Supremo Tribunal de Justicia that resulted in the impeachment of its chief magistrate and the expulsion of three deputies from the state legislature. The following year he was overthrown temporarily by a rival group, but was restored by the central government.[65]

While rival revolutionary factions competed for power at the state level and the central government sought to extend its control over Chihuahua, the prerevolutionary municipal political bosses fought to retain their power. Through the 1920s several maintained their positions successfully. In isolated subregions in the western and southwestern parts of the state, the old elite dominated by virtue of its overwhelming economic power and geography. Both the Becerras and Rascóns, for example, ruled their home grounds from the middle of the nineteenth century and had been steadfast allies of Luis Terrazas, the boss of Chihuahua for much of the Porfiriato. The Becerras of Urique, a mining center in southwestern Andres del Río district, continued to rule through the middle of the decade, strengthening their hold by marrying a daughter to Governor Jesús Antonio Almeida. The Rascóns of Uruachic, Rayón district, dominated local politics and the economy into the 1930s. The Samaniegos, political bosses of Ciudad Juárez during the Díaz era and close allies of Terrazas, like Becerras, extended their influence through marriage. No fewer than five postrevolutionary municipal presidents of Juárez were relations.[66]

Even in subregions where the revolution had begun or had drawn fervent backing, some of the old bosses stayed in power. In revolutionary-hotbed Coyame, the same family that held the post of municipal president in 1906–1908 held it in 1929.[67] In Janos, the first pueblo to arise in 1910, essentially the same local power structure existed in the late 1920s as had been there in 1910. The same families (Rentería, Baeza, and Echeribe) ran local politics and the major hacendados (Baeza, Azcarate, and Zozoya) kept their lands.[68] In fractionalized Guerrero district, another birthplace of the revolution, the same families that had vied for local influence for a half century—Casavantes, Ricos, Dozals, Ordoñez, Domínguez, and Caraveos—continued to do so.[69]

At least on the surface, all Chihuahua earned for a decade of civil war was another decade of chaos. In ten years, no individual or group firmly controlled state politics. No governor finished his term. The central government, even under the harsh direction of Calles, was unable to bring order to the unruly state. Legislatures quarreled with governors. Governors battled military zone commanders and the courts. There was no peace.

Underneath, however, were the beginnings of crucial changes. With the devastation of agriculture and the ruin of small mineholding and mining in isolated regions, political and economic power shifted decisively (even more dramatically than during the Porfiriato) toward the central core of the state and Ciudad Juárez. Mining was concentrated in the central subregion from Santa Eulalia south to Parral. Juárez generated large amounts of money through gambling and liquor. Furthermore, there was a generational shift. The original revolutionaries were dead, in exile, or retired. Of all Chihuahuan governors after 1920 only Ignacio C. Enríquez, Marcelo Caraveo, and Rodrigo M. Quevedo were significant military leaders in the revolution. Characteristically, the new leaders—and the three above as well—were less dedicated revolutionaries than "freebooters." Caraveo and Quevedo were brilliant opportunists. New bases of power had also emerged: peasants and labor organizations. In their efforts to consolidate control of political power, Enríquez and Obregón had started to tap them. To his detriment, Almeida had ignored them. León brought them into a structured organization.

The Chihuahuan case exemplified general political conditions in Mexico. Politics in most states were fragmented and tumultuous. One state, Nayarít, had five governors in 1925 alone. The central government was often able to topple an unacceptable leader or group, but just as often unable to sustain them. Obregón and Calles compromised with state bosses, because when confronted with three major rebellions (de la Huerta, Cristero, and Escobar) in ten years they desperately needed military allies. The revolutionary principles of land reform labor rights frequently gave way to expediency. New leaders, many of whom had come late to the revolution, saw politics as an opportunity for enrichment. As landowners and industrialists, they worked against reform. Their growing alienation from peasants and workers contributed to the conflict and instability.

The Chihuahuan case points us to several conclusions about the character of Mexican politics during the 1920s. First, the central government had not consolidated its control over the states. This did not mean, however, that it was bereft of influence or that its influence was not growing. Second, the importance of coercive power was paramount. It was no accident that governors Enríquez and Almeida arose from the *defensas sociales* and that Caraveo was the military zone commander. Third, very little had changed on the municipal level. The old bosses retained control. Fourth, because of adverse economic conditions, political instability, lack of centralized control in the states by the federal government or the municipalities by the state government, and unwillingness on the part of the new leadership to jeopardize their newly acquired property, reform did not proceed at a rapid pace except when a military threat made it politically expedient. Finally, the decade was beset by violence. Mexico would need Cárdenas and peace to heal its wounds and to rebuild.

Notes

The author wishes to thank the Tinker Foundation, the American Council of Learned Societies/Social Science Research Council's Joint Committee on Latin American Studies, and the Rutgers Research Council for their support of the larger project of which this is a part.

1. J. B. Stewart to Secretary of State (hereafter cited as SS), 17 Februaray 1922, U.S. National Archives, Record Group 59, General Records of the Department of State (hereafter cited as USNARG 59), Decimal Files, Internal Affairs of Mexico, 1910–1929, 812.52T2/6; Manuel A. Machado, *The North Mexican Cattle Industry, 1910–1975* (College Station: Texas A & M University Press, 1981), 31–32; Lorenzo Meyer, *Historia de la Revolución Mexicana, 1928–1934: El conflicto social y los gobiernos del maximato* (México: El Colegio de México, 1978), 288; Pedro Saucedo Montemayor, *Historia de la ganaderia en México* (México: UNAM, 1984), 94.

2. *El Periódico Oficial del Estado de Chihuahua* (hereafter cited as POC), 8 July 1922, 5; C. Harper, American vice-consul, "Crop Conditions in Ciudad Juárez, 1923," 29 December 1923, USNARG 84, Ciudad Juárez, 861, 1923, vol. 5; Robert M. Ott, American vice-consul, Chihuahua City, "Agricultural Resources of the State of Chihuahua," 24 July 1931, USNARG 84, Chihuahua City, 861, 1931, 7; Thomas McEnelly, American consul, "Review of Commerce and Industry for the Quarter Ending September 30, 1927," 7 November 1927, USNARG 84, Chihuahua City; Manuel Aguilar Saenz to McEnelly, 8 April 1925, USNARG 84, Chihuahua City: McEnelly to to Julio Ornelas, 17 February 1927, USNARG 84, Chihuahua City, 861.3; "Review of Commerce and Industry for the Quarter ending September 30, 1924," 18 October 1924, USNARG 84, Chihuahua City; Unofficial estimates. J. B. Stewart to SS, 17 February 1922, USNARG 59, 812.52T52/6; *Boletín Comercial* (Ciudad Chihuahua), 15 July 1924, 24.

3. "Review of Commerce and Industry for the Quarter Ending March 31, 1927,"

27 April 1927, U.S. National Archives, Records of the Department of State, Record Group 84, Correspondence of the American Consulates (hereafter cited as USNARG 84), Chihuahua City.

4. "Review of Commerce and Industry for the Quarter Ending September 30, 1924," 18 October 1924, USNARG 84, Chihuahua City; McEnelly to Department of State (DS), 7 January 1925, USNARG 84, Chihuahua City; Dye, "Economic Report for Ciudad Juárez for the Quarter Ending June 30, 1926," USNARG 84, Ciudad Juarez, 610.1, 1926, 3; "General Economic Report, April-July, 1928," U.S. National Archives, Record Group 165, U.S. Military Intelligence Reports: Mexico, 1919–1941, No. 2231, Reel 9.

5. McEnelly, "Review of Commerce and Industry for the Quarter Ending December 31, 1924," 27 January 1925, USNARG 84, Chihuahua City.

6. Governor Ignacio C. Enríquez to Torreblanca, Private Secretary to the President (PSP), 9 July 1923, México, Archivo General de la Nación, Ramo de Presidentes, Obregón-Calles (hereafter cited as O-C), 101-P-10; David J. D. Myers, American consul, "Report on the Financing of Construction of Water Works in Chihuahua," 7 December 1928, USNARG 84, Chihuahua City, 1926, 5.

7. Chihuahua, Secretaría General de Gobierno, Sección Estadística, *Boletín Estadística del Estado de Chihuahua*, No. 3, Años de 1923–24 (Chihuahua: Imprenta del Gobierno, 1926), 86; Comite Directivo para la Investigación de los Recursos de México, *La industria minera en el estado de Chihuahua*, Boletín no. 7 (México: n.p., 1946), p. 8; McEnelly, "Review of Commerce and Industry for the Quarter Ending December 31, 1924," 27 January 1925, USNARG 84, Chihuahua City.

8. R. F. Manahan, "Historical Sketch of the Mining Operations of the American Smelting and Refining Company in Mexico," unpublished ms., 1948, provides an excellent summary of Asarco's acquisitions during this period.

9. The first three centers were dominated by ASARCO.

10. *Informe* of the Presidente Municipal of Batopilas, J. M. Morales, 26 March 1921.

11. *El Paso Times*, 11 February 1922, 3, and 17 February 1922, 12; letter to R. H. Smith, 10 February 1922, Mexican Northwestern Railway Papers, John H. McNeely Collection, box 11, Univeristy of Texas at El Paso.

12. Letter to R. Home Smith, 2 October 1922, President, Mexican Northwestern Railway Papers; *El Paso Times*, 30 September 1922, 1, and 1 October 1922, 1.

13. G-2 Report, "Stability of Government and Revolutionary Activities," 29 December 1923, USNARG 165, 4367, Reel 1; Obregón to Enríquez, 30 January 1924, AGNO-C, 101-R2-P; *El Paso Times*, 31 January 1924, 1; *La Patria* (El Paso), 11 February 1924, 1, and 18 March 1924, 1. It is clear from the accounts in *La Patria* and the *El Paso Times* that neither Villa nor Chao fared very well, suffering defeat after defeat.

14. "Review of Commerce and Industry for the Quarter Ending 30 June 1924," USNARG 84, Chihuahua City.

15. *El Correo de Chihuahua*, 11 July 1925; *El Paso Times*, 14 November 1926, 1; Dye, "Political Report for Ciudad Juarez for January 1927," 7 February 1927, USNARG 84, Ciudad Juarez, 800, 1927, 3.

16. *El Continental* (El Paso), 18 June 1927, 2.

17. G-2 Report, "Mexico Political: Stability of Governmment, Armed Revolutionary Movements throughout the Republic from January 1 to February 1928," 16 February 1928, USNARG 165, 1942, Reel 2; G-2 Report, "Armed Revolutionary Movements from February 1 to March 1928," 23 March 1928, USNARG 165, 1996, Reel 2.

18. *La Voz de Parral*, 5 March 1929, 6 March 1929, and 7 March 1929; G-2, "Armed Revolutionary Movements," 14 May 1929, USNARG 165, 2392, Reel 2; Enrique Leikens, Consul General of Mexico, El Paso, to John W. Dye, American consul, Cuidad Juárez, 26 March 1929; México, Archivo General de la Nación, Ramo de Presidentes, Portes Gil, 3/343, 5613; General José Luis Amezcua, Jefe del Estado Mayor de la Jefetura de Operaciones Militares de Chihuahua to Secretario A. Roldán, 22 June 1929, AGN, Portes Gil, 617, 11180.

19. Francisco R. Almada, *Gobernadors del Estado de Chihuahua* (México: Imprenta del Cámara de Diputados, 1950), 525–31; Armando B. Chávez M., "Hombres de la Revolución en Chihuahua," unpublished ms., University of El Paso, 84–85.

20. Harry B. Ott, vice-consul, "Economic Report for the Chihuahua Consular District, January to April 1923," 31 May 1923, USNARG 84, Chihuahua City; Enríquez to Obregón, 20 October 1921, AGN-OC, 731-Ch-1; Francisco R. Almada, "Preliminares del Sistema Nacional de Riego Número Cinco," *Boletín de la Sociedad Chihuahuense de Estudios Históricos* 10:5 (1958), 1–5.

21. Linda B. Hall, "Alvaro Obregón and the Politics of Mexican Land Reform, 1920–1924,: *Hispanic American Historical Review* 60 (May 1980): 226; Octavio Santibañez, Secretario Interno, Partido Nacional Agrarista, to Obregón, 14 July 1923, AGN-OC, 701-Ch-3.

22. Ibid.

23. Files 812.52T27/1-40, USNARG 59, Decimal Files and Expediente 806-T, AGN-OC deal with the Terrazas–McQuatters transaction. Machado, *Cattle Industry*, summarizes the affair.

24. *El Periódico Oficial del Estado de Chihuahua*, 28 July 1923, p. 2 (Chúviscar), 11 August 1923, p. 1 (San Andrés), 16 June 1923, p. 4 (Bachíniva), 16 December 1922, 2–3 (Namiquipa).

25. Acuerdo de la Secretaría de Hacienda y Crédito Público, 4 June 1923, Agustín Moye to Obregón, 3 October 1923, Moye to Obregón, 23 November 1923, and Serafín Legarreta to Obregón, 27 July 1926, AGN-OC, 818-P-13.

26. McEnelly, to Alexander Wedell, American consul-general, 3 December 1924, USNARG 84, Chihuahua City.

27. Asarco to Obregón, 19 September 1923, Ignacio Enríquez to Obregón, 19 September 1923, and Enríquez to President, 1 October 1923, AGN-OC, 407-A-12;

William Parker Mitchell, American consul, to SS, 19 September 1923, Mitchell to SS, 3 October 1923, USNARG 84, Chihuahua City.

28. "Review of Commerce and Industry for the Quarter Ending June 30, 1924," USNARG 84, Chihuahua City; J. Juan Rivas and G. Romero to Obregón, 4 March 1923, AGN-OC, 307-E-10.

29. Almada, *Gobernadores*, 557.

30. Reinaldo Talavera to President, 19 May 1924, E. Cervantes to Obregón, 20 August 1924, Ricardo Ruiz to President, 5 December 1924, letter to Calles, 12 December 1924, AGN-OC, 407-S-28; McEnelly to SS, "Labor Troubles at Santa Eulalia Mining District," 13 May 1924, USNARG 84, Chihuahua City.

31. Almada, *Gobernadores*, 559–61; Chávez M. "Hombres," 9.

32. *El Correo de Chihuahua*, 6 October 1925, 1, and 21 August 1925, 4.

33. *El Correo de Chihuahua*, 4 September 1925; McEnelly, "Review of Commerce and Industry for the Quarter Ending 30 September 1925," 19 October 1925, USNARG 84, Chihuahua City.

34. McEnelly to SS, 14 May 1924, USNARG, 84, Confidential Files, 1922–1928.

35. "Annual Report on Commerce and Industry for 1926," USNARG 84, Confidential Files, 1922–1928.

36. Ibid.; McEnelly to SS, 20 April 1927, USNARG 84, Confidential Files, 1922–28.

37. Extracto del Informe general Estado que guardan los terrenos que comprenden el latifundio Terrazas propiedad de la Caja de Préstamos para Obras de Irrigación y Fomento de la Agricultura, S.A., enclosure to Ing. Manuel Romero González, Banco Nacional de Crédito Agrícola, S.A., to President Pascual Ortiz Rubio, 7 November 1930, AGN, Ramo de Presidentes, Ortiz Rubio, 24 (1930) 13564.

38. "Review of Commerce and Industry for the quarter Ending 31 December 1924," 27 January 1925, USNARG 84, Chihuahua City; McEnelly to SS, 26 November 1924, USNARG 84, Chihuahua City; Lázaro Canares, Secretario Exterior, Confederación Obrera de Chihuahua, to Calles, 21 January 1925, AGN-OC, 707-Ch-5.

39. McEnelly to SS, 29 June 1926, USNARG 84, Chihuahua City.

40. Almeida to Diputado Francisco García Carranza, 12 November 1925, AGN-OC, 428-Ch-12.

41. McEnelly, "Report on Commerce and Industry for the Quarter Ending September 30, 1927," 7 October 1927, USNARG 84, Chihuahua City; *El Paso Times*, 16, 17, 19, 20, and 21 April 1927; Ernest Gruening, *Mexico and Its Heritage* (New York: The Century Company, 1928), 410–12; Jean Meyer, *Historia de la Revolución Mexicana, Periódo 1924–1928: Estado y Sociedad con Calles* (México: El Colegio de México, 1977), 184.

42. Dudley Ankerson, *Agrarian Warlord, Saturnino Cedillo and the Mexican Revolution in San Luis Potosí* (DeKalb: Northern Illinois University Press, 1984); Heather F. Salamini, *Agrarian Radicalism in Veracruz* (Lincoln: University of Nebraska Press, 1971).

43. Lázaro Canales, Secretario Exterior, Confederación obrera de Chihuahua, to President, 21 January 1925, AGN-OC, 707-Ch-5.
44. *El Correo de Chihuahua*, 8 September 1925, 1.
45. "Annual Report on Commerce and Industry for 1926," USNARG 84, Confidential Files, 1922–1928; Armando B. Chávez M., *Sesenta anos de gobierno municipal: jefes políticos del distrito Bravos y presidentes municipales del municipio de Juárez, 1897–1960* (México: Gráfica Cervantina, 1959), 221–31.
46. H. F. Arthur Schoenfeld, counselor, U.S. Embassy, to McEnelly, 26 April 1927, USNARG 84, Confidential Files, 1922–1928.
47. Gruening, *Mexico and Its Heritage*, 411.
48. Meyer, *Estado y sociedad con Calles*, 184; *El Paso Times*, 20 April 1927, 8.
49. *El Continental*, 17 April 1927, 1.
50. *El Paso Times*, 17 April 1927, 1.
51. *El Paso Times*, 9 May 1927, 1; Meyer, *Estado y sociedad con Calles*, 184.
52. McEnelly to James R. Sheffield, U.S. Ambassador, 6 May 1927, USNARG 84, Confidential Files, 1922–28; *El Paso Times*, 19 April 1927, 8.
53. Meyer, *Estado y sociedad con Calles*, 182–83.
54. Enclosure to David J. D. Myers to SS, 7 December 1927, USNARG 84, Chihuahua City, 1928, 5; McEnelly, "Report on Commerce and Industry for the Quarter Ending September 30, 1927," 7 November 1927, USNARG 84, Chihuahua City.
55. Almada, *Gobernadores*, 568–70; Chávez M., "Hombres," 47–48; Marcelo Caraveo, "Memorias del General Marcelo Caraveo," unpublished ms., 1931, University of Texas at El Paso.
56. Confidential Enclosure to Myers to SS, 7 December 1927, USNARG 84, Chihuahua City.
57. Caraveo, "Memorias," 210–63.
58. Almada, *Gobernadores*, 571–73.
59. W. J. McCafferty, American consul, Chihuahua City, "Political Conditions in Chihuahua during Months of May, June, and July, 1929," 30 July 1929, USNARG 59, Decimal files, 812.00 Chihuahua/32.
60. Ibid.; Ing. Luis L. León to President, 25 April 1929, AGN, Ramo de Presidentes, Portes Gil, 3/340, 7038; McCafferty, "Political Conditions in Chihuahua during August 1929," 31 August 1929, USNAR 59, Decimal files, 812.00 Chihuahua/34.
61. León purchased a part of the Terrazas estate. See correspondence in AGN, Ortiz Rubio, 24 (1930) 13564 and 24 (1930) 13187; León to President, 10 November 1930, AGN, Ortiz Rubio, 24 (1930) 13681; Luis León, *La doctrina, la táctica, y la política agraria de la Revolución Mexicana* (México: Talleres de El nacional Revolucionario, 1931), 4–11, cited in Albert L. Michaels, "Mexican Politics and Nationalism from Calles to Cardenas" (Ph.D. diss., University of Pennsylvania, 1966).

62. Almada, *Gobernadores*, 572.

63. "Political conditions in Chihuahua, September 1929," 4 October 1929, USNARG 59, Decimal files, 812.00 Chihuahua/41; *El Continental*, 27 December 1929, 6.

64. Eyler N. Simpson, *The Ejido: Mexico's Way Out* (Chapel Hill: University of North Carolina Press, 1937), 610–11.

65. McCafferty, "Political Conditions in Chihuahua, October 1929," 31 October 1929, USNARG 59, Decimal Files, 812.00 Chihuahua/42; Memorandum dated October 1929, AGN, Portes Gil, 6/500; *El Paso Times*, 26–29 June 1930.

66. For a more detailed discussion of the Becerras, Rascóns, and Samaniegos: Mark Wasserman, "Strategies for Survival of the Porfirian Elite in Revolutionary Mexico: Chihuahua during the 1920s"; and Wasserman, *Capitalists, Caciques, and Revolution: The Native Elite and Foreign Enterprise in Chihuahua Mexico*, 154–1911 (Chapel Hill: Univeristy of North Carolina Press, 1984), 39, 137, 24, 35, 38, and 53.

67. *El Periódico Oficial del Estado de Chihuahua*, 15 February 1906, 6–7, 15 January 1908, 7, 23 January 1910, 10, 26 October 1919, 9, and 30 November 1929, 6; Chihuahua, *Directorio General de Municipios* (Chihuahua: p., 1927), 340; Chihuahua, Secretaria de Gobierno, Sección Estadistica, *Chihuahua 1934*, 93; *El Correo de Chihuahua*, 17 March 1904, 2.

68. *El Periódicio Oficial del Estado de Chihuahua*, 9 January 1908, 5, 21 September 1929, 12, 21 December 1929, 5, 23 November 1929, 12, 12 October 1929, 12–13; *Chihuahua 1934*, 116; José María Ponce de León, *Directorio Industrial, etc. del Estado de Chihuahua* (Chihuahua: Imp. El Chihuahuense, 1907), 119; Chihuahua, *Directorio General de Municipios*, 359–61; *El Correo de Chihuahua*, 28 November 1923, 2, and 8 December 1925, 3.

69. *El Periódico Oficial del Estado de Chihuahua*, 12 January 1908, 6, 23 January 1910, 8–9, 30 November 1929, 5; *Chihuahua 1934*, 113–14; Chihuahua, *Directorio General de Municipios*, 353–57, 359; *El Correo de Chihuahua* 15 December 1925, 1.

TLAXCALA

SIGNOS.

CIUDAD *Capital de Estado*
CIUDAD *Cab. de Distrito*
Villa *Cab. de Distrito*
Villa *Cab. de Municip.*
Pueblo *Cab. de Dist.*
Pueblo *Cab. de Municip.*
Pueblo
Hacienda
Rancho

10

Tlaxcala

Consolidating a Cacicazgo

Raymond Th. J. Buve

This chapter analyzes the emergence and consolidation of a regional ruling group during the 1920s. Mainly of civilian descent, the members of this group succeeded in displacing the earlier revolutionary military chiefs and successfully defusing the original popular basis of the revolutionary chiefs, a highly militant peasantry which had vested interests in land and autonomy acquired during the Armed Revolution.

The first section will summarize findings from earlier reserach on the origin and development of the Tlaxcalan revolutionary leadership, its final incorporation into Constitutionalist ranks and the demise of the autonomous revolutionary movement.[1] During these years of crisis for the local revolutionary movement, a new civilian leadership emerged that came to power with the Sonorenses in 1920. Against many odds, a highly militant peasantry among them, they succeeded in consolidating their position between 1920 and 1925 into a *cacicazgo* which, at first sight, is not unlike other postrevolutionary *cacicazgos* of the 1920s. How did they manage to do it and what was their relationship to the Sonorenses? These questions will be tackled in the later sections.

The most distinguishing feature of state-level power politics in the 1920s was the high incidence of conflict and violence, due, to a considerable degree, to the social and political conditions created by the revolution and the Sonorenses' attempt to control or redress them. The Armed Revolution (1910–1917) and the slow process of consolidation of the revolutionary regime gave not only ample room for a mosaic of revolutionary movements strongly different from each other in terms of their roots, objectives, and results, but also fostered the evolution of regional *cacicazgos* from among the competing revolutionary chieftaincies in the states. When Obregón came to power, he and his successor Calles faced a myriad of revolutionary power struggles between regional contenders who tried to forge or maintain their *cacicazgos*, entering into shifting alliances with rival political groups at the federal level. Given their lack of control over the army, Congress, and the states, Obregón and Calles realized the necessity of maintaining an equilibrium and carefully playing one contender against the other as long as the federal government would be unable to impose its will over all of them. This equilibrium was frequently threatened by disruptive issues like the presidential succession, the church–state conflict, and the relations with the United States.[2]

Under these circumstances, attempts to gain control over state governments and to prevent rivals from doing so required careful calculations and prudent maneuvering on the part of the Sonorenses. Even under President Calles, dislodgement of a strong governor-cacique (Jalisco, 1925–1926) or an attempt to create order by imposing it on a trusted governor on a state ripped apart by local conflict (Puebla, 1924–1927) sometimes took years. The president, his cabinet members, rival political groups in Congress, labor or peasant leadership, and military commanders all tended to manipulate state-level conflict with an eye on the national issues of the moment. At the same time, local political leadership, the ruling groups, and their political enemies did not hesitate to grab the opportunities offered by political mobilization around a hot national issue to gain whatever support they could get at the federal level or in adjacent states. In short, local conflict had its immediate ramifications on the other levels and vice-versa. Obregón and Calles made ample use of it in their policy to gain control at the state level.[3]

Given the Sonorenses' firm intention to strengthen their grip on the states, governors with an eye on the establishment of a *cacicazgo* often rebelled in the end against deliberate attempts to erode their local power base and to make them more and more dependent on federal recognition and legitimation. Even those who stayed loyal always tried to maintain the autonomy they had acquired at the risk of harboring ambitions incongruent with the growing power of the federal government. From the Sonorenses' point of view, it may have been far more attractive to promote local ambitious leadership with a weak local power base and strongly dependent on federal support. It could be more reliable and useful not only for federal control on their native states or as a watchdog or basis in the struggle of the federal government for control over adjacent states, but also, especially in Calles's case, as a means to clamp down on local labor and land-tenure disputes which threatened his more and more restrictive views on social reform.[4]

The case of Tlaxcala in the 1920s seems to be a nice example. Here, the emergence of a ruling group was able to establish a dependent *cacicazgo* with strong federal support in the face of a militant peasantry and was on the threshold of political crisis in the state of Puebla.

Revolutionary Leadership and the Making of a Militant Peasantry

At the end of the Porfiriato the state of Tlaxcala had within its boundaries two different types of agrarian structure. In the north, large estates covered the electoral districts of Ocampo, Morelos, and Juárez, two-thirds of the state's territory and about one-third of its population. Commercial agriculture was based on the cultivation of wheat, barley and corn, cattle raising, pulque production, and the exploitation of forests for timber, firewood, and charcoal. Most of the haciendas depended on resident labor and, to a minor degree, on permanent or seasonal laborers from neighboring and often nearly landless villages.

Revolutionary leadership, however, came from central and south Tlaxcala, where a different type of agrarian structure prevailed. This region became the main basis of the Tlaxcala Revolutionary Movement (TRM)[5] and the *patria chica* of most of its leaders. By 1910, the rising demand for land and labor had seriously reduced the natural resources of the indigenous village communities, changing their population from subsistence cultivators to a geographically and occupationally mobile work force. The village-based peasants of central and south Tlaxcala were to a considerable degree integrated as small producers, artisans, and workers in the large commercial agricultural and industrial complex which had its center in Puebla City and extended along the railroad lines to Apizaco, Texmelucan and Atlixco (see Map 10.1). Peasant households combined subsistence agriculture on tiny plots with home industries, weekly or seasonalbe labor on haciendas, and daily or weekly commuting to the factories. They became urban industrial workers "whose roots were in the lands and the rural villages." Commercial agriculture on medium-sized and often irrigated properties and industrial activities in the small towns along the railroads were mostly controlled by the Puebla oligarchy, partly of Spanish descent. Alienation of land and water, higher taxes on small cultivators, reduced piece-wages, dismissals, the *tienda de raya* or truck system, and police repression all contributed to a vigorous peasant tradition of protest. Peasant resistance was strongly influenced by the values and goals of the workers' movements along the Veracruz–Mexico City axis.[6]

Within this framework of restiveness and protest the revolutionary leadership in central and south Tlaxcala and the adjacent districts of Puebla originated. Many of the Tlaxcalan leaders like Máximo Rojas and Anastasio Meneses were smallholders, textile workers, and peddlers. Domingo and Cirilo Arenas herded the family flock and, like Antonio and Octavio Hidalgo, were factory workers. Many of them were receptive to the fairly radical and PLM-inspired Maderista movement of Aquiles Serdán in Puebla. Its strong response on the hot issues of land and labor gave the movement roots among peasants and workers, teachers and students.[7] While the Maderista radicals in Puebla failed to gain influence and power after Díaz fell, those in Tlaxcala succeeded in building a strong-based Maderista political party and came to power with a government program which reflected the demands and support of the Puebla radicals. It asked for "the return of stolen lands to communities, the abolition of the land tax for smallholders, the foundation of agricultural colonies for landless peasants, better labor conditions for workers, and the punishment of Porfirista officials guilty of repression and murder."[8]

The election of peasant worker Antonio Hidalgo as governor triggered a fairly unique process of political mobilization and polarization. After only a year of political struggle the shocked Tlaxcalan elites were able to bring down Hidalgo's government. With the onset of the counterrevolution in 1913 repression began, and the surviving Maderista radicals went into hiding or resorted to guerrilla warfare. However, unlike the nearby Zapata movement, the Tlaxcalan revolutionaries, like their Puebla friends, lacked a strong unanimously accepted leadership and had never been able to gain sufficient political autonomy to realize their major goals. Only after long deliberations was Máximo Rojas, a veteran from the Maderista revolution, accepted as commander of the Tlaxcalan revolutionary forces.

As was to be expected, after Huerta's fall in July 1914, the small and rather loosely unified Tlaxcalan revolutionary forces were forthwith incorporated into the Constitutionalist armies. Rojas was appointed provisional governor and military commander and promoted to general, but none of his fellow officers obtained the desired rank of general.[9]

Personal ambitions, a zeal for autonomy, and social revenge against landlords and local Huertistas finally provoked a major schism among the Tlaxcalan revolutionaries. On 12 November, 1914, Domingo Arenas, one of Rojas's senior officers, declared for Zapata. He took most of the officers and men with him and clearly had the support of many village leaders, workers, and peasants in the center and southwest of Tlaxcala. Rojas remained with Carranza, but he only kept the loyalty of a few officers, mostly fellow villagers, who were officials from his own government and the leadership of the recently founded Constitutionalist party, the successor of the extinct Maderista Party. They were to be the leading officials in the Tlaxcalan Constitutionalist government after 1914. In fact, the small Rojas group of early 1915 was the cradle of the *familia revolucionaria,* which was to gain power and keep it throughout the 1920s.

Within a year, however, constitutionalist military successes seriously endangered Arenas's agrarista ideal: direct restitution of lands to village communities and the foundation of agricultural colonies of resident workers on haciendas. In December 1916, Arenas and his troops rejoined Carranza, and Arenas's new position as military commander of the upper Atoyac River basin in Puebla and Tlaxcala gave him, for the time being, the de facto autonomy he needed to realize his ideals under the protection of his own troops. A detailed analysis of the interests involved in Arenas's unification with Carranza, Arenista leadership, and land reform can be found elsewhere and will not be discussed here.[10] What does concern us here is the impact of Arenas's return in the Constitutionalist camp on Tlaxcalan revolutionary politics.[11]

Rojas's position was far from strong at the end of 1916. He only held the position of local military commander and was mistrusted by the state governor, a Carranza appointee, and superior Constitutionalist authorities. He was elected as deputy for Tlaxcala to the Constituent Convention of Querétaro, but the convention refused to recognize him. Nevertheless, the Rojas group showed a clear intention to become the ruling revolutionary group in Tlaxcala and tried to impose their political will and their candidates for local office. From this point of view, they seem to have persistently opposed the attempts to bring Arenas back in the Constitutionalist camp. The fact that commander Rojas was completely left out of the negotiations with Arenas perfectly illustrates his rather weak and marginal position. By spring 1917 Arenas was *the* symbol of agrarianism for the land-hungry peasants of Tlaxcala and completely dominated the south and west of the state. His far-reaching desires for autonomy and his large-scale land distribution would, no doubt, have brought about a confrontation with Carranza if he had not been murdered in August 1917. Carranza immediately saw his chance for consolidation of Constitutionalist power in Tlaxcala, a necessary precondition for the constitutionally required elections of a state government and deputies. Arenas troops were transferred to other states, not without difficulties, and a new governor of non-Tlaxcalan origin, General Luis M. Hernández, was commissioned to establish Constitutionalist authority in Arenista territory and return the haciendas to the owners. Village communities were entitled to present petitions for land to the governor, but had to resume production on the hacienda under fair labor or sharecropping arrangements, while awaiting final presidential decision on their petitions for land. Governor Hernández and the Local Agrarian Commission (CLA) did their utmost to accelerate procedures, no doubt with a clear eye on the political loyalty of the peasants. But the National Agrarian Commission (CNA) and President Carranza did not heed their intentions. the Arenas legacy—

dozens of village communities and agricultural colonies resisting the devolution of "their" hacienda lands to the owners—remained therefore the hot issue of Tlaxcalan electoral politics for years to come. Carranza's reticence in land distribution severely hampered Rojas and his Partido Liberal Constitucionalista (PLCT) in their electoral campaign to gain the peasant vote. On the other hand, the deadlock in land distribution strengthened the political base of Arenista leadership. Within a few weeks after Arenas's death, a group of (mostly civilian) Arenista leaders grasped the possibilities for gaining solid electoral support among a peasantry that felt threatened. The Arenista Partido Liberal launched as candidate for governor one of Arenas's most respected officers, Anastasio Meneses. The Arenista villages clung to their leader. The elections had to be rigged to give Rojas at least a majority in his state legislature.

The Tlaxcalan Constitutionalists in Power

Although Rojas became constitutional governor of Tlaxcala in June 1918, the position of the Tlaxcalan Constitutionalist revolutionary family was still far from consolidated. Its leadership was weak and internally divided; its relations with President Carranza, never the best, gradually worsened; and it was unable to control the militant popular masses in the most densely populated parts of the state.

As mentioned before, Rojas never rose to the level of a strong and widely accepted leader. He was continuously liable to the rivalry of revolutionary leaders who wanted to influence or control him. By 1917 Antonio and Octavio Hidalgo had been able to emerge above their other rivals; they had Rojas accepted by the PLCT as their candidate for the governorship and had him finally elected. During Rojas's term, Antonio Hidalgo was senator and Octavio was secretary general of the state government. In the words of the opposition, "they politically administered señor Rojas" together with General Macario M. Hernández, a Maderista co-revolutionary of Rojas who had risen to an important federal military command. Other contenders like Maderista writer Modesto González Galindo and Gerzayn Ugarte, President Carranza's private secretary and a Tlaxcalan Porfirista deputy who had joined Hidalgo in 1911, found their ambitions for office blocked, and they joined the Arenista opposition party, the PLT, which was still solidly entrenched in the southwestern municipalities.[12]

By 1918 the rural situation in central, south, and west Tlaxcala seemed to be dominated by village-based agrarista power domains linked to the rival Arenistas and Rojistas. In this situation, Governor Rojas proved virtually powerless, checked by opposing interests. Tlaxcalan hacendados continuously pressed President Carranza with their numerous complaints about armed agraristas who resisted their attempts to regain control of their properties. Carranza refused to heed Rojas's urgent pleas to confirm the pending petitions for land, and he ordered the Rojas government again and again to follow proper procedures and return the lands to the owners. Rojas, however, was unable and probably even did not want to dispossess the agraristas, since this would have cost him the loyalty of Rojistas and thwart all his attempts to gain the support of the Arenista peasants. Lack of control over rural areas also reduced the major source of income for Rojas's government: the taxes to be paid by the pulque or grain producing estates. Many owners refused to pay as long as the state government proved unable to guarantee their possessions as well as law and order. [13]

On the other hand, the delicate rural situation in Tlaxcala and the adjacent southern part of Puebla, characterized by insufficient control, offered ample opportunites for the emergence of rival person- or group-centered clientelist systems at the village level. This was, first of all, due to the fact that the existing interests of agraristas remained in jeopardy because of Carranza's refusal to recognize their possessions. What was more, many agrarista leaders were probably well aware of the fact that the amount of land they already controlled often surpassed the rather narrow limits of Carrancista land reform. Carranza never intended to repartition whole haciendas, like Arenas sometimes did. Landless laborers, moreover, never figured among the beneficiaries-to-be of Carrancista land distribution. Second, in densely populated parts of Tlaxcala and adjacent southern Puebla intervillage conflict over land and water was common. The occupation of estate lands or the demarcation of ejidos on hacienda lands donated to a community often provoked, and sometimes revived, serious conflict between villages or between villages and haciendas. This was especially the case when occupation or donation implied that local sharecroppers or rural laborers were to lose their plots and jobs because of the donation of "their" hacienda lands to a neighboring village. In the upper Atoyac River basin of Puebla and Tlaxcala, this intervillage competition was complicated by the issue of access to the irrigation systems. Finally, one has to take into account the problem of public safety. This was not only a problem for landlords or administrators, but just as well for small cultivators and laborers who risked assaults by *bandoloeros*, robbing soldiers or *cabecillos*, who looked for funds, arms, food, and animals. As a consequence, factions within village agrarista leaders with their followers, especially if they had been able to control large amounts of hacienda lands and production, all looked for political alliances and support to defend their vested interests and to dislodge others.[14]

Rojas, no doubt, saw how he could exploit these opportunities, and he succeeded in winning the support of a number of Arenista villages by protecting the interests of the local Arenista faction in keeping the lands they already controlled. However, lack of federal assistance made it impossible for him to protect their interests beyond level of tacit and, as far Carranza was concerned, illegal recognition of the status quo. In fact, there is some evidence to show that Rojas was only able to obtain a minimum level of control by either catering to the Arenists or bringing their local enemies to power, transferring the agrarista possessions to the new Rojistas, an act equally illegal in Carranza's eyes.[15]

While Rojas was struggling for rural control, Rafael Apango and Ignacio Mendoza gradually rose to power within the Rojas ruling group and rivaled the Hidalgo's. Like the Hidalgos they had been partisans of the Armed Revolution in 1911. They never rose to military prominence and started their careers with Rojas as municipal presidents and medium-level officials (1915–1916). When González Galindo and Ugarte clashed with Rojas and the Hidalgos, Mendoza became Rojas's campaign leader for the governorship and became a Rojista deputy himself in 1918.[16]

Obregón's decision to become a candidate for president and his rupture with Carranza intensified the struggle for power between Rojistas and Arenistas, and at the same time, triggered conflict within the Rojas ruling group. To begin with, the Rojas group had good reasons for joining Obregón in 1920. Carranza, no doubt, had supported Rojas in coming to power in 1918 but, as we have seen before, he mistrusted the Tlaxcalan revolutionaries. He saw Rojas compared to Arenistas at best as "el mal menor," the least bad. when General Luis M. Hernández started his pacification of the Arenista zone, Rojas's own troops had no role in the campaign, and Ugarte became the state's special representative before the federal governement. In addition, Carranza refused to heed Rojas's urgent pleas for land distribution, while his private secretary, Ugarte, supported the Arenistas after Rojas came to power. When Rojas's most important advisors, Antonio Hidalgo and General Macario M. Hernández, were arrested in April for their suspected Obregonista loyalties, Rojas publicly declared his support for Obregón and joined his forces. Subsequently, Mendoza took over as provisional Obregonista governor of Tlaxcala.[17]

The Arenista opposition party, PLT, split over the issue of Carranza's successor. Part of its leadership and deputies hoped to win political power with Carranza and refused to join Obregón. With Carranza's defeat and General

Rojas stationed outside the state, Mendoza saw his chance to impose his will on the Arenista "traitors of the country" and his own rivals within the government party PLCT. The Carrancistas were thrown out of office, and Mendoza saw to it that all the Arenista municipalities voted for Obregón. The government party choose Apango, a client and associate of Mendoza, as candidate for governor, and the disappointed Antonio Hidalgo left the PLCT. By March 1921, Mendoza had been able to have Apango elected governor and impose his candidates in the municipal and state elections. For sure, the Arenistas resisted. Their candidate for governor, Arenista General Antonio Mora, rebelled twice and was caught. He was shot like Cirilo Arenas, Domingo's brother, who had rebelled against Carranza in 1918–1919. *Ayuntamientos* and village agrarian committees complained by the dozens, sending petitions to *gobernación* and the president or asking for federal military protection, but to no avail. [18]

Consolidating a Cacicazgo:
Federal Support in Exchange for Unconditional Loyalty

Between 1920 and 1925 most of the rivals of Apango and Mendoza in the ruling group disappeared, and most of the opposition was eliminated or co-opted. Since Apango and Mendoza consistently remained on the side of Obregón and Calles, their rivals and the opposition often found no other options but to rebel or join Obregón's or Calles' political enemies. But even if they obtained support of some of Obregón's or Calles' allies, it did not serve them.

Dissatisfied agraristas of Arenista origin quite often participated in the assaults and small-scale rebellions which took place in Tlaxcala and adjacent parts of Puebla during the early 1920s. Some of them volunteered to fight in the De la Huerta rebellion in 1923–24, and this gave Apango and Mendoza ample opportunity for a severe crackdown on restive agraristas. As we shall see later on, the only hope for agraristas of Arenista origin lay with the strong peasant movement which, under the leadership of Manuel P. Montes, emerged in the Puebla district of Huejotzingo–Texmelucan, one of the original bulwarks of the Arenas movement, a stronghold of the rebellious Cirilo Arenas in 1918, a refuge for Tlaxcalan Arenistas after 1920. [19]

Within the Tlaxcalan ruling group the original Rojas clique soon disappeared from state-level politics. Antonio Hidalgo lost, as we have seen, his struggle with Mendoza on the issue of Rojas's succession in 1920. Octavio Hidalgo likewise lost in the 1924 elections for governor, which brought Mendoza to the governor's chair as Apango's successor. Modesto González Galindo, moving back and forth between the ruling group and the opposition, gambled after the De la Huerta rebellion on the prestigious Agrarista and Labor parties. In Tlaxcala, he lost with them. Macario M. Hernández, another contender in the 1920 struggle to become the ruling PLCT candidate for governor, joined De la Huerta and lost with him. Máximo Rojas, who, under pressure from Mendoza, had opted for his friend Apango instead of his mentors Antonio Hidalgo or Macario M. Hernández, died in combat while fighting De la Huerta. Ugarte made a timely switch to Obregón in 1920 and did his utmost to mobilize federal political interests against Apango and Mendoza. In 1923–1924, however, as an important leader of the national Partido Nacional Cooperatista (PNC), he lost with his party on the issue of the presidential succession and had to leave Tlaxcala to Mendoza. By 1926 agrarista and labor leaders had been either eliminated or co-opted, and a small Mendocista in-group controlled the state government and legislature, congressional seats, municipal councils and presidencies. (See Table 10.1)[20]

What was the role of the Sonoreneses in the struggle of Apango and his mentor Mendoza to consolidate their power? There are no indications that Obregón was particularly impressed by Apango's qualities or policies, but he nevertheless supported Apango in decisive moments of state level crisis because, as we will see, it served his regional and national interests. In the case of Calles and Mendoza, a much stronger axis of common or complementary interests offered Mendoza the opportunity to establish a dependent but, in terms of local control, strong *cacicazgo*. The options for the opposition were, therefore, increasingly limited. It could try to align itself with dissatisfied

Table 10.1
The Mendocista In-Group[21]

Ignacio Mendoza	State Deputy, Governor and Senator (1918–1934)
Rafael Apango	Predecessor of Mendoza as Governor Senator (1921–1930)
Lic. Zainos y Lumbreras	Friend of Mendoza, Secretary General and intellectual mentor of Apango's government, Federal Deputy (1921–1930)
Adrian Vásquez	State Deputy and successor of Mendoza as Governor (1925–1933)
Lic. Moisés Huerta	State and Federal Deputy, Senator (1918–1936)
Carlos F. de Lara	State and Federal Deputy (1923–1932)
Felipe Xicóhtencatl	Party leaders and State Deputies, for 9 to 12 years
J. Natividad Nava	
Heriberto Vásquez	
Fernando Carvajal	

labor and agrarian interests within Tlaxcala or with interests in neighboring states or at the federal level. However, if these interests were at odds with the Mendocistas they also ran the risk of being at odds with those of Obregón and Calles.

The first thing the Tlaxcalan opposition groups tried to do was to profit from the increased power and prestige of local labor and agrarian leaders who had supported Obregón against Carranza in 1920. Zapatista leaders, incorporated in the Obregonista military and civilian bureaucracy, had founded the Partido Nacional Agrarista (PNA) as a mass peasant organization to contend for political office at the federal and state level. In Tlaxcala, however, they failed. Mendoza and Governor Apango cleverly manipulated the fact that a group of agrarian leaders from the Arenista party had sided with Carranza in 1920. Brandished as traitors to the cause of Obregón, the agraristas' potential for political mobilization was seriously reduced. Harassed agraristas fled to Texmelucan; others went to jail; and if we believe the Pelecista (Pro PLCT) newspaper *El Gladiador*, many village leaders, even in Arenista strongholds like Hueyotlipan, left the PLT and joined the government party.[22]

In Puebla, however, the situation was quite different. The state government stumbled from one crisis into another and maintained, at best, a fragile equilibrium between region-based interests like those of northern Puebla and Tehuacán caciques, labor- and agrarista-based leadership in the Atoyac River basin and the still powerful Puebla City interests in commerce, industry, and agriculture. Unlike Tlaxcala, the power and prestige of the state government was seriously undermined by its partisanship for Carranza in 1920 and De la Huerta in 1923. In both years the state government was ousted, while labor and agrarista leaders who had supported Obregón and Calles won power and prestige and became the new contenders in the political arena. During Carranza's presidency, both in the Tlaxcala and Puebla part of the Atoyac River basin, Arenas land grants and the land invasions by village communities were in danger. William O. Jenkins, landowner and American consular agent in Puebla, estimated that by 1920 about half of the estates in this district had been returned to the owners, due to the joint pressure of Carranza, a conservative state government, and the strong Puebla-based, mainly Spanish interests in agriculture. In 1920, Manuel P. Montes, a local agrarista leader who had been able to organize the hard-pressed agrarista village communities in his Confederacion Social Campesina "Domingo Arenas" (1921),[23] joined another Puebla agrarista leader José María Sánchez against Carranza. Sánchez was a deputy of rural-worker origin and enjoyed the support of the Puebla workers, the CROM syndicate at Puebla City, and the peasants of the Atoyac River basin. With firm federal support of Obregón and Calles, and in spite of the fierce resistance by the Puebla-based elites, Sánchez became governor of the state in 1921. He introduced an ambitious and costly program of reforms, to be paid for by heavy taxations on private enterprise. The Sánchez program triggered acute political polarization in Puebla. On the other hand, it provoked what Obregón called a "disarmed or pacific rebellion" of the "good and Catholic society."[24] Shopkeepers and artisans closed their doors, factory owners threatened to close down, and landowners appealed to the federal government. On the other hand, it promoted intense labor and agrarista mobilization. Workers attempted to seize factories, and unemployed textile workers invaded haciendas and asked the governor to hand them over for agricultural colonies. Village agraristas occupied hacienda lands, and administrators were insulted in the streets of Texmelucan.[25]

The southern and central Tlaxcalan interests in industry and agriculture, intimately linked to Puebla firms and families, and the Tlaxcalan state government were seriously worried about the Puebla situation. Tlaxcalan industrial labor was strongly influenced by Puebla syndicates, and it was barely represented in PLCT leadership and government. Furious agraristas, supported by Montes's "Domingo Arenas" confederation, threatened the secretary general of Apango's government, Lic. Florencio Zainos y Lumbreras, who made sniping remarks about "agraristas furibundos" (frenzied agraristas) to the press. Apango sent state troops to Tlaxcalan villages near the border to arrest agrarista village leaders, and he threatened to suppress any industrial unrest.[26]

Although Calles and the CROM did not hide their sympathy for Sánchez, the federal government apparently grew increasingly worried about the delicate political situation in Puebla. By early 1922 Froylan C. Manjárrez, a federal deputy for Puebla and one of the national leaders of the PCN, saw his chance to dislodge Sánchez and gain control of the state government for himself and the rising PCN. In March 1922 Sánchez was ousted by the Puebla state Congress and Manjárrez took over, beginning with a purge of Sanchista officials.[27] The many complaints of landowners and administrators as well as the reports of Jenkins make it clear that Manjárrez proved unable to gain control over the Huejotzingo–Texmelucan district, dominated by Montes's peasant organization, which claimed control over ninety-six villages, a number of them in Tlaxcala.[28]

Manjárrez also became a key activist in the 1922 attempt of the PCN to dislodge the PLC from its dominant position in the federal Congress and in the states. A coalition of the Cooperatista Party and the Agrarista and Labor parties, at that time supported by the *Gobernación* secretary, Calles, succeeded in ousting the national level PLC from its dominant position in Congress. At the state level mamy Pelecista parties were ousted from power, with the support of Secretary Calles. In Tlaxcala, Mendoza and Governor Apango now faced joint action from hostile federal interests allied to their local opposition. The PCN, and especially leaders from its Puebla branch, sought an alliance with the ailing PLT and tried to revive the party. At the same time, the national Agrarista and Labor parties did their best to oppose "tiranello" Mendoza, his strong-arm Pelecista boys, and Apango's regional forces in the municipal, state, and federal elections of 1921 and 1922. The Agrarista Party made it clear that all the villages, which had received land grants from the government or were about to receive them, should join the Agrarista Party. Since the PLT, supported by the national and Puebla Cooperatistas, held the same intentions regarding Tlaxcalan agrarista villages, the alliance was rather uneasy.[29]

The outcome of the struggle probably reflects the Sonorense policy of maintaining careful equilibrium between opposing forces while consolidating power. They recognized the quite different roles of the local branches of national parties as aggregates of specific state-level interests, and intended to deploy them in their consolidation policies. In the case of Tlaxcala, after the demise of the federal PLC, Apango and Mendoza had to acknowledge the inevitability of leaving most of the federal congressional seats to political enemies: "although the Tlaxcalan people do not elect them, they triumphed in Mexico."[30] As a consequence, the credentials of elected PLCT Senators Máximo Rojas and Macario M. Hernández were annulled in Mexico, and Rojas's protests were rather brusquely rejected by President Obregón.[31] One year later, however, Apango and Mendoza did succeed in maintaining their political control at the state and municipal level, when the federal and Puebla Cooperatistas attempted to oust the Pelecista government party during the elections for state deputies in the spring of 1923. The PLT, strengthened by the support of the PNC, the now anti-Mendocista Tlaxcalan federal deputies and senators, and other local opposition groups, allied with the federal Agrarista and Labor parties in an attempt to gain a congressional majority. Before the elections the PLC asked the Puebla chief of military operations, General Juan Andreu Almazán, for his protection against Pelaecista repression. Almazán refused, however, and the Tlaxcalan opposition parties complained forthwith about large-scale fraud and repression. Political violence was at least partly due to the strong resurgence of agrarian conflict sometimes deliberately elicited by the local opposition and its out-of-state allies. When Governor Apango was about to announce victory for the PLCT, Puebla and and Mexico City–based strong-arm boys of the Cooperatista Party occupied the state legislature and intended to dislodge the Pelecistas. The invaders were ejected by police forces, but the struggle over the electoral results dragged on for months. Governor Apango, supported by Calles, successfully resisted the attempts of the Tlaxcalan opposition, allied to the Cooperatista bloc in the federal Congress, to have him convicted by a grand jury and recognize a Cooperatista-dominated legislature. The imbroglio was finally solved in favor of the Tlaxcalan ruling group. This was due, most probably, to the fact that the cooperatistas tended to fall apart on the issue of presidential succession and lost the support of the National Labor and Agrarian parties. What may have been more important, Governor Manjárrez of Puebla, one of the engineers of the attempt to dislodge the PLCT, was a close friend of De la Huerta; and it is quite likely that President Obregón, by summer 1923, did not want a dependable local ruling group to be dislodge by a friend of De la Huerta.[32]

The issue of presidential succession had quite different political consequences at the Puebla and Tlaxcala state level. It could have ripped apart the Tlaxcalan ruling group in the way it happened in Puebla or other states. Both Rojas and Apango were not really in favor of Calles as presidential candidate in 1923. They stayed, however, in line with the federal government, especially after Calles's firm support in 1923 and in 1925.[33] In Puebla, however, the issue of presidential succession resulted in another major crisis. Governor Manjárrez made strong propaganda in favor of De la Huerta.[34] When the rebellion broke out in December 1923, Manjárrez was first arrested, but after his release he joined the rebels. Rebel troops soon occupied Puebla. The battle of Puebla brought more arms, power and prestige to Montes, Sánchez, and several former Zapatista generals who organized peasant and worker battalions to help the federal government in retaking the city of Puebla. Montes alone had eighteen hundred armed members of his "Domingo Arenas" Confederation and intended to maintain control of the Huejotzingo—Texmelucan district.[35] In nearby Tlaxcala, labor and agrarista leadership had no chance to challenge the state government. They had never been able to profit from the major political crises of 1920 and 1923–24 in terms of gaining local power or autonomy as their Puebla counterparts had. The stable and loyal Tlaxcalan ruling revolutionary group had been able to monopolize federal support and recognition. While J. M. Sánchez, the CROM leadership, and the agrarista leaders in Puebla considered themselves the victors over a disgraced state government and fought over its legacy, setting up three different state governments (in 1925), Mendoza, with federal support, cracked down on all of their Tlaxcalan counterparts or co-opted them in his political machine.

After the de la Huerta rebellion, the Tlaxcalan ruling group faced the considerably stronger position of the national Agrarista and Labor Parties and the CROM, who now wanted to penetrate Mendoza's domain and sought to align themselves with the enemies of the Tlaxcalan ruling group. In April 1924 the Tlaxcalan Labor Party was founded; in June, the local Agrarista Party, in the presence of Montes. Both parties were partly made of dissenters from the PLCT, including a few state deputies. The Labor Party even succeeded in rallying behind it a number of important municipal councils like industrial Apizaco. It also tried to wrest Rojas—who had just died in combat—as *the* peasant—worker revolutionary symbol from the ruling group.[36] With an eye on the coming gubernatorial elections, the Agrarista and Labor parties in Tlaxcala, the PLT, and a few minor groups united in an ad hoc Allianza de Partidos Revolucionarios. The Allianza postulated Octavio Hidalgo, now an ex-Pelecista, as candidate for governor against PLCT candidate Mendoza. The united opposition found its basis not only among the traditionally anti-Mendoza agrarista leaders of ex-Arenista territory, but also among strong peasants and workers from central Tlaxcala and eastern villages who were clearly dissatisfied with land reform and labor policies. The local federation of the CROM refused to support Mendoza, who, in their view, "was walking with the clergy and the landlords."[37] Finally, in September 1924, against Apango's wishes, Obregón appointed the Zapatista general Genovevo de la O as chief of military operations in the state of Tlaxcala, and the local agraristas tended to consider him as their protector.[38]

With the help of two-thirds of the state deputies and the state *gendarmerie,* and with the municipal councils purged, Mendoza, "El Director intellectual del actual Gobernador,"[39] (the intellectual director of the present governor) tried to win the municipal and gubernatorial elections in late 1924. Campaigning was violent on both sides, and the partisans of the Allianza continuously asked De la O for protection. Governor Apango accused De la O of helping the opposition, and General De la O stressed that it was his duty to protect civilians and opposition leaders against the assaults of a state government which wanted to push the election of Mendoza.[40]

The PLCT majority in the state legislature recognized Mendoza's victory. Election results in traditionally hostile municipalities were annulled and provisional councils installed, often in the presence of state forces. Armed agrarians from the southwest, supported by Montes from Texmelucan, and Laborites from the Apizaco–Puebla industrial zone clashed with state forces, Pelecista agrarians and strong-arm boys. By early 1925, the outgoing governor Apango accused the Allianza of rebellion; and President Calles, flooded by dozens of complaints, sent Cabinet Minister Luis N. Morones to solve the problem in Tlaxcala in favor of Mendoza. Calles probably had good reasons for doing so. Puebla and Tlaxcala had suffered several rebellious outbursts in late 1924. Moreover, the federal government had lost control over the political situation in Puebla, where Sánchez, Montes, and the CROM were at each other's throats and Calles could, no doubt, use a stable state government in Tlaxcala under a dependent and, therefore, loyal Callista governor. Morones made it clear to the representatives of forty-three villages and eight factories that sabotage of the Mendoza government smacked of rebellion and would not be tolerated by President Calles. The Allianza assured Morones that it abhorred rebellion and that it was prepared to accept Mendoza as governor, but insisted on free elections for state deputies in February 1925. Agraristas and laborites were prepared to give up their arms if the governor's forces would also be disarmed. On the day of his inauguration as governor, Mendoza fiercely protested against the possible disarmament of his forces. He badly needed them "in virtue of the fact that my Government lacks the full respect that it is legally due."[41] This lack of respect was stressed again during the February elections. The opposition tried to install its own legislature, this time in Mexico City. Tlaxcalan agrarista leaders became more and more involved in Montes's organization, which used its administrative services to hold reunions in Texmelucan. The Mendocista deputies of the southern districts of Tlaxcala complained about joint local agrarista–Montista assaults, robberies of ballot boxes, and large joint protest meetings of the Agrarista Party and Montes's "Domingo Arenas." As was to be expected, one of Montes's major enemies of the moment, José María Sánchez, offered his support to Mendoza.[42]

In spite of continuing violence and unrest, Mendoza was able to consolidate his position with continuing firm federal support. In February 1925, none of the candidates of the opposition was able to reach office. General De la O was transferred in late 1925, and by the end of that year Mendoza was in control of virtually all the municipalities.

After Morones's visit in early 1925, the Tlaxcalan CROM and Labor party made their peace with Mendoza and his enemies left the organizations. The Mendocista CROM gained control over factories and many ejidos, and saw to loyal voting patterns. To strengthen his grip, especially at the grass roots, he reorganized the government party into a Partido Socialista, established according to the model of Tabasco strong-man Garrido Canabal and operated like an "auténtico pulpo" (a real octopus).[43]

The issue of Obregón's reelection threatened to provoke a clash between Apango, now a federal senator and Governor Mendoza. Governor Mendoza clearly supported the election of his friend and client Adrian Vásquez, who had served as a state deputy during Mendoza's governorship. Apango, however, showed a strong desire to be reelected as governor. This clash reflects, on the one hand, the dependency of the Tlaxcalan ruling group on the Sonorenses and, on the other hand, the room for political maneuvering afforded by the intention of Obregón and Calles to alternate in national power. Since Mendoza had enjoyed Calles's full support throughout his governorship, Apango hoped to strengthen his position by becoming a fervent partisan of Obregón, Calles's choice for the 1928–1934 presidential term and elected in 1928. But Obregón's murder in July 1928 strengthened the position of staunch Callista Mendoza, who was not able to have Adrian Vásquez Sánchez elected (1929–1933).[44] Under Mendoza and his handpicked successor, Adrian Vásquez, the Agrarista Party fell upon hard times. It had never been able to cope with the paradoxical situation created for it by President Calles in early 1925, when it was forced to agree to a governor generally perceived as the local symbol of antiagrarismo. Local agraristas therefore often tended to stay out of the party or were attracted by the powerful Montes, who even became governor of Puebla in November 1926 and now seemed to be in total control of the whole Huejotzingo–Texmelucan district. With staunch support for Montes's enemies, especially the CROM, and as we shall see in the next section) an iron grip on ejido committees, Mendoza intended to construct a *cordon sanitaire* in south Tlaxcala. Montes's governorship, however, was short-lived. In June 1927 he was evicted and murdered shortly afterward. Now the CROM took over, and Tlaxcalan agraristas lost their external political support.[45]

After 1930, however, the position of the Tlaxcalan ruling group weakened, mainly because of their resistance against the growing interference of Calles's Partido Nacional Revolucionario (PNR) in state-level political mobilization and organization. When President Pascual Ortiz Rubio and Calles disagreed about Vásquez's successor in 1932, the PNR encouraged the debilitated and partly exiled Tlaxcalan opposition to launch a candidate for governor opposed to the ruling group. After a fierce electoral struggle and federal intervention, the PNR sponsored candidate Adolfo Bonilla, a former local Arenista chief and for years a federal officer outside Tlaxcala. Bonilla became governor of Tlaxcala in 1933 and liquidated the political machine and hierarchy of the erstwhile ruling group.[46]

Consolidating a Cacicazgo: *How to Defuse a Militant Peasantry?*

The relations of the Tlaxcalan ruling group with the agraristas changed significantly when the revolutionary chiefs of peasant–worker origins lost their dominant position, beginning with the death of Arenas (in 1917) and culminating with the death of Rojas (in 1924). With Apango and Mendoza, power and office came into the hands of a new group of mainly urban and civilian leaders, who were partly of professional origins and much less bound to village-level peasant interests.

One of the major problems of this newly emerging shift within the Tlaxcalan ruling group was the consolidation of their control over a hostile peasantry who saw its access to land and its autonomy, acquired during the Arenas years, seriously threatened by the Carranza government. As governor, Rojas had been unable to protect their interests, but he had also been unable to interfere with still-standing agrarista interests at the village level. In this delicate situation, Apango took the reins of government at a moment in revolutionary history when the power and prestige of agraristas in Central Mexico were on the rise because of their support for Obregón and Calles. The considerable span and scope of Montes's peasant movement in Puebla served as a fine example of successful political mobilization and it was precisely with the peasantry of this agrarista stronghold that the campesinos from the south and west of Tlaxcala had much in common. It served them as a basis for action and refuge. How then, in a political climate characterized by the rising prestige and legitimacy of agrarismo, was the Tlaxcalan ruling group under Apango and Mendoza able to defuse the strong mobilization efforts of a hostile peasantry, which received support from Puebla and federal agrarista interests and was manipulated by the political enemies of the Tlaxcalan ruling group?

First, we must distinguish between the northeast of Tlaxcala and the southwest. The haciendas in the former region had largely remained outside Arenas's territory. Moreover, until the 1930s, agrarian legislation excluded rural laborers who lived on haciendas and comprised the majority of the peasants northeast of Tlaxcala. Apart from a few villages known for strong agrarista interests, political control had more to do with the landlords than with the peasants. It is clear from the correspondence that here the landlords did their best to cultivate their relations with the revolutionary ruling group (through special services, presents, and payments). Moreover, both the state government and the landlords had more worries about labor and production than about agrarismo.[47] The real problem of control concerned the village-based peasantries in the south and west, where prolonged and autonomous peasant mobilization during the revolutionary years and the Carrancista threat to peasants' newly acquired access to land had created a high degree of militancy. The obligation to gain or regain land by way of slow and cumbersome procedures and disappointing results often generated resentment which could easily flare up in open conflict, sometimes between villages, sometimes with the government, and often with both at the same time.[48] How did Apango and Mendoza cope with this problem?

During Obregón's presidency, *caciquismo agrario*—strong local agrarista leaders dominating the countryside with their own armed guards—was well known in states where the revolution had generated strong peasant mobilization. Sánchez and Montes in Puebla were exemplary. Apango and Mendoza, however, apart from some of their rhetoric, never promoted agrarismo and tried to check the virtual autonomy of defiant local agrarista leaders like those in the municipalities of Zacatelco, Nativitas, Lardizabal and Hueyotlipan. Apango's government saw agrarian radicalism, in the words of Government Secretary General Florencio Zainos y Lumbreras, as a "perpetual struggle against the authorities" and a drag on the economic recovery of the state of Tlaxcala because it could seriously affect tax income from land and agricultural products: Apango "has not done much in the division of land, and this is due to the frenzied agraristas who do not take into account that, since Tlaxcala is purely agricultural, it would be imprudent to cut off the only source of revenues that the Executive has. . ."[49] Apango's conservative policies were sometimes quite at odds with Obregonista land reform policies. He clashed several times with the federal CNA and even had difficulties with presidential orders. Mendoza and Vásquez, his successors, stayed fully in line with the ups and downs in the agrarian policies of Presidents Calles, Portes Gil, and Ortiz Rubio. It was Governor Vásquez who, first in accordance with Portes Gil, granted provisional ejidos to about thirty villages and who, of course, had dutifully adhered to the Socialist government party. In 1931, now in accordance with Ortiz Rubio, he formally ended land reform in Tlaxcala and became notorious for his antiejido declarations to the press.[50]

Apango and Mendoza may have been anything but agraristas, but they grasped the unique opportunities for what Antonio Díaz Soto y Gama once called making the ejido "un instrumento de política" (a political instrument). Petitions for land, land distribution, the corresponding bureaucratic interventions ad procedures, and the formal obligations imposed by law made peasants more dependent on the government than ever before. As a result of quick presidential decisions on land grants and the reestablishment of the provisional possession, villages received ejido lands between 1920 and 1925. Although the majority of these petitions had been entered before 1920, the actual distribution of land and the corresponding rise in local peasant mobilization and conflict offered the ruling group a fertile field for clientist politics. The same holds for ejido administration. Once in legal possession of hacienda lands, the ejidatarios had to pay the corresponding land tax, and their ejido administrative committee faced the cumbersome task of defining the amount of tax to be paid by each ejidatario according to the size of his plot and the quality of its soil. Conflict was rampant, and within a few years so many ejido committees were behind in their tax payments and liable to embargoes on their crops that the state government recognized the impossibility of executing the embargoes. In practice, it became policy to condone accumulated tax debts in exchange for a firm promise to start with a clean bill. As one can understand, this policy could be used in enforcing political loyalty at the village level.[51]

No wonder that in the densely populated parts of Tlaxcala competing political factions emerged. Village-level interest groups, based on *barrio*, family, and friends, mobilized around the issue of access to land and water. When the actual distribution of land set in, agraristas and those who opposed them—sharecroppers "incondicionales del hacendado" (puppets of the hacendado) and *fraccionistas*, those who preferred to buy a plot from the landlord—all tried to defend their interests and to outdo the other parties. This resulted in shifting networks of ad hoc alliances between various peasant factions at the village level or inter-village level and representatives of the ruling group or its political enemies inside and outside Tlaxcala.[52]

For example, let us consider the municipality of Nativitas. The villages of Nativitas nearly all entered petitions for land in 1916 and 1917. In competition with each other and with the many villages in the surrounding municipalities, they claimed the fertile haciendas in the Atoyac–Zahuapan Valley. A number of these villages had received land grants under Arenas, but by 1918 the returning landlords attempted to force the peasants into sharecropping and labor arrangements. Communities became split between agrarista and their opponents, and the competition over scarce resources triggered serious intervillage conflicts. Since most of the local hacendados, many of whom were members of the Puebla elite, succeeded in delaying the land reform procedures, the villages often had to wait for years before they finally gained legal possession of the lands. This resulted in prolonged "warming-up" periods for internal conflict, deteriorating relations with the agrarian bureaucracy and the state government, and finally, attempts by the exasperated agraristas to take the land by force.

One by one, the agrarista committees of La Concordia (1918), Michac (1921), Atoyatenco and Tepetitla (1922), Xochitecatitla, and Capulac (1923) began to consider themselves as "victims of our goverment and of the agrarian offices of the State."[53] La Concordia agraristas violently resisted the return of a hacienda to the owner; Michac, Atoyatenco and Tepetitla, supported by Montes's C.S.C. "Arenas," decided to take haciendas by force; and the agrarista committees of Xochitecatitla and Capulac, both disappointed by prolonged procedures without results, finally turned to organizations not linked to the ruling revolutionary group. The former committee asked Montes for help, and the latter went to the Liga de Comunidades Agrarias dominated by Manjárrez's Cooperatista Party in Puebla.

Apango retaliated immediately by sending troops and arresting committees or having them harassed by armed Pelecistas, "esbirros del gobierno" (constables of the government).[54] Faustino Carranco, the PLCT deputy for Nativitas imposed by Apango (1923–1927), did his utmost to bring ejido committees—those who administered ejidos and those who had asked for ejidos but had not yet received them—to loyal voting patterns and membership of the PLCT. The opposition accused him of making false promises for the quick resolution of petitions (La Concordia, Xochitecatitla), putting pressure on ejido committees (Michac), imposing *faenas* (tasks) on unwilling agraristas (Nativitas), and even murder (Atoyatenco). Resistance was so strong that Apango and Mendoza were forced to annul the municipal, gubernatorial, and deputy elections of 1924 and 1925, and to impose Pelecista municipal councilors and agents in Nativitas.[55]

Who were these Pelecistas at the village level? This question, in my view, brings us to the major reasons for the final success of the Tlaxcalan ruling group in consolidating its control over a restive peasantry, especially in the southwestern half of the state. Such reasons have to do with the internal conflict between ejido "haves and haves not" and intervillage conflicts in which one group or the other became invariably linked to and manipulated by the political enemies of the ruling group. In the municipality of Nativitas, for example, the original agrarista group in most villages had been able to control the distribution of ejido plots and to reserve the best plots for committee members, their families, and friends. They became an ejido elite that often tried to exclude the ex-sharecroppers and laborers, who had stayed with the landlords, from the ejido. These ejido "have nots" tried, again and again, to remove the administrative ejido committees and to redistribute the plots, as in La Concordia, Tepetitla, and Atoyatenco. For their part, the ejido elites did their utmost to prevent these proceedings or to patronize an initiative of the "have nots" to ask for an extension of the ejidos.[56] In all these initiatives, however, the cooperation of the state government was important, if not crucial. José Natividad Nava, Carranco's successor as deputy for Nativitas (1927–1933), chaired the local Agrarian Committee which had to prepare the governor's resolutions on land grants. It served as a key mechanism in enforcing loyalty on those who asked for government support.

In a number of cases, however, loyalty was short-lived or did not come about. First of all, it was virtually impossible to satisfy the demands of both parties in a conflict over scarce natural resources. Secondly, the Tlaxcala state government was often unable to push a case at the federal level of the bureaucracy or it did not want to do so because of its essentially antiagrarista attitude. In those cases where the ruling group succeeded in winning the loyalty of the peasants, even in former Arenista territory, it tended to be the loyalty of ejido elites. There is ample proof in the files of several investigated municipalities in Tlaxcala that in situations of the growing scarcity of land the ejido elites tended to safeguard their vested interests in an alignment with the consolidated ruling group. This does not imply that the process was a peaceful one. There was always the threat of embargo on crops for overdue tax payments; leaders hostile to the government could be forced out of office; and Mendoza, especially, was accused of planning deliberate assaults on administrative committees he did not yet control, like Tenanyecac, Atoyatenco, and Xochitecatitla in 1925.[57]

With the ruling group and the ejido elites reinforcing each other's positions, a *coup d'ejido* by local "have nots" or by other opponents of the ejido elite generally had little chance for success. In spite of its frequent interventions in Nativitas, the Agrarista Party never succeeded in dislodging a *gobiernista* ejido elite. The only case of successful dislodgment, this time against the wishes of the Agrarian Party, had to do with La Concordia (1924), where the ejido elite happened to be decidedly anti-Apango. It had quarreled for years with the state government over hacienda lands and refused to consent in a redistribution of ejido plots requested by landless peasants who had joined the PLCT. Being anti-Apango, the ejido elite had no problem in soliciting the support of the Agrarista Party, of the labor party, of Montes, and even of presidential candidate Calles who had been asked to intervene by the anti-Apango federal deputies for Tlaxcala. Meanwhile, the PLCT promised the "have nots" of La Concordia the extra plots still in the hands of the ejido elite if they would vote for the government party in the municipal and gubernatorial elections of late 1924. The ejido elite, in the end, lost its control over the ejido committee and the plots to the Pelecistas.[58]

The Tlaxcalan ruling group was clearly able to profit from the increasing number of peasants in need of government mediation, be it for a land grant, obtaining or keeping a plot in an existing ejido, getting tax reduction, or preventing an embargo on the crop. To this we can add the often obvious risks and small results of an alliance with the political enemies of the ruling group, since the latter controlled the local agrarian and the state bureaucracy. No wonder, then, that the opposition lost many agrarista committees and that the number of peasants adhering to the government party grew to more than twenty thousand by 1926, if we are to believe its officials.[59] Between 1922 and 1924 Tlaxcala was plagued by a number of small-scale rebellions, and opposition agrarista committees had to make it clear that they had not been involved. When agraristas of Atoyatenco joined de la Huerta, the leaders were murdered shortly afterwards.[60] The final blow, however, was President Calles's strong support of Mendoza against the attempts of a joint opposition sustained by Montes and by the federal Agrarian and Labor parties. On the basis of case studies from Nativitas and from a number of villages in Hueyotlipan and Calpulalpan, we can conclude that Mendocistas were in control of the ejidos by the late 1920s. They either belonged to the original ejido elite or had been able to enter the ejido elite as local-level clients of the ruling group. This phenomenon was, no doubt, strongly promoted both by Calles's determined policy to check "agrarismo furibundo" and by the decrease in land distribution. When the Mendocista *cacicazgo* was finally dismantled in 1933, this implied a large-scale purge of ejido administrative committees all over Tlaxcala.[61]

Mendoza's growing control over the ejido administrative committees, and the fact that his political enemies and their allied organizations lacked federal support, explain the relatively scant success of mass peasant organizations whose strength lay outside Tlaxcala. Apango succeeded in preventing most of the southern Tlaxcalan villages from joining Montes's "Arenas" confederation and the Liga de Comunidades Agrarias of Puebla. With the help of Pelecista ejido committees (quite often ejido elites) and a purged, now *gobiernista* federation of the CROM, Mendoza was able to check to a considerable degree the influence of Montes in the south ot Tlaxcala. Together with Úrsulo Galván and several others, Montes founded the radical Liga Nacional Campesina (1926) and aimed at a true national organization which, of course, had to include Tlaxcala. Tlaxcalan delegates were involved in the foundation of the LNC, and in late 1927 Mendoza even permitted the LNC to organize the first peasant congress in Tlaxcala. One wonders why a governor who was earlier branded as "walking with the clergy and the landlords" suddenly welcomed a radical peasant organization. One factor may have been that President Calles initially welcomed the LNC as yet another element in his policy to maintain a balance between opposed interests. At that moment, the CROM was very strong, and in Tlaxcala as well. One also has to remember that by then, Montes had already been ousted as governor and had been murdered, while the CROM was making severe inroads into the strongholds of the "Arenas" confederation. One year later (1928), Mendoza clashed with the LNC when it proved to be increasingly anti-Calles after the murder of president-elect Obregón.[62] In addition, landlord reaction to the LNC was wholeheartedly negative. They sent a committee to ask Mendoza for counteracting measures, and the governor received them reassuringly. His successor, governor Vásquez, even started to promote on a small scale the organization of rural laborers on the northern haciendas, much to the chagrin of the owners. However, like Mendoza, he never used the *sindicatos* for agrarista purposes. Political and electoral control seemed more important, and moreover, the *sindicatos* served the aim of reminding hacendados of the power of the governor. The landlords' worries were, however, not unfounded, for the late 1920s saw a number of labor conflicts on the haciendas and eastern village agraristas in Ixtenco and Zitlaltepetl harassed hacienda employees. However, the real upsurge of agrarista committees did not begin before 1932. It was changes in agrarian legislation and the PNR-sponsored campaign against another Mendocista candidate for governor in Tlaxcala that triggered the agrarista movement on the haciendas in the north and east.[63]

Conclusion

The rise of a mainly civilian revolutionary ruling group in Tlaxcala after 1918, the development of its local power base, its relations to the federal government, and the stability of its rule—unlike the situation in many other states, none of the governors were evicted between 1918 and 1933—show that the Tlaxcalan ruling group resembles the PNR type of officialdom more than the postrevolutionaary *cacicazgos* of the 1920s.

The crucial differences seem to lie in the power base of the Tlaxcalan ruling group, its relations to the federal government, and its strategies and tactics of political mobilization and control.

To begin with, Apango and Mendoza's power and prestige were not based on their merits during the Armed Revolution. They had only minor roles, and like the Rojas group in general, they had serious troubles with Arenas's legacy: the militant peasantry of the southwestern part of the state. Apango and Mendoza's popular base must have been rather limited when they gained power in 1920. During the early 1920s Apango's restrictive agrarian and labor policies, which even clashed with Obregón, kept alive a strong local opposition that welcomed external initiatives to topple their enemies from government power. The electoral struggle of 1924 makes it clear that local agraristas, industrial workers, and the parties alledgedly representing them were unified in their attempts to prevent Mendoza, Apango's "director intellectual," from gaining power. If Apango and Mendoza's government had such a weak popular base and, to cite again Mendoza's words, "lacked all respect," how did they reach the rather unique (for the 1920s) level of stable government, characterized by *continuismo* in the best Callista tradition?

The answer seems to lie in their relations to Obregón and Calles, and in their Sonorense style of political mobilization and control. Their relations to the Sonorenses were defined not so much by an obviously strong popular base which would have forced Obregón and Calles to take them into account at least for the time being, as by the near absence of this popular base. Federal support seems to have been so crucial for Apango and Mendoza that it could secure their constant loyalty. Obregón's support was neither strong nor unequivocal, but Apango and Mendoza were fortunate because their state was situated on the threshold of a permanent major headache for the fedearl government: the unruly state of Puebla. Next to their usefulness as a watchdog or *cordon sanitaire* against possibly contagious Puebla events, it may have been significant for their political survival that their terms as governor happened to coincide with the presidential terms. Therefore, the inevitable mobilization efforts of emerging rivals in the second half of a term in office, and the equally strong efforts of the new incumbent to consolidate his power, coincided at the state and federal level. This coincidence probably saved Apango in 1923 from eviction, and it certainly kept Mendoza in power against the popular opposition movement in early 1925. Moreover, Apango and his mentor Mendoza seem to have been to a certain extent, precursors of the mid- and late-Sonorense policies which aimed at stable and dependent state governments, economic reconstruction along capitalist lines, and "no grand restructuring of society."[64] This would explain why Apango clashed with early Obregonista agrarian policies, while his mentor Mendoza fitted nicely in Calles's views on law, order, and social reforms. After twelve years in power (1920–1932), Mendoza's downfall as "mini jefe máximo" of Tlaxcala was brought about within three months. He did something which an official, dependent on federal recognition could not do: he refused to heed Calles's policies regarding Tlaxcala and the PNR.

Apango and Mendoza were strongly dependent on federal support. The considerable time span of this support gave them the opportunity to implement at the state level, albeit slowly, the strongly clientist strategies of co-optation and repression deployed by the Sonorenses in their attempts to mobilize and control the peasantry. No doubt, Apango disliked the agraristas furibundos; but his own government party must have remembered Rojas's ordeal when he was unable to bring Carranza to quick decisions on land grants; and Apango must have been keenly aware of the instrumental value of Obregonista land distribution for local control. Already in 1921 agrarista leaders at the village level began to realize the possible convenience of joining the government party, pushed and pulled as they were by repressive or co-optative politics. Mendoza, backed by Calles's restrictive land reform policies and his firm intention to impose order, was able to wrest the ejido as a political instrument from the hands of the opposition. When land distribution in Tlaxcala dropped to near zero and dissatisfied landless peasants grew in numbers, both those who held ejido plots and those who did not looked more and more to the ruling group. The former wanted their ejido tenancy guaranteed; the latter wanted redistribution of plots or an extension of the ejidos. Moreover, the ejido elites, local agrarista leaders who had taken special care of themselves, their friends, and family, soon found out that their illegal extra plots would best be guaranteed with government protection. Within the limited framework of late Sonorense land reform policy and its strong commitment to order, land invasions were to be exemplarily punished. Additional ejidos were not to be expected and the existing distribution of ejido land became more and more the focus and issue of village level peasant mobilization, to be manipulated in state-level clientelist politics. This helps to explain why an essentially antiagrarista ruling group was able to control and defuse a militant peasantry without any substantial extension of ejidos.

Notes

1. Raymond Th. J. Buve, "Peasant movements, caudillos and land reform during the Revolution (1910–1917) in Tlaxcala, Mexico," *Boletín de Estudios Latino-americanos y del Caribe* 18 (1975): 112–52; Buve, "Neither Carranza nor Zapata: The Rise and Fall of a Peasant Movement which Tried to Challenge Both, Tlaxcala, 1910–1919," in *Riot, Rebellion and Revolution: Rural Social Conflict in Mexico*, ed. Freidrich Katz (Princeton: Princeton University Press, 1988), 338–75; Juan Felipe

Leal and Margarita Menegus, "Los trabajadores de las haciendas de Maxaquiahac y el Rosario, en los albores de la revolución agraria 1910–1914," *Historia Mexicana* (hereafter cited as HM) 122 (1981): 233–78. The information on Puebla is based on David G. LaFrance, "Madero, Serdán y el movimiento revolucionario en Puebla," HM, 115 (1980): 472–512; LaFrance, "A People Betrayed: Francisco I. Madero and the Mexican Revolution in Puebla" (Ph.D. diss., Indiana University, 1984).

2. Romana Falcón, *Revolución y caciquismo: San Luis Potosí, 1910–1938* (México: El Colegio de México, 1984), 14–16; Hans Werner Tobler, *Die Mexikanische Revolution* (Frankfurt: Suhrkamp Verlag, 1984), vol. 3, chap. 1; Alan Knight, *The Mexico Revolution*, vol. 2: *Counterrevolution and Reconstruction* (Cambridge: Cambridge Univeristy Press, 1986).

3. Jean Meyer, *Estado y sociedad con Calles. Historia de la revolución mexicana, 1924–1928* (México: El Colegio de México, 1977), 175–197.

4. Antonio Ugalde, "From Hacienda to PRI," in *The Caciques*, ed. R. Kern (Albuquerque: University of New Mexico Press, 1973), 119–35; Enrique Krauze, *La reconstrucción económica. Historia de la revolución mexicana, 1924–1928* (México: El Colegio de México, 1977), 123–30.

5. The term *Tlaxcala Revolutionary Movement* is not used here in the sense of a unified movement or one formal organization (a situation which only existed for a short period), but is used to give a name to the combined parties, factions, and bands which surged between 1910 and 1918.

6. Rodney Anderson, *Outcasts in their Own Land: Mexican Industrial Workers, 1906–1911* (DeKalb: Northern Illinois University Press, 1976), 320.

7. The most important teachers were José Rumbia, secretary of Antonio Hidalgo, Porfirio del Castillo, secretary of Máximo Rojas, and Andrés Angulo, secretary of Domingo Arenas.

8. Buve, "Neither Carranza nor Zapata," sec. 1, 341–46; La France, "A People Betrayed," 155, 194, 154–279.

9. Buve, "Neither Carranza nor Zapata," sec. 1; LaFrance, "A People Betrayed," chap. 7.

10. Buve, "Neither Carranza nor Zapata," sec. 2, 350–54.

11. Below follows a short summary of revolutionary political developments between 1915 and 1918, taken from Buve, "Neither Carranza nor Zapata," sec. 2.

12. Porfirio del Castillo, *Puebla y Tlaxcala en los días de la Revolución* (México, 1953), 188–90; "Acta declaración pro Carranza," 11 November, 1914, Archivo General del Estado de Tlaxcala (hereafter cited as AGET), Fondo Revolución-Régimen Obregonista (hereafter cited as FRRO), leg. Hacienda y Guerra (hereafter cited as HyG) 1914; Crisanto Cuellar Abaroa, *La revolución en el estado de Tlaxcala* (México: INERM, 1975), vol. 2, passim; *El Constitucional, semanario político, organo del PLCT*, Tlaxcala, 26 August 1917 and 23 September 1917; *Carta Abierta, la campaña electoral en Tlaxcala*, México, 22 August 1918, fdo. Gerzayn Ugarte,

Antonio Meneses; on Ugarte, see Central de Estudios de Historia de México (hereafter cited as CEHM), Fondo Venustiano Carranza (Hereafter cited as FVC): C96-10926, C111-12725, C119-13467, C133-15224.

13. Many complaints of owners are found in AGET/FRRO, legs. 237 to 249, HyG 1918; Buve, "Neither Carranza nor Zapata," sec. 2; Buve, "Agricultores, Dominación Política y Estructura Agraria," in *Haciendas in Central Mexico from late Colonial Times to the Revolution* ed. R. Buve (Amsterdam: CEDLA, 1984), 239–40, 245–49, 250.

14. For the problem of Arenista attempts to have their possessions recognized, see Buve, "Neither Carranza nor Zapata," sec. 2; Buve, "Boerenmobilisatie en Landhervorming tijdens en na de Mexicaanse Revolutie: De vallei van Nativitas, Tlaxcala tussen 1910 en 1940," (Amsterdam: CEDLA, 1977); AGET/FRRO, October 1917 leg. Justicia y Gobierno (hereafter cited as JyG), January 1918 leg. 261 HyG; *Al Pueblo Tlaxcalteca* (pro-Rojas pamphlet), México, October 1919.

15. See Rojas's attempts to gain peasant support in Arenista strongholds in West Tlaxcala, in Buve, "Neither Carranza nor Zapata," sec. 2.

16. *El Constitucionalista*, 26 August and 23 September 1917; del Castillo, *Puebla y Tlaxcala*, 188–90; Cuellar, *La revolución en el estado de Tlaxcala*, vol. 2, passim. Apango became municipal president of Apetatitlan (in 1915), and Mendoza president of Apizaco (in 1914). Apango was a member of Rojas's Consejo de Guerra Permanente, a post reserved for trusted friends of Rojas. Apango was physician in Rojas's brigade and Mendoza was paymaster. Both Apango and Mendoza were members of the first Local Agrarian Commission in 1915.

17. CEHM, Fondo Pablo González (hereafter cited as FRG), C18, C19; see the numerous complaints about Rojas in the correspondence of Governors Del Castillo and Machorro with Carranza in CEHM/FVC, F21, C27-C74, C80, C90, C95, C100, C106; Ez. M. Gracia, "Síntesis de Historia Tlaxcalteca" (SHT), unpublished ms. 253–56; Javier Garciadiego Dantan, "El movimiento Arenista en la Revolución Mexicana," unpublished ms., 1980, 46; Decreto 130, Gob. Suplente Ign. Mendoza, 21 May 1920, U.S. National Archives, Washington, D.C. (hereafter cited as NAW), Decimal File 1910–1929 (hereafter cited as DF), 812.00: 24101; W. O. Jenkins, Consular Agent, Puebla to George T. Summerlin, U. S. Legation, Mexico City, 10 May 1920; Cuellar, *La revolución en el estado de Tlaxcla*, 2:127–29; Del Castillo, *Puebla y Tlaxcala*, 244, 276–78; *El Universal*, 4 March 1920.

18. For complaints, see Archivo General de la Nación, Ramo Presidentes Obregón–Calles (hereafter cited as AGN/OC), leg. 241-C.A 31; *El Universal*, 4 March 1920; Del Castillo, *Puebla y Tlaxcala*, 265–66; Andres Angulo, *Carta abierta a los ciudadanos presuntos diputados del Colegio electoral del Congreso de la Unión*, 26 August 1920; *El Civilista* (Órgano de los partidos Civilista y anti-militarista), 19 February 1920; M. González Galindo, *Carta Abierta Negra traición se sierne sobre el Estado de Tlaxcala*, 1 December 1920; *Alerta Cuidadanos*, February 1921,

in Colección de folletos Revolucionarios (CFR), Tlaxcala; *El Demócrata*, 9 September 1920; *El Disco Rojo* (periódico político liberal del PLC), Tlaxcala, 4 December 1920; *Excélsior*, 5 and 27 January, 2, 9, 20 and 23 April, 5 and 11 May, and 22 July 1921.

19. On rebellions, see Telegraphic Bulletins Mexican War Department (hereafter cited as TB/MWD) to all military commanders from 15 March to 15 December 1922, in Dispatches George T. Summerlin, Mexico, to Secretary of State, Washington, NAW/DF, 812.00: 25474 onward; *El Universal*, 22 February 1919; *El Demócrata*, 4–6 March 1920; on Montes, see Facundo Arias González, "Historia de las relaciones del movimiento obrero con el campesino: El caso de la CROM y de la Confederación Social Campesina 'Domingo Arenas,' " unpublished ms., October 1985; interviews with Ez. M. Gracia, Rojista state deputy, 1918–1923, and Luis Reyes Armas, Mendocista politician, both in January and April 1968.

20. AGN/OC, leg. 241-AD-34 (Hidalgo); *El Disco Rojo*, 4 December 1920; Del Castillo, *Puebla y Tlaxcala*, 277; Gracia, "Sintesis de Historia Tlaxcalteca," 258–60; Georgette José, *El relevo del caudillo* (México: El Caballito, 1982), 35; interviews with Ez. M. Gracia, October 1967, and Mrs. Ángulo, daughter of Arenista leader Andrés Ángulo, February 1981.

21. See Mario Ramírez Rancano, "El Socialismo en Tlaxcala," *Secuencia* 5 (1986); 61–81; E. M. Gracia, "Síntesis de Historia Tlaxcalteca," 279–82; Convocatoria y Estatuos PLCT, 2 March 1920; Interviews with Ez. M. Gracia, October 1967.

22. *El Gladiador* (Órgano del PLC de Tlaxcala), January–May 1922; interviews with Candelario Reyes (CNA delegate in Tlaxcala), April 1968.

23. On Montes, see Arias González, "Historia de las relaciones del movimiento obrero con el campesino," and Jenkins to Claude I. Dawson, Mexico City, 8 December 1923, enclosed in Summerlin to Secretary of State, 12 December 1923, idem., 4, 20 and 30 January 1924, enclosed in Dawson to Secretary of State of 6 and 23 January, and 1 February 1924, NA/DF 812.00: 26661, 26767, 26933, 26971; Julio Cuadras Caldas, *Mexico Soviet* (Puebla: Santiago Loyo, 1926), 483–85; interviews with Reyes, April 1968 and November 1979.

24. *Excélsior*, 16 October 1921.

25. On Sánchez, see Del Castillo, *Puebla y Tlaxcala*, 285–96; *Excélsior*, 26–27 May, 16–17 June, 16 October, 26 December 1921, and 13 January 1922; *El Demócrata*, 22–23 September, and 4 October 1921.

26. For case studies of villages in the municipalities of Lardizabal and Nativitas bordering the state of Puebla, see Buve, "Boerenmobilisatie en Landhervorming tijdens en na de Mexicaanse Revolutie"; *Excélsior*, 14 and 20 January 1922; interviews with Amado C. Morales (CROM leader), November 1967; Buve, "Jefes menores de la Revolución Mexicana, y los primeros avances en la consolidación del Estado Nacional: El caso de Tlaxcala (1910–1920)," paper AHILA, Florence, May 1985, 19–20.

27. On Calles, see TB/NWO, 21 November 1922; and interview in *Excélsior*, 15

September 1922; *Excélsior* and *El Demócrata*, January–March 1922; and Del Castillo, *Puebla y Tlaxcala*.

28. Cuadras Caldas, *México Soviet*, 326, 483–85, 503; Arias González, "Historia de las relaciones del movimiento obrero con el campesino;" AGN/OC, 241-AD-34 (Texmelucan).

29. John W. F. Dulles, *Yesterday in Mexico: A Chronicle of the Revoluution, 1919–1936* (Austin: University of Texas Press, 1961), 132–34; Gracia, "Síntesis de Historia Tlaxcalteca," 256–58; *El Gladiador*, 15 February 1922; *El Latigo* (Semanario Político de Combate, anti-Apango), México, January-February 1923; *Manifiesto* (Mexican Labor Party), 6 June 1922; *A los Ciudadanos Tlaxcaltecas Independientes*, 22 September 1922; *Manifiesto PLT, adherido al Partido Cooperatista Nacional*, October 1922; *Manifiesto a los municipios de Nativitas, Tetlalahuca y Tepeyanco* (anti-PLCT), December 1922; *Duro Don Saturnino*, 1 March 1923; *Partido de la Juventud Tlaxcalteca*, 1 January 1923; interviews with Ez. M. Gracia, November 1967.

30. *El Gladiador*, 15 February 1922.

31. Gracia, "Síntesis de Historia Tlaxcalteca," 257.

32. AGN/OC, leg. 818-X-8, 408-T-31 (1923); *Manifiesto* (PLCT published a series of telegrams exchanged between the Tlaxcalan state government and the Chief of Military Operations in Puebla–Tlaxcala, 23 February 1924), in CRF, Tlaxcala; on agrarian conflicts, see TB/MWO, 24 january 1923; *El Demócrata*, 14 February 1923, published a memorial by the Governor of Tlaxcala to the Secretary of Gobernación, idem., 17 March 1923; *El Universal*, 23 and 30 March, 20 April, and 13 July 1923; *Excélsior*, 26 February, 3, 9, 16, 18, 20, 22, and 24 March, 2 April, 30 May, and 3 August 1923; Dulles, *Yesterday in Mexico*, 191, 223–24.

33. Interviews with Ez. M. Gracia, November 1968; Antonio Hidalgo, December 1967; and Luis Reyes Armas, January 1968.

34. Meyer, *Estado y sociedad con Calles*, 93–96; interviews with Ez. M. Gracia, October–November 1967.

35. Del Castillo, *Puebla y Tlaxcala en los días de la Revolución*, 299–303. Del Castillo collaborated with Manjarrez's government and left politics with the outbreak of the De la Huerta rebellion; Cuadras Caldas, *México Soviet*, 483–86; Gracia, "Síntesis de Historia Tlaxcalteca," 259–60; Jenkins reports December 1923–January 1924, earlier referrred to; AGN-OC, 408-P-16, leg. 1, file on political struggles in Huejotzingo district; *El Mundo*, "el único diario librae de Puebla," año 3, tomo 14, 24 December 1923 and 10 January 1924.

36. *El Combate* (Periódico trisemanario de información y Política, Puebla), 20 November 1924; *Lucha Social* (órgano del Partido Laborista de Tlaxcala), Aprin–June 1924; October–November 1924; *El Combate* (órgano del PNA, México), 21 June 1924, interveiws with Luis Reyes Armas, April 1968.

37. Tel. Partido Laborista Tlaxcalteca to President Calles, 12 January 1925.

38. *El Gladiador*, 20 July, 3 September, and 2 October 1924; AGN-OC, 408-T-33 file on the electoral struggle in Tlaxcala; *Convención, Alianza de Partidos Revolu-*

cionarios, 25 October 1924; Tel. Part. Lab. Tlaxcala to Pres. Calles, 12 January 1925; *Lucha Social*, op. cit., interview with Amado C. Morales, November 1967. Apango wanted General Fausto Topete as Chief of Military Operations; see *Lucha Social*, 24 May 1924 and 17 May 1924.

39. Secretario municipal Partido Laborista Apizaco to Luis N. Morones.

40. AGN-OC, 408-T-33, is full of protests of alianza partisans and Pelaecistas about generalized violence. On de la O, see: Informe General Genevevo de la O to Pres. Obregón, México, 18 November 1924; Tel. Gob. R. Apango to Pres. Obregón, 20 November 1924; Informe Manuel Lira, Srio. Mpal. Part. Lab. Apizaco to Srio. de Industria y Trabajo, Luis N. Morones, 5 February 1925.

41. Tel. Gob. Tlaxc. to Pres. Calles, 16 January 1925; AGN-OC, 408-T-33: Tel. Sen. A. Meneses, México to Pres. Calles; Tel. Luis N. Morones, Tlax. to Pres. Calles, México, 16 january 1925; Acta Tel. Gob. I Mendoza, Tlax. to Pres. Calles, México, 16 January 1925; Tel. Alianza, Tlax. to Pres. Calles, México, 14 January 1925; and Tel. Pres. Calles to Alianza, 15 January 1925. *La Crónica* (Diario de información), 11 December 1924.

42. AGN-OC, 408-T-33: CSC "Domingo Arenas," Texm. to Pres. Calles, méxico, 25 February 1925; Tels. Gob. G. N. Tirado, Puebla, to Pres. Calles, México, 24 and 25 February 1925; Dip. Octavio Hidalgo a.o. México to Pres. Calles, 15 March 1925; Tels. Tlax. Politicians to Gobernación, México, 15 March 1925; Tel. Vecinos San José Atoyatenco, Tlax. to L. N. Morones, Mexico, 19 January 1925; *La Gaceta* (Diario Independiente, México), 22 January 1925.

43. Ramírez Rancano, "El socialismo en Tlaxcala," 69–70.

44. AGN-OC, 408-T-33: Informe Manuel Lira cit., Ez. M. Gracia, "Síntesis de Historia Tlaxcalteca," 279–82; Buve, "State Governors and Peasant Mobilization in Tlaxcala," in *Caudillo and Peasant in the Mexican Revolution* ed. D. A. Brading (Cambridge: Cambridge University Press, 1980), 231–233; and interview with Amado C. Morales, November 1967.

45. González, "Historia de las relaciones del movimiento obrero con el campesino," *El Universal*, 21 April 1926; and *Excélsior*, 30 June 1927, Montes had affiliated committees in the municipalities of Nativitas, Lardizabal, and Ixtacuixtla.

46. Buve, "State Governors and Peasant Mobilization in Tlaxcala," 233–35; *El Pueblo* (Semanario del Partido Reivindicador de Tlaxcala), 1 November 1930 (anti-PST and Gob. Vásquez).

47. Rojas and Octavio Hidalgo received regular presents and payments; see AHT-UIA: 1.1.9.36, 37 and 28, Correspondence of the Management of Haciendas Mazaquiahuac and El Rosario, Tlaxco, with state government Tlaxcala. See, also, Buve, "Peasant Mobilization and Reform Intermediaries during the 1930s: The Development of a Peasant clientele around the Issues of Land and Labour in a Central Mexican Highland Municipio, Huamantla, Tlaxcala," in *Jahrbuch fur die Geschichte von Staat. Wirtschaft und Gesellschaft Lateinamerikas* 17 (1980), 355–95.

48. Buve, "Boerenmobilisatie en Landhervorming tijdens en na de Mexicaanse

Revolutie"; and Buve, "Mobilización campesina y reforma agraria en los valles de nativitas, Tlaxcala (1917–1932)," in *El trabajo y los trabajadores in la historia de México* ed. Cecilia Frost, et al. (México: El Colegio de México, 1979), 533–64.

49. Zainos y Lumbreras, cited in *Excélsior*, 14 January 1922.

50. *Excélsior*, 14 January 1922; *La Vida Nueva*, August 23, dedicated in its Tlaxcala number an article to Apango's prudent agrarian policies of, for example, not inciting the peasants; interviews with Ez. M. Gracia, deputy under Apango, November 1967; Apango had serious conflicts with the CNA and its delegate in Tlaxcala under the radical S. G. Miguel M. López Schwertfeger. See TB/MWO, 20 December 1922, in Summerlin, México, to Secretary of State (NAW-DF 812.00:26161) and *El Latigo* (semanario político de combate, México), 11 February 1923, on anti-agrarian policies of the state government; *El Demócrata*, 8 November 1922, *Excélsior*, 24 November 1922, *El Pueblo* (Semanario del Partido Reivindicador Tlaxcalteca), 1 November 1930. For a eulogy on governor Vásquez's work, see *El Noticiero* (Periódico de Información, Tlaxcala), 13 February 1932, where land reform is not even mentioned. *El Noticiero* was *gobiernista*.

51. Archivo Secretaría de la Reforma Agraria (ASRA) 4943: DT 115-124 Report Candelario Reyes, CNA delegate in Tlaxcala, on the problems of tax payments, 30 December 1920; Informe Gobernador Rafael Apango 1921–1922; 77ff; Informe Gobernador Adolfo Bonilla, 1934–1935: 67ff; *Excélsior*, 5 November and 10 December 1921; Buve, "Peasant mobilization and reform intermediaries" 120–23 and case studies; Ramírez Rancano, "El Socialismo en Tlaxcala," 73–74.

52. Eric R. wolf, "Patrones políticos entre campesinos latinoamericanos," in *Problemes Agraires en Ameriques Latines*, (CNRS, Paris, 1967), 173–89.

53. President Agrarian Committee, Atoyatenco to President Obregón, 1 November 1922, ASRA 5003 DT 213.

54. Michac, Atoyatenco, Tepetitla: ASRA 5003 DT 214-422, correspondence and telegrams between ejido committee, Governor Apango, S.C. CNA and Mexican War Office; La Concordia: buve, "Movilización campesina y reforma agraria," 551–61; Xochitecatitla: ASRA 4973: AL 185-186, 194, 197, AT 50, 55, 58. The committee for expansion of ejidos first requested Montes's intervention and, afterward, that of the PNA during 1923; Capulac: ASRA 5026: DT 21-22, 24, 25, 46, correspondence of ejido committee with P.D.P. Tlaxcala and S.G. CNA in Mexico City, interventions Liga de C.A.

55. Carranco: ASRA 4973: AT 181 on electoral promises, ASRA 4943: 32, 45, 47, 52, correspondence of Federal Agrarista and Labor deputies for Tlaxcala with President CNA and Secretary of Agriculture, Mexico, on electoral promises La Concordia; *El Latigo*, 11 February 1923 on *faenas*; Michac: ASRA 4986: AT Aurelio M. Peña, Fed. Deputy Tlaxcala to President CNA, 6 March 1923; for other complaints, see AGN/OC: 408-T-33 Nativitas.

56. For exasmple, see *Excélsior*, 7 July 1921 (Calpulalpam), 3 October 1921 (Cuauhtelulpam), and 1 February 1922 (Xalostoc). In Nativitas we found clear cases of

ejido elites: Milagro, Atoyatenco, Michac, Xochitecatitla, and Concordia. Landless exaparceros and agraristas tried to get rid of administrative committee president Perfecto Hernández, first Arenista and from 1923 Pelaecista. He refused redistribution of plots together with the established ejido elite. See SRA-DTA 114d. In Atoyantenco the agrarista leadership stayed anti-*gobiernista* and the "have nots" joined the PLCT, but Apango refused extension of ejidos, claiming no land was available. Ejido elite and landless peasants remained anti-*gobiernista* and were persecuted by Mendoza in 1925. See ASRA 5003: DT 213-295.

57. ASRA 5003:L DT 293 complaint ejido admin. com. to President CNA, 16 April 1925.
58. ASRA 4943: DR 2o 13-231 (March 1923 to July 1924). When the PNA finally realized they were protecting the ejido elite, PNA federal leadership was embarrassed; see DT 2o 188.
59. See *El Gladiador*, 20 February 1922, a clearly Pelaecista newspaper, but the trend is confirmed by the Nativitas case studies and by Ramírez Rancano, "El socialismo en Tlaxcala," 69.
60. *El Mundo*, Puebla, cit., and ASRA 5003: DT 2o 293, cit.
61. Buve, "State Governors and Peasant Mobilization in Tlaxcala," 232.
62. Meyer, *Estado y sociedad con Calles*, 94, 102; Moisés González Casanova, *La Confederación Nacional Campesina* (México: Costa Amic, 1968), 130–32; González Arias, "Historia de las relaciones del movimiento obrero con el campesino."
63. Buve, "State Governors and Peasant Mobilization," 234–36; Buve, "Peasant mobilization and Reform Intermediaries," and Ramírez Rancano, "El Socialismo en Tlaxcala," 76–77.
64. Knight, *The Mexican Revolution*, 2: 513.

Part III

Conclusion

11

Nationalizing the Revolution

Culmination and Circumstance

Stuart F. Voss

Temporal perspective has been fundamental to the differing interpretations of the purpose, significance, and reality of the Mexican Revolution. The delineation of the boundaries of the "revolutionary process"—the duration of the underlying historical forces and of the principal causative factors—reveals, in large part, the underlying assumptions of the particular interpretation. Do forces germinated in the immediate past satisfactorily explain that process? Are factors arising from the circumstances of the revolutionary period itself better able to account for the working out of the revolution? Does the revolution encompass the determination of other historical issues or conflicts? Is the revolution itself part of a larger historical process that culminates in the revolutionary or postrevolutionary period?[1]

The orthodox view of the revolution makes a clear demarcation of the armed struggle begun in 1910 from the preceding Porfirian era and establishes the character of the modern revolutionary movement as a popular, agrarian, and nationalist struggle for social justice. Of equal importance has been the linkage of various phrases of the post-1910 period into a tightly woven revolutionary process which leads, for some, to the contemporary era. Though this orthodox interpretation resolutely locates the causes for the revolution in the so-called evils of the Porfiriato, the revolution itself is the product of the historical forces at work during the post-1910 decades.

A more recent, revisionist interpretation views the revolution from a much different temporal perspective. Its adherents are struck by what they see as the continuities between the Porfiriato and post–World War II Mexico. Thus, from a longer perspective than that of the orthodox school, their inquiry centers on how the "revolutionary years" of 1910 to 1940 (or 1946) shaped the creation of a centralized, capitalistic modern state, which began its formation during the Porfiriato. There are, in effect, two revolutions for the revisionists. One, which failed, was a radical, popular, and nationalist transformation of Mexican society aimed toward transmuting the changes wrought by the

Porfiriato and in eliminating the vestiges of the old order. The other, which succeeded, was a modernizing, capitalistic movement (often labeled bourgeois), intended to broaden access to, to reduce foreign control over, and to make more productive the modern capitalistic and governmental structures initiated in the late nineteenth century. However, there is little consensus among the revisionists on when and why, exactly, the one revolution failed and the other triumphed.[2]

In contrast to both the orthodox and the revisionist historians are those who see historical forces and conflicts of much longer duration at work in the revolution itself, or at least accompanying it. Jean Meyer concludes that the Cristero Revolt by Catholics among the popular classes was the culmination of a nearly two-hundred-year struggle between the church and an anticlericalist state for predominance in Mexican society. That revolt of the late 1920s, Meyer contends, was a formidable alternative to the Constitutionalist revolutionary movement which was then consolidating its power. According to Albert Michaels, the Sinarquista movement born in the late 1930s saw the revolution of 1910 as the last in a series of revolutions that had destroyed the colonial order, a "Golden Age" which they hoped to resurrect. Paul Garner notes how the Oaxaca Sovereignty Movement of 1915–1920 considered itself part of a long struggle, dating back to the early nineteenth century, to erect and then preserve a liberal and federal Mexico.[3] Alvaro Obregón, in a manifesto announcing his candidacy for the presidency in 1920, also saw the revolutionary struggle as part of a much longer conflict: "Ever since our country began its first liberating movement, the Mexican family has been divided into two political parties, one formed by the oppressors and the other by the oppressed." In the first (which he identified as Conservative), Obregón included "the opulent, the upper clergy, the privileged foreigners." The second (Liberal) comprised "the great majority of the Mexican family."[4]

Along with the issue of duration in the revolutionary process is the question of whether the unfolding of the revolution was planned or accidental, contemplated or unintended. Was that process the product of the intentions of its principal protagonists (whether movements, cliques, or individuals), and determined according to their relative resources and capabilities? Or was it more the result of an accumulation of responses to circumstances and opportunities of the moment, with often unanticipated consequences? To put it another way, did the turning points of the revolutionary years (be they 1915, 1920, 1929, 1934–35, 1940, or 1946) mark the stages at which the competing forces triumphed or succumbed in the intended march toward their goals? Or did those turning points denote more the junctures at which, for expediency, those forces took initiatives that altered the course of the revolution, with unforeseen results?[5]

Viewing the Mexican Revolution as part of a long continuum, and in terms of unintended consequences of expedient responses to immediate circumstances, suggests that the revolutionary years from 1910 into the 1940s saw the culmination of two long-standing, intertwining conflicts in the historical evolution of the nation. At issue were the beneficiaries of political power and economic resources and the geographic scale upon which those social interests were best served. Integral to these two conflicts was the question of what political structures or mechanisms could best bring the desired results.

From the independence wars there had been a fundamental division in the desired social stratification of Mexican society: one that was to be firmly based on hierarchy versus one that was to be organized generally along egalitarian lines. The precise composition and interrelations of the social groupings (or classes) in the contending societal conceptions have altered. So too have their apologists and partisans. In the former, successive orders or classes were to be dependent on and subordinate to those above them, with ascending degrees of privilege and descending obligations of deference. Political initiative was to be narrow, access to economic resources and their benefits quite differentiated, and social mobility limited. In the latter, there was to be wide latitude in the pursuit of opportunity and in the extent of participation. What was egalitarian was choice, not necessarily outcome. Decision-making in the allocation of resources and in the exercise of political initiative was to be broad-based and social movement within the society fluid.

The term *popular* has frequently appeared in the debate concerning this conflict over the proper social stratification of society, among the participants themselves and among scholars. Customarily, the term has been employed as an antithesis to *hierarchy*. But the root meaning of the word centers on that which pertains to or is engaged in by the people at large. And in postindependence Mexico (and in Latin America generally), the great majority of the people constituted what came to be called most commonly the "plebe," the "masses," or the "popular classes." If something were "popular," it meant that it included or derived from these people, as distinct from the minority constituting the middle and upper sectors of society. In economic, social, and political terms it connoted inclusion, with the popular classes' interests considered on a continuing and integral basis. That gave them a stake in society beyond mere physical survival. Culturally, "lo popular" implied respect for the values, attitudes, and forms of expression of the popular classes. In socioeconomic and political terms, an egalitarian ordering of society necessarily implied "lo popular." Yet culturally, when it entailed the organization of society on a national scale, the linkage was not so certain. By comparison, a hierarchical ordering of society could be popular-based, when it respected and preserved the diversity of popular cultural expression and when it considered the popular classes as integral, deserving components of the society.

The second conflict entailed the proper scale for the primary organization and functioning of Mexican society. On the one hand, there was the conception of Mexico as a society whose institutions and social groups should be national in scope and identity, directed by a centralized state. On the other hand, there existed the vision of Mexico as a federation of autonomous regional subsystems, which were to be united in their common historical experience and in their commitment to support one another's right in allocating resources, perquistes, and control as each saw fit, and under some general, agreed-upon guidelines.[6] At issue was not simply the division of political power at the national (federal), state (regional), and local levels; but more comprehensively, the questions of the scope in which decisions were made and had their effect upon the broad spectrum of life's concerns, of the range of social organization and interaction, and of the scale and prioritization of identities.

These two conflicts over the ideal ordering of Mexican society have generally been treated separately by scholars. One exception is the thesis put forth by August Spain thirty years ago that the experience of the early and mid-nineteenth century led to the alignment of federalism with "democracy" and centralism with oligarchic control. Such a thesis overlooks the emergence of regional caciques such as Santiago Vidaurri and Juan Alvarez, who (usually) affirmed federalism while presiding over a hierarchically ordered local society, often founded upon a popular base. Moreover, by the time of the Restored Republic at least, though egalitarian-oriented politicians professed their continued adhesion to a federal Mexico, the meaning of the word in operative terms was being transposed from confederative to national.

The liberal–national Mexico conceived during the Reforma and altered during the Restored Republic proved to be an unworkable contradiction. Regionalism could not be subordinated to nationalism without destroying federalism in the process. In confronting the problems of economic stagnation and public disorder, the majority of Liberal politicians at the national level sought the creation of a highly centralized political machine, whether out of ambition, necessity, or both. Politically, this emerging centralized state was built upon the reciprocal exchange of patronage for political subordination with notable cliques and caciques in the various states, foreclosing efforts made at fostering a more egalitarian society. Economically, it began to pursue nationalist goals, particularly in the control of basic natural resources, in infrastructure, and in education.[8] The regime fashioned by Porfirio Díaz was the full-blown expression of this executive centralism, of national liberalism gone awry.

The Porfiriato, however, also demonstrated that state-centralized power, combined with a hierarchically based society that made no provision for maintaining a popular base, was destined to failure in the long run. Díaz fostered the creation of the requisite infrastructure for developing a national market and secured national control and allocation of most basic natural resources. He also tried, with much less success, to foster the diffusion of a national culture, primarily through education. The principal effect of this policy was to widen the cultural distance between the popular classes and the *gente decente* (notables and middle sectors) and to menace the diversity of popular expression at the regional and local level.

Those economic policies (and, to a much lesser extent, Porfirian cultural initiatives) wrought profound economic and social changes in most areas of the country. They dislocated—if not destroyed—the various working agreements and understandings that underlay the traditional subsystems within the regions. In part, this was due to the enhancement of the economic and political power (though *not* the authority) of the notable family cliques and individual caciques within their region. By the turn of the century, those hierarchical subsocieties were being maintained increasingly only by force. Moreover, the very strengthening of the internal power of the regional ruling groups worked to fortify regionalism. The alliance-based nature of the Díaz centralized state—whereby he tolerated their internal control as long as they did not threaten his supremacy nationally—meant that "the national regime's [direct] contributions to and demands upon the populace were still too meager to disturb the regional hierarchy."[9]

Indeed, it is ironic that the very aggrandizement of economic and political power at the regional level by these ruling cliques—at the expense of the popular classes generally, and increasing numbers of prominent families and their poor relations more particularly—came to be seen as the singular handiwork of the Díaz regime in Mexico City. That became the rationale behind which many a revolutionary *jefe* sought to maintain regional autonomy while employing that Porfirian-enhanced power within the region for their own ends. Romana Falcón's portrait of the Barragáns in San Luis Potosí (included in this volume) illustrates well such a figure.

Porfirian Reprise: Sorting out the Possibilities

The revolution of 1910 unleashed armed struggles in varying degrees of intensity and scope throughout most parts of the country. Their primary effect was to destroy the national state on which the Porfirian hierarchical order rested. In the initial phase, the regional and local revolts that came to align themselves with Francisco Madero's antireelectionist crusade were, above all, expressions of opposition to the Porfirian centralized state. They sought to redress the balance of geopolitical power that had increasingly—for some, alarmingly—shifted away from the regions (vis-à-vis the national government) and the localities (vis-à-vis the satellite political machines tied to the Díaz regime). In some regions and localities, that loss of power or autonomy had become coupled with economic grievances. From this view, the expanding power of the national state, to the detriment of everyone else in the society, had benefited a few groups unfairly: principally, the ruling political cliques, foreign capitalists, and a rising group of immigrant entrepreneurs. Leadership of these germinal rebel groups came from disaffected notables and an increasing number from the middle sectors (often the notables' poor relations). They employed the customary methods of popular mobilization: material incentives; inherited deference; and, when necessary, the leverage of implied or direct threat. [10]

In their leadership style and in their fundamental concern with regional and local prerogative, even autonomy, these initial disparate rebellions paralleled those of the Restored Republic, which in time aligned themselves with Porfirio Díaz in the Tuxtepec Revolt (1876–1877). In their political expression, the link with nineteenth-century liberalism was frequently professed, usually in the sense of reconstituting what they believed had been subverted by the Porfirian regime. However, that subversion did not include the legacy of a hierarchical ordering of society. If anything, the Porfiriato had strengthened it. But Díaz had narrowed access to the upper levels of the hierarchy, which they wanted reversed. There were also grievances from below that many felt should be addressed, though in due process and in due time, providing it did not threaten the foundations of the hierarchy. [11]

Unlike the Tuxtepec years, however, there also appeared after 1910 an expanding number of rebellions aimed at important segments of the existing order. Their adherents also sought local autonomy, initially manifested in the settling of accounts regarding the abuses of local authorities. Their loss of autonomy in the Porfirian centralization of control had not only been political. Economically, the spreading commercialization and industrialization of the economy in a national framework had left them caught increasingly in a web of dependent insecurity. The economic difficulties brought on by the conversion to the gold standard, the financial crisis of 1907, and widespread crop failures aggravated that insecurity, for some beyond the toleration point. As governmental authority eroded and the contagion of social tensions and consciousness spread from 1911 through 1914, these local insurrections turned to redressing that dependent insecurity: better working conditions; access to land; fairer and more secure tenant and sharecropper contracts; and seizure of goods.

Though some of the leaders of these local, egalitarian-oriented insurgent bands were indigenous, most were professionals, business people, or landowners of modest means. Emerging revolutionary *jefes*, such as ranchero Saturnino Cedillo in southeast San Luis Potosí and schoolteacher Alberto Carerra Torres in a neighboring district in Tamaulipas, closely identified with the rising discontent and parochial concerns of the popular classes. Relying on strong personal relationships with their followers and respect for their military skills, these "popular" revolutionary *jefes* emerged as dispensers of justice and disbursers of booty. Though Emiliano Zapata amalgamated a fairly homogeneous movement of communal villagers, based in Morelos, most of these egalitarian-oriented bands remained heterogeneous in composition and parochial in concern. They drew their support largely from hamlets, villages, and small towns. Most became only tentative affiliates of the larger revolutionary movements that arose. Geopolitically they would have felt most comfortable with Zapata's vision of a parliamentary federation of regions, comprised of autonomous municipalities.[12] Socially, in most regions the distinctions between village farmer, sharecropper, peon, artisan, day laborer, and industrial worker had become more blurred. Identities and survival strategies among the popular classes overlapped considerably, in individual lives and among members of families.[13]

Despite their adhesion to local and regional autonomy, most of the larger revolutionary movements with which these egalitarian-oriented bands affiliated advocated the recreation of the national society being forged during the Porfiriato. The Huertistas, Felicistas, and Carrancistas all basically sought as well the maintenance of the Porfirian hierarchy with its strong modernizing orientation. They differed in the personnel of their leadership and the degree to which the grievances of popular elements needed to be addressed. The radical Constitutionalists, led by Obregón militarily and Francisco Múgica legislatively, also sought a nationalizing society directed by a centralized state. But the popular unrest that helped to provoke the revolution, and which broke the bounds of traditional restraints in full force during the course of the fighting, convinced them that such a centralized national state required a popular base.[14] What was left undetermined among the radical Constitutionalists was whether that popular-based national society would move in the direction of egalitarianism or toward the creation of a new hierarchy.

The culmination of the armed phase of the Mexican Revolution (1914–1916) saw the triumph of a revolutionary movement that was national, urban, and based in the middle and upper sectors. The Constitutionalists alone had moved beyond their regional origins to create a national constituency. By 1920, the leadership of that national movement had been narrowed to those whose base had been in northwest Mexico (commonly labeled the Sonorans).[15] The Constitution of 1917 created a strong interventionist state, empowering it to pursue several options toward the reconstruction of Mexican society. In nationalist terms, it authorized the total secularization of society and the reduction of foreign control over sectors of the economy. In egalitarian terms, it sanctioned the reform of landholding and of employer–worker relations. The Sonorans had the alternative of pursuing these options or of deferring on them. Yet the national regime they headed possessed neither the internal cohesion, fiscal capacity, nor control over political resources to enforce a coherent program drawn from those constitutional options. Post-1917 conditions presented them with severe constraints.[16]

The decade of armed struggle had weakened the dominant groups of the Porfiriato. However, the attenuation of their interests varied substantially, depending upon the sector and locale. In Oaxaca and Tamaulipas, for example, the notables' economic dominance remained largely intact. The hegemony of Monterrey's powerful, industrially oriented network of prominent families lacked only the prior procapitalist guarantee of governmental allies.[17] Moreover, in areas where dislocations had been exacting, elements of the old hierarchy proved adept at maneuvering within the parameters set by the emerging revolutionary order to regain their former position. In Chihuahua, the Terrazas family and their allies in various districts restored a sizable portion of their prerevolutionary wealth and influence. Then, too, there were the new aspirants to notability, using the dislocations of the revolution to acquire wealth and status. They included a growing number of those who had fought in the name of the revolution, but who were being recruited into the remaining Porfirian establishment.[18]

Foreign interests also made their presence felt. The Sonorans were confronted with the more immediate problem of diplomatic dependency to secure and maintain external support, lacking any solid fiscal or political base of their own. In the long term, the legacy of economic dependency from the

Porfiriato went unabated. Foreign capital still controlled key sectors of the economy.[19]

Though the Roman Catholic church was a subordinate partner in the Porfirian establishment, it represented a formidable opponent to the Sonorans. During the Porfiriato it had "reconquered" the countryside and had begun to mobilize the faithful politically and economically, led by a generation of lay people trained by the clergy. After a century of anticlericalist aggression, including the recent armed struggle, the Sonorans found the Catholic church more vigorous than ever. It was determined to resist a centralized state that sought to institute an all-encompassing secular nationalism, and which had created a broad range of popular organizations to do so. Yet the church was not a monolith. Ideology and social milieu separated the clerical hierarchy, the devout urban and middle sectors, and the faithful among the popular classes.[20]

In addition to these segments of the Porfirian hierarchy, the Sonoran-led ruling group was constrained in pursuing the options for the creation of an interventionist national state by mobilized, organized groups among the popular classes calling for a redress of long-standing inequities. They were fragmented spatially between the urban and the rural; occupationally, between small proprietor, sharecropper, rural laborer, and communal villager in the countryside, and between day laborer, factory worker, and domestic in the cities; ideologically, between those most committed to the Catholic faith, to "Marxian class struggle," and to traditional clientele relations.

But above all, the Sonorans found themselves restricted by the resurgence of regionalism. The decade of armed struggle had removed the constraints of the Díaz centralized state on the enhanced power of those in control at the regional level. At the same time, it had broken the monopoly on that regional (and local) power exercised by established notable families and individual caciques. Thus, the Sonorans confronted a myriad of regional (and often local) forces struggling, individually or in combination, to maintain a hierarchy or to create a more egalitarian-based regional subsystem. They had emerged within the parameters created by the Porfiriato in terms of the region's or locale's particular socioeconomic structures and its social elements, and by the revolutionary armed struggle in terms of the location of political initiative.[21]

The Sonorans' political savvy lay partly in their recognition of the constraints on their goal of creating a new national state with exclusive control spatially and sectorally, though not without some costly trial and error. In addition, they perceived that the most effective way to work around those constraints (in the short term, at least) was to secure as many alliances as possible with those who represented popularly based groups. When necessary, they also sought out elements of the old hierarchy as allies. For both the revolutionary groups and their adversaries, scattered regionally and locally throughout the country, had increasingly come to understand that they needed intermediaries to negotiate with those above them who were trying to consolidate power (at the state level and nationally).

The prerogative of intermediaries varies according to time and place. The degree of leverage they and their clients possess is crucial. The line between being an intermediary and a leader is often blurred and crossed. A client's potent political or economic power and shared experiences or beliefs can reduce an intermediary to the function of a dependent, or representative, agent. On the other hand, a client's vulnerability can provide an intermediary with considerable autonomy. Inadequate political or economic resources (especially in dealing with those operating on a larger scale), lack of cohesion, or intractable circumstances can even reduce the client to dependency.

In the preceding century, hacendados, caciques (local bosses), and regional caudillos had become patrons for groups among the popular classes reacting to social dislocation, and among the *gente decente* in times of political turmoil. Many of the *jefes* who had emerged from the revolutionary struggle had served an intermediary function in the groups they led in this traditional and patronal manner. Others had arisen as more charismatic, personally linked leaders, who, as the scale of their followers' involvement in the revolution increased, acted as intermediaries.[22] After 1920, both types of revolutionary *jefes* found themselves having to yield their function of go-between to a new kind of intermediary. Leaders generated from within mobilized popular constituencies and elements of the old hierarchy increasingly sought direct ties with these new political brokers (for want of a better term). These new intermediaries generally possessed neither private economic leverage, affective ties, or personal loyalty to secure relations with their clients. Their authority derived almost solely from their ability to broker clients' interests with outside forces and obtain results: to market their clients' political stock (in the form of electoral or armed force) in exchange for payment on their demands (in promises, at least, if not in concrete terms). The political brokers used programs, organized parties, and bureaucratic posts to build their clientele and to increase their leverage over them.[23]

The new *políticos* took advantage of the unstable geopolitical and social equilibriums resulting from a decade of fighting and political mobilization. Most had served in the revolutionary armies or in politically supporting roles. In social origin, they were intermediaries between the popular classes and the notable—in great part from the urban middle sectors, offspring of professionals, small merchants, and *empleados*. And they quickly moved into the relative political vacuum between the localities and Mexico City. They constituted an alternative intermediate level for political initiative, organization, and authority.[24] The national Congress after 1918 became the arena, the barometer for the unstable political equilibrium. And through the fledgling national political parties, or as direct representatives of revolutionary *jefes*, the new political brokers increasingly came to occupy the congressional seats.[25] The degree of their autonomy—vis-à-vis the various groups they served and the ruling clique in Mexico City—was a function of the competition for the intermediary role, the strength of initiative within their client groups, and the proximity of the brokers' objectives to those of their constituencies.

The Sonorans astutely read this changing makeup among the intermediaries who represented the myriad of local and regional constituencies that had arisen in the wake of the revolution, especially those with popular bases of support. The alliances the Sonorans negotiated with intermediaries were based primarily on two criteria: the firmness of the latter's loyalty or their dependency (as versus their inclinations toward autonomy); and the strength of the popular support (political and/or armed) they could wield in support of the national regime. The series of revolts through the 1920s threatened the permanence of the new interventionist national state. Nevertheless, it provided the opportunity to gauge the relative strengths and weaknesses of the revolutionary *jefes* and political brokers, individually and comparatively.[26] In the short term, alliances with the revolutionary *jefes* took priority. Though their loyalty and dependency was often circumspect, they still controlled the largest share of the popular constituencies. Yet in the long run, the new political brokers offered a surer avenue for the consolidation of the national regime. The ties to their constituent groups were less direct and largely impersonal. Few could martial armed units. That made them more vulnerable to dependence on the national ruling group.[27]

For nearly a decade the Sonorans sorted out and tested alliances personally negotiated with regional (and often local) intermediaries. In the process, they forged a personalist governing coalition which reestablished to a large degree the centralized state apparatus of the late Porfiriato. In strategy and tactics, they were strikingly similar to the Porfiristas in the decade following the Tuxtepec Revolt. Díaz and his associates over the following decade had forged alliances that bound regional ruling groups to their national regime. First Tuxtepec chieftains, then loyal zone commanders, and finally pliant *políticos* (increasingly those "imported" into the region) served as intermediaries. Yet the constituencies in the two personalist, *caudillista* systems were dissimilar. Díaz had solicited the backing of notable networks, relying on their customary subordination of the popular classes in the localities. Obregón and Calles were forced to take into account the demands of popular-based groups mobilized for radical change in the socioeconomic system. Whereas political clubs had served Díaz as instruments of communication with and control of the notable networks, Obregón and Calles turned to national parties in their relations with the mobilized elements of the popular classes. Constitutionally, like Díaz, the Sonoran presidents maneuvered to reverse the revolutionary commitment to no reelection. Their alliances were broad and secure enough with the intermediaries by the time of the 1926–1928 Congress to reintroduce a single, nonimmediate reelection to the presidency (January 1927). A year later, a six-year term was reinstituted and unlimited reelection, but with a proviso of alternation. The latter reflected the legacy of the ruling triumvirate in Porfirian Sonora rather than the national Díaz regime, and perhaps the relative strengths and mutual needs of Obregón and Calles as versus those of Díaz and Manuel González.[28]

By the summer of 1928, with Obregón's reelection, the Sonoran diarchy had tenuously succeeded in reconstructing the Porfirian personalist centralization of the national state. But they had done so in the end by working within the unstable political equilibrium generated by the decade of armed struggle, not by persistently challenging and transforming it. The Constitution of 1917 had given the Sonorans legal authorization to enhance national power at the expense of the regions and localities, and to destroy the old hierarchical order. And they had established the bureaucratic machinery and statutory legislation for intervention in the economy toward national autonomy, in landholding toward more widespread ownership, in employer–labor relations toward a greater share of benefits for workers and more productive cooperation, and in church–state relations toward the complete subordination of ecclesiastical affairs. But in nationalizing the society they could move very little beyond the Porfiriato. In the choice of direction between hierarchy and a more egalitarian society, they were indecisive. They recognized the requisite of establishing the modernizing Mexican society they sought on a broad popular base. Yet they failed either to meet egalitarian demands in more than token fashion or to incorporate the popular classes directly into the state apparatus.

Obregón, more moderate in approach, pursued only the agrarian option with any firm resolve. Calles initially pressed labor's interests, in an alliance with Luis Morones's *Confederación Regional Obrera Mexicana* (CROM), and sought to establish greater control over foreign capital. More radically, he used manifestations of clericalist resistance to bureaucratic emasculation and secular nationalism to launch an all-out effort to destroy the Catholic church as an important cultural and ideological force in Mexican society. But Obregón, and even more Calles, found that foreign capital was necessary to quell insubordinate regional forces (especially to combat the Cristero Rebellion), and (along with Porfirista entrepreneurs) to maintain economic recovery and capitalist development.[29] Moreover, the Sonorans retained the nineteenth-century liberal focus on expanding access to the upper levels of wealth and status. Egalitarian issues and programs never passed beyond being expedient vehicles to secure popular class support or acquiesence.

Obregón's assassination a few weeks after his reelection exposed the vulnerability of the Sonorans' reconstruction of a centralized national state through a personalist, *caudillista* regime. Moreover, it became clear within the succeeding twelve months that the Cristeros had not only achieved a military stalemate. They had also instituted an effective autonomous government over much of west central Mexico. Worse still, there was the prospect that the Cristeros might join forces with the urban-based opposition election campaign forming around José Vasconcelos. Separately or combined, the two represented the first serious challenge originating outside the Constitutionalist revolutionary coalition since 1915. The revolutionary *jefes* felt their local and regional dominance gravely threatened. Obregón's personal prestige and popularity had bound them together. Their response to this sudden negative turn of events was to search for a new national *caudillo*.[30]

The Obregonista generals' initial move was to unite around Aarón Sáenz, Obregón's chief of staff and close associate, as presidential successor. In the end, they yielded to Calles's bid for singular personalist power without the presidency and to incorporation into the official national party he created as the vehicle to realize his ambition. Calles's influence in the Obregón-led ruling coalition had been through his political and administrative abilities, not through his military genius, regional roots, or charisma. The revolutionary *jefes* lacked solidarity. Moreover, for most, the conservation of local supremacy took primacy over the power to shape decisions at the national level. These two realities played into Calles's hands. Both they and he viewed the new *Partido Nacional Revolucionario* pragmatically, as a limited and expedient institutionalization of the personalist, *caudillista* system. For the revolutionary *jefes*, it was the most likely guarantee to preserve the unity within the ruling coalition and their individual dominance regionally, in the face of serious opposition from several directions. For Calles and his associates, it was the only practical means, given the circumstances, to elevate themselves to the center of power in the personalist system then governing the coalition. More inclined to this mechanism for improving the structure and continuity of the ruling coalition were the emerging political brokers, especially those who served as intermediaries in the Congress. They had risen to prominence far more through impersonal relations and political structure than through personalism and economic or military leverage.[31]

Until then, such formal national political organizations were regarded as "national tendencies" that ideologically grouped factions with perceived complementary interests around a national leader, usually the president or an aspirant to the office. Obregón appears to have toyed with the creation of an all-encompassing party. But suspicions of its constraints on his political maneuvering and doubts about its feasibility, given the widespread struggles for power then current, led him to decide not to pursue it.[32] Now, in late 1928, facing the prospect of soon being without the power of the presidency, and without a strong personal following among the revolutionary *jefes*, Calles and his circle of close associates needed to move beyond such accepted conceptions of an inclusive national party. These circumstances required a controlled forum for negotiating political power in the selection of candidates and the determination of policies, one which centered on Calles as arbiter.

Accordingly, the Calles circle labored to establish two overriding axioms for the functioning of the PNR. Party discipline, through a vertical party structure, was crucial. Decision-making was centered in a National Executive Committee, extending downward to state, district, and municipal levels of party organization. Nevertheless, the PNR's founding tenets reveal that Calles was only partially able to move beyond the long-standing regional basis of political organization. Whether this was owing to necessity or the limitations of a Porfirian politican mentality, or both, is not clear. Conceding a respect for local autonomy, the party at the municipal and district levels remained personalist. The party's link with popular groups was only indirect and at the discretion of caciques and political brokers. Only the national level was sufficiently institutionalized. The state level, controlled by the military commanders and governors, quickly became the zone of transition and conflict between the two contrary forms of political functioning. No more than Díaz did Calles overcome the local–regional basis of political organization.

The second axiom was the establishment of "sides." Calles set forth a party ideology that was ecumenical, claiming the inheritance of nineteenth-century liberalism and of the various revolutionary movements whose programs for change were embodied in the Constitution of 1917. This facilitated the co-optation and integration of opponents to the national regime, while attaching the stigma of "reactionary" or "counterrevolutionary" to all of those who maintained resistance.[33] By drawing such wide ideological bounds for the PNR, Calles made party membership less ideologically based and yet more politically consequential. Party membership became the prime mechanism for enforcing party discipline. The potency of party membership as a disciplinary sanction first became significantly manifest in the struggle in Congress in 1930 between the Calles circle and the allies of newly elected President Pascual Ortiz Rubio for control of the election-certification process.[34]

Assisting Calles's consolidation of national power through the PNR was the successful elimination of the regime's three principal challenges in the wake of Obregón's assassination. The Escobar Revolt (March 1929), of Obregonista dissidents unreconciled to the PNR's rejection of Sáenz's candidacy, was suppressed. The Cristero Rebellion collapsed a few months later with the bishops' conditional surrender to the Calles administration after two years of transitory negotiations. And the Vasconcelos campaign for interim president that fall gave out in the face of the PNR's quickly demonstrated electoral organization and muscle backed by the force of the army.[35] The turn of events in 1929—which pared the threat to the ruling coalition's control nationally and to the local and regional dominance of its revolutionary *jefes* individually—coincided with the initiation of a national political organization under Calles's successful management. The Porfirian personalist scheme for a centralized national state had been provided a limited institutionalization. It had made Calles the "jefe máximo" and his political circle a ruling clique. But it had also sown the seeds for a profound change in Mexican politics, seeds that would germinate in a climate of world depression and popular disillusionment. In the relations between region and nation, and in the establishment of a national regime with a popular base, the seeds would bear fruit; but in construction of a more egalitarian society, they would not.

Intended and Unintended Institutionalization: Forging a National, Popular-based Society through a Corporativist Framework

The *Maximato*—the oligarchic rule of the Callista political machine—revealed the unworkability of the limited institutionalization of the Porfirian personalist scheme for a centralized national state and of the reconstitution of societal hierarchy without an integrated popular base. The post-1917 unstable equilibrium, which the Sonorans had exploited to gradually consolidate their power nationally, was coming undone. Important segments of the old oligarchy had begun to recover from their weakened position. They were joined by an emerging group of new capitalists (including many revolutionary *jefes* and office holders). Moreover, Calles's growing accommodation with them from the last years of his presidency had led to an increasing suspension of reforms which, though limited, had begun to redistribute economic resources and leverage. It had also resulted in a greater dependence on foreign capital, especially that of the United States. Ortiz Rubio's policy inclinations reinforced these tendencies. At the same time, the PNR, in practice, quickly proved to be nothing more than a mechanism for indirect control of the popular classes through local bosses, and its ideology of a singular revolution became merely a homogenized myth. Yet popular-based organizations at the regional level survived, expanded, and became increasinly interlinked.[36]

The *Maximato* failed to institutionalize Calles's intended personalist national regime. However, that expedient and initial step of institutionalization embodied in the PNR, combined with changing historical circumstances in the early and late 1930s, led to the crystallization of a new political order; one which was truly national in scope and popular-based in conception and structure, but essentially dedicated to the consolidation of a postrevolutionary elite, coalescing around a ruling clique—the "Revolutionary Family"—and sitting atop a modernizing, national, and hierarchical society.

Paradoxically, Lázaro Cárdenas became the central transitional figure in that transformation of Mexican society that Calles had unknowingly set in motion. Cárdenas presided over the most radical phase of Mexico's postrevolutionary development. Yet Cárdenas was the architect of the corporatist system of interest representation and the nationalization of society that provided the institutional framework for the new hierarchical order which crystallized in the 1940s. Cárdenas was a *político* with strong convictions, but also one who pragmatically responded to the opportunities and necessities of the historical situation. Conviction propelled Cárdenas toward effective popular participation and a more equitable distribution of resources and opportunity, in concert with an institutionalized, state-directed, and modernizing national society within a corporatist framework. In the early and mid-1930s, circumstances encouraged the coupling of these two goals. In the late 1930s, circumstances forced him pragmatically to choose between them. He intended the decoupling to be temporary. However, as will Calles before him, the intentions of Cárdenas's successors and the very institutionalization he had crafted converted a short-term expediency into a long-term direction.

The initial PNR vertical structure of coordinating committees at the subnational levels fostered the emergence of small *Maximatos*. A local or state cacique headed a political circle employing a tight personal solidarity to establish or conserve its influence and to convert the party bureaucracy into a ruling oligarchy. Calles strove to depose those *Maximatos* that resisted PNR interference in political organization at the state level, which were designed to supplant regional parties and to demobilize popular groups.[37] However, Calles met with only partial success.

Important revolutionary *jefes* like Saturnino Cedillo (San Luis Potosí) and Juan Andreu Almazán (Nueva León) and political brokers such as Emilio Portes Gil (Tamaulipas) and Cárdenas (Michoacán) preserved their control. Even those who had yielded to PNR interference presented Calles with a rapidly developing problem. To a new generation of *políticos*, many schooled in the regional "laboratories" of the 1920s, the Callista *Maximatos* were coming to resemble the political exclusivity of the Porfiriato. To accommodate them, Calles once more expediently turned to an institutional adjustment in 1933. To widen the base and to create mobility in the directing circles of the PNR and in the government, individual party membership was established and no reelection was reinstituted.[38]

In a parallel fashion, Calles responded to the resurgence of popular mobilization. The *Maximato* had fragmented popular groups, but had made little headway in demobilizing them. The brazen manipulation and aggrandizement of the PNR political circles, along with the reversal in agrarian and labor reform policies, had spread disillusionment among the popular classes. The effects of the Depression increased that alienation. Unionization and peasant organization expanded, along with significant steps toward unification in 1933–1934. Segments among the middle sectors, professionals and business people especially, were also becoming politicized against the *Maximato*.[39] To head off the rising alienation of the popular groups and their possible mobilization by opponents of the regime, as well as to curb the growth of a dissident left wing within the PNR, Calles devised a party platform for the 1933 presidential nominating convention. The Six-Year Plan returned the Sonoran-led revolutionary coalition to the commitments for reform through state intervention authorized by the Constitution of 1917.[40]

Calles was yielding to political reality. Through his close confidant, Abelardo Rodríquez, who had been elected provisional president by Congress following Ortiz Rubio's resignation (September 1932), Calles began to implement some provisions of the Six-Year Plan, particularly in agrarian policy. Ortiz Rubio's antiagrarian legislation was set aside. Agricultural workers were made eligible for land distribution. A Department of Agrarian Affairs was created.

Rodríguez also incorporated young *políticos* into the party apparatus. Yet in the selection of a candidate for the 1934 presidential elections, Calles made his most calculated and expedient decision. He settled on Cárdenas as the best option to contain the growing dissidence within the party and the rising alienation of the popular classes. Calles preferred Manuel Pérez Treviño, then PNR president and a political broker become bureaucrat who had been a key player in all of Calles's maneuverings to consolidate his control. Pérez Treviño had the support of most of the government bureaucracy, and his lack of any substantial power base meant that he would be beholden to Calles. Nevertheless, the "jefe máximo" realized that Pérez Treviño's imposition might divide the PNR irrevocably. He believed that by maintaining the party's unity, he retained the instrument to control the presidency, as the last six years had demonstrated.[41] And he calculated that Cárdenas was best able to quell popular discontent, bind dissident elements firmly to the party apparatus, and yet loyally work within the policy limits that Calles established.

The "jefe máximo," however, had not ceded enough to the demands of the moment. Rather, his expedient adjustments set in motion forces he could not control. The young *políticos* he made room for in the party aligned themselves with Cárdenas. Increasingly they became political, then bureaucratic, brokers for the popular groups who responded to Cárdenas's candidacy. The Six-Year Plan, which was intended to confine the policy initiatives of the new president, became the rationale for a vigorous commitment to fulfill the promises of the 1917 Constitution. The presidential candidate, whose selection was designed to ameliorate rising popular discontent, instead used the campaign and his first months in office to mobilize and galvanize the popular classes to an unprecedented extent. And in the end, the limited institutionalization, intended to cement the Sonorans' personalist, *caudillista* regime around Calles, had so steadily depersonalized politics that when the *jefe máximo* attempted to bring to heel the dynamic new president, few stood by him. Through the latter half of 1935, Cárdenas employed the institutional prerogatives of the presidency to the fullest. Forced to choose, a solid majority in the army, in the government bureaucracy, in the Congress, and in the subnational levels of the PNR opted for the institutionalizing regime rather than the personalist Callista clique that had conceived it.[42]

Calles's demise did not mean a wholesale discontinuity in policy. Both he and Cárdenas believed that a secularizing cultural revolution was necessary to dismantle the old order, especially among the peasants. The Cristero Rebellion had both confirmed and hardened that belief. Calles had initiated (in the revision of Article 3) the explicit mandate of the teaching of socialist principles in the primary and secondary schools advocated in the Six-Year Plan.[43] Calles and Cárdenas appear to have also shared a commitment to a reformed capitalist economy, one which fostered an autonomous (or national) development through its vanguard of small and medium producers and through substantial state intervention. Calles came to this policy more pragmatically and in response to conditions generated by the Depression, especially the rising economic discontent. Cárdenas sought to infuse his convictions about greater popular participation, economic equity, and national integration into the policy to help break the oligarchic structure of the country and to broaden the national market.[44]

Both Calles and Cárdenas believed in the primacy of an interventionist national state and an all-encompassing political party for the unity and development of the nation. But the relation of the popular classes to that state and party became the pivot on which Cárdenas turned in a radical new direction. Calles had seen the PNR as a means to achieve permanent national control for the ruling clique of the Sonoran-led revolutionary coalition. For Cárdenas, however, politics could not be nationalized unless the society was nationalized. And without a real measure of participation and integration into that state and party, the sundry popular organizations scattered throughout the country would not be brought under effective national control. Cárdenas envisaged functional groups transcending regional subsystems as the fundamental basis of nationalizing Mexican society. Their political and social integration as well as their national identity and loyalty depended, in turn, upon the mediating role of the state. That role, he believed, ultimately resided in the president as final arbiter.[45]

That corporatist, nationalizing vision was not what had galvanized support around Cárdenas in the contest for the PNR nomination. Regional caciques such as Cedillo, Almazán, and Tomás Garrido Canabal (Tabasco) allied with Cárdenas as a way to arrest the centralizing force of the Callista clique, which had deposed many of their counterparts. His support of reform (especially agrarian reform) and of popular participation in a time of mounting economic and social unrest appears to have led regional popular power at the expense of regional autonomy. As first PNR president, and then Minister of War, Cárdenas was an agent of that centralizing policy.[46] The *políticos* of the left wing of the PNR (labeled as progressive or radical by different sources) were more receptive to Cárdenas's nationalizing vision. They shared his belief that the incorporation of the popular classes was a *sine qua non* for the survival of the party they aspired to lead and for the revolution it claimed to represent. There would prove not to be such unanimity among them over the desirability and efficacy of Cárdenas's more radical egalitarian reforms.[47]

As president, Cárdenas set about instituting a corporatist framework that would institutionalize the efffective participation of the popular classes, while simultaneously nationalizing them as sectoral clienteles. Under the stimulus of the interventionist state, a single, nationally comprised interest group would be sanctioned as the sole legitimate representative of each sector of society. The national state, and ultimately the president, would intervene in the economy to mediate among these certified national interest groups and to promote the larger common interest of the nation. To facilitate that intervention, Cárdenas secured passage of legislation that would consolidate public control over private interests.[48]

Though wracked by factionalism (both ideological and personal), the labor movement among urban workers already constituted a national functional interest group. Cárdenas made clear his commitment to back labor in its struggle with employers to improve workers' living conditions. But in return, he called upon workers to unite into a single organization. Through government intervention in contract disputes, subsidies, and periodic harassment of unions refusing to affiliate, he worked toward the unification of the movement as a client of the state, culminating in the creation of the Confederación de Trabajadores de México (CTM). By blocking labor's initiative to organize rural and government workers, Cárdenas was able to organize the two as separate functional groups. Agricultural workers were subsumed under the Confederación Nacional Campesina (CNC), in which membership of all ejidatarios was made mandatory by law. Public employees were organized into several functional groups and merged into what would become the Confederación Nacional de Organizaciones Populares (CNOP) in 1943.[49]

Simultaneously, Cárdenas worked to bring the PNR into conformity with this incorporation of the popular classes as an institutionalized base of support for the national state. The PNR was to become an official instrument of the state, mediating now between the popular sectoral organizations instead of between diverse geographic and personal factions of the revolutionary coalition. Cárdenas's initial step was to affiliate the popular organizations with the party and to incorporate their leaders into the party and state bureaucracies. Then, in 1938, he moved to a more definitive inclusion of the popular classes. Membership in the metamorphosed party (now called the Partido de la Revolución Mexicana, the PRM) returned to being only indirect, but now through membership in the functional organizations being sanctioned by the national state. Competition for political office was to be within and among nationally organized sectors of the society, and no longer among local and regional multistrata coalitions. But in reality, the indigenous leaders and political brokers of the popular organizations negotiated over candidate positions with caciques and personalist political circles at the state and district levels, who remained lodged in the direct structure of the party. The former were soon reduced to the role of dependent intermediaries, even agents, for the national state. Their interests merged with those of the revolutionary regime, the main axis of political life, through the official party and through the national state.[50]

This fundamental political realignment would significantly enhance the power of the institutionalized national state in subsequent years. It secured the right to sanction competing groups, and it acquired considerable direct administrative control through the specific regulatory powers of government departments over the sectors.[51] Perhaps most importantly, it established strong and direct links with the general populace, bypassing the customary regional and district organization of their lives. The geographic layers of Mexican society, which had insulated and bonded various socioeconomic and cultural elements in a variety of subsystems, were being stripped away. This made possible an unprecedented degree of national integration and centralized power.

The corporatist framework was creating national-level institutional loyalties and identities; however, it was not necessarily forging direct ideological linkages with the general citizenry. Cárdenas employed the official popular sectors (principally the CNC and CTM)[52] and the government bureaucracy (most notably the Ministry of Education in the promotion of "socialist" education as a national curriculum) to generate those direct ideological linkages. He was determined to break the old order's hold on the mind-set of the popular classes. The prejudices and slavish attitudes of the past would give way to a new consciousness, through which the popular classes would organize themselves, defend their interests, and arrive at a strong commitment toward the nation and the official party which labored in its (and their) behalf. In the end, a new equilibrium among the social sectors would be attained, making viable a modernizing, nationalized, and more egalitarian Mexico.[53]

Yet by the end of the decade the new equilibrium was far from being realized. Resistance to Cárdenas's vision of a new Mexico had been steadily growing within as well as outside the regime. There was opposition to his direct linkages with popular elements. Local powers-that-be took advantage of his pragmatic instincts and inclinations for compromise, especially in his efforts to undermine those judged too independent of the national state. Defenders of the old order had been able to survive with considerable strength by adapting to the changing circumstances. Most telling, perhaps, was the renewed disillusionment among the popular classes with the "official" revolution and its ruling "family."

Whether supporters of Cárdenas's reforms or not, there were those for whom his strategy of establishing direct ties with (and eventual control over) popular groups constituted a threat of profound and lasting consequences. Despite their old friendship, despite the embodiment of many of his radical agrarian movements' ideas in the Cardenista program, and despite Cárdenas's continuing efforts to negotiate a compromise, Adalberto Tejeda unsuccessfully resisted the steady drive of local Cardenistas, backed by the full weight of the PNR, to take control of his Veracruz agrarian league. Saturnino Cedillo was driven from the Cárdenas cabinet and to an easily quashed rebellion. A charismatic *jefe* in southeast San Luis Potosí during the armed struggle, in the 1920s he had become a traditional, paternalistic cacique for the whole state. Though he helped in securing Cárdenas's presidential nomination, he soon rejected the imposition of socialist education and saw the collective ejido as a Soviet imitation (in contrast to his own military colonies as a model for the nation). But above all, he fought the president's attempt to take over the country's main peasant organization (the Confederación Campesina Mexicana), which he dominated. Economically, culturally, and politically, his base of power was threatened. With the revolt's failure, the previously autonomous agrarian block was merged into the new CNC, the official campesino client of the regime.[54]

Numerous regional and local authorities, in particular, sought to combat the inroads of "socialist" education. Often it was because they were in connivance with those who had a stake in the old order (including *padres de familias*) and/or because it put their own material interests in danger. Equally important, it seems, they were opposing what they perceived as an instrument for the further centralization of power. They wanted to keep the expanding educational bureaucracy and maintain control of the emerging teachers' unions within their own domains.[55]

At times, the Cárdenas regime itself put obstacles in the way of forging direct links between Mexico City and subnational popular organizations. Whether because of personal ties or political necessity, Cárdenas, like the Sonorans, cut deals with elements of the old hierarchical order. Wealthy rancheros and hacendados were spared expropriation of their lands in the face of campesino demands and legal claims.[56] The president also negotiated a compromise with one of the pillars of the old order, the hierarchy of the Roman Catholic church. By the beginning of 1936, he had come to understand that the antireligious campaign renewed by the PNR in 1933 was dividing the popular classes and undermining his own links to them, as well as strengthening the hand of those opposed to his radical reforms generally. He moderated his policies. Blatant anticlericalist measures were set aside, extremists in the states were reined in, and private schools began to reopen.[57]

The truce between Cárdenas and the Roman Catholic church manifested not only the president's political instincts for compromise with opponents of the new revolutionary order. It also revealed the latter's ability to survive in strength through a growing adaptability to the altering circumstances of the second half of the decade. A modification of the church's position toward the revolution began. A reduced number of the faithful among the popular classes did continue to carry on guerrilla warfare in the mountains of the western Sierra until 1940. Nevertheless, the moderate wing of the clergy and lay leadership reconciled the legacy of progressive Catholic reform dating back to the late nineteenth century with the revolution's tenets of developmental nationalism and the need for social reform. They drew the line, however, at any attempt to imbue those tenets with what they considered socialism. Cárdenas's moderating stance on anticlericalism and Pope Leo XI's call for reconciliation strongly influenced their thinking.[58] Even among Catholics who could not swallow the fundamental changes brought by the revolution there was adaptation. The Sinarquista movement (Unión Nacional Sinarquista) led by zealous young professionals reached out to secure a popular base among the campesinos. It advocated land distribution (though into private properties) and opposed armed rebellion. Among reactionary Catholics of the urban middle and upper strata, who had no inclinations to "dialogue" with the campesinos, the founding of the Partido Accionista Nacional (PAN) provided a means for national political expression.[59]

Resistance to Cardenismo was particularly gathering force among Mexico's large entrepreneurs. The 1931 battle with the government over the codification of Article 123 (concerning labor—employer relations) had spawned a fledgling national business movement resolved to limit the power of the national revolutionary regime. The Callista clampdown on labor militancy and fragmentation within the labor movement in the early 1930s did lessen the business magnates' sense of imperative. But Cárdenas's support of strikes and labor unification rekindled their resolve, especially after the president personally intervened in Nuevo León (in February 1936) to break the Monterrey network's long-standing hegemony over workers and to declare his national labor policy. The inner circle of the Monterrey network had formed the leadership core of the national business movement. The symbolism and significance for both sides was explicit. Supported by large entrepreneurs around the country and employing propaganda, moles, co-optation and intimidation, the Monterrey network largely succeeded in rolling back Cardenismo from the state by the end of 1937.[60]

Another secular-based center of opposition had also begun to form. It was a coalition of interests whose objection was not to the revolution *per se*, but to their exclusion from its political power and to the direction in which it was heading under Cárdenas by the late 1930s. The accumulation of frustrated revolutionaries during the years of armed struggle had continued through the sorting-out process of the 1920s and the split within the PNR in the transition from Calles to Cárdenas. However, the organization of the popular classes nationally and sectorally through government and party sanction—supported and managed by public functionaries subservient to the president—gave a far greater sense of permanency and finality to the exclusion from power wrought by the periodic shifts in control of the ruling clique. These revolutionary veterans—politically on the "outs" but economically seeking to consolidate their new-found interests—were joined by notables of the old hierarchy who had made their peace with the Sonoran-led revolutionary coalition. Also part of this coalition of interests were the steadily expanding middle sectors, many of whom had initially supported Cárdenas's attack on privilege and monopoly. Within this coalition there was divergence on the degree of openness and fluidity within the upper levels of a hierarchical ordering of society. There was, however, a convergence of belief on the necessity of discipline and passivity among the lower levels if continued material progress was to be assured. Labor militancy agrarian reform, socialist education, and religious persecution were all stimulants for and symptoms of the challenge from below which Cárdenas had provoked.[61]

These centers of opposition to the Cárdenas reforms—whether regional or national, traditional or postrevolutionary, clerical or secular—became magnets in the late 1930s and attracted growing numbers of workers and peasants disillusioned with Cardenismo. The discontent among organized workers stemmed from the increasing governmental restraints on militant job-action (especially as it affected wages) and the paternalism of PMR labor leaders.[62] More disaffection was surfacing in the countryside. Campesinos found themselves under the thumb of bureaucrats who controlled access to credit, determined production and marketing decisions, and often engaged in corruption in the process. They feared the cultural effects of socialist education on their children.[63] To the ejidatarios' discontent was added the disillusionment of those who heightened expectations for obtaining land went unfulfilled.[64]

The popular classes' disillusionment and the opposition's strength in the last years of Cárdenas's presidency were not only a response to his radical reforms. They were also fed by new circumstances, both internal and external, which Cardenismo itself had in part generated. Economic difficulties were forcing Cárdenas to choose between conflicting demands that previously he had been able to accommodate. The favorable diplomatic and ideologic climate were rapidly eroding with the onset of World War II.

Deficit financing to fund Cárdenas's social programs and public improvements had spawned an accelerating inflation, which by the end of the decade had left most Mexican workers with decreased real income. By early 1937, a process of decapitalization had set in. Large entrepreneurs and foreign investors would not buy Cárdenas's premise of expanding national markets through rising worker income; and they had grown alarmed at the real and potential effects of labor militancy, nationalization of some industries, and agrarian reform. Cárdenas's decision to nationalize the oil industry (in March 1938) compounded these economic difficulties. The trade imbalance worsened markedly. Retaliatory measures by North American and British interests as well as declining commodity prices (especially for minerals) reduced exports. A decline in agricultural production reduced exports further and even necessitated food imports. As revenues declined and debt mounted, the government was less and less able to finance reforms and economic activity. All this, plus the accelerating inflation, made the popular classes more dissillusioned and militant. A vicious circle was setting in.[65]

The international climate reinforced this increasingly negative domestic situation facing the Cárdenas government. The invigoration of the Right in various European countries, particularly the rising strength of the Fascists, undercut the Popular Front aura and socialistic temper that has surrounded Cardenismo. This was evidenced in the intensely hostile reaction of the middle sectors to the granting of asylum to Leon Trotsky, to the unrestricted immigration of Spanish Republicans, and to new educational reform legislation (1939). The Nazi–Soviet Pact and the outbreak of World War II narrowed Mexico's economic and diplomatic options to the point where restoration of closer ties with the United States seemed the only viable diplomatic alternative.[66]

Faced with this new set of circumstances, and with an opposition expanding in numbers and militance, Cárdenas became more pragmatic in policy and more exclusive in priorities. He moderated the radical parts of his reformist agenda. The socialistic tone of educational policy was withdrawn in practice.[67] Land reform was curtailed, while special support was given to private landowners. Cárdenas pressured labor to increase productivity in the national interest and to set aside the primacy of pursuing class interests.[68]

The pressure of these changing internal and external circumstances were forcing Cárdenas to choose between goals and constituencies that at least temporarily could no longer be reconciled.[69] That he placed highest priority on the solidification of a national, modernizing society—with an integrated popular base and directed by an autonomous institutionalized state—seems borne out by his response to the circumstances his government confronted in the late 1930s. The open question was whether in the long term the egalitarian disposition initiated at the national level by Cárdenas would continue as one of the twin bases of the modernizing Mexican society which was by then in formation. The extent to which it would continue as such depended on several variables: the corporatist institutional framework he had constructed; the commitment of those who would inherit its direction; the strength of the opposition; and the larger global circumstances that would follow. Though the latter was beyond Cárdenas's control, the other three variables were very much affected by his actions. By the end of his presidency, the corporatist framework and the opposition's strength were far more forces with which to contend than to shape. What remained decisive for Cárdenas to influence was the commitment of his successors to an egalitarian as well as national, modernizing society.

Institutional Permutation: Solidification of a National, Modernizing Hierarchical Society

The pragmatic response to the question of presidential succession in 1928–1929 had resulted in a change of direction in the evolution of the postrevolutionary Mexican state and society. Calles's creation of a national revolutionary party had set in motion an ongoing depersonalization of Mexican politics that soon surpassed his limited intentions. Cárdenas had sought to expand that institutionalization process by extending it to the popular classes, in an effort to guarantee their effective participation and to institute egalitarian reforms that would secure their interests in a capitalist economy. By 1940, it was also evident that his institutional initiative had not turned out as he had contemplated. There was a similar parallel in the selection of a successor. The impact of the worldwide Depression had reinforced the growing opposition to Calles's curtailment of reforms. This forced him to move temporarily toward the center and to opt for one he thought in the short run could contain the opposition and in the long run would prove loyal enough to follow policy guidelines as Calles determined them. The circumstances of the late 1930s had strengthened the mounting opposition to Cárdenas's radical reforms. He too moved temporarily to the center, but far more to preserve his reform program than his own personal hold on national power. He settled on a successor who he calculated would maintain the unity of the party until the crisis had passed and who would endorse the resumption of Cardenismo. Both Calles and Cárdenas were unwilling to risk fracturing the revolutionary coalition irrevocably—and thereby quite possibly its control of the centralized national state—by engaging in an all-out struggle with the opposition within and outside the party.

The corporatist framework, by which Cárdenas had extended the institutionalization of the national state and of an all-encompassing party, had incorporated a popular base for both. It had not, however, created a political constituency capable of securing his radical reforms. Large segments of the state and party, especially its bureaucratic leadership, had reached the conclusion that Cárdenas's implementation of the Constitution of 1917 had gone beyond what was desirable and prudent. In 1934–1935, institutional loyalty and self-interest had led them to support the president in his showdown with the "Jefe máximo." Now that same institutional loyalty and self-interest led these military, legislative, and administrative bureaucrats, headed by Portes Gil, to settle on a candidate who would continue the retreat from Cardenismo, which had been temporarily initiated by the president himself. To rekindle popular militancy—especially given the waxing strength and beginnings of coalescence among the various elements of the opposition—was to threaten national unity, economic development, and the dominance of the institutionalizing revolutionary regime. The ties of these PRM conservatives and moderates with the numerous subnational caciques, whose influence party reorganization had not removed, strengthened this disposition. So too had the institutionalization of the leaders of popular groups within the party sectors. The corporatist framework had made their incumbency more dependent upon their linkages with the state and party bureaucracy—which many thus sought to join—than to their popular constituencies. The ability of the sectoral structure to convey directly the popular will had been negated.[70]

The conservative and moderate leaders of the PRM feared that Cárdenas, despite his recent moderating stance, would, in the end, support Francisco Múgica. He possessed a distinguished revolutionary career as popular reformer and nationalist, had been a close associate of the president over many years, and was committed to extending the Cardenist reforms. But it was just that uncompromising radical conviction, the intense reaction it provoked among the opposition, and his impeccable integrity that gave them grave concern. To counter Múgica's expected candidacy, they began promoting General Manual Avila Camacho, the Minister of Defense. Avila Camacho had been a loyal functionary with few enemies within the party, and he was a moderate. They were joined by important segments of the PRM's left wing. The leaders of the CTM and CNC, who most spoke for the popular classes within the party, gave their tentative support to Avila Camacho a month before the party nominating convention in early 1939. This converted him from potential nominee to favorite. Apparently, they rationalized that Avila Camacho was a necessary unifying, administrative transitional figure in a time of approaching world war and mounting rightist opposition, consolidating the work of Cardenismo until it could be resumed.[71]

Cárdenas, in the end, appears to have reached a similar conclusion. He faced what was the most serious political challenge to the ruling revolutionary clique since 1928–1929. Internationally, the spreading conflagration of world war heightened the potential for instability. He could not contain the growing expressions of support for Avila Camacho without resorting to a presidential imposition. Cárdenas seems to have concluded that to choose Múgica was to risk a fatal split in the party, an intensification of the opposition to his reform program, and a necessary cooperative agreement with the United States. Avila Camacho, he could fairly safely calculate, would maintain the interventionist national state and continue economic development. That he would preserve and expand the egalitarian component of Cardenismo was far more a gamble and a hope of Cárdenas' part.[72]

Cárdenas determined that he could neither rely on, nor risk, popular will and action to secure his presidential preference within the party. The very corporatist framework that had institutionalized their incorporation had rendered their interests and facility to act dependent upon the support of party leaders and government bureaucrats. And once accepting Avila Camacho's candidacy, Cárdenas employed the full leverage which the corporatist framework provided to dispel manifestations of support for Múgica.[73] Yet Cárdenas soon became alarmed at the potential of the popular will among the general electorate to undo his efforts to obtain the optimal succession given the circumstances.

General Almazán, the candidate of the previously divergent elements of the opposition—business magnates, alienated revolutionary veterans, the PAN and other Catholic nationalists, and notables of the old order in general—was generating increasing popular support. He was profiting from the growing discontent and disillusionment among the popular and middle sectors as economic difficulties mounted and bureaucratic whim and corruption went unchecked.[74] Cárdenas had promised Almazán that the popular will would be respected, assuming that the opposition's prior record of disintegrative squabbling and its failue to generate popular support would undermine this candidacy as well. But as that assumption proved incorrect, the government countered with repression and electoral manipulation. The president was convinced that the opposition's victory would fractionalize the PRM, dissipate worker and campesino support for his reforms, and open the door to the reactionary right, undoing all that he had accomplished. But in going back on his commitment to fair elections, Cárdenas had closed off the only remaining institutional avenue for effective popular participation.[75]

Short of rebellion, Cárdenas had returned the popular classes he had mobilized in the mid-1930s to powerlessness, within the party and in the general electorate. For whatever his precise motives, Cárdenas, in response to immediate circumstances, had left the commitment to an egalitarian-based modernizing society at the discretion (and convictions) of the ruling party clique, and more immediately, of his successor, Manuel Avila Camacho. Ironically, in the 1940s, the popular classes would assume a wholly passive function, as Calles had intended a decade before. They were to be solely beneficiaries, dependent upon an exclusive ruling group, acting through a growing institutional apparatus which alone determined and addressed their needs.[76]

Cárdenas apparently saw the moderation of reforms in the late 1930s and the manipulation of the election of 1940 as a necessary detour in the course that he had initiated upon assuming the presidency. Avila Camacho, it seems clear, viewed them as the proper direction for the revolution to follow. The new president understood the value of retaining the corporatist framework, of maintaining the national integration of campesinos and urban workers through functional sectors as a popular base for the regime. But his commitment to egalitarian reforms was only as it served the purposes of an interventionist national state. And the latter objectives increasingly seemed to coincide with the mutually reinforcing interests of public functionaries and of a narrowing group of impresarios (domestic and foreign, familial and corporate). The circumstances arising from the Second World War buttressed this departure from Cardenismo.

Avila Camacho initiated the departure in his presidential campaign, as Cárdenas had signaled his change of course from Calles six years before. The PRM had reaffirmed the Cárdenas program in a new six-year plan (of November 1939), though with some moderation. Yet Avila Camacho called for the replacement of class struggle with social harmony; communal-collective agriculture with support for the individual producer: strident nationalism with an invitation to foreign capital to assist in Mexico's development; and vigorous pursuit of anticlericalism with a defusion of the religious question, even to the point of publicly professing that he was a believer. He was, in short, offering the Catholic church, private property, and foreign capital an acceptable place within the revolution. Indeed, except for the issue of state intervention, Avila Camacho and Almazán differed little in their campaign approach.[77] This left the popular classes vulnerable and opponents of Cardenismo with an opportunity to seize the initiative.

The quickening spread of global conflict gave national unity a greater imperative, strengthening the power, prestige, and prerogative of the president in the process. Politically, congressional granting of the power to suspend constitutional rights gave Camacho considerable leverage in demanding sacrifices and compromises from powerful interest groups. A change in the electoral law in 1945 took that process out of the hands of municipal and state authorities and placed its custody in a new national agency. Programs to meet the demands of war mobilization—and the expansion of the bureaucracy to implement them—extended the direct contact of the national state with the general citizenry. The war effort also was employed to reestablish unity within the Revolutionary Family and to foster working relations with many revolutionary veteran opponents. Symbolic of this was the gathering of all presidential office holders since 1920 at the 1942 Independence Day celebrations in a show of unity.[78]

In the economy, the national state's intervention intensified. The drastic reduction in imports, the demand for strategic materials, and the necessity of self-sufficiency in basic commodities and consumer goods put a premium on an enlarged and more efficient productive capacity. The Avila Camacho government established a national development corporation (*Nacional Financiera*) to direct capital toward industrial expansion. Through legislation and funding, it strove to create additional agricultural resources and to improve existing ones.[79]

Avila Camacho also invoked the crisis circumstances of the war to justify and dictate the removal of egalitarian reforms from the programmatic equation for Mexico's emerging modern society. He did not dismantle the institutional popular base, though he altered Cárdenas' framework so as to strip it of any potentially effective popular participation. The "popular sector" of the party (largely middle class in composition) was integrated so as to parallel and check the worker and campesino sectors. Party activity became more individualized (including official membership), allowing still more access to the middle class and to business groups. The influence of the sectors in the internal selection of candidates was officially diminished. The Cardenista vocabulary was abandoned, the second Six-Year Plan scuttled, and the practice of adopting a party platform discontinued. Renovation of party and government personnel greatly reduced the number of leftist advocates. Cárdenas's PRM was reduced to being solely an electoral instrument of the state, and was renamed the Institutional Revolutionary Party, or the PRI.[80]

The popular classes were rendered impotent not only within the party, but in the functioning of their organizations in the national society. Lombardo Toledano, the Marxist head of the CTM, was replaced by the pliant Fidel Velázquez. Labor militancy was also dampened by the modification of the Federal Labor Law.[81] Workers' administration of the nationalized railways was replaced by a government-controlled bureaucracy, and guarantees against nationalization were extended to encourage industrial enterprises. Similar guarantees were given to private landowners, large and small. Collective ejidos were cut off from credit. The CNC became wholly a bureaucratic apparatus.[82]

While the commitment to a popular-based modern Mexico was being abandoned under the Avila Camacho presidency, a consensus around a new hierarchical order was crystallizing. It involved the fusion of interests of elements of the old order, the successful revolutionary entrepreneurs, and the public functionaries who had never accepted Cardenismo or had grown tired of it. The consensus had germinated at least by the Cárdenas years, perhaps earlier. But the war years brought it to fruition, and it was now linked intrinsically with a national state-directed society.[83]

Avila Camacho's policies enabled entrepreneurs to take the intiative they had lost under Cardenismo by effectively holding the popular organizations in check. His working agreement with the United States brought not only financial and technical aid from that country, but attractive arrangements for foreign investment to be mixed with domestic capital. The Avila Camacho administration also extended tax exemptions and other stimulants, especially to industry. A narrowing segment of entrepreneurs benefited disproportionately. So too did a number of public functionaries.[84] Having found that their political careers no longer depended upon the realization of the Cardenista reforms and that their bureaucratic control of popular organizations was all that was required, they had begun fusing their interests with those of domestic and foreign entrepreneurs.[85]

The mechanisms, or locales, for this fusion process were varied. Most visible were the entrepreneurial—bureaucratic linkages in the national state itself.

Though initiated before 1940—most notably during the Cárdenas years—the exigencies of the war years accelerated and solidified their development.[86] Less immediate and more subtle was the role of education in this fusion of hierarchical interests. For the generation of the armed phase of the revolution, those who had shared military and militant experiences on and off the battlefield, had also forged political and economic linkages. By 1940, certain educational institutions were becoming an important source of common experiences for the postrevolutionary generation.[87] More lasting, though less tangible on the surface, were familial ties that had begun to fuse these hierarchical interests. Kinship had been a critical element in the concentration of power among the notables of the old order.[88] The role of education and family underlines the importance of a generational transition during the 1940s in the fusion of these interests, who by that decade were bent upon forging a new hierarchical order. The offspring of these elements, whether products of such ties or forgers of the linkages themselves, were coming into prominence by 1940. In the last half of the decade, during what has commonly been labeled the "Alemán Generation," they took the initiative in guiding the revolutionary regime. They solidified and extended the policies of the Avila Camacho administration which had constituted a marked departure from Cardenismo.[89]

The presidency of Miguel Alemán saw the solidification of a new hierarchical order that reduced egalitarian reform to a nostalgic memory, a propaganda tool, a token of hope. Individual, private initiative—in alliance with the national state—would prove to be primal in the building of modern Mexican society. Translated into economic policy and practice, that meant a decline in government social expenditures and a significant rise in economic expenditures, whose benefits accrued above all to the narrowing segment among domestic entrepreneurs. While industrial production nearly doubled, inflation continued its escalation from the war years, and real wages declined as labor militancy was suppressed when necessary. Land distribution ground to a virtual halt. Overall, the redistribution of wealth toward the middle and upper classes that advanced markedly during the Avila Camacho years became even more pronounced.[90]

The excesses in official corruption and lavish consumption by those at the top of the new hierarchy led to mounting popular resentment and intellectual criticism. The Revolutionary Family pulled back to the comparatively more balanced course marked out by Avila Camacho. They settled on Adolfo Ruiz Cortines as successor, a bureaucrat of proven moderation and probity. They initiated a slight redress in benefits for workers and campesinos.[91] The "compromise of 1952," however, was one of emphasis, not of fundamental direction. The headlong rush toward the new hierarchy during the Alemán years had raised the prospect that the commitment to egalitarian reforms—by then only a remnant of the Cardenist revolutionary equation—was being utterly abandoned. Its retention as form instead of substance, propaganda instead of conviction, has been an essential buttress for the continued nationalization of society by the interventionist state.

The war years of the 1940s marked the decisive consolidation of the institutional national state. Pragmatically conceived by Calles (and in limited terms), and metamorphosed by Cárdenas through a corporatist framework, it was completed by Avila Camacho. Institutionally, operationally, and ideologically, the president had become preeminent in the government and the official party, directing an interventionist state apparatus that reached into most facets of Mexican life and ultimately governed them. The result of the process was a national ordering of society. The long-standing conflict over the proper scale for the primary organization and functioning of Mexican society had been settled. The regional subsystems, which had been invigorated by the armed phase of the revolution, were finally dismantled as the integrative and encompassing governants of people's lives. There would be challenges to the PRI's hegemony in the years ahead, centered in various states and regions. Their aspirations, however, would not be for regional autonomy, but rather to change the national directions that shaped their interests.

Cárdenas's corporatist structures had greatly facilitated this nationalization of Mexican society, augmented by the diffusion of state-directed infrastructure and mass communications. Those structures, in particular, had brought the popular classes under the firm control of the national state. Yet his commitment to egalitarian reforms had also been important in mobilizing the popular classes behind an interventionist national state. The old hierarchy, weakened by the armed revolutionary struggle and regional revolutionary "laboratories" of the 1920s, was damaged beyond repair by the aggressive Cardenista implementation of the 1917 Constitution. Nevertheless, the longstanding conflict over social stratification was not consummated in favor of an egalitarian-based Mexican society.

When immediate circumstances forced him to choose, Cárdenas trusted the good intentions of those like himself who directed the national institutionalized state—not the effective participation of the popular classes through independent leaders and an accountable electoral system—to ensure the egalitarian character of a national and modernizing Mexico. However, after 1940 the Revolutionary Family had other intentions. They were disposed to the creation of a new hierarchy, interfaced with a strong interventionist national state. They retained Cárdenas's corporatist framework, along with some egalitarian rhetoric in the official ideology. But it would only serve as a mechanism for control of Mexico's rural and urban masses.

Until his death, Cárdenas challenged the intentions of the Revolutionary Family, obtaining some benefits from campesinos and workers from time to time. Yet he continued to uphold the corporatist party system, modified by Avila Camacho. That he did so, and that so many of those with popular, egalitarian convictions after him have done so, perhaps helps to explain why the national, modernizing, and hierarchically based society that crystallized in the 1940s has endured for nearly a half-century.

Notes

1. The "immediate past" corresponds to that portion of the past directly experienced, varying in duration with the various demographic cohorts that comprise the population. "Distant past" refers to the past not directly experienced.

2. For some (Adolfo Guilly, *The Mexican Revolution*, translated by Patrick Camiller [London: Verso Editions and New Left Books, 1983]), a social revolution begun during the armed struggle was interrupted, giving way to a triumphant bourgeois revolution. Nevertheless, the latter was forced to integrate significant reforms into the juridical structure of the country as it began to construct the postrevolutionary Mexican state beginning in 1920. Nora Hamilton (*The Limits of State Autonomy: Post-Revolutionary Mexico* [Princeton, N.J., Princeton University Press, 1982]), also sees 1920 as an important turning point, but for the development of a national bourgeoisie and the formation of many of the major institutions of contemporary Mexican capitalism. Others, as we have already seen in this volume, see the 1920s as a "laboratory" for the revolution, building upon the popular and radical movements that arose during the preceding phase of armed struggle. For them, the years beginning in 1929 are a crucial demarcation line. Thereafter, the new economic and political order became institutionalized, accompanied by the creation of an official revolutionary ideology, a phase completed by the end of the Second World War.

   Thomas Benjamin, "The Leviathan on the Zocalo: Recent Historiography of the Postrevolutionary Mexican State," *Latin American Research Review* (hereafter cited as *LARR*) 20:3 (September 1985): 195–218, provides a good survey of recent literature for the period 1920–1946. Other bibliographic essays on the revolution include: Alan Knight, "The Mexican Revolution," *History Today* 30 (May 1980): 28–34; and Barry Carr, "Recent Regional Studies of the Mexican Revolution," *LARR* 15:1 (January 1980): 3–14.

3. Jean Meyer, *The Cristero Rebellion: The Mexican People Between Church and State, 1926–1929*, trans. Richard Southern (Cambridge: Cambridge University Press,

1976); Albert L. Michaels, "Fascism and Sinarquismo: Popular Nationalisms Against the Mexican Revolution," *Journal of Church and State* (hereafter cited as *JCS*) 8:2 (Spring 1966): 234–50; Paul Garner, "Federalism and Caudillismo in the Mexican Revolution: The Genesis of the Oaxaca Sovereignty Movement (1915–1920)," *Journal of Latin American Studies* (hereafter cited as *JLAS*) 17:1 (May 1985): 114–33.

4. Alvaro Obregón, *La caída de Carranza: de la dictadura a la libertad*, ed. José Vasconcelos (México, 1920), in Charles Cumberland, *The Meaning of the Mexican Revolution*, (Lexington, Mass.: D. C. Heath Co., 1967), 10.

5. Contrasting views on this perspective are seen in Hamilton, *Limits of State Power*; and in Alejandra Lajous, *Los orígenes del partido único en México* (México: Universidad Nacional Autónoma de México [hereafter cited as UNAM], 1981).

6. Paul Drake, "Mexican Regionalism Reconsidered," *Journal of Inter-American Studies and World Affairs* (hereafter cited as *JIASWA*) 12:3 (July 1970): 402–3.

7. August O. Spain, "Mexican Federalism Re-visited," *Western Political Science Quarterly* 9:3 (September 1956): 620–32. Faced with what they saw as a growing unruliness among the popular classes, their disinclination to trust in the judgement and supervision of those to whom they had customarily deferred, the "gentry" became ever more committed to a centralized state to provide the maximum control over the popular classes. In response, Spain contends, the leaders of "popular" causes increasingly reached the conclusion that "democracy" was better served by a federal system that emphasized the autonomy of the states and local initiative.

The expansion of regionalism from independence to 1880 is stressed by Angel Bassols Batalla, *México: formación de regiones económicas* (México: UNAM, 1979).

8. Laurens B. Perry, *Juárez and Díaz: Machine Politics in Mexico* (DeKalb: Northern Illinois University Press, 1978), 5, 339–53. Garner, in "Federalism and Caudillismo," 114–24, shows the persistence (indeed, strengthening) of the existing hierarchy of Oaxacan society in the wake of the failure of national liberalism. A more detailed case study of that failure can be found in Stuart F. Voss, *On the Periphery of Nineteenth Century Mexico: Sonora and Sinaloa, 1810–1877* (Tucson: University of Arizona Press, 1982), chaps. 7–9.

9. Drake, "Mexican Regionalism," 403–4. Oaxaca was one region that appears to have undergone limited economic and social change during the Porfiriato. Nevertheless, the political power of the ruling groups was strengthened. That reinforced regionalism found expression in the Oaxaca Sovereignty Movement during the revolution. Garner, "Federalism and Caudillismo," 116–26.

10. John Tutino, *From Insurrection to Revolution in Mexico: Social Bases of Agrarian Violence, 1750–1940* (Princeton: Princeton University Press, 1986); Diana Balmori, Stuart F. Voss, and Miles Wortman, *Notable Family Networks in Latin America* (Chicago: University of Chicago Press, 1984), 123–28.

11. Romana Falcón, "Charisma, Tradition, and Caciquismo: Revolution in San Luis

Potosí,'" in *Riot, Rebellion and Revolution: Rural Social conflict in Mexico* ed. Friedrich Katz (Princeton: Princeton University Press, 1986), 421–25. The Oaxaca Sovereignty Movement saw itself as the latest in a series of defenses of the federal liberal structure that had emerged through the course of the nineteenth century and had been embedded in the Constitution of 1857. The sovereignty it sought was Oaxaca's right to conserve its hierarchical subsystem. Garner, "Federalism and Caudillismo," 118–33.

12. Tutino, *Insurrection to Revolution*, 275–325; Falcón, "Charisma, Tradition, and Revolution," 426–31; John Womack, Jr., *Zapata and the Mexican Revolution* (New York: Alfred Knopp, 1969).

13. Barry Carr, "The Mexican Communist Party and Agrarian Mobilization in the Laguna, 1920–1940: A Worker–Peasant Alliance?" (paper presented to the Meeting of the Latin American Studies Association, Boston, October 1986), 5–14; for Tlaxcala, see Raymond Buve, chap. 10 this volume; for west central Mexico, see Meyer, *Cristero Rebellion*, 86, 92–94, 101–11. See, also, Paul J. Vanderwood, "Building blocks but Yet No Building: Regional History and the Mexican Revolution," *Mexican Studies Estudios Mexicanos* 3:2 (Summer 1987): 427–28.

14. Linda B. Hall, "Alvaro Obregón y el partido único mexicano, *Historia Mexicana* (hereafter cited as *HM*) 29:4 (April-June 1980): 602–3, 614–19. Ian Jacobs, in *Ranchero Revolt: The Mexican Revolution in Guerrero* (Austin: University of Texas Press, 1982), sees the armed struggle in that state as an extension of the nineteenth-century regional and national conflict.

15. See Tutino, *Insurrection to Revolution*, chap. 3.

16. Hamilton, *Limits of State Autonomy*, 61–63.

17. Ibid., 63, 79–84 101; Heather Fowler Salamini, "Tamaulipas" chap. 8, and Paul Garner, "Oaxaca" chap. 7 this volume; Alex M. Saragoza, *The Monterrey Elite and the Mexican State, 1880–1940* (Austin: University of Texas Press, 1988), 109–13.

18. Hamilton, *Limits of State Autonomy*, 84–90. In Chihuahua, the Terrazas family and their allies in various districts restored a sizable portion of their prerevolutionary wealth and influence; see Mark Wasserman, "Persistent Oligarchs: Vestiges of the Porfirian Elite in Revolutionary Chihuahua" (paper presented at the VI Conference of Mexican and U.S. Historians, Chicago, September, 1981). In the village of Azteca, Morelos, the ex-caciques regained control of village politics and resources for a time; see Oscar Lewis, *Pedro Martínez: A Mexican Peasant and His Family* (New York: Random House, 1964), 119–61. Local hacendados in the Zacupu Valley, Michoacán, secured the support of federal troops to resist and then undermine local agrarianists; see Paul Friedrich, *Agrarian Revolt in a Mexican Village* (Englewood Cliffs, N.J.: Prentice-Hall, 1970), 98–119. For the army's role in the recovery and protection of the notables' interests, see Hans Werner Tobler, "Peasants and the Shaping of the Revolutionary State, 1910–1940," in Katz, *Riot, Rebellion and Revolution*, 505–10.

19. Hamilton, *Limits of State Autonomy*, 69–74, 101.

20. James W. Wilkie, "The Meaning of the Cristero Religious War Against the Mexican Revolution," *JCS* 8:2 (Spring 1966): 214–33; Meyer, *Cristero Rebellion*, 6–32.

21. Gilbert Joseph, "Mexico's Popular Revolution: Mobilization and Myth in Yucatán, 1910–1940," *Latin American Perspectives* (hereafter cited as *LAP*) 6:3 (Summer 1979): 46–50; Romona Falcón, "Veracruz: los limites del radicalismo en el campo (1920–1934), *Revista Mexicana de Sociología* (hereafter cited as *RMS*) 41:3 (July-September 1979): 671–73.

22. Raymond Buve, "Políticas locales: el caso de Tlaxcala," *Revue Francaise D'Histoire D'Outre Mer* 66:3/4 (1979): 356–62. In Yucatán, Felipe Carrillo Puerto's regional socialist movement came to rely on the new rural caciques as intermediaries in its efforts to mobilize the peasantry. Joseph, "Mobilization and Myth in Yucatán," 54–60.

23. In this volume, Garner, chap. 7, provides examples of the traditional intermediaries in the caciques of the Oaxaca Serrano. Wasserman and Fowler Salamini, chaps. 9 and 8, show the traditional and charismatic revolutionary *jefes* giving way to the new political brokers in the 1920s. Saragoza, in *Monterrey Elite*, 114–25, 135, 151–52, and 169, details the Monterrey notable network's search for an intermediary to guarantee a procapitalist stance by the state government. Aarón Sáenz provided only temporary service, but General Juan Andreu Almazán proved to be the near reincarnation of Bernardo Reyes during the Porfiriato.

24. In this volume, Fowler Salamini, chap. 8, and Buve, chap. 10; and Jacobs, *Ranchero Revolt*, offer good examples of these new political brokers in Tamaulipas, Tlaxcala, and Guerrero.

25. Lajous, *Partido unico*, 27–28, 32; Lajous, "El partido nacional revolucionario y el Congreso de la union," *RMS* 41:3 (July-September 1979), 651–53.

26. The alliance Obregón made with Cedillo in the Agua Prieta Revolt was reinforced by the latter's effective employment of the military–agricultural colonies he organized, in defense of the Sonoran-led regime in the revolts of 1923, 1927, and 1929. Victoria Lerner, "Los fundamentos socio-económicos del cacicazgo en el México postrevolucionario: el caso de Saturnino Cedillo," *HM* 29:3 (January-March 1980): 411–17. Similarly, the delahuertista Revolt (1923) demonstrated to the national authorities the loyalty, effectiveness, and necessity of the agrarian batallions organized by Adalberto Tejeda's "radical movement in Veracruz; see Falcón, "Veracruz," 673–74. In contrast, the same revolt left the Michoacán agrarian leader Primo Tapia and his followers straddling the fence and switching sides seven times, which incurred the permanent enmity of Calles. When, in promoting agrarianism throughout the state and beyond, he openly spoke out against Calles, he became a marked man (brutally tortured and killed in 1926); see Friedrich, *Agrarian Revolt*, 105–12, 124–28.

27. In this volume, Buve, chap. 10, illustrates well the Sonorans' alliance with two

urban middle-sector intermediaries in Tlaxcala, based on the latter's demonstrated loyalty and growing dependence.

28. Luis Javier Garrido, *El partido de la Revolución institutionalizada (medio siglo de poder político en México): la formación del nuevo estado (1928–1945)* (México: Siglo Veintiuno, 1982), 20–62, 72–73, 99; Lajous, *Partido único*, 13–19; Lajous, "Partido nacional y el Congreso," 65, dismantle these political parties when they began to restrict the Sonorans' personalist autonomy or no longer did their bidding; see Lorenzo Meyer, "La Revolución Mexicana y sus elecciones presidenciales: una interpretación (1911–1940)," *HM* 32:2 (October-December 1982), 165–71]. In Sonora, the pattern of alternation was maintained for thirty years, though Luis Torres was the dominant figure in the ruling triumvirate; see Stuart F. Voss, "Towns and Enterprise: A History of Urban Elites, Sonora and Sinaloa, 1830–1910," (Ph.D. diss., Harvard University, 1972), 281, 341, 448–49].

29. Hamilton, *Limits of State Autonomy*, 67–103; J. Meyer, *Cristero Rebellion*, 17–47; Wilkie, "Cristero Religious War," 218–25.

30. J. Meyer, *Cristero Rebellion*, 58–66; Lajous, *Partido único*, 33–39.

31. Lajous, *Partido único*, 15–41; L. Meyer, "Elecciones presidenciales," 171–78; Lajous, "Partido nacional y el Congreso", 652, 656–663. Lajous contends that the conversion of the Bloque Revolucionario Obregonista into the Bloque Nacional Revolucionario, in late September 1928, implies that the intermediaries in Congress accepted the institutional forms Calles was then working out, leading to the creation of the PNR that winter.

32. Garrido, *Partido de la Revolución*, 101; Hall, "Obregón y el partido único," 602–22. Lorenzo Meyer, in "Elecciones presidenciales," 168, claims that Calles first proposed such an all-encompassing national party in 1926 to prepare for the official candidacy of Obregón, but events led the project to be shelved.

33. Garrido, *Partido de la Revolución*, 63–102; Lajous, *Partido único*, 38–69.

34. Lajous, "Partido nacional y el Congreso," 658–67.

35. Lajous, *Partido único*, 70–79.

36. David Raby, "La contribución del Cardenismo al desarrollo del México Actual," *Economía Política* 9:4 (October-December 1972): 13–15; Garrido, *Partido de la Revolución*, 99, 173–74; Guillermo Palacios, "México en los años treinta," in *América Latina en los Años Treinta*, ed. Luis Antezana E. et. al. (México: UNAM, 1977), 523–32; Hamilton, *Limits of State Autonomy*, 104–8. The resilience of the Monterrey network and their rapidly growing influence among the private sector nationally, and in resistance to the national revolutionary coalition, is detailed in Saragoza, *Monterrey Elite*, 151–69.

37. Lajous, *Partido único*, 86–88; Garrido, *Partido de la Revolución*, 172–73. The Tlaxcalan political machine of Ignacio Mendoza, who had maintained a consistent loyalty to the Sonorans since 1920, was liquidated when it tried to resist PNR penetration; see Buve, this volume chap. 10.

38. Lajous, *Partido único*, 155–56; Benjamin, this volume chap. 4; Ricardo Pozas

Horcasitas, "La consolidación del nuevo orden institucional en México (1929–1940)," in Pablo González Casanova, *América Latina: Historia de Medio Siglo* (México: Siglo Veintiuno, 1981) 2:266–70. No immediate reelection at the congressional level had the additional benefit of preventing the intermediary political brokers from establishing personal bases of power. Nevertheless, Calles postponed this constitutional change until 1933. He wanted those of proven loyalty elected in July 1932 to oversee the selection and election of the next candidate for the presidency; see Lajous, "Partido nacional y el Congreso," 668.

39. Palacios, "México en los añōs treinta," 523–28; Hamilton, *Limits of State Autonomy*, 108–16; Wayne Cornelius, "Nation Building, Participation, and Distribution: The Politics of Social Reform under Cardenas," in *Crisis, Choice, and Change: Historical Studies of Political Development* ed. Gabriel Almond et. al. (Boston: Little, Brown, and Co., 1973), 413–14; Werner Tobler, "Peasants and the Revolutionary State," 516; Pozas Horcasitas, "Nuevo orden institucional," 271, 277–82. The Depression opened new opportunities for political mobilization as working conditions hardened in the Laguna district; see Carr, "Mexican Communist Party," 19–20. Deteriorating working conditions and remuneration stimulated unionization among teachers; see John A. Britton, "Teacher Unionization and the Corporate State in Mexico, 1931–1945," *Hispanic American Historical Review {HAHR}* 59:4 (November 1979):674–90]. Small and medium business people faced continued competition from foreign capital and the difficulties of the Depression, and in addition, they were hit with a tax surcharge in 1931; see Palacios, "México en los años treinta", 523–28.

40. Hamilton, *Limits of State Autonomy*, 121–24; Palacios, "México en los años treinta," 528–32; Lajous, *Partido único*, 178–80. Calles compromised further by accepting revisions in the Six-Year Plan that made it more reformist, particularly in agrarian policy.

41. Pozas Horcasitas, "Nuevo orden institucional," 283–84, 287–88; Cornelius, "Politics of Social Reform," 437–43; L. Meyer, "Elecciones presidenciales," 179–83; Lajous, *Partido único*, 175–76, 178.

42. Cornelius, "Politics of Social Reform," 437–55; Lajous, *Partido único*, 176–78.

43. Lyle Brown, "Mexican Church–State Relations, 1933–1940," *JCS* 6:2 (Spring 1964): 202–10; Marjorie Becker, "Black, White, and Color: Cardenismo and the Search for a Campesino ideology," *Comparative Studies in History and Society* 29:3 (July 1987): 453–56; J. Meyer, *Cristero Rebellion*, 203–4.

44. Victoria Lerner, "El reformismo de la decada de 1930 en México," *HM* 26:2 (October-December 1976): 188–91, 194–206; Nora Hamilton, "The State and the National Bourgeoisie in Postrevolutionary Mexico, 1920–1940," *LAP* 9:4 (Fall 1982): 31–33; Joe Ashby, "The Role of Organized Labor in the Mexican Revolution: The Years of Lázaro Cárdenas," *Indiana Social Studies Quarterly* 22:1 (Spring 1969):79. The Depression generated new conditions which widened the existing entrepreneurial sectors (that of industry, in particular) and encouraged

the greater involvement of the national state in the economy. A series of government measures were instituted between 1933 and 1938 to assist this "small bourgeoisie," implemented during the decade by a cadre of sympathetic public functionaries, themselves of modest origins.

45. Charles H. Weston, Jr., "The Political Legacy of Lázaro Cárdenas," *The Americas* 39:3 (January 1983): 387–90. Cárdenas's corporatism derived from a cultural–political tradition with deep roots in Mexican history and from certain corporatist features of the 1917 Constitution (that is, recognition of classes, the state's obligation to protect and promote their interests through a body of rules, and granting, within the law, special rights to groups.

46. Benjamin, this volume chap. 4; Lajous, *Partido único*, 173–76; Carlos Martínez Assad, "La rebellión cedillista o el ocaso del poder tradicional," *RMS* 41:3 (July-September 1979): 712–13. Cárdenas was the chief beneficiary of both the popular unrest and the official party's attack on regional autonomy. His relations with the radical agrarian movement of Tejeda in Veracruz illustrate this paradox. As Minister of War, Cárdenas directed the disarming of the rural forces that undergirded Tejeda's control in the state. Yet he inherited the support of the agrarian moderates whom the PNR had pried away from Tejeda's agrarian league; see Falcón, "Veracruz," 681–98.

47. Palacios, "México en los años treinta," 538–39; Hamilton, *Limits of State Autonomy*, 116–20. Cárdenas also attracted those who resented the prolonged Sonoran control of the revolutionary coalition and their lack of inclusion in Calles's inner circle; see Lajous, *Partido único*, 156, 176–77.

48. Weston, "The Cárdenas Legacy," 389–91; Pozas Horcasitas, "Nuevo orden institucional," 312–13. The most important of these interventionist laws were those concerning the nationalization of property (30 August 1935), expropriations (6 October 1936), and the regulation of chambers of commerce and industry (27 August 1936).

49. Weston, "The Cárdenas Legacy," 392–95; Ashby, "Organized Labor," 70–72, 76. The organization of laborers and peasants in the Laguna district demonstrates well the decisive role played by governmental intervention in establishing the CNC as the dominant organization in the rural sector; see Carr, "Mexican Communist Party," 20–27. The intersindicalist struggles based upon ideology and personalism, as well as the divisions between local and federal, and rural and urban schools made the education sector one of the most difficult to organize into a singular, dependent national-interest group. Here, too, Cárdenas employed direct intervention and even threats in to promoting a unified sector of teachers, which in the end was converted into an appendage of the national state; see Jorge Mora Forero, "Los maestros y la práctica de la educación socialista," *HM* 29:1 (July-September 1979): 142–60; and Britton, "Teacher Unionization and the Corporate State," 680–87.

50. Garrido, *Partido de la Revolución,* 177–301; Cornelius, "Politics of Social Reform," 462–66.

51. Weston, "The Cárdenas Legacy," 395–98; Drake, "Mexican Regionalism," 404–5. In Guerrero, a series of governors from 1929 to 1941 sought to rebuild an independent power base and to restore the *cacicazgo* of the nineteenth century. Unlike Calles, Cárdenas undermined the basis of the challenge. Through the imposition of radical agrarian reform, he achieved a significant degree of direct political control over the campesinos. Using the CNC as the organization structure, he created a new power base within the state. A new generation of Guerrero *políticos* understood the new reality. They abandoned any pretensions to regional autonomy and assumed the role of agents of the national state in managing the sectors of the official party. See Jacobs, *Ranchero Revolt*, 127–37, 145–64; Joseph, "Mobilization and Myth in Yucatan," 362–71; and Buve, "Políticas locales," 362–71. The Laguna district appears to be the exception to this general pattern. With ideological cohesion and political intermediaries chosen largely from within, the peasant organizations retained an important measure of autonomy vis-à-vis the new corporatist clientele structure that Cárdenas instituted through the CNC; see Judith Hellman, "The Role of Ideology in Peasant Politics: Peasant Mobilization and Demobilization in the Laguna region," *JIASWA* 25:1 (January 1983): 7–13].

52. Hamilton, "State and National Bourgeoisie," 32; Ashby, "Organized Labor," 76–79; Lerner, "Reformismo," 198–201; Richard Roman, "Railroad Nationalization and the Formation of *Administración Obrera* in Mexico, 1937–1938," *Inter-American Economic Affairs* 35:3 (1981): 4–10, 22.

53. John Britton, "Urban Education and Social Change in the Mexican Revolution, 1931–1940," *JLAS*, 5:2 (November 1973), 225–42; Michael Burke, "The University of Mexico and the Revolution," *The Americas* 34:2 (October 1977): 267–73; Josefina Vázquez de Knauth, "La educación de los años treintas," *HM* 18:3 (January-March 1969): 412, 419–20; Victoria Lerner, "Historia de la reforma educativa, 1933–1945," *HM* 29:1 (July-September 1979): 94–95, 99–104. Neither Vazquez nor Lerner (nor any of the other sources consulted) conclude that either Cárdenas or his advisors intended to use educational reform to transform the country into a socialist regime. Becker, "Cardenismo and the Search for a Campesino Ideology," 453–60, details the intrusion of the Cardenista ideological campaign into an island village in Lake Patzcuaro, Michoacán. Garner, this volume chap. 7, notes the Cardenista program's subversion in the Oaxacan Serrano of cacique control and of the traditional order in general.

54. Falcón, "Veracruz," 696–698; Falcón, "Charisma, Tradition, and Caciquismo," 420–21, 439–47; Martínez Assad, "La rebelión cedillista," 712–18. Cedillo also opposed the government's support of workers' strikes as excessive and fostering disorder.

55. Lerner, "Reforma educativa," 103–4, 116–17; Forero, "La práctica de la educación socialista," 140–42, 150–52.

56. In the Sierra de Jacala of Hidalgo, few farms were eligible for expropriation. But Cárdenas's closest political ally there was also a wealthy ranchero who opposed any redistribution of land. Not a single piece of property was converted into ejidos for the hard-pressed landless peasants; see Frans J. Schryer, "From Rancheros to Pequeños Propietarios: Agriculture, Class Structure and Politics in the Sierra de Jacala, Mexico," *Boletín de Estudios Latinamericanos y del Caribe* 34 (1983): 53–54. In San Luis Potosí, federal troops backed large landowners who still occupied distributed lands in the face of campesino protests. Cedillo, who for more than a decade had a close working alliance with the state's notables, found his former allies in Cárdenas's camp when he openly defied Mexico City; see Martínez Assad, "La rebelión cedillista," 718–28; Lerner, "Cacicazgo: el caso de Cedillo," 431–37.

57. Albert Michaels, "Modification of Anti-Clerical Nationalism under Cárdenas," *The Americas* 26:1 (July 1969): 44–53; Michaels, "El nacionalismo conservador mexicano desde la Revolución hasta 1940," *HM* 16:2 (October-December 1966): 222–23; Lerner, "La reforma educativa," 116–18.

58. J. Meyer, *Cristero Rebellion*, 205–6, 211; Michaels, "Anti-Clerical Nationalism," 44–47, 51–53; Michaels, "El nacionalismo conservador," 222–23.

59. Michaels, "El nacionalismo conservador," 223–26, 229–30; Michaels, "Fascism and Sinarquismo," 241–47.

60. Saragoza, *Monterrey Elite*, 165–91.

61. Michaels, "El nacionalismo conservador," 215, 230–34; Michaels, "Las elecciones de 1940," *HM* 21:1 (July-September 1971): 100–113; "The Crisis of Cardenismo," *JLAS* 2:1 (May 1970): 70–77; Hamilton, *Limits of State Autonomy*, 214–15, 254–60.

62. Michaels, "Las elecciones de 1940," 123; Roman, "Railroad Nationalization," 5–8; Hamilton, *Limits of State Autonomy*, 244–54.

63. Michaels, "El nacionalismo conservador," 229–30; Joseph, "Mobilization and Myth in Yucatán," 61; Lewis, *Pedro Martínez*, 260–74; Lerner, "Reforma educativa," 98–99. The *indigenista* novel, a vehicle of protest born during this decade, captured the general suspicions of rural folk toward such efforts by "outsiders"; see Donald L. Schmidt, "The Indigenista Novel and the Mexican Revolution," *The Americas* 33:4 (April 1977): 654.

64. Buve, "Políticas locales," 366–67; Schryer, "Rancheros to Pequeños Propietarios," 53–54; Raby, "Contribución del Cardenismo," 33–35.

65. Michaels, "Chrisis of Cardenismo," 53–65; Lerner, "Reformismo," 207–8; Palacios, "México en los años treinta," 535, 543–44; Hamilton, *Limits of State Autonomy*, 239–40; Cornelius, "Politics of Social Reform," 466–69.

66. Michaels, "Crisis of Cardenismo," 70–79; Lerner, "Reforma educativa," 118–19; Vazquez, "La educación socialista," 421–22.

67. Vazquez, "La educación socialista," 421–423; Lerner, "Reforma educativa," 120–21.

68. Michaels, "Crisis of Cardenismo," 59–70. The railroad industry offers a poignant example of Cárdenas's pragmatic shift in priorities. Confronted with financial crisis and labor strife in the industry, he nationalized it, and then after considerable negotiation, he instituted workers' management (1937–1938). But by sharply delimiting their control over the railroads, under conditions which would unavoidably compel them to carry out cutbacks and enforce wage discipline, Cárdenas was able to maintain his reformist ideological framework while forcing the railway workers to straighten out the industry in the national interest. Roman, "Railroad Nationalization," 5–14.

69. There is little disagreement among historians that Cárdenas turned back from radical reform during the last years of his presidency. The debate concerns why he did so. For some, Cardenismo was only the customary alliance of the political "outs." The mobilized popular organizations served only as a political instrument, whose interests were to be discarded when the necessities of political power dictated it; see, Alicia Hernández Chavez, *La mecánica cardenista*, vol. 16 of *Historia de la Revolución Mexicana* (México: El Colegio de México, 1979. For others, the political structures through which Cardenas institutionalized revolutionary power took pimacy over the spirit and goals of his reforms. When the former was threatened, the latter had to yield; see Tzvi Medin, *Ideología y praxis política de Lázaro Cárdenas* (México: Siglo Veintiuno, 1972, 1976]. A third view is that Cárdenas's radical restructuring of society was undermined by the structural limitations in which it operated: the resistance of domestic and foreign capitalism, the contradictions within the political coalition which supported him, and the formation of a strong conservative faction within the revolutionary state; see Hamilton, *Limits of State Autonomy*.

70. Pozas Horcasitas, "Nuevo orden institucional," 316–17; Hamilton, *Limits of State Autonomy*, 254–59; Weston, "The Cárdenas Legacy," 397–400, 404.

71. Hamilton, *Limits of State Autonomy*, 260; Raby, "Contribución del Cardenismo," 23–33. Raby contends that Lombardo Toledano, head of the CTM, oppposed Múgica because of his rumored association with Leon Trotsky, and probably because he was too radical for Lombardo Toledano's efforts, at that time, to balance the Moscow Popular Front line with the favor of the PRM ruling group.

72. Pozas Horcasitas, "Nuevo orden institucional," 316–17; Michaels, "Las elecciones de 1940," 80–83, 90–99.

73. Michaels, "Las elecciones de 1940," 80–82; Weston, "The Cárdenas Legacy," 397–400.

74. Hamilton, *Limits of State Autonomy*, 261–67; L. Meyer, "Elecciones presidenciales," 183–92. While Almazán and the core of his opposition sought curtailment of national state intervention and egalitarian reforms, Almazán's appeal to the popular classes included equal support to ejidos and small property, the protection of workers' rights and the independence of their leadership, as well as full rights for women.

Up to 1936, the Monterrey notable network had only sought to strike a deal with the national state to secure local hegemony. But when Cardenismo made clear that the ruling revolutionary group would not do so, they moved nationally to weaken the national state and to curtail Cárdenas's reforms. Almazán had been their regional ally for more than a decade, and they were one of his principal backers; see Saragoza, *Monterrey Elite*, 186–96, 202.

75. Michaels, "Las elecciones de 1940," 131–34; Weston, "The Cárdenas Legacy," 404.

76. Guillermo Palacios, "Calles y la idea oficial de la Revolución Mexicana," *HM* 22:3 (January-March 1973): 274–75.

77. Michaels, "Las elecciones de 1940," 114–21; Hamilton, *Limits of State Autonomy*, 261–67.

78. Howard F. Cline, *The United States and Mexico* (New York: Atheneum, 1965), 269–70, 283, 325–26. Several ex-presidents were given important posts in the defense effort, most notably Cárdenas as Minister of Defense.

79. Ibid., 284–91; Hamilton, *Limits of State Autonomy*, 267–68.

80. Garrido, *El partido de la Revolución*, 301–60. The war-efforts demands for military efficiency and readiness enabled Cardenas to divorce the military from politics. The military sector of the party was abolished and the military block in Congress was disbanded. "Political" generals were retired; see Cline, *U.S. and Mexico*, 276.

81. Ibid., 357–59; Raul Trejo Delarbe, "The Mexican Labor Movement: 1917–1975," trans. Anibal Yanez, *LAP* 3:1 (Winter 1976): 144–45.

82. Cline, *United States and Mexico*, 288–90; Hamilton, *Limits of State Autonomy*, 268–69; Garrido, *Partido de la Revolución,* 359. In education, Avila Camacho gradually opened the door to private initiative and removed ardent proponents of socialist education from the bureaucracy. Article 3 was reformed to remove the overtly Marxist aspects of the curriculum in favor of the ideals of family, social harmony, and, above all, national unity; see Lerner, "Reforma educativa," 120–23; Britton, "Teacher Unionization and the Corporate State," 687–89.

83. Nora hamilton, "State and National Bourgeoisie," dates the origins of the consensus back to the 1920s.

84. Cline, *United States and Mexico*, 272–74, 285–87; John Womack, Jr., "The Spoils of the Mexican Revolution," *Foreign Affairs* 48:4 (July 1970): 679–80.

85. Lerner, "Reformismo," 191; Buve, "Políticas locales," 368–69. Ruben C. Carrizosa and his associates from a district in Tlaxcala smoothly made the transition from Cardenismo to advancement in the Camacho administration. Two rose to the governship of the state (in 1946 and 1952).

86. Hamilton, *Limits of State Autonomy*, 267–69. The national state, through its expanding regulatory powers and agencies, had become essential to capital formation. Entrepreneurs and public functionaries interfaced more directly through interlocking directories that resulted from joint state–private ventures.

Moreover, the recruitment from the state to the private sector received new impetus.

87. Roderic A. Camp, "Education and Political Recruitment in Mexico: The Alemán Generation," *JIASWA* 18:3 (August 1976): 295–315; Camp, *Mexico's Leaders: Their Education and Recruitment* (Tucson: University of Arizona Press, 1980), 25–25, Chaps. 5 and 6. The National Preparatory School and the National University, in particular, fostered these ties among *políticos* and bureaucrats, and less directly with entrepreneurs.

88. Roderic A. Camp, "Family Relationships in Mexican Politics: A Preliminary View," *Journal of Politics* 44 (August 1982): 848–62; Wasserman, "Persistant Oligarchs," 1–2, 5–7, 11–13. The evidence is as yet sparse and often fragmentary— revealed in novels, secondary details, and historiographical asides, as well as in a few pioneering monographic studies. But it suggests that family linkages, consciously sought out, were an important medium for the fusion of the interests of the old order and successful revolutionary entrepreneurs, and of these with public functionaries.

89. Luis Medina, *Civilismo y modernización del autoritarismo,* vol. 20 of *Historia de la Revolución Mexicana* (México: El Colegio de México, 1979), 62–79, 93, 176–94.

90. James W. Wilkie, *The Mexican Revolution: Federal Expenditure and Social Change* (Berkeley: University of California Press, 1970), 84–85, 128–40, 158–59; Womack, "Spoils of the Revolution," 679–80; Frank Brandenberg, *The Making of Modern Mexico* (Englewood Cliffs, N.J.: Prentice-Hall, 1964), 100–106; Judith Adler Hellman, *Mexico in Crisis,* 2d ed. (New York: Holmes & Meier, 1983), 92–93; Raby, "Contribución del Cardenismo," 41.

91. Brandenberg, *Modern Mexico,* 106–12.

12

Regionalizing the Revolution:

The Many Mexicos in Revolutionary Historiography

Thomas Benjamin

"They entered Mexico, by way of Villa de Guadalupe, the cavalry of Lucio Blanco: men of the proletariate class, dark skinned campesinos, some dressed every which way, others hardly dressed at all, except for triple cartridge belts slung across their chests. . . . That which marched before our eyes was Mexico, the real Mexico in all of its terrible reality."[1] Génaro Fernández McGregor's description of provincial Carrancistas descending upon Mexico City, and the famous photograph of Zapatistas ("their physical features did not reflect the satisfaction and natural pride of the conqueror"[2]) drinking coffee in Mexico City's plush eatery Sanborns in 1914, highlight one aspect of the regional significance of the Mexican Revolution: provincials conquering the center. Another aspect, armies of the central government shattering the calm of provincial life, was just as significant. Constitutionalist General Jesús Agustín Castro, following his incursion into Chiapas in 1914, declared: "Chiapanecan cowards, while the North is struggling, you are enjoying peace, but I will teach you to feel the effects of the Revolution."[3] The importance of provincial Mexico in the remaking and rethinking of the nation during and immediately following the revolution would be difficult to exaggerate.

"It has not been a national revolution in the sense that all of the country participated in the same movement and at the same time," wrote Frank Tannenbaum in 1933. "It has been local, regional, sometimes almost by counties."[4] As a result, the revolution has been reported, chronicled, and analyzed from local, regional, and provincial perspectives from the beginning.[5] Many recent commentators on revolutionary historiography view, however, the outpouring of subnational studies by academic historians from the late 1960s to the 1980s as a fundamental break with the national and centralist tradition of Mexican historiography. Yet the recent boom in subnational historiography is built upon a substantial and long-lived, if not always appreciated or critically distinguished, foundation of historical writing on the provinces of the revolution. What has changed in recent decades is not historians' discovery of regional history or even that "historians consider the Mexican Revolution as a regionalized phenomenon," as Sérgio Ortega Noriega contends.[6] What is new is the wider acceptance by historians of Tannenbaum's view that there were multiple Mexican revolutions across the length and breadth of the country.

While there are several good provincially focused historiographical essays, as well as bibliographies of local, regional, and provincial studies on the revolution, there is no comprehensive description and analysis of this vast historical literature. This essay provides a beginning.[7]

"Fuera de México Todo es Cuautitlán"

The Porfirian historians, by and large, were not interested in provincial, regional, or local history either before or following the revolution.[8] Most were residents of the capital city and, writes John Rutherford, "the inhabitants of Mexico City came, under Porfirio Díaz, to assume an even more condescending attitude towards the inhabitants of the rest of the Republic than the inhabitants of capital cities usually do towards their fellow-countrymen."[9] This attitude was reflected in the well-known put-down, "fuera de México todo es Cuautitlán": beyond Mexico City every place is [the insignificant ranchería] Cuautitlán. Luis Pérez Verdía, a Jalisciense historian, complained in 1911 of the intellectual centralization exercised by Mexico City.[10] The few regional studies which were published during the late Porfiriato[11] downplayed regionalism and "tried to make Mexicans from different sections of the republic feel loyalty to the nation."[12]

The Porfirians, however, did contribute unknowingly to the regionalist historiography of the revolution by their production of numerous state geographies and statistical compilations. The most ambitious effort, a twenty-volume series entitled "Geografía y Estadística de la República Mexicana," was authored by Alfonso Luis Velasco and published by the Secretaría de Fomento between 1889 and 1895.[13] Nearly ten years later, the Mexico City publishing house, Vda. de Ch. Bouret, began a similar series called "La República Mexicana" but produced only six slim volumes betwen 1908 and 1912.[14] Other volumes, which were generally ordered by state governors and printed by state government printing presses, were designed to demonstrate regional progress in order to attract Mexican and foreign investment and enterprise. These *compendios, noticias, reseñas*, and *diccionarios* have been invaluable to postrevolutionary historians in understanding regional land tenure, agricultural and industrial production, trade and commerce, demographic trends, and more.[15]

Dazzled by the glitter of positivism, however, the authors of these data bases provided little or no analysis of provincial society and economy. That task, fortunately, was taken up by enterprising or muckraking foreigners. Karl Kaerger's two-volume *Landwirtschaft und Kolonisation in Spanischen Amerika* (1901–1902), of which a large portion of the second volume is devoted to Mexico, analyzes agriculture in different regions: henequén in Yucatán; cacao in Tabasco; tobacco and coffee in Veracruz, Oaxaca, and Chiapas; sugar in Morelos; cereals in central Mexico; and cotton and cattle in northern Mexico.[16] This book, according to Friedrich Katz, "is the most complete report that has been written about [labor] conditions in the Mexican countryside during the Porfiriato."[17] The most famous muckraking analysis of regional labor conditions in Mexico, John Kenneth Turner's *Barbarous Mexico* (1910), focused on coffee plantations in El Valle Nacional in Oaxaca and henequén haciendas in Yucatán. *Barbarous Mexico*, according to historian Ramon D. Chacon, "represents a contemporary indictment of Porfirian Mexico and a valuable source for understanding the dispossession and exploitation of the Indians, especially the Yaquis and Mayas. The book is particularly useful to examine the issues of debt peonage slavery and the attitudes of henequen hacendados vis-a-vis their Indian workers."[18]

Analyzing the Revolution: "We Have Understood Our Heterogeneity"

The regional significance of the Mexican Revolution was widely appreciated during the revolution itself. "During the Mexican presidential campaign of 1909–1910 and the Maderista revolution," writes John Womack, Jr., "local heroes suddenly became figures of national prominence."[19] Mexico City, the center, became identified with Porfirismo, then Huertismo, followed by Carrancismo; while the hydra-headed revolution emerged from such obscure and not so obscure places as Casas Grandes, Gómez Palacio, Sahuaripa, Huitzuco, Anenecuilco, and many more. Through its several permutations, the revolution swept through all regions, countless localities, and in and out of Mexico City, "a wind that tore men and women from their roots and whirled them far from their settled dust and their old cemeteries and their quiet villages."[20] As a result, noted Ramón Beteta in 1937, "with the Revolution, our greatest force, we have discovered ourselves; analyzing the Revolution, we have understood our heterogeneity, our lack of unity."[21]

Many of the first accounts of the revolution were penned by participants and observers from their provincial perspectives. Each had a political point to make, a heroic tale to tell, or an atrocity to report. Custodio Valverde, for example, defended the motives and actions of the Guerrerense Maderista and Carrancista Julián Blanco. José Domingo Ramírez Garrido did the same for Tabasqueña Carrancista Luis Felipe Domínguez. *Memorias* have continued to be published since the epic revolution, even into the 1980s.[22] Documented accounts, while not always more objective, naturally were far fewer in number.[23]

The view of the revolution as seen by the leaders, "los revolucionarios," in their memoirs and autobiographies is quite different from that of the revolutionized, "los revolucionados," as discovered in regional and local accounts, testimonies, historical novels, and *corridos*, according to Luis González and others. During the tumultuous decade of 1910–1920 the revolution was not yet viewed universally as one comprehensive process of revindication. In contrast to Luis Cabrera's famous definition "La Revolución es la Revolución," which was made in reference to the Maderista Revolution, for many "everyday Mexicans" then and later the revolution was plural. As one revolutionary-era *corrido* illustrated:

> One sees many hard things
> in these revolutions:
> destructions, burnings,
> beatings and hangings.[24]

González concludes: "The general run of people observed distinct revolutionary actions in space and in time" and "discerned many 'revoluciones' since that of Madero."[25]

During the 1920s and 1930s regionalism was in vogue in intellectual circles, and "the course of Mexicanism was leading inevitably to the province,"[26] Laboratories of the revolution in such states as Yucatán, Tabasco, and Veracruz tested the limits of social reform and regional autonomy. Social anthropologists led by Manuel Gamio came to the conclusion that the lingering socioeconomic problems of Mexico's diverse ethnic groups could only be effectively addressed region by region, not by broad national policies.[27] National economic development required state intervention adjusted to the distinct and different problems, conditions, and requirements of Mexico's various regions.[28] "We may say," wrote Harry Bernstein, "that the *científico* stress upon science for the benefit of central Mexico is being replaced by the application of many social sciences to the different regions of Mexico under a planned, integrated understanding of the Mexican scene."[29]

As the postrevolutionary state consolidated and institutionalized its power, however, the historical Mexican Revolution began to take on a more singular and national cast. The regionalized struggles of 1910–1917 came to be viewed as "la Revolución maderocarrancista."[30] Books published by "revolutionary" state governments tended to explicate the particular regional contribution to the origin and development of "la Revolución."[31] The federal Agrarian Department published a geography of Tabasco in 1930, for example, justifying "the integration of Tabasco into the Mexican Revolution."[32]

The regional revolutions which received the most attention by writers were the Zapatista movement of Morelos ("el Estado mártir de la Revolución," according to Gildardo Magaña) and the central highlands and the Villista movement of north-central Mexico.[33] In both cases, however, the primary focus of contemporaries, later chroniclers, and historians has been the two individuals of mythic proportions rather than their regional struggles.

Emiliano Zapata and Zapatismo are the subjects of a substantial literature.[34] During the violent decade Zapata, referred to as the "Atila del Sur" and the Mexican Genghis Khan, "was one of the most discussed individuals of his time, and perhaps, the most vilified."[35] Books by J. Figueroa Doménech, Antonio D. Melgarejo, Lamberto Popoca y Palacios, Héctor Ribot, and Atenor Sala portrayed the Zapatista Revolution as murderous, rapine, savage, and out of control.[36] Zapata's heroic status was confined largely to his followers in Morelos and the surrounding regions and "only found its way into print and common acceptance when he became respectable and harmless by dying."[37]

During the 1920s and 1930s Presidents Alvaro Obregón and Lázaro Cárdenas appropriated Zapata and Zapatismo as an important foundation of Obregonismo, later Cardenismo, and thus shoring up the revolutionary legitimacy of their governments. After 1919 Zapata, the symbol of agrarian revolution, overshadowed Zapatismo, the regional insurrection for land and liberty, in the historical accounts. Aurelio Palacios (1924) placed Alvaro Obregón and Plutarco Elías Calles in a favorable light as supporters of Zapatismo. Similarly, Carlos Reyes Avilés (1928) characterized Zapata as the "apóstol del agrarismo" and the "first Obregonista." To Germán List Arzubide (1927), Zapata was the symbol of agrarian struggle everywhere in Mexico; "Emiliano Zapata, is now a symbol: the mortal man, by his work has been transformed into an idea." Sergio Valverde (1933) told the story of Zapatismo in order to attack Carranza, to praise Obregón, and to criticize the then current "reactionary" governor of Morelos.[38]

The first serious efforts to understand Zapata and his regional movement did not appear until the mid-1930s and 1940s. Baltazar Dromundo's biography (1934) protrayed Zapata as a tragic hero, excessively parochial and intellectually unprepared to effectively solve the agrarian problem.[39] Zapata's secretary and intellectual advisor, Gildardo Magaña (who possessed the Zapatista archive), wrote three volumes of his *Emiliano Zapata y el Agrarismo en México* in the mid-1930s, which were published first by the Partido Nacional Revolucionario. Eventually five volumes were published, although the chronicle was still incomplete since the narrative stopped in late 1914.[40] Magaña's work, according to Womack, was "the first obviously documented study of the Zapatista movement and the role of its chief." To Arias Gómez, "perhaps the essential objective of this work would be to free Zapata from abuses, to analyze the cause from its most remote origin; to challenge the faction that had 'officialized' the character of the caudillo and his movement, as the incarnation of illegality."[41]

The first genuinely local history of Anenecuilco, Zapata's pueblo, was published in 1943. Jesús Sotelo Inclán's *Raíz y Razón de Zapata. Anenecuilco* was, according to Alicia Olivera de Bonfil and Eugenia Meyer, "the first formal attempt, from the point of view of investigation, to undertand the agrarian movement of the South, within an appropriate historical framework."[42] Sotelo Inclán, a school teacher, sought to look beyond the myth of Zapata, the heroic leader, and uncover the historical and social context which gave rise to Zapatismo. His book is about the origins of Zapatismo and does not even touch upon the revolutionary struggle of 1911–1919. The historian explained: "There was a pueblo behind him and the tragedy of the pueblo and the struggle of the pueblo was much larger, infinitely larger than that of one man, and that is how I explained Zapata."[43]

Numerous favorable biographies and popular histories of Zapata and Zapatismo were published following the Second World War. As with most of the earlier accounts, however, the mythic hero overshadowed the regional struggle.[44] In 1960 the first analysis of Zapatismo by a professional historian, Francois Chevalier, was published in Mexico.[45] John Womack, Jr., in his widely acclaimed *Zapata and the Mexican Rvolution*, published in 1969, expertly placed Zapata in his provincial context.[46] Womack's Zapata was a conservative revolutionary forced into insurrection to preserve his local village society. "In choosing to study the locally limited movement of Zapata," writes the novelist Carlos Fuentes, "Womack has pinpointed precisely what the Revolution was about at its profoundest level. . . . He understands Zapatismo as the history, not of exotic 'peasants,' but of campesinos, people from the fields who did not, in the larger senses of the term, feel culturally deprived but, rather, were conscious that a social and political opportunity was given them to realize, in actuality, the latent promises of their local culture."[47]

Since Womack's study, and in part because of it ("whose history is based only on what the Zapatistas and Obregonistas told him," writes Womack's severest critic, Pablo González) the Zapata counterlegend has reappeared. González, son of the Carrancista general, purports to document Zapata's complicity in the assassination of Madero and other crimes. José de la Lux Valdés argues that Zapata was a "terrible bandolero" who caused ten thousand deaths. Miguel Angel Peral portrays the real Zapata as a paranoid bandit and criminal degernate, and Armando Ayala Anguiano presents him as a traitorous cacique.[48] More important contributions to the historiography of Zapatismo, however, are provocative syntheses of Zapatismo[49] and several volumes of documents and testimonies, and studies of postrevolutionary Morelos.[50]

"The legend of the Mexican Revolution which achieved widest circulation inside and outside Mexico during and after his lifetime," writes John Rutherford, "was that of Pancho Villa."[51] Like Zapata, Villa was a revolutionary leader of mythic proportions as well as a *caudillo* of a regional revolutionary movement. And even more than Zapata, most of the vast historical literature concerning Villa focuses upon the man, not the regional revolution he led.[52]

The first, and still one of the best, books about Pancho Villa was written by the American revolutionary journalist, John Reed, in 1914. In *Insurgent Mexico* Reed wrote about his few months with Villista forces and Villa, in Chihuahua in late 1913 and early 1914.[53] The book, according to Jim Tuck, "is part fact and part fabrication. Reed did not so much invent as embroider. He was not above embellishing incidents, even to the extent of creating fictitious characters and arbitrarily changing their identities when it suited his purpose." With this caveat, Tuck praises Reed's sympathetic and "magnificently true-to-life" portrait of Villa and his report of Villa's government of Chihuahua. "The poetic quality of *Insurgent Mexico*," Tuck writes, "derives directly from Reed's magnificent gifts as a descriptive writer and his burning commitment to the villista cause."[54]

To contemporaries in Mexico, Villa and Villismo were subjects of intense controvery. *Científico* Francisco Bulnes saw Villa as "a beast or a maniac, spreading fire and destruction in his pathway."[55] Ramón Puente, a close advisor to Villa, on the other hand, countered Carrancista allegations of wrongdoing by ghostwriting Villa's self-serving memoirs.[56] Rafael F. Muñoz, a reporter from *Universal Gráfico*, continued Puente's version of Villa's memoirs for the years from 1916 to 1923.[57]

Following Villa's assassination in 1923, the "Centaur of the North"—in contrast to Zapata—remained as controversial as ever. Friends and foes continued their quarrel with the production of a considerable historical literature.[58] To José Vasconcelos, writing in 1940, "no few writers have glorified [Villa] and suffer from a complex of moral complicity with the criminal."[59] On the fiftieth anniversary of the Mexican Revolution of 1910, General (ex-Villista Major under Felipe Angeles) Federico Cervantes M. published a book in defense of the reputation of Villa, "who has been the object of vilification on the part of his enemies."[60]

The primary source of all biographical treatments of Villa is Martín Luis Guzmán's series of memoirs, *Memorias de Pancho Villa* (1938–1964).[61] Based in part on the personal archive of Villa, Guzmán's version of Villa's memoirs is lengthy and detailed, vivid and boastful, and (it is generally agreed) a literary, if not a historical, masterpiece. Through Guzmán, Villa narrates his life and revolutionary exploits until defeat by Obregón at Celaya in April 1915. "Everything in this book," writes Ermilo Abreu Gómez, "has the force of a double aesthetic value: reality and invention. Everything is captured in a picture of such profundity that, once you have entered it, it lives, bleeds, dreams. . . . Martín Luis Guzmán created with the *Memorias de Pancho Villa* a master work of the Mexican province."[62]

Equally important, although less well known, is Silvestre Terrazas's serialized account "El Verdadero Pancho Villa," which was published between 1944 and 1955.[63] Terrazas was a loyal and close collaborator of Villa in Chihuahua. His account of Villa is both memoir and history, based on memories (his own and others) and documents from his own archive. "The portrait that Terrazas draws of Villa," writes historian Friedrich Katz in his introduction of a recent edition of this work, "is complex." Villa's personality, political ideology, plans for reforms, and more are described in this "extremely revealing work."[64]

In the 1960s Alberto Calzadíaz Barrera produced the most comprehensive biography of Villa and chronicle of Villismo to date. The three volumes of *Hechos reales de la Revolución mexicana* (1961–1965), based on interviews of numerous Villista and Carrancista veterans, is a substantial effort to demonstrate that Villa was a true revolutionary, the military leader most responsible for the overthrow of Huerta, and not the responsible party in the break with Carranza.[65] Marte R. Gómez, at about the same time, demonstrated the agrarianism of Villismo in a study of agrarian reform in the Villista north.[66]

The numerous popular biographies and histories of Villa and the División del Norte published in the 1960s and 1970s, nearly all of which are sympathetic, demonstrate a new consensus regarding the Chihuahuan revolutionary.[67] In 1966 the name of Francisco Villa was inscribed in gold letters, as an official national hero, in the national Cámara de Diputados. This took place thirty-five years after Zapata's official promotion into the pantheon of national heroes.

A statue of Villa was unveiled three years later in the glorieta at Cuauhtémoc and División del Norte in Mexico City. Like the statue, Villa remains larger than life for most Mexicans, the mythic Centaur of the North.[68]

As late as 1979, however, historian Friedrich Katz noted that "we still do not know what forces Villa really represented and what social changes (such as agrarian reform or measures regarding labor) he did nor did not implement while in power."[69] For over two decades, Katz has been working to correct this deficiency by patiently placing Villa back into his regional setting. Although his regional history of Villismo ("what will probably be the most ambitious and solid study which can be prepared about villismo"[70]) is still in progress, he has published several articles and chapters. In contrast to the great bulk of Villa historiography, Katz focuses upon the regional movement rather than the legendary man. As a result he is revitalizing the image of Villa (and Villismo) as a genuine social reformer and revolutionary (as well as a *caudillo* in the nineteenth-century mold), and thereby contributing significantly to our understanding of the social dynamics of the Mexican Revolution.[71]

"Villa and Zapata were not the only ones," noted William Spratling in 1932. "In all the sierras and valleys of Mexico, each region had its own revolutionary hero."[72] Thanks to provincial pride and government pesos, many of the stories of these heroes and their revolutions have been chronicled.

The Institutionalization of Provincial History

The consolidation of the postrevolutionary Mexican state by the 1940s, often referred to as the "institutionalization of the revolution," completed the centralization of politics, the economy, and, to a considerable extent, culture. "The vision of the National Mexican State presupposed a withering away of provincial pecularities in favor of a much wider enterprise," writes novelist Carlos Fuentes. The national revolution "felt it had to centralize energies in order to transform a heterogeneous society and create a modern infrastructure in a country lacking in communications, electric power, and administrative coordination."[73] During the 1940s the status of Mexico's provinces "ceded to the preeminence of urban and industrial culture at the heart of a strong but abstract nationalism easily organized in Mexico City."[74] To Célia Herrera, a Chihuahuense author in 1939, "la Provincia Mexicana which caused the triumph of the 1910 Revolution . . . has been abandoned and forgotten by all the governments that have come to power."[75]

As national policy undermined provincial power and interests, public and private cultural institutions emphasized the importance of provincial history and culture. The decline and political marginalization of the "other Mexicos" prompted a new but innocuous resurgence of cultural and historicist regionalism. The state institutionalized not only the Mexican Revolution but also provincialism, rendering both harmless and insignificant.

The institutionalization of provincial history found expression in a number of ways. Beginning in 1933, the Congreso Mexicano de Historia held periodic conferences in prominent provincial cities. "The main merit of the Congress," according to Eugenio del Hoyo, "was that of promoting and orienting studies of regional history."[76] A decade later, at the Congress held in Jalapa, José Ignacio Dávila Garibi noted that "in the last ten years, there has been work, in the city as well as in the States, with real tenacity and enthusiasm. New routes have been opened into the retarded and in some parts, still virgin territory of regional history."[77] After the Second World War several academic centers and institutes devoted to regional history were established, notably in Jalisco, Michoacán, Nuevo León, and Puebla.[78] Local, regional, and regional history was promoted at the first meeting of the Congress of Historians of Mexico and the United States held in Monterrey, Nuevo León, in 1949.[79] In 1951, at the meeting of the Congreso Científico Mexicano, Wigberto Jiménez Moreno said: "I hope that more importance will be given to regional history, corresponding to the view of many Mexicos."[80] Also in 1951, former president General Abelardo L. Rodríguez, Aarón Sáenz, and Governor Ignacio Soto established the Archivo de la Revolución, Sonora's contribution to revolutionary historiography, in order to assist in the preparation of a study of Sonora in the revolution under the direction of Manuel González Ramírez.[81] The first Congreso de Historia Regional was held in Mexicali, Baja California, in 1956, and was supported by the state government.[82]

The 1940s and 1950s constituted a virtual "golden age" of the discovery of state and municipal archives. Prompted by concerns regarding the poor state of Mexican archives as a result of the destruction caused by the revolution (Manuel Aguirre Berlanga counted 230 local archives that had been destroyed),[83] historians, archivists, and bibliographers began to explore and describe regional and local archives.[84] The Museo Nacional de Historia, located in the Castillo de Chapultepec, in 1950 began to microfilm state archives in order to preserve the documents and facilitate research in regional history.[85] Beginning in the 1950s the new historical journal *Historia Mexicana*, published by El Colegio de México, encouraged regional history with a series of articles on state and municipal archives called "La historia y sus instrumentos." Eventually, articles about Jalisco, Michoacán, Nuevo León, Oaxaca, Durango, and San Luis Potosí were published. (See the appendix for citations.)

The institutionalization of provincial history was not identical with professionalization. Most historians of the provinces in Mexico from the 1930s to the 1960s were provincials generally and journalists, politicians, antiquarians, literati, and "minor historians," "aficionados more or less self-educated," in the words of Rafael Montejano y Aguiñaga.[86] These amateur provincial historians rarely advanced beyond factual chronicle, subjected prevailing interpretations of the revolution to rigorous analysis, or consulted a wide range of documentary sources and employed such scholarly accouterments as footnotes and bibliographies. "What little [local political history] that does exist," noted Albert Michaels in 1969, "has been the result of local historians trying to glorify their home towns or states."[87] The relative unimportance of academic regional and provincial history in Mexico prior to the 1960s is reflected in the absence of citations in an article on revolutionary history written between 1940 and 1965.[88] Academic local history fared little better, despite the popularity of community studies.[89]

Midcentury also constituted the age of comprehensive multivolume state histories, chronicles really, which were generally published by state governments.[90] Many regional histories at midcentury were revisionists of a sort, seeking to demonstrate the revolutionary character of their *terruno*. José Fuentes Mares's well-written and -researched . . . *Y México se refugió en el desierto* sought to disprove the "revolutionary belief" that Chihuahua's Terrazas clan was Porfirista and that the insurrection in that state in 1911 was aimed as much against the Terrazas latifundio as against Díaz.[91] Oaxaca's premier historian, Jorge Fernando Iturribarría, was motivated "to demonstrate to the public opinion of Oaxaca and the country the fallacy, so unjustly propagated— and so damaging—that we Oaxaqueños have been enemies of the Mexican Revolution."[92] And Sonora's Antonio G. Rivera exalted "Sonoran heroism" and emphasized that the revolution in its violent phase was won by Sonorense soldiers and in its constructive phase was directed by Sonorense statesmen.[93]

Moisés T. De la Peña, and a team of researchers, published a series of regional economic studies during the 1940s and early 1950s which were quite historically detailed and have proven indispensable to subsequent historians.[94]

The most ambitious effort in the institutionalization of provincial history was initiated in 1953 with the creation, by President Adolfo Ruiz Cortines, of the Patronato del Instituto Nacional de Estudios Históricos de la Revolución Mexicana, a dependency of the Secretaría de Gobernación. The presidential decree establishing the Patronato explained that its purpose was to acquire all kinds of documents and testimony regarding the revolution, to plan and edit works of historical investigation, and to promote a better understanding of the revolutionary era. The Patronato's director, Salvador Azuela, reminded his compatriots in 1963 that Mexican history, particularly the history of the revolution, was made in the provinces, beyond Mexico City, in Cuautitlán and other important places.[95] During the 1960s, 1970s, and 1980s the publishing arm of the Patronato, the Biblioteca del Instituto Nacional de Estudios Históricos de la Revolución Mexicana, produced twenty state histories of the Mexican Revolution.[96]

The quality of this series is uneven, as is true for most multiauthor series. Francisco R. Almada's lengthy and well-researched volumes on Chihuahua and Sonora explore the social and economic origins of regional insurrection as well as detail the military and political events of the Maderista, Villista, and Constitutionalist revolutions. Eugenio Martínez Núñez's seventy-seven-page account of the revolution in San Luis Potosí, on the other hand, is politically superficial and overly fixated with his state's claim as "the cradle of the Revolution." Most authors subscribe to the essential unity of the Mexican Revolution ("la Revolución maderocarrancista," in the phrase of Guillermo Palacios) and view local and provincial events not as distinct or autonomous insurrections or revolutions but as important episodes that contributed to the national drama. Most authors concur as to the benefits the revolution provided their states, except Everardo Gámiz Olivas who bitterly noted that "thousands of those fighters [of Durango] that offered their lives in order to obtain conquests which they still do not enjoy, slip into the last stage of their lives in oblivion and misery."

These state histories are useful since they chronicle the central events, introduce the main actors, and reproduce important documents of the Mexican Revolution in each state. And, as George J. Rausch, Jr., comments on Jesús Romero Flores's study of Michoacán and, perhaps unknowingly but accurately, on the series in general:

Although the place of Michoacan in the revolution was neither unique nor particularly significant, the book is perhaps valuable for that very reason. It s a well-written study of the revolution in a fairly typical state which reflects the chaos, changes in personal fortunes, shifting political influences and ultimately stability and progress that made up this important phase of the Mexican Revolution.[97]

The distinguishing feature of most provincial and regional histories of the revolution prior to the 1970s was the interpretation of the Mexican Revolution as a unified, singular, and national movement of revindication, "la idea unitaria de la Revolución."[98] As Vicente Fuentes Díaz wrote in his history of

Guerrero: "The 1910 Revolution had a national character in which local incidents unavoidably ceded their importance, as great as they were, to the general spirit and immense perspectives that impelled the movement."[99]

The Fragmented Revolutions of the Academics

Beginning in the mid-to-late 1960s and continuing to this day, the provinces of the Mexican Revolution have been inundated by professionally trained Mexican and foreign academic historians. Influenced by the romantically rebellious times, disillusioned by the apparent lack of social progress of modern Mexico, and outraged by the Mexican government's bloody repression of the 1968 student movement, the academics sought the origin of the undesirable present and found it in the failures of the Mexican Revolution. As much as earlier historians found local, regional, and provincial evidence for the unquestioned successes of the revolution, the new wave of academics discoverd in the provinces the reasons for its failures, contradictions, and disappointing consequences.

The academic discovery of provincial history in the 1960s, according to Henry C. Schmidt, was the result of "doubt over the wisdom of emphasizing the macro-level of the Revolution."[100] It was also the result of professors and students at state universities seeking relevant history; for the Seminar of Contemporary History at the Universidad Veracruzano, in 1960, "doing the History of the Revolution in Veracruz has as the first objective that of understanding the actual circumstances of Veracruz."[101]

Equally important was the publication during the 1960s of the works of several influential precursors of provincial revisionism.[102] Lowell L. Blaisdell, Michael C. Meyer, and James D. Cockcroft took the popular approach of political biography and each gave it a regional twist. Luis González's *Pueblo en vilo,* the history of an insignificant municipio in Michoacán, portrayed the revolution not as a glorious liberation or transformation but as an unpleasant intrusion of hunger, brigandage, and immorality effecting little lasting change. Of greatest impact, however, was John Womack's eloquent *Zapata and the Mexican Revolution*, which depicted a genuine agrarian revolutionary movement, a regional revolution, which persistently struggled against "revolutionary" and counterrevolutionary governments for ten years.[103] These studies by academic historians not only called into question the prevailing—and official—interpretation of the Mexican Revolution as a unified movement and triumphant revindication, but also served as methodological models for the next generations of doctoral students in Mexico, the United States, and Europe.

In the wake of the precursors came a new surge of institutionalization of provincial history. The Mexican missionary of local history, Luis González, issued his "invitation to microhistory" repeatedly at historical conferences in the late 1960s and 1970s, including the Primer Encuentro de Historiadores de Provincia held in San Luis Potosí in 1972.[104] At that same conference, the Asociación Mexicana de Historia Regional, A.C., was established. At the second meeting of provincial historians in 1974, also held in San Luis Potosí, María Elena Bribiesca Sumano lamented the paucity of regional centers and institutes of history and the terrible condition and service of local and regional archives.[105] Since then, however, there has been a virtual explosion of institution building in the Mexican provinces. The National Institute of Anthropology and History (INAH) established twelve regional centers of investigation in the mid-1970s. In the late 1970s and early 1980s institutions such as the Centro de Estudios de la Revolución Mexicana 'Lázaro Cárdenas,' A.C. (in Jiquilpan de Juarez, Michoacán), the Centro de Estudios Historicos of the Universidad Veracruzana (Jalapa), El Colegio de Michoacán (Zamora), El Colegio de Jalisco (Guadalajara), El Colegio de la Frontera Norte (Tijuana), and El Colegio de Sonora (Hermosillo) were established with government assistance.[106] These new, and other existing, institutions have trained and employed regionalist historians and initiated publication of many excellent state historical journals and monograph series.[107] "I firmly believe," José Ma. Muriá writes, "that institutions such as [El Colegio de Michoacán] are the model for copying throughout provincial Mexico so that they become true centers of subversion conducive to revolutionize regional historiography."[108]

Finally, the efforts that have been made since 1977 under the Sistema Nacional de Archivos to organize, index, preserve, microfilm, and modernize state and municipal archives has been nothing short of phenomenal.[109]

Regional studies have not been singularly responsible for the development of the revisionist interpretation of the Mexican Revolution as a failed popular revolution or as a triumphant bourgeois movement which has become so important in the 1970s and 1980s.[110] Local, regional, and provincial studies, however, have discredited the image of the singular and unified revolution, "la Revolución maderocarrancista." The academic historians of the 1970s and 1980s have taken Frank Tannenbaum's advice, given in the 1930s, that "a true history of the Revolution would detail the little obscure movements as they developed and gathered force and importance in localities, fought their battles and disappeared, to come to the surface again another place."[111] As a result, the prevailing image has become that of a fragmented revolution or revolutions. "At present," writes Romana Falcón, "no one speaks anymore of a general revolution, but of multiple revolutions, each one with its different roots, protagonists, ideals, reach, and enemies."[112]

Most recent provincial and regional studies of the revolution fall within the traditional periodization of 1910–1940, naturally, and especially the 1910s and 1920s. Although most authors at least touch upon the origins of the Mexican Revolution, Mark Wasserman's *Capitalists, Caciques and Revolution* represents perhaps the most detailed and analytically sophisticated study of the roots of the revolution in a key region. Wasserman argues, contrary to Fuentes Mares, that the Terrazas economic empire—and its connections to foreign enterprise and the national regime—generated the discontent which led to insurrection in Chihuahua in 1910 and after. In the excellent concluding chapter, Wasserman compares Chihuahua with other Mexican regions to explain why the mass insurrection, which became a revolution, began in Chihuahua and why it succeeded.[113] An important complementary study by Francois-Xavier Guerra maintains that the Maderista insurrection of 1910–1911 was generated primarily in the modernized mining zones of the north. "Is the revolution of 1910–1911 an agrarian revolution?" asks Guerra. "Yes, unquestionably in its last stage and in some regions. But first and foremost it is the rebellion of the most modern zones of Mexico. Its spearhead are the regions and the mining cities, those where modernization was at the same time the most precocious and the most extended."[114]

A more provocative interpretation of the origins of the revolution, based on the provincial example of San Luis Potosí, is offered by Romana Falcón. She contends that in that state the insurrections of 1910–1911 were led not by workers or campesinos but by members of the comfortable classes—landowners and the urban middle class—who successfully prevented the potential leaders of the popular classes from taking charge of the regional revolutionary movement and promoting their class demands.[115]

The Maderista Revolution, studied as a national movement and government by Charles C. Cumberland, Stanley R. Ross, and José C. Valadés in the 1950s and early 1960s, has been divvied up into its provincial parts in the 1970s and 1980s. The provincial origins of the 1910 revolution have been examined by Thomas Benjamin (Chiapas), Francie R. Chassen and Héctor Gerardo Martínez Medina (Oaxaca), David LaFrance (Puebla), Gilbert M. Joseph and Allen Wells (Yucatán), John H. McNeely (Morelos), William K. Meyers (the Comarca Lagunera), and Robert Sandels and Mark Wasserman (Chihuahua), among others.[116] The role of state governments in the period 1911–1913 has been researched by William H. Beezley (Chihuahua and Coahuila), Susan M. Deeds (Sonora), David LaFrance (Puebla), Peter V. N. Henderson (Oaxaca), and Douglas W. Richmond (Coahuila).[117] Beezley's 1979 essay on Maderismo is especially interesting since he persuasively contends that the revolutionary government essentially failed in the provinces, thus making it vulnerable to a coup d'etat in the capital, because "Madero had failed to reach rural Mexico."[118]

The revolution on the Mexican–United States border has long attracted the attention of historians on both sides of the border and shows no sign of abating. Most studies have focused, writes Oscar J. Martínez, "on descriptive narratives of revolutionary events in individual northern Mexican state, on the origin of the conflict in selected localities, on personalities, or on sensational incidents thatoccurred in the borderlands."[119] Recently, however, scholars have mined archives newly discovered on both sides of the border to produce more credible and, in some cases, provocative histories.[120]

One of the outstanding, and most influential, regional histories of the "epic revolution" is Héctor Aguilar Camín's *La frontera nómada*. This study of Maderismo and Carrancismo in Sonora (1910–1914), painstakingly researched in state and national archives, explains Sonorense military victory and revolutionary ideology in regional (rather than primarily ideological or class) terms. The entrepreneurial drive of the middle-class revolutionaries of Sonora, as well as the absence of a village peasantry in the northwest, explains the Sonorense emphasis of economic progress over social justice. Dependence upon state power and organization (even during the disintegration of the national state in 1913–1914) and a paid army, as opposed to the Zapatista "confederation of armed communities," made the Sonorenses militarily powerful as well as experienced state builders.[121] Thus Héctor Aguilar Camín contends, writes Henry C. Schmidt, "that the consensus view of the 1910–17 Revolution as controlled essentially by Zapatista agrarianism and the northern semi-populist Villistas is distorted, since it was really the Sonora group who were imposing their world on the peasant center and establishing the future course of the country."[122]

In central Mexico, recent regional studies have presented a schizophrenic revolution during the 1910–1920 decade. In some regions and localities, historians see a grass-roots agrarian revolt.[123] Elsewhere, other—and more— historians see little more than factional disputes (often long standing) for power among landowners and others of the middle and elite classes and a kind of conservative mobilization of campesinos. In Tlaxcala, Hidalgo, the Veracruz Huasteca, Guerrero, Jalisco, and Michoacán, agrarian struggle and class conflict took a back seat to factional disputes among landowners and the rise of new caciques.[124] In the state of San Luis Potosí, historians differ on the nature of the events of the epic revolution. Dudley Ankerson and Beatriz Rojas argue that the Cedillo brothers and Alberto Carrera Torres, rancheros, led radical-ized agrarian rebellions. Romana Falcón, on the other hand, stresses the tra-ditional (clientelist) nature of Saturnino Cedillo's regional power and denies the existence of "a true agrarista movement."[125]

Many of the recent provincial studies of the epic revolution have focused on peripheral states or struggles where the revolution impinged upon the prov-ince rather than the other way around. Counterrevolutionary (or state-autonomy) movements have been examined in Oaxaca and Chiapas, emphasizing local continuity with Porfirian politics and society and also the brutal treatment of locals by Carrancista armies.[126] In Yucatán, the imposition of "the Revolution" —Constitutionalism and General Salvador Alvarado—in 1915 has been stud-ied rather extensively, demonstrating the moderate reformism (and moderate success) of the Alvarado regime and its relevant model for postrevolutionary populist institutionalization.[127]

The postrevolutionary 1920s and 1930s have received considerable atten-tion, and perhaps the most incisive analysis, by regionalist historians over the past fifteen years.[128] The "institutionalization of the Mexican revolution," not long ago favorably considered as the gradual implementation of the prom-ises of the 1917 Constitution, is now viewed as an ominous process of politi-cal centralization, destructive of provincial autonomy, popular mobilization, and a revolutionary transformation of land tenure. The revolutionary rise and eventual downfall of powerful and/or radical provincial *caudillos* (as well as independent regional agrarian movements), such as Felipe Carrillo Puerto, Primo Tapia, Adalberto Tejeda, Tomás Garrido Canabal, and Saturnino Cedillo, is the subject of many of the best subnational histories published in the 1970s and 1980s.[129] Jean Meyer's volumes on the Cristero Rebellion showed how a popular regional insurrection in the 1920s (the last of the Mexican revolu-tions) was repressed by the leviathan state, thus accelerating "the moderniza-tion of politics."[130] "In the long run," summarizes Ian Jacobs in his study of Guerrero, reflecting the revisionist and total view of the revolution, "the cen-tral achievement of the Mexican Revolution was to establish the absolute pri-macy of the national state."[131]

Related studies on postrevolutionary agrarian movements have demonstrated why radical regional organizations failed and why others with much less ambi-tious objectives succeeded. Paul Friedrich, Heather Fowler Salamini, and Gil-bert M. Joseph have written, in effect, an outstanding trilogy of unsuccessful movements in, respectively: Michoacán, Veracruz and Yucatán. Heather Fowler Salamini, in *Agrarian Radicalism in Veracruz*, examines the rise and fall of the Veracruz agrarian movement and underscores the potential political value of popular peasant mobilization as well as its fragility in hands other than the national state. Whereas Salamini stressed the importance of political relationships between agraristas and powerful state and national politicians in the rise (and, for that matter, fall) of agrarian movements, Paul Friedrich, in his pioneering study, *Agrarian Revolt in a Mexican Village*, emphasized kinship in the organization of agrarianism and the vulnerability of a movement without a powerful patron. Gilbert Joseph in *Revolution from Without*, on the other hand, sees the failure of Yucatán's "socialist experiment" closely related to the decline of the region's export economy.[132] Ann Craig's study of a successful movement in Jalisco posited the critical importance of both national government support and local popular organization.[133]

The role played by agrarian movements and state-sponsored land reform in the centralization and consolidation of a powerful national state has been one of the most important fruits of regional research. Several studies have demonstrated how agrarian reform "from above and without" served to divide peasants, demobilize agraristas, and tie ejidatarios to the new state. Alan Knight, referring to Frans Schryer's study of rancheros in Pisaflores, Hidalgo, writes: "Once more, we see how the agrarian 'struggles' of the institutional revolution have been—not just co-opted and manipulated—but even initiated by local politicians on the make."[134]

Many recent local, regional, and provincial histories of Mexico provide analyses over the (more or less) *longue durée*. This perspective, almost without exception, brings historians to a Tocquevillian interpretation of the revolution emphasizing continuity in modern (Porfirian, revolutionary, and postrevolutionary) Mexican history.[135]

Wigberto Jiménez Moreno's judgment that "without good regional and local history, you cannot have good national history," while obviously sensible, is now proving to be demonstrably true. Friedrich Katz's *The Secret War in Mexico* (1981), which focuses primarily on the Mexican skullduggery of the Great Powers, contains a book within a book, an excellent account of "four regional revolutions and various revolts of less importance."[136] Katz's multinational archival research for this book is legendary, but as his notes show, he made good use of both the recent and early provincial and regional historiography of the revolution.[137] In his novel reinterpretation of the Porfiriato and the coming of the revolution, *Le Mexique; de l'Ancien Régime a la Revolution* (1985), Francois-Xavier Guerra acknowledged that his work was possible thanks to the researches of John Womack, Jr., Luis González, and many other local, regional, and provincial studies.[138] Alan Knight's antirevisionist history of the epic revolution of 1910–1920, *The Mexican Revolution* (1986), is intended as, in the author's words, "a national history which both takes into account local and regional variations, and also delves below the level high politics and diplomacy." On both counts he succeeds admirably, in large part thanks to, as he also acknowledges, the wealth of published work on the revolution, particularly the numerous provincial, regional, and local histories.[139] Finally, for the moment at least, John Tutino's *From Insurrection to Revolution in Mexico* (1986) carefully analyzes the social and regional bases of agrarian violence and insurrection in Mexico from the eighteenth century to the Mexican Revolution. While Tutino is at home in the archival sources of late colonial and early independent Mexico, his interpretation of the Porfirian and revolutionary eras is based substantially on recent local, regional, and provincial studies.[140]

As these four magisterial national histories clearly demonstrate, the history of the Mexican Revolution is being boldly reinterpreted through comparative analysis. In no small way, the achievements of these four historians rest upon a solid foundation of local, regional, and provincial historiography, the product of the often difficult and intense journeyman's labor of the field. Recent subnational studies of the Mexican Revolution have, it is true, produced ambiguous, inconsistent and often contradictory result. While some topics and places are neglected, others are redundantly researched and restudied. In overviewing the spatial complexity of the Mexican Revolution, there may be temptation to "dissolve the Revolution into an anomic chaos."[141] The antidote, as this volume hopes to show, is comparative analysis.

Notes

1. Genaro Fernández McGregor, quoted in Carlos Monsiváis, "La aparición del subsuelo: Sobre la cultura de la Revolución Mexicana," *Historias* 8–9 (Enero–Junio 1985): 171.
2. Francisco Ramírez Plancarte, *La ciudad de México durante la Revolución Constitucionalista* (México, 1932), 249.
3. Luis Pola, "Por el honor de Chiapas," *El Sur de México* (Tapachula, Chiapas), 12 April 1945.
4. Tannenbaum, *Peace by Revolution: An Interpretation of Mexico* (New York, 1933), 121.
5. This raises two problems related to terminology. First, the terms "region" and "regional" (denoting an indefinite large area possessing some kind of coherence and identity) and "province" and "provincial" (denoting administrative territories of a national state) can be usefully differentiated. These terms often are used interchangeably, and many scholars, myself included, employ the term "regional

history" to describe all subnational history. The majority of works considered in this essay are about federal states and thus fall into the category of, strictly speaking, provincial history. This problem permeates the historiography discussed here and cannot be expunged. Second, despite the regionalized and plural nature of the events of 1910–1920 and after, terminology has long been and remains singular. Bowing to tradition and general use, in this essay I refer to the events of the second decade of the twentieth century as the Mexican Revolution.

6. Sérgio Ortega Noriega, "Hacia la regionalización de la historia de México," *Estudios de Historia Moderna y Contemporánea de México* 8 (1980), 11.

7. The best historiogrpahical essays (in chronological order of publication) are: Luis González y González, *Invitación a la microhistoria* (México: SepSententas, 1973) and *Nueva invitación a la microhistoria* (México: Sep/80, 1982); Enrique Florescano, "Minucias para una historia mayor," *Nexos* (Junio de 1978), 23; Douglas W. Richmond, "Regional Aspects of the Mexican Revolution," *New Scholar* 7:1/2 (1979): 297–304; Barry Carr, "Recent Regional Studies of the Mexican Revolution," *Latin American Research Review*, 15:1 (1980): 3–14; Ma. de la Luz Parcero, *Introducción Bibliográfica a la Historiografía Política de México, Siglos XIX y XX* (México: Universidad Nacional Autónoma de México, 1982), chapter 3, "El Proceso Histórico Regional," 129–87; Romana Falcón, "Las revoluciones mexicanas de 1910," *Mexican Studies/Estudios Mexicanos* 1:2 (Summer 1985): 362–88; Edingardo Aguilar Cerrillo and Patricia Salcido Canedo, "Desde la microhistoria, referencias bibliográficas en torno a al Revolución Mexicana," *Revista Mexicana de Ciencias Políticas y Sociales* 31:122 (Octubre-Diciembre 1985): 167–77; Mark T. Gilderhus, "Many Mexicos: Tradition and Innovation in the Recent Historiography," *Latin American Research Review* 22:1 (1987): 204–13; Alma M. Garcia. "Recent Studies in Nineteenth- and Twentieth-Century Regional Mexican History," *Latin American Research Review* 22:2 (1987): 255–66; Linda Hall, "The Mexican Revolution and Its Aftermath: Perspectives From Regional Perspectives," *Mexican Studies/ Estudios Mexicanos* 3:2 (Summer 1987): 413–20; and Paul J. Vanderwood, "Building Blocks But Yet No Building: Regional History and the Mexican Revolution," *Mexican Studies/Estudios Mexicanos* 3:2 (Summer 1987): 421–32. For provincially specific historiographical essays and bibliographies, see the appendix.

8. "Las deficiencias explicativas de la historiografía del siglo XIX pueden deberse, en parte, al desconocimiento de la realidad regional de México, en un periodo en que lo regional ocupa el primer plano." Ortega Noriega, "Hacia la Regionalización de la Historia de México," 10. See, also Thomas Benjamin and Marcial Ocasio-Melendez, "Organizing the Memory of Modern Mexico: Porfirian Historiography in Perspective, 1880s–1980s," *Hispanic American Historical Review* 64 (May 1984): 333, 338–39.

9. John Rutherford, *Mexican Society during the Revolution: A Literary Approach* Oxford: Oxford University Press, 1971), 265.

10. Luis Pérez Verdía, quoted in José Ma. Muriá, "Notas sobre la historiografía regional jalisciense en el siglo XX," *Relaciones* 3 (Primavera de 1982), 69–70. Muriá discusses the Porfirian-era "brain drain" from Jalisco to Mexico City, in "Historiadores jaliscienses en la capital. Notas sobre su obra," *Secuencia* 2 (Mayo/Agosto 1985): 34–39.

11. There are only a handful of books, for example, listed in the massive bibliographies on the Porfiriato by Daniel Cosío Villegas. See Cosío Villegas, "El Porfiriato: su historiografía o arte histórico," *Extremos de América* (México: Tezontle, 1949); "Nueva historiografía política del México moderno," *Memoria de El Colegio Nacional* 5:4 (1965): 11–176, with special attention to Part 3, "Historias Particulares," 65–82; and "Ultima bibliografía política de la historia moderna de México," Ibid., 7:2 (1970): 41–222.

12. Frederick C. Turner, *The Dynamic of Mexican Nationalism* (Chapel Hill: University of North Carolina Press, 1968), 102n. There are a few and distinguished exceptions; see: Elías Amador, *Bosquejo histórico de Zacatecas* (Zacatecas, 1906–1912), 2 vols.; Eligio Ancona, *Historia de Yucatán* (México, 1880); Manuel Moro, *Historia de San Luis Potosí* (San Luis Potosí, 1892–1910), 3 vols.; and Luis Pérez Verdía, *Historia particular del Estado de Jalisco* (Guadalajara, 1910–1911), 3 vols.

13. Alfonso Luis Velasco, *Estado de México*, tomo 1; *Estado de Sinaloa*, tomo 2; *Estado de Veracruz*, tomo 3; *Estado de Nuevo León*, tomo 4; *Estado de Guanajuato*, tomo 5; *Estado de Michoacán*, tomo 6; *Estado de Morelos*, tomo 7; *Estado de Querétaro*, tomo 8; *Estado de Oaxaca*, tomo 9; *Estado de Guerrero*, tomo 10; *Estado de Tlaxcala*, tomo 11; *Estado de Tamaulipas*, tomo 12; *Estado de Durango*, tomo 13; *Estado de Sonora*, tomo 14; *Estado de Zacatecas*, tomo 15; *Estado de Campeche*, tomo 16; *Estado de Aguascalientes*, tomo 17; *Estado de Colima*, tomo 18; *Estado de Coahuila*, tomo 19; *Estado de Chiapas*, tomo 20.

14. Martín Pérez F., *Reseña Geografía y Estadística. Sonora, Chihuahua, Coahuila, Nuevo León, y Tamaulipas* (1908); Rafael de Alva, *Coahuila. Reseña Geografía y Estadística* (1909); Rafal de Alva, *Chihuahua. Reseña Geografía y Estadística* (1911); Luis Pérez Milicua, *Veracruz. Reseña Geografía y Estadísticaa* (1912); and León Diguet, *Territorio de Baja California. Reseña Geografía y Estadística* (1912).

15. Examples of this genre include: Pedro Larrea y Cordero, *Gran cuadro histórico, político, geográfico, biográfico y estadístico del Estado de Veracruz* (Veracruz, 1880), and *Gran cuadro histórico, político, geográfico, industrial y religioso de la ciudad de Tlaxcala y del Estado de su nombre* (Tlaxcala, 1886); Joaquín Romo, *Guadalajara. Apuntes históricos, biográficos, estadísticos y descriptivos de la capital del estado de Jalisco* (Mexico, 1888); Ramón Rabasa, *El estado de Chiapas: geografía y estadística* (México, 1895). Valuable comprehensive volumes include: Emiliano Busto, *Estadística de la república mexicana, estado que guarden la agricultura, industria, minería, y comercio* (México, 1880); J. Figueroa Domenech, *Guía general descriptiva de la república mexicana. Tomo II: Estados y territorios federales* (México, 1899); Lázaro Pavia, *Los estados y sus gobernantes. Ligeros apuntes históricos, biográficos y estadísticos* (México,

1890); Manuel Rivera Cambas, *México pintoresco, artístico y monumental* (México, 1880–1883) 3 vols.; John R. Southworth, *El directorio oficial de las minas y haciendas de México. Descripción general de las propiedades mineras y de las haciendas y ranchos de aquellos estados y territorios donde se han podido obtener datos fidedignos de la República Mexicana* (México, 1910); and R. Zamacona, *Reseña histórica, estadística y comerciala de México y sus estados* (México, 1892).

16. Kaerger, *Landwirtschaft und Kolonisation in Spanischen Amerika* (Leipzig, 1901). The section on Mexico is translated into Spanish by Pedro Lewin and Gudrun Dohrmann, in *Agricultura y colonización en México en 1900* (México: Universidad Autónoma Chapingo and Centro de Investigaciones y Estudios Superiores en Antropología Social, 1986).

17. Katz, *La servidumbre agraria en México en la época porfiriana* (México: Ediciones Era, 1980), 10.

18. Turner published a series of articles called "Barbarous Mexico" in the *American Magazine, Appeal to Reason, International Socialist Review*, and *Pacific Monthly* in 1909 and 1910. These articles subsequently were published in book form as *Barbarous Mexico* (Chicago, 1910, and New York, 1911). It was introduced by Daniel Cosío Villegas in "Lección de la Barbarie" and published in Mexico as "México Bárbaro," *Problemas Agrícolas e Industriales de México* 7:2 (abril-junio de 1955): 19–158. Chacon, "John Kenneth Turner, Barbarous Mexico, and the Debate about Debt Peonage Slavery in Yucatan during the Porfiriato," *Peasant Studies* 13 (Winter 1986): 98. Also see the commentaries by Eugenia Meyer, "En torno a John Kenneth Turner," *Boletín del Instituto Nacional de Antropología e Historia*, no. 36 (1969): 19–21; and Rosalía Velázquez, "Turner: un historiador de la revolución" *Casa del Tiempo*, 2:21 (mayo de 1982): 27–34.

19. Womack, review of Michael C. Meyer, *Mexican Rebel: Pascual Orozco and the Mexican Revolution* (Lincoln, 1967), in *Hispanic American Historical Review*, 48:2 (May 1968): 304.

20. Colonel García, in Carlos Fuentes, *The Old Gringo* (New York: Farrar Straus Giroux, 1985), 102.

21. Ramón Beteta, *The Mexican Revolution, a Defense* (México: DAPP, 1937), 18–19. Similarly, Henry C. Schmidt argues, "the Revolution elevated the province to major importance in the new hierarchy of national values." Schmidt, "Héctor Aguilar Camín and the Interpretation of the Mexican Revolution," *New World: A Journal of Latin American Studies* 1:1 (1986): 84.

22. See, for example: Gregorio Torres Quintero, *Apuntes sobre la última campaña electoral; la Revolución Falseada* (México, 1911); Luis Espinosa, *Rastros de Sangre, historia de la Revolución en Chiapas* (Tuxtla Gutiérrez, 1912); Lamberto Popoca y Palacios, *Historia del vandalismo en el Estado de Morelos* (Puebla, 1912); Ramón Puente, *Pascual Orozco y la Revuelta de Chihuahua* (México, 1912); José Juan Tablada, *Historia de la Campaña de la División del Norte* (México, 1913); José Diego Fernández, *Discursos en el Senado. La Revolución de 1910. Golpe de Estado en Morelos* (México,

1914); José Domingo Ramírez Garrido, *La esclavitud en Tabasco* (San Juan Bautista, 1915); Silvestre Dorador, *Mi Prisión, la Defensa Nacional y la verdad del caso; Una página para la Historia de la Revolución Constitucionalista en Durango* (México, 1916); J.M. Marquez, *El Veintiuno. Hombres de la Revolución y sus hechos* (Oaxaca, 1916); Rodolfo G. Robles, *Sinaloenses en campaña* (Culiacán, 1916); Custodio Valverde, *Julián Blanco y la revolución en el estado de Guerrero* (México, 1916); Salvador Alvarado, *Mi actuación Revolucionaria en Yucatán* (Paris-México, 1918); José Guerra y García, *Apuntes históricos de la revolución constitucionalista en Tamaulipas* (Tampico, 1918); C. Valenzuela, *Sonora y Carranza* (México, 1921); Félix Fulgencio Palavicini, *Mi vida revolucionario, 1906–1927* (México, 1937); José G. Zuno, *Reminiscencias de una vida* (Guadalajara, 1956–1972), 3 vols.; Angel Moreno Ochoa, *Semblanzas Revolucionarios* (Guadalajara, 1959–1965), 2 vols; José Fuentes Mares, *La revolución mexicana: memorias de un espectador* (México: Joaquin Mortiz, 1971).

23. For example, Carlos R. Menéndez, *La primera chispa de la Revolución Mexicana. El movimiento de Valladolid en 1910* (Mérida, 1918); and Clodoveo Valenzuela and Amado Chaverri M., *Sonora y Carranza* (México, 1921).

24. Luis González, "La Revolución Mexicana desde el punto de vista de los revolucionados," *Historias* 8–9 (Enero-Junio 1985): 12.

25. Luis González, "La Revolución Mexicana desde el Punto de Vista de los Revolucionados," *The Mexican Forum* 5 (October 1985): 4. Also see Michael C. Meyer, "Habla por ti mismo, Juan: Una propuesta para un método alternativa de investigaión," *Historia Mexicana* 22 (enero-marzo 1973): 396–408; William H. Beezley, "In Search of Everyday Mexicans in the Revolution," *Revista Interamericana de Bibliografia*, 33:3 (1983): 366–82; and Alicia Olivera de Bonfil, "La Versión Popular de la Revolución Mexicana," in *VIII Jornadas de Historia de Occidente: La Revolución y la Cultura en Mexico* (Jiquilpan de Juárez, Michoacán: Centro de Estudios de la Revolución Mexicana, 1986), 33–41. This view is supported by oral history accounts and the testimonies of surviving participants. See Ricardo Pozas's "ethnological recreation," *Juan Perez Jolote: Biografía de un Tzotzil* (México: Fonda de la Cultura Económica, 1952), translated as *Juan the Chamula* (Berkeley: University of California Press, 1962); Santiago Martínez Hernández, *Tiempos de Revolución: La Revolución Mexicana en el Sur de Veracruz vista por un campesino zoque-popoluca* (México, 1982); Eugenia Meyer, "Hablan los villistas," *Antropología e Historia: Boletín del Instituto Nacional de Antropología e Historia* 3 (julio-septiembre 1978): 7–39; Oscar J. Martínez, ed., *Fragments of the Mexican Revolution: Personal Accounts from the Border* (Albuquerque: University of New Mexico Press, 1983); and *Mi pueblo durante la revolución*, 3 vols. (México: Instituto Nacional de Antropología e Historia, 1985).

26. Henry C. Schmidt, *The Roots of Lo Mexicano: Self and Society in Mexican Thought. 1900–1934* (College Station: Texas A & M Press, 1978), 101.

27. Guillermo de la Peña, "Los estudios regionales y la antropología social en Mexico," *Relaciones* 2 (Otono de 1981): 49–52.

28. *Regiones económico agrícolas de la República Mexicana (Memorias Descriptivas)* (Tacubaya, D.F.: Secretaría de Agricultura y Fomento, 1936).

29. Harry Bernstein, "Regionalism in the National History of Mexico," *Acta Americana* 2 (October-December 1944): 314.

30. Guillermo Palacios, "Calles y la idea oficial de la Revolución Mexicana," *Historia Mexicana* 22:3 (enero-marzo 1973): 263–69.

31. Crisanto Cuellar Abaroa, *Juan Cuamatzi. Indio tlaxcalteca, precursor de la Revolución Mexicana* (Tlaxcala, 1935); Rafael Díaz de León, *Homenaje a Juan Sarabia* (San Luis Potosí, 1932); and Gustavo López Gutiérrez, *Chiapas y sus epopeyas libertarias* (Tuxtla Gutiérrez, 1932), 2 vols.

32. Salvador Teuffer, *Datos geográficos de Tabasco* (México, 1930).

33. There is also a considerable historical literature on the Magonistas, the Partido Liberal Mexicano, somewhat regionally focused primarily on San Luis Potosí and Baja California. See James D. Cockcroft, *Intellectual Precursors of the Mexican Revolution, 1900–1913* (Austin: University of Texas Press, 1968); Lowell L. Blaisdell, *The Desert Revolution: Baja California, 1911* (Madison: University of Wisconsin Press, 1962); Salvador Hernández padilla, *El magonismo: historia de una pasión libertaria, 1900–1922* (Mexico: Ediciones Era, 1984); and W. Dirk Raat, *Revoltosos: Mexico's Rebels in the United States, 1903–1923* (College Station: Texas A & M University Press, 1981); as well as their notes and bibliographies.

34. On the historiography of Zapata and Zapatismo see: Maria Eugenia Arias Gómez, "Algunos cuadernos históricos sobre Emiliano Zapata y el Zapatismo (1911–1940)," in *Emiliano Zapata y el Movimiento Zapatista* (México, 1980), 183–280; Lola E. Boyd, "Zapata in the Literature of the Mexican Revolution," *Hispania*, 52:4 (December 1969): 903–10; Boyd, *Emiliano Zapata en las letras y el folklore mexicano* (Madrid, 1979); Jorge Gurría Lacroix, "Historiografía sobre Emiliano Zapata," *Memorias de la Academia Mexicana de la Historia* 20 (1973): 246–66; Robert P. Millon, *Zapata: The Ideology of a Peasant Revolutionary* (New York, 1969), appendix, "The Literature on the Zapatista–Carrancista Conflict," 133–141; Rodolfo F. Pena, "Zapata: El mito contra la historia," *Solidaridad* 3 (1960): 29–31; and John Womack, Jr., *Zapata and the Mexican Revolution* (New York, 1969), "Bibliographical Note," 413–23.

35. Arias Gómez, "Algunos cuadernos históricos sobre Emiliano Zapata y el Zapatismo," 199.

36. Figueroa Domenech, *Veinte meses de Anarquía. Segunda parte de la Revolución y sus Héroes* (México, 1913); Melgarejo, *Los Crímines del Zapatismo* (México, 1913); Popoca y Palacios, *Historia del bandalismo en el estado de Morelos. ¡Ayer como ahora! ¡1860! ¡1911! Plateados–Zapatistas* (Puebla, 1912); Ribot, *El Atila del Sur. Novela histórico-trágica* (México, 1913); and Sala, *Emiliano Zapata y el Problema Agrario en la República Mexicana* (México, 1919). Alfonso Taracena criticized Zapata in order to shore up the reputation of Francisco Madero, in *La Tragedia Zapatista. Historia de la Revolución del Sur* (México, 1931).

37. Rutherford, *Mexican Society during the Revolution*, 148. This view is supported by Carlos J. Sierra, "Zapata. Señor de la tierra, capitan de los labriegos," *Boletín Bibliográfico de la Secretaría de Hacienda y Crédito Público*, suplemento al no. 361 (15 de Febrero de 1967): 1–24.

38. Palacios, *Historia Verídica del célebre guerrillero del sur, Emiliano Zapata* (Orizaba, 1924); Reyes Aviles, *Cartones Zapatistas* (México, 1928); List Arzubide, *Emiliano Zapata. Exaltación* (Jalapa, 1927), 36; and Valverde, *Apuntes para la historia de la Revolución y de la política en el Estado de Morelos* (México, 1933).

39. Dromundo, *Emiliano Zapata, Biografía* (México, 1934). On the fiftieth anniversary of the Plan de Ayala, Droumundo published a revised biography, *Vida de Emiliano Zapata* (México, 1961).

40. Magaña, *Emiliano Zapata y el Agrarismo en México* (México, 1934–1937), 2 vols; a third volume was published posthumously in 1946, and Carlos Pérez Guerrero completed the final two volumes which were published in 1952. Four other personal testimonies should be mentioned: Antonio Díaz Soto y Gama, *La revolución agraria del Sur y Emiliano Zapata, su caudillo* (México, 1960); Marte R. Gómez, *Las comisiones agrarias del Sur* (México, 1961); Genovevo de la O, "Memorias," *Impacto*, 31 December 1949 and 29 January 1950; and Octavio Paz Solorzano [father of the poet], "Emiliano Zapata," in José T. Meléndez, ed., *Historia de la Revolución Mexicana* (México, 1936), vol. 1. This chapter has been republished with an introduction by Octavio Paz as *Tres revolucionarios, tres testimonios. Tomo II:: Zapata* (México: Collección Biografía, 1986).

41. Womack, Jr., *Zapata and the Mexican Revolution*, 419; Arias Gómez, "Algunos Cuadernos Históricos Sobre Emiliano Zapata y el Zapatismo," 263–64.

42. Sotelo Inclán, *Raíz y Razón de Zapata. Aneneuilco. Investigatión histórica* (México, 1943); Alicia Olivera de Bonfil and Eugenia Meyer, *Jesús Sotelo Inclán y sus conceptos sobre el movimiento zapatista (entrevista)* (México, 1970), 5.

43. *Jesús Sotelo Inclán y sus conceptos sobre el movimiento zapatista*, 11.

44. Mario Mena, *Zapata* (México, 1959); Porfirio Palacios, *Emiliano Zapata. Datos biográfico-históricos* (México, 1960); Silvano Barba González, *La lucha por la tierra. Emiliano Zapata* (México, 1960); Alberto Morales Jiménez, *Zapata* (México, 1961); Robert Paul Millon, *Zapata :The Ideology of a Peasant Revolutionary* (New York, 1969); Saul Chavez Peralta, *Emiliano Zapata: crisol de la Revolución mexicana* (México, 1972); Roger Parkinson, *Zapata: A Biography* (New York, 1975).

45. Chevalier, "Un factor decisivo de la revolución agraria de México: el levantamiento de Emiliano Zapata (1911–1919)," *Cuadernos Americanos* 110:6 (Noviembre 1960): 165–87.

46. Womack, Jr., *Zapata and the Mexican Revolution* (New York, 1969); and the Spanish translation by Francisco González Aramburu, *Zapata y la revolución mexicana* (México, 1969). Womack talks about his work on Zapata in Henry Abelove et al., eds., *Visions of History* (New York, 1984), 247–51.

47. Fuentes, "Viva Zapata," *New York Review of Books*, 13 March 1969, 6.

48. González, *Zapata. Reaccionario y traidor* (Saltillo, Coahuila, 1974), 7; Luz Valdés, *El mito de Zapata* (Saltillo, Coahuila, 1974); Ángel Peral, *El Verdadero Zapata* (México, 1975); and Ayala Anguiano, *Zapata y las grandes mentiras de la revolución mexicana* (México: Editorial Vid, 1985).

49. Adolfo Gilly. *La revolución interrumpida. México, 1910–1920: una guerra campesina por la tierra y el poder* (México, 1971), see chapter 3, "El zapatismo," and chapter 8, "La Comuna de Morelos," 49–86 and 235–308; an English translation has been published as *The Mexican Revolution* (London, 1983), and Ramón Eduardo Ruiz, *The Great Rebellion: Mexico, 1905–1924* (New York, 1980), see chapter 13, "Emiliano Zapata: The Unorthodox Rebel," 199–212.

50. Josefina E. de Fabela, ed., *Emiliano Zapata: el Plan de Ayala y su Política agraria* (México, 1970); Miguel León Portilla, *Los manifiestos en nahuatl de Emiliano Zapata* (México, 1978); *Documentos ineditos sobre Emiliano Zapata y el Cuartel General* (México, 1979); Rosalind Rosoff and Anita Guilar, *Así firmaron el plan de Ayala* (México, 1976); Salvador Rueda Smithers, "Oposición y subversión" testimonios zapatistas," *Historias* 3 (enero-marzo de 1983): 3–32; *Ejército Libertador del Sur (1911–1923). cuadernos del Archivo Histórico de la UNAM* (México, 1988); also see the interviews conducted by the Archivo de la Palabra del Instituto de Investigaciones Dr. José Luis Mora, Mexico City. Studies of postrevolutionary Morelos include: Laura Helguera Resendiz, Sinecio López, and Ramón Ramirez, *Los Campesinos de la Tierra de Zapata* (México: SEP-INAH, 1974–1976), 3 vols.; Arturo Warman, . . . *Y venimos a contradecir: Los campesinos de Morelos y el estado nacional* (México: Ediciones de Casa Chata, 1976), which has been translated as, *"We Come to Object": The Peasants of Morelos and the National State* (Baltimore: Johns Hopkins University Press, 1980); and Guillermo de la Peña, *Herederos de promesas. Agricultura, política y ritual en los Altos de Morelos* (México: Ediciones de Casa Chata, 1980), which has also been published in English as *A Legacy of Promises: Agriculture, Politics, and Ritual in the Morelos Highlands of Mexico* (Austin: University of Texas Press, 1981).

51. Rutherford, *Mexican Society during the Revolution,* 152.

52. On the historiography of Villa, see Nancy Brandt, "Pancho Villa: The Making of a Modern Legend," *The Americas* 21:2 (October 1964): 146–62; Enrique Beltrán, "Fantasía y Realidad de Pancho Villa," *Historia Mexicana* 16 (julio-septiembre 1966): 71–84; Guadalupe Villa Guerrero, "Francisco Villa: Historia, Leyenda y Mito" (tesis, Universidad Nacional Autónoma de México, 176); and Arturo Langle Ramirez, *Los primeros cien años de Pancho Villa* (México, 1980).

53. Reed, *Insurgent Mexico* (New York, 1914); the book was translated and published in Mexico by the Fondo de Cultura Popular as *México insurgente* in 1954. Reed's articles on Mexico have been published by Jorge Ruffinelli, *Villa y la Revolución Mexicana. John Reed en México* (México, 1983). Nearly twenty years later, another American journalist, Edgcumb Pinchon, wrote a similarly sym-

pathetic biography: *Viva Villa!: A Recovery of the Real Pancho Villa: Peon, Bandit, Soldier, Patriot* (New York, 1933).

54. Tuck, *Pancho Villa and John Reed: Two Faces of Romantic Revolution* (Tucson: University of Arizona Press, 1984), 104, 115, and 103. See also Jorge Rufffinelli's lengthy and excellent commentary on Reed's reportage on Mexico: "John Reed en la Revolución Mexicana," in *Villa y la Revolución Mexicana*, 11–106.

55. Bulnes, *The Whole Truth About Mexico: President Wilson's Responsibility* (New York, 1916); see also Frederico P. Robledo's *El constitucionalismo y Francisco Villa a la luz de la verdad* (Matamoros, 1915).

56. Puente, *Vida de Francisco Villa. contada por él mismo* (Los Angeles, 1919). Puente later published expanded versions of Villa's memoirs: *Memorias de Pancho Villa, narradas por él mismo* (México, 1923); *Hombre de la Revolución: Villa (Sus auténticas memorias)* (Los Angeles, 1931); and *Villa en pie* (México, 1937). Villa's friend Elías L. Torres wrote *Vida y Hazañas de Pancho Villa* (México, 1921).

57. Muñoz, *Memorias de Pnacho Villa* (México, 1923). Several years later, Muñoz wrote a novel about a small group of Villista soldiers: *¡Vámonos con Pancho Villa!* (Madrid, 1931).

58. Friends include Teodoro Torres, Jr., *Pancho Villa, Una vida de romance y de tragedía* (San Antonio, 1924); Villa's widow, Luz Corral Vda. de Villa, *Pancho Villa en la intimidad* (México, 1948); two Villista veterans, Luis and Adrián Aguirre Benavides, *Las grandes batallas de la División del Norte. Al Mando del General Francisco Villa* (México, 1964). Foes include Carrancista General Manuel W. González, *Contra Villa: Relatos de la campaña de 1914–1915* (México, 1935); the sister of Carrancista Maclovio Herrera, Celia Herrera E., *Francisco Villa ante la historia* (México, 1937); and the nephew of Venustiano Carranza, Gen. Alberto Salinasa Carranza, *La Expedición Punitiva* (México, 1936), who, surprisingly, gives grudging respect to Villa.

59. Vasconcelos, review of Celia Herrera, *Francisco Villa ante la historia*, in *Timón*, 11 May 1940.

60. General Federico Cervantes M., *Francisco Villa y la Revolución* (México, 1960). A similar memoir–history is Luis Aguirre Benavides, *De Francisco I. Madero a Francisco Villa: Memorias de un revolucionario* (México, 1966).

61. Guzmán, *Memorias de Pancho Villa*, 1. *El hombre y sus armas* (México, 1938); 2. *Campos de batalla* (México, 1939); 3. *Panoramas políticos* (México, 1939); 4. *La causa del pobre* (México, 1940); 5. *Adversidades del bien* (México, 1964). The book was first serialized in *El Universal* in 1936. The first four volumes were published by Ediciones Botas, and the fifth volume was published by the Compañía General de Ediciones. A condensation and translation by Virginia H. Taylor was published by the University of Texas Press: *Memoirs of Pancho Villa* (Austin, 1965).

62. Abreu Gómez, "Martín Luis Guzmán: Crítica y Bibliografía," *Hispania* 35 (1952); 71.

63. Silvestre Terrazas, "El Verdadero Pancho Villa," *Boletín de la Sociedad Chihuahuense de Estudios Históricos*, vols. 5–8 (1944–1955).

64. Silvestre Terrazas, *El verdadero Pancho Villa. El Centauro del Norte . . . sus heróicas batallas y acciones revolucionarias*, Presentación de Friedrich Katz, Biografía de Silvestre Terrazas por Margarita Terrazas Perches (México: Ediciones Era, 1985), 12–13.

65. Calzadíaz Barrera, *Hechos reales de la Revolución mexicana*, 2 vols. (México, 1961); *Hechos reales de la Revolución mexicana*. 2 vols. (México, 1961); *Hechos reales de la Revolución Mexicana*. vol. 3: *El fin de la División del Norte* (México, 1965); and *Porqué Villa atacó a Columbus* (México, 1972).

66. Gómez, *La Reforma Agraria en las Filas Villistas: Años 1913 a 1915 y 1920* (México, 1966).

67. Robert Blanco Moheno, *Pancho Villa, que es su padre* (México, 1969); Angel Rivas López, *El verdadero Pancho Villa* (México, 1970); José Grigulevich, *Pancho Villa* (Habana, 1970); Eugenio Toussaint Aragón, *Quien y como fue Pancho Villa* (México, 1979); Luis Garfias M., *Verdad y leyenda de Pancho Villa: vida y hechos del famoso personaje de la Revolución mexicana* (México, 1981). The most recent anti-Villa interpretation is by Rodrigo Alonso Cortés, *Francisco Villa, el quinto jinete del Apocalipsis* (México, 1972). Provocative syntheses have been written by Adolfo Gilly. *La revolución interrumpida*, chapter 4, "La División del Norte," 87–118; and Ramón Eduardo Ruiz, *The Great Rebellion*, chapter 12, "Francisco Villa: The Mexican Robin Hood," 185–98.

68. Pere Foix, *Pancho Villa* (México, 1970), 270; and Ilene V. O'Malley, *The Myth of the Revolution: Hero Cults and the Institutionalization of the Mexican State, 1920–1940* (New York: Greenwood Press, 1986), 111–12.

69. Katz, review of Jessie Peterson and Thelma Cox Knoles, eds., "Pancho Villa: Intimate Recollections by People Who Knew Him" (1977), in *American Historical Review* 84 (June 1979); 887.

70. Segundo Portilla y Héctor Aguilar Camín "¿A Donde Ibamos con Pancho Villa? Un Dialogo con Friedrich Katz sobre Política y Administración," *Siempre!*, 12 January 1977, ix. A more recent interview is "Volvámonos con Pancho Villa: Una entrevista con Friedrich Katz," *Nexos* 9 (Noviembre 1986): 37–48.

71. Katz, "Peasants in the Mexican Revolution of 1910," in Joseph Spielberg and Scott Whiteford, eds., *Forging Nations: A Comparative View of Rural Ferment and Revolt* (East Lansing: Michigan State University Press), 61–85; "Agrarian Changes in Northern Mexico in the Period of Villista Rule, 1913–1915," in James W. Wilkie, Michael C. Meyer, and Edna Monzon de Wilkie, eds., *Contemporary Mexico: Papers of the IV International Congress of Mexican History* (Berkeley and Mexico City: University of California Press and El Colegio de México, 1976), 259–73; "Pancho Villa and the Attack on Columbus, New Mexico," *American Historical Review* 83 (February 1978): 101–30; *Pancho Villa y el ataque a Columbus* (New Mexico-Chihuahua: Sociedad Chihuahuense de Estudios Históricos, 1979);

"Villa: Reform Governor of Chihuahua," in George Wolfskill and Douglas Richmond, eds., *Essays on the Mexican Revolution: Revisionist Views of the Leaders* (Austin: University of Texas Press, 1979), 26–45; "Pancho Villa, peasant movements and agrarian reform in northern Mexico," in *Caudillo and Peasant in the Mexican Revolution* ed. D. A. Brading (Cambridge: Cambridge University Press, 1980), 59–75; and *The Secret War in Mexico: Europe, The United States and the Mexican Revolution* (Chicago: University of Chicago Press, 1981).

72. William Spratling, *Little Mexico* (New York: Jonathan Cape and Harrison Smith, 1932), 105.

73. Fuentes, "Viva Zapata," 8.

74. Schmidt, "Héctor Aguilar Camín and the Interpretation of the Mexican Revolution," 84.

75. Herrera, *Francisco Villa ante la historia*, 8.

76. Hoyo, "Historiografía Mexicana en el Siglo XX," *Humanitas*, 20, (1979): 238–39. Each Congress was held in a provincial city, and at least one session was devoted to the history of that state and region.

77. José Ignacio Dávila Garibi, *Los estudios históricos regionales como base de la historia general del país* (México, 1943), 9. Wigberto Jiménez Moreno noted, in the Congress celebrated in Guanajuato in 1945, that "habían venido consagrando particular atención a la historia de regiones y Estados." See "Comentario" (Historia del Tema Regional y Parroquial), *Investigaciones contemporáneas sobre historia de México: Memorias de la tercera reunión de historiadores mexicanos y norteamericanos, Oaxtepec, Morelos, 4–7 noviembre de 1969* (México: Universidad Nacional Autónoma de México, El Colegio de México, and University of Texas at Austin, 1971), 271.

78. Robert Potash, "Historiography of Mexico Since 1821," *Hispanic American Historical Review* 40 (August 1960): 404.

79. *Memoria del Primer Congreso de Historiadores de México y los Estados Unidos, celebrado en la ciudad de Monterrey, Nuevo León, México, del 4 al 9 de septiembre de 1949* (México, 1950).

80. Jiménez Moreno, "50 años de historia mexicana," *Historia Mexicana* 1 (enero-marzo 1952): 454.

81. The most important publication of the Archivo de la Revolución is the multivolume *Fuentes para la historia de la Revolución Mexicana* (México: Fondo de Cultura Económica, 1954–1959), 5 vols.

82. Gobierno del Estado de Baja California, *Memoria del primer Congreso de Historia Regional* (Mexicali, 1958), 2 vols.

83. Vito Alessio Robles, *Bosquejos históricos* (México, 1937); Manuel Aguirre Berlanga, "Investigaciones sobre los archivos públicos," *Divulgación Historia* 2 (15 de enero de 1941): 153–56; idem. (15 de marzo de 1941): 257–60; "El lamentable abandono de los archivos de México," *El Universal*, 1 May 1941; Vito Alessio Robles, "Los archivos de la República Mexicana," *Excélsior*, 12 June 1941; and "Los archivos y la historia," *El Universal*, 15 June 1943.

84. The most important contribution was Manuel Carrera Stampa's *Archivalía Mexicana* (México, 1952). Also, see: Guillermo Flores Muñoz, "Los archivos de Durango," *Divulgación Histórica* 6 (15 de julio de 1943): 164–66; "El Archivo de Historia de Michoacán," *Anales del Museo Michoacano* (septiembre de 1944): 108–9; Woodrow Borah, "Archivo de la Secretaría Municipal de Puebla, Guía para la consulta de sus materiales," *Boletín del Archivo General de la Nación* 13 (abril-junio de 1942): 207–39; and idem. (julio-septiembre de 1942):: 423–64; Juan de Dios Pérez Galaz, "Reorganización del Archivo General del Estado," *Orbe* (Mérida) (abril-mayo 1945): 12–13, 16.

85. Agustín Millares Carlo, *Repertorio bibliográfico de los archivos mexicanos y de los europeos y norteamericanos de interés para la historia de México* (México, 1959): 192–93.

86. Rafael Montejano y Aguiñtaga, "Métodos de Investigación de la Historia Regional," *Estudios de historia del noreste*, Presentados al Congreso de Historia del Noreste de Mexico, 1971 (Monterrey: Sociedad Nuevoleonesa de Historia, Geográfica y Estadística, 1972), 18. The background of the most prominent provincial historians is given in Ernesto de la Torre Villar, *Lecturas Históricas Mexicanas*, tomos 3–4 (México, 1969); also see Jack Ray Thomas, *Biographical Dictionary of Latin American Historians and Historiography* (Westport, Conn.: Greenwood Press, 1984), 89–90, 192–93, 294–95; Muriá, "Notas sobre la historiografía regional jalisciense en el siglo XX," 73.

87. Albert Michaels, "Commentary" [Historiografía de la vida política], *Investigaciones contemporáneas sobre historia de México*, 498.

88. Out of a total of fifty citations, Stanley Ross included four regional histories, none of which were written by professionally trained historians. See Ross, "Historia polí tica: La Revolución Mexicana," *Veinticinco años de investigación histórica en México*, 1, special issue of *Historia Mexicana* 15 (octubre 1965-marzo 1966): 425–45. John Womack, Jr., in his discussion of "Mexican Political Historiography, 1959–1969," has nothing to say of regional history except the need for studies of "the Revolutionary governments in certain states like Oaxaca, or Sonora or Tamaulipas." *Investigaciones contemporáneas sobre historia de México*, 481. Michael C. Meyer, for example, writing in 1972 noted that "the cultivation of state and local history is still in its infancy in Mexican Revolutionary historiography, although it is beginning to attract the interest of a young generation of scholars." Meyer, *Huerta: A Political Portrait* (Lincoln, 1972), "Bibliographical Essay," 253–54.

89. Howard Cline, "Mexican Community Studies," *Hispanic American Historical Review* 32 (May 1952): 212–42. An emphasis on the "temporal dimensions" of community life, as opposed to the anthropological perversion called "ethnographic present," was detected a quarter-century later by William B. Taylor, "Revolution and Tradition in Rural Mexico," *Peasant Studies* 5 (October 1976): 31–37.

90. Jorge Fernando Iturribarría, *Historia de Oaxaca*, (Oaxaca, 1935–1956), 4 vols; Alvaro Gamboa Ricalde, *Yucatán desde 1910* (Veracruz and México, 1943–1955),

3 vols; Jorge Luis Melgarejo Vivanco, *Historia de Veracruz* (Veracruz, 1950), 5 vols; Bernardino Mena Brito, *Reestructuración histórica de Yucatán* (México: Editores Mexicanos Unidos, 1965–1969), 3 vols; Arnulfo Ochoa Reina, *Historia del Estado de Durango* (1958); Everardo Peña Navarro, *Estudio histórico del Estado de Nayarit* (México, 1946), 2 vols; Jesús Romero Flores, *Historia de Michoacán* (México, 1946), 2 vols; Salvador Sánchez Colín, *El Estado de México* (México, 1951), 2 vols; Manuel B. Trens, *Historia de Chiapas* (México, 1942); Trens, *Historia de Veracruz* (Jalapa, 1949–1950), 6 vols; Primo Feliciano Velázquez, *Historia de San Luis Potosí* (México, 1946–1948), 4 vols.

91. José Fuentes Mares, . . . *Y México se refugió en el desierto: Luis Terrazas: Historia y destino* (México, 1954), xxiii–xxiv. See the critical review by Rosa Peralta, "Historia, Destino y Desierto," *Historia Mexicana* 3 (abril-junio 1954): 612–17.

92. Jorge Fernando Iturribarría, *Oaxaca en la Historia* (México, 1955), x. Moisés Ocho Campos of Guerrero wanted to affirm that "the people of the South never were Porfirista." Ocho Campos, *Historia del Estsado de Guerrero* (México, 1968), 271.

93. Antonio G. Rivera, *La revolución en Sonora* (México, 1969), 9, 11.

94. Moisés T. De la Peña y otros, *Campeche Económico* (México, 1941); *Zacatecas Económico* (México, 1944); *Chihuahua Económico* (México, 1945), 3 vols; *Veracruz Económico* (México, 1946), 2 vols; *Guerrero Económico* (México, 1948), 2 vols; and *Chiapas Económico* (México, 1951), 4 vols.

95. Salvador Azuela, "El rescate de la provincia," *El Imparcial* (Hermosillo, Sonora), 10 de Septiembre de 1962.

96. See *Catálogo de Publicaciones: Instituto Nacional de Estudios Históricos de la Revolución Mexicana* (México: Secretaría de Gobernación, 1987). The state studies in chronological order of publication are: Atenedoro Gámez, *Monografía Histórica sobre la Génesis de la Revolución en el Estado de Puebla* (1960); Everardo Gámiz Olivas, *La Revolución en el Estado de Durango* (1963); Francisco R. Amada, *La Revolucion en el Estado de Chihuahua*, 2 vols. (1964–1965); Héctor R. Olea, *Breve historia de la Revolución en Sinaloa* (1964); Jesús Romero Flores, *Historia de la Revolución en Michoacán* (1964); José Guadalupe Zuno, *Historia de la Revolución en el Estado de Jalisco* (1964); Eugenio Martínez Núñez, *La Revolución en el Estado de San Luis Potosí* (1964); Edmundo Bolio, *Yucatán en la Dictadura y la Revolución* (1967); Ildefonso Villarelo Vélez, *Historia de la Revolución Mexicana en Coahuila* (1970); Alfonso Francisco Ramírez, *Historia de la Revolución en Oaxaca* (1970); Francisco R. Almada, *La Revolución en el Estado de Sonora* (1971); Leonardo Pasquel, *La Revolución en el Estado de Veracruz*, 2 vols. (1971); José Ángel Aguilar, *La Revolución en el Estado de Mexico*, 2 vols. (1972); Manuel González Calzada, *Historia de la Revolución Mexicana en Tabasco* (1972); Ricardo B. Núñez, *La Revolución en el Estado de Colima* (1973); Crisanto Cuéllar Abaroa, *La Revolución en el estado de Tlaxcala*, 2 vols. (1975); Manuel M. Moreno, *Historia de la Revolución en Guanajuato* (1977); Manuel Frías Olvera, *Historia de la Revolución Mexicana en el Estado de Puebla* (1980); Luis Rubluo, *Historia de la Revolución mexicana en el estado*

de Hidalgo, 2 vols. (1983–1985); Octavio Gordillo y Ortiz, *La Revolución en el estado de Chiapas* 1986).

97. George J. Rausch, Jr., review of Jesús Romero Flores, *Historia de la Revolución en Michoacán*, in *Hispanic American Historical Review* 45 (November 1965): 629–30. Albert Michaels is less generous, referring to the "mostly superficial volumes" of the INEHRM, "Commentary," 498.

98. Francisco José Ruiz Cervantes maintains that "it was only by the 1970s when some investigators began to work with the idea that the revolution had different meanings at distinct moments and locations." See "Seis libros sobre la Revolución en Oaxaca," *Revista Mexicana de Sociología* 44:1 (Enero-Marzo de 1982): 341.

99. Vicente Fuentes Díaz, *La Revolución de 1910 en el Eestado de Guerrero* (México, 1960), 1.

100. Schmidt, "Héctor Aguilar Camín and the Interpretation of the Mexican Revolution," 84.

101. Xavier Tavera Alfaro, Jorge Alberto Manrique, and David Ramírez Lavoignet, "La razón de escribir una historia de la Revolución en Veracruz," *La Palabra y el Hombre: Revista de la Universidad Veracruzana* 16 (Octubre-Diciembre 1960): 160–61.

102. Michael C. Meyer, "Perspectives on Mexican Revolutionary Historiography," *New Mexico Historical Review* 44 (April 1969): 174; and Stanley R. Ross, "Twentieth-Century Mexican History: An Overview from the United States," in Wilkie et al., eds., *Contemporary Mexico*, 785–86.

103. Lowell L. Blaisdell, *The Desert Revolution: Baja California, 1911* (Madison: University of Wisconsin Press, 1962); Michael C. Meyer, *Mexican Rebel: Pascual Orozco and the Mexican Revolution, 1910–1915* (Lincoln: University of Nebraska Press, 1967); James D. Cockcroft, *Intellectual Precursors of the Mexican Revolution, 1900–1913* (Austin: University of Texas Press, 1968); Luiz González, *Pueblo en vilo. Microhistoria de San José de Gracia* (México: El Colegio de México, 1968); and Womack, Jr., *Zapata and the Mexican Revolution* (1969).

104. Luis González, "El Arte de la Microhistoria," in *Invitación a la microhistoria*, 8. The II Encuentro was held in San Luis Potosí in 1974, the III Encuentro in Monterrey in 1976, and the IV Encuentro in Saltillo in 1979. Agustín Jacinto complained of the regionalism—northern control—within the Association. See "EL AMEHRAC y la historia regional," *Relaciones* 1 (Invierno de 1980): 141–45.

105. María Elena Bribiesca Sumano, "La Necesidad de la Creación de Institutos, Centros y Sociedades de Historia Regional para la Formación de los Investigadores de Provincia," in *II Encuentro de Historiadores de Provincia . . . Memorias* (San Luis Potosí: Asociación Mexicana de Historia Regional, 1975), 50.

106. The journal *Históricas,* in sections called "Provincia," provides news of provincial universities and archives and their efforts on behalf of provincial Mexican history. Luis González, "La Enseñanza de la Historia en el Colegio de Michoacán," *Boletín de el Colegio de Michoacán* 2 (Abril-Junio 1979); "El Colegio de Michoacán,"

Historia Mexicana 32 (Abril-Junio 1983): 577–96. Most theses on themes of regional history continue to be produced in institutions located in Mexico City and environs. See *Catálogo de Tesis sobre Historia de México* (México: comite Mexicano de Ciencias Históricas, 1976); *Segundo Catálogo de Tesis sobre Historia de México* (1984); *Addenda al Segundo Catálogo* (1985), and *II Addenda al Segundo Catálogo* (1987). More than one-half of the projects in regional history by Mexican academics listed in the recent *Guía Internacional de Investigaciones sobre México/International Guide to Research on Mexico* (Tijuana and La Jolla: El Colegio de la Frontera Norte and Center for U.S.–Mexican Studies, University of California, San Diego, 1986, and the 1987 edition) are by investigators based in provincial institutions.

107. Esteban Krotz, "Las revistas de la provincia mexicana: un panorama preliminar," *Relaciones: Estudios de Historia y Sociedad* 8 (invierno de 1987): 85–98; and Enrique Florescano Mayet, "Problemas actuales de la difusión de la historia y de la formación de los historiadores," *Memoria del VI Encuentro Nacional de Estudiantes de Historia, Noviembre de 1983* (México, 1984), xiv–xv.

108. José Ma. Muriá, "Problemas del historiador provinciano," Históricas 3 (Mayo-Agosto 1980): 36.

109. See Sérgio Ortega Noriega, "Archivos históricos regionales y locales. Un proyecto de catálogo," *Boletín del Archivo General de la Nación*, tomo I:2 (Julio-Septiembre, 1977), 33–34; Stella González C., "Desarrollo del Inventario Nacional de Archivos Municipales y Parroquiales," *Memoria de la V Reunión Nacional de Archivos Administrativos e Históricos, Estatales y Municipales* (México: Archivo General de la Nación, 1982), 64–69; and Victoria San Vicente Tello, "Las Perspectivas en la Organización de los Archivos Históricos Nacionales," *Memoria de la IX Reunión del Sistema Nacional de Archivos* (México: A.G.N., 1986), 51–54. For progress in specific states, see José Luis Alanis Boyso, "Los archivos municipales del Estado de México," *Historia Mexicana* 28 (Abril-Junio 1979): 567–95; Angélica Inda and Ándres Aubry, "Los Archivos Municipales de Chiapas," *Memoria de la VI Reunión . . .* (México: A.G.N., 1983), 40–45; David G. LaFrance, Fred Lobdell, and Maurice Leslie Sabbah, "Fuentes históricas para el estudio de Puebla en el siglo XX," *Historia Mexicana* 27 (Octubre-Diciembre 1977): 260–72; Leticia Martínez C., "El Archivo General del Estado de Nuevo León en su Contexto Actual," *Memoria de la V Reunión . . .*, 160–72; Alfonso Martínez Rosales, "El Archivo Histórico del Estado de San Luis Potosí," *Historia Mexicana* 33 (Octubre-Diciembre 1983): 318–36; Cynthia Radding de Murrieta, "Preservación de los archivos históricos de Sonora," *Antropología e Historia* 3 (enero-marzo 1979): 65–76; Rodolfo Ruz Menéndez, "Los archivos del Estado de Yucatán (México)," *Yucatán: Historia y Economía* 5 (Marzo-Abril 1982): 42–49; as well as the following journals published by state and municipal archives: *Archivo Histórico del Estado Lic. Antonio Rocha* (San Luis Potosí); *Boletín Archivo General del Estado, Sección Historia* (Nuevo León); *Boletín del Archivo General del Estado de México; Boletín del Archivo*

Histórico Municipal (León, Guanajuato); *Boletín del Archivo Histórico Pablo L. Martínez* (La Paz, Baja California); and *Boletín del Archivo Histórico de Jalisco.*

110. David C. Bailey, "Revisionism and the Recent Historiography of the Mexican Revolution," *Hispanic American Historical Review* 58 (February 1978): 62–79.

111. Tannenbaum, *Peace by Revolution*, 148.

112. Falcón, "Las revoluciones mexicanas de 1910," 363. "In sum one cannot speak of a Mexican Revolution, of a movement that included the entire country but of a multiplicity of small 'revolutions' of dissimilar origins, with different objectives and protagonists." See Romana Falcón, "La Revolución mexicana y la busqueda de la autonomía local," in *Poder local, poder regional* ed. Jorge Padua N. and Alain Vanneph (México: El Colegio de México, 1986), 107.

113. Mark Wasserman, *Capitalists, Caciques and Revolution: The Native Elite and Foreign Enterprise in Chihuahua, Mexico, 1854–1911* (Chapel Hill: University of North Carolina Press, 1984). The regional origins of the revolution are explored by several historians in *Other Mexicos: Essays on Regional Mexican History, 1876–1911* ed. Thomas Benjamin and William McNellie (Albuquerque: University of New Mexico Press, 1984).

114. Francois-Xavier Guerra, "Territorio minado (Más álla de Zapata en la Revolución Mexicana)," *Nexos* 6 (mayo de 1986): 31–47, quote from 47; and "La révolution mexicaine: d'abord une révolution minière?, *Annales: Economies, Socities, Civilisations* 36 (1981), 785–814. The mining industry during the revolutionary decade is discussed by Linda B. Hall and Don M. Coerver, "La frontera y las minas en la Revolución Mexicana (1910–1920)," *Historia Mexicana* 32 (enero-marzo 1983): 389–421.

115. Romana Falcón, "¿Los origenes pouplares de la Revolución de 1910? El caso de San Luis Potosí," *Historia Mexicana* 29 (octubre-diciembre 1979): 197–239.

116. Thomas Benjamin, "Revolución interrumpida: Chiapas y el interinato presidencial, 1911," *Historia Mexicana* 30 (julio-septiembre 1980): 79–98; Francie R. Chassen, "Los prescursores de la revolución en Oaxaca," in Víctor Raul Martínez Vásquez, ed., *La revolución en Oaxaca, 1900–1930* (Oaxaca, 1985); David LaFrance, "Madero, Serdán y los albores del movimiento revolucionario en Puebla," *Historia Mexicana* 29:3 (enero-marzo 1980): 472–512, and "Puebla: Breakdown of the Old Order," in Benjamin and McNellie, *Other Mexicos*, 77–106; Gilbert M. Joseph and Allen Wells, "Summer of Discontent: Economic Rivalry among Elite Factions during the Late Porfiriato in Yucatan," *Journal of Latin American Studies* 18 (1986): 255–82; Héctor Gerardo Martínez Medina, "Génesis y desarrollo del maderismo en Oaxaca, 1909–1912," in Martínez Vásquez, *La revolución en Oaxaca*; John N. McNeely, "The Origins of the Zapata Revolt in Morelos," *Hispanic American Historical Review* 46 (May 1966): 153–60; William K. Meyers, "La Comarca Lagunera: Work, Protest, and Popular Mobilization in North Central Mexico," in Benjamin and McNellie, *Other Mexicos*, 243–74, and "Second Division of the North: Formation and Fragmentation of the Laguna's Popular Movement, 1910–1911," in *Riot,*

Rebellion, and Revolution: Rural Social Conflict in Mexico ed. Friedrich Katz (Princeton, 1988), 448–86; Robert Sandels, "Antecedentes de la Revolución en Chihuihua," *Historia Mexicana* 24 (enero-marzo 1975): 390–402; Mark Wasserman, "The Social Origins of the 1910 Revolution in Chihuahua," *Latin American Research Review* 15:1 (1980): 15–38.

117. William H. Beezley, *Insurgent Governor: Abraham Gonzalez and the Mexican Revolution in Chihuahua* (Lincoln: University of Nebraska Press, 1973), "Governor Carranza and the Mexican Revolution in Coahuila," *The Americas* 33 (July 1976): 50–61, and "State Reform during the Provisional Presidency: Chihuahua, 1911," *Hispanic American Historical Review* 50 (August 1970): 524–37; Susan M. Deeds, "José María Maytorena and the Mexican Revolution in Sonora," *Arizona and the West* 18 (Spring 1976): 21–40, and idem. (Summer 1976): 125–48; David LaFrance, *Francisco I. Madero and the Mexican Revolution in Puebla* (Wilmington, Del.: Scholarly Resources, 1989), "Francisco I. Madero and the 1911 Interim Governorship in Puebla," *The Americas* 42 (January 1986): 311–31; and "Failure of Reform: The Maderistas in Puebla, 1911–1913," *New World* 1 (1986): 44–64; Peter V.N. Henderson, "Un gobernador maderista: Benito Juárez Maza y la revolución en Oaxaca," *Historia Mexicana* 24 (enero-marzo 1975): 372–89; and Douglas W. Richmond, "Factional Strife in Coahuila, 1910–1920," *Hispanic American Historical Review* 60 (February 1980): 49–68. Gilbert M. Joseph and Allen Wells are presently examining this period in Yucatán for a projected study entitled "Summer of Discontent, Seasons of Upheaval: Elite Politics and Rural Rebellion in Yucatan, 1897–1915."

118. William H. Beezley, "Madero: The 'Unknown' President and His Political Failure to Organize Rural Mexico," in *Essays on the Mexican Revolution: Revisionist Views of the Leaders* ed. George Wolfskill and Douglas W. Richmond (Austin: University of Texas Press, 1979), 1–24, quote from 20. A similar but more critical interpretation is given by Moisés González Navarro, "Madero: La Revolución Contra los Campesinos," *El Buscón* 15 (1986): 51–76.

119. Oscar J. Martínez, ed., *Fragments of the Mexican Revolution: Personal Accounts from the Border* (Albuquerque: The University of New Mexico Press, 1983), 9. Also, see Charles C. Cumberland, "The United States–Mexican Border: A Selective Guide to the Literature of the Region," *Rural Sociology* 25:2 (June 1960): 1–239, in particular, "The Mexican Revolution of 1910," 20–25; Ellwyn R. Stoddard, Richard L. Nostrand, and Jonathan P. West, *Borderlands Sourcebook: A Guide to the Literature on Northern Mexico and the American Southwest* (Norman: University of Oklahoma Press, 1983); and Daniel Manny Lund, "Apuntes para una historiografía de la frontera del Norte," *Revista Mexicana de Ciencias Políticas y Sociales* 28:113–114 (Julio-Diciembre de 1983): 111–34.

120. Don M. Coerver and Linda B. Hall, *Texas and the Mexican Revolution: A Study in State and National Border Policy, 1910–1920* (San Antonio: Trinity University Press, 1984), and *Revolution on the Border: The United States and Mexico, 1910–1920*

(Albuquerque: University of New Mexico Press, 1989); Charles H. Harris, III, and Louis R. Sadler, "The Plan of San Diego and the Mexican–United States War Crisis of 1916: A Reexamination," *Hispanic American Historical Review* 58 (August 1978): 381–408, and "Pancho Villa and the Columbus Raid: The Missing Documents," *New Mexico Historical Review* 50:4 (October 1975): 335–46; Friedrich Katz, "Pancho Villa and the Attack on Columbus, New Mexico," *American Historical Review* 83 (February 1978): 101–30; Dirk Raat, *Revoltosos: Mexico's Rebels in the United States, 1903–1923* (College Station: Texas A & M University Press, 1981); and James A. Sandos, "The Mexican Revolution and the United States, 1915–1917: The Impact of Culture Conflict in the Tamaulipas–Texas Frontier Upon the Emergence of Revolutionary Government in Mexico," (Ph.D. diss., University of California, Berkeley, 1978).

121. Héctor Aguilar Camín, *La frontera nómada: Sonora y la revolución mexicana* (México: Siglo XXII, 1977); and "The Relevant Tradition: Sonoran Leaders in the Revolution," in *Caudillo and Peasant in the Mexican Revolution* ed. D. A. Brading (Cambridge: Cambridge University Press, 1980), 92–123. To a certain extent, Aguilar Camín's interpretation was sketched out some years earlier by Barry Carr, "The Peculiarities of the Mexican North, 1880–1928: An Essay in Interpretation," Institute of Latin-American Studies, University of Glasgow, Occasional Papers no. 4, 1971. Linda B. Hall and Douglas W. Richmond have further contributed to our understanding of Constitutionalism as a "northern faction" in their excellent political biographies. See Hall, *Alvaro Obregón: Power and Revolution in Mexico, 1911–1920* (College Station: Texas A & M University Press, 1981); and Douglas W. Richmond, *Venustiano Carranza's Nationalist Struggle, 1893–1920* (Lincoln: University of Nebraska Press, 1983).

122. Henry C. Schmidt, "Hector Aguilar Camin," 87.

123. See Womack, *Zapata and the Mexican Revolution*, for Morelos; Paul Friedrich, *Agrarian Revolt in a Mexican Village* (Englewood Cliffs, N.J.: Prentice-Hall, 1970), for Naranja, Michoacán; Jean Meyer, "Historia del reparto agrario en Nayarit, 1915–1934," *Encuentro* 3 (Abril-Junio 1986): 43–56, for Nayarit during 1912–1913.

124. Brading, *Caudillo and Peasant in the Mexican Revolution*. See Brading's introduction and the concluding essay by Hans Werner Tobler. Ramon Eduardo Ruiz, in a review of the volume, writes: "To ascribe the rebellion simply to agrarian discontent distorts the picture. . . . In truth, the essays demonstrate, what took place was mass mobilization under the control of the caudillos, frequently of backgrounds and aspirations at odds with those of their rural followers." Ruiz, *Hispanic American Historical Review* 61 (August 1981): 532. Also see Raymond Th. J. Buve, "Peasant movements, caudillos and land reform during the Revolution (1910–1917) in Tlaxcala, Mexico," *Boletín de Estudios Latinoamericanos y del Caribe* 18 (June 1975): 112–52, and " 'Neither Carranza nor Zapata!': The Rise and Fall of a Peasant Movement that Tried to Challenge Both, Tlaxcala,

1910–19," in Katz, *Riot, Rebellion, and Revolution,* 339–75; Frans J. Schryer, "The Role of the Rancheros of Central Mexico in the Mexican Revolution (The Case of the Sierra Alta de Hidalgo)," *Canadian Journal of Latin American Studies* 4:1 (1979): 21–41; Heather Fowler Salamini, "Caciquismo and the Mexican Revolution: The Case of Manuel Peláez," VI Conference of Mexican and United States Historians, Chicago, 1981; Ian Jacobs, "Rancheros of Guerrero: The Figueroa brothers and the Revolution," in Brading, *Caudillo and Peasant in the Mexican Revolution,* 76–91; and Fabían González, "Sociedad y política en el Estado de Jalisco durante la Revolución Mexicana," *Controversia* (Guadalajara), 1:1 (1976), 43–74.

125. Dudley Ankerson, *Agrarian Warlord: Saturnino Cedillo and the Mexican Revolution in San Luis Potosi* (DeKalb: Northern Illinois University Press, 1984); Beatriz Rojas, *La Pequeña Guerra: Los Carrera Torres and los Cedillo* (Zamora, Michoacán: El Colegio de Michoacán, 1983); and Romana Falcón, *Revolución y caciquismo. San Luis Potosí, 1910–1938* (México: El Colegio de México, 1984), and "Charisma, Tradition, and Caciquismo: Revolution in San Luis Potosí," Katz, *Riot, Rebellion, and Revolution,* 338–447.

126. Paul Garner, "Autoritarismo revolucionario en el México provincial: el carrancismo y el gobierno preconstitucional en Oaxaca, 1915–1920," *Historia Mexicana* 34 (octubre-diciembre 1984): 238–99; Garner, "Federalism and Caudillismo in the Mexican Revolution: The Genesis of the Oaxaca Sovereignty Movement (1915–20)," *Journal of Latin American Studies* 17 (1985): 111–33; Francisco José Ruiz Cervantes, *La Revolución en Oaxaca: El movimiento de la Soberanía (1915–1920)* (México: Fondo de Cultura Económica, 1986); Thomas Benjamin, "Chiapas Contrarrevolucionario: Regional Rebellions and the Mexican Revolution in Chiapas, 1910–1920," unpublished manuscript; Alicia Hernández Chavez, "La defensa de los finqueros en Chiapas, 1914–1920," *Historia Mexiana* 28 (enero-marzo 1979): 335–69; Antonio García de León, "Lucha de clases y poder político en Chiapas," *Historia y Sociedad* 22 (1979): 57–88.

127. Ramón D. Chacón, "Yucatán and the Mexican Revolution: The Pre-Constitutional Years, 1910–1918" (Ph.D. diss., Stanford University, 1982); James C. Carey, *The Mexican Revolution in Yucatan, 1915–1924* (Boulder: Westview Press, 1985); Gilbert M. Joseph, *Revolution from Without: Yucatan, Mexico, and the United States* (Cambridge: Cambridge University Press, 1982); Enrique Montalvo Ortega, "Caudillismo y estado en la Revolución Mexicana: El gobierno de Alvarado en Yucatán," *Nova Americana* 2 (1979): 13–36; Francisco José Paoli, *Yucatán y los orígenes del nuevo estado mexicano. Gobierno de Salvador Alvarado, 1915–1918* (México: Ediciones Era, 1984); and Douglas W. Richmond, "Salvador Alvarado and the Yucatán during the Mexican Revolution, 1914–1920," *Maryland Historian* 15:2 (Fall-Winter 1984): 1–10.

128. In 1969 Albert Michaels suggested the need for studies of the Salvador Alvarado and Felipe Carrillo Puerto regimes in Yucatán, the Tomás Garrido Canabal

regime in Tabasco, and the Cedillo movement and government in San Luis Potosí. Such studies have since been published. "Commentary," 498–99.

129. Joseph, *Revolution from Without;* Friedrich, *Agrarian Revolt in a Mexican Village;* Romana Falcón, *El agrarismo en Veracruz: La etapa radical, 1928–1935* (México: El Colegio de México, 1977); Romana Falcón, Soledad García, *La semilla en el surco: Adalberto Tejeda y el radicalismo en Veracruz, 1883–1960* (México: El Colegio de México, 1986); Alan M. Kirschner, *Tomás Garrido Canabal y el movimiento de los Camisas Rojas* (México: SepSetentas, 1976); Carlos Martínez Assad, *El laboratorio de la revolución: el Tabasco garridista* (México: Siglo XXI, 1979); Ankerson, *Agrarian Warlord;* and Falcón, *Revolución y caciquismo.* Also see Carlos Martínez Assad, "Los caudillos regionales y el poder central," *Revolucionarios fueron todos* (México: SEP/80, 1982), 147–233.

130. Jean Meyer, *La Cristiada* (México: Siglo XXI, 1974), 3 vols.; *Apocalypse et Revolution au Mexique. La guerre des Cristeros, 1926–1929* (Paris: Editions Gallimard-Julliard, 1974); and *The Cristero Rebellion: The Mexican People between Church and State, 1926–1929* (Cambridge: Cambridge University Press, 1976), 216–17.

131. Ian Jacobs, *Ranchero Revolt: The Mexican Revolution in Guerrero* (Austin: University of Texas Press, 1982), 112. This is an example, according to Alan Knight, of "a kind of statolatry, which now pervades a good deal of recent historical studies." Knight criticizes this and other teleologies in "The Mexican Revolution: Bourgeois? Nationalist? Or Just a 'Great Rebellion'?" *Bulletin of Latin American Research* 4:2 (1985): 1–37.

132. Friedrich, *Agrarian Revolt in a Mexican Village;* Salamini, *Agrarian Radicalism in Veracruz;* and Joseph, *Revolution from Without.*

133. Ann L. Craig, *The First Agraristas: An Oral History of a Mexican Agrarian Reform Movement* (Berkeley: University of California Press, 1983). Also see Raymond Th. J. Buve, "Movilización campesina y reforma agraria en los valles de Nativitas, Tlaxcala (1917–1923): Estudio de un caso de lucha por recuperar tierra habidas durante la revolución armada," in Elsa Cecilia Frost et al., eds., *El trabajo y los trabajadores en la historia de México* (México and Tucson: El Colegio de México and University of Arizona Press, 1979), 533–64; and Carlos García Mora, "Tierra y Movimiento Agrarista en la Sierra Purhepecha," *Jornadas de Historia de Occidente. Movimientos populares en el occidente de México, siglos XIX y XX* (Jiquilpan, Michoacán: Centro de Estudios de la Revolución Mexicana, 1980), 47–101.

134. Alan Knight, review of Schryer, *The Rancheros of Pisaflores,* in *Journal of Latin American Studies,* 197. Also see Ankerson, *Agrarian Warlord;* Buve, "State Governors and Peasant Mobilization in Tlaxcala," in Brading, *Caudillo and Peasant in the Mexican Revolution,* 222–44; Falcón, *Revolución y caciquismo;* Jacobs, *Ranchero Revolt;* Heriberto Moreno García, *Después de los latifundios (La desintegración de la gran propiedad agraria en México). III Coloquio de Antropología e Historia Regionales, Agosto 5–8 de 1981* (México: El Colegio de Michoacán, 1982); and Susan Walsh Sanderson, "La política de la reforma agraria en México: nexos locales, estatales

y nacionales," *Revista Mexicana de Sociología*, 42:1 (Enero-Marzo de 1980): 131–52.

135. See the books of Dudley Ankerson, *Agrarian Warlord;* Guillermo de la Peña, *Herederos de promesas;* Romana Falcón, *Revolución y caciquismo;* Ian Jacobs, *Ranchero Revolt;* G. M. Joseph, *Revolution from Without;* Frans J. Schryer, *The Rancheros of Pisaflores;* Arturo Warman, . . . *Y venimos a contradecir;* and two which have not been previously cited: Thomas Benjamin, *A Rich Land, A Poor People: Politics and Society in Modern Chiapas* (Albuquerque: University of New Mexico Press, 1989); and Antonio García de León, *Resistencia y útopia: Memorial de agravios y crónica de revueltas y profecías acaecidas en la provincia de Chiapas durante los últimos quinientos años de su historia* (México: Ediciones Era, 1985), 2 vols.

136. Jean Meyer, "Friedrich Katz: entre la Mata Hari y el imperialismo," review of *The Secret War in Mexico*, in *Nexos* 6 (Febrero de 1983): 53–58.

137. Also see Katz's interesting synthesis of the agrarian and regional structures of Porfirian Mexico (although one based more on primary sources than monographic studies), "Labor Conditions on Haciendas in Porfirian Mexico: Some Trends and Tendencies," *Hispanic American Historical Review* 54 (February 1974): 1–47; and republished in Mexico with relevant documents as *Servidumbre agraria en México en la época porfiriana* (México: Sep-Setentas, 1976, and Ediciones Era, 1980).

138. Francois-Xavier Guerra, *Le Mexique, de l'Ancien Regime a la Revolution* (Paris: Editions L'Harmattan, 1985), 2 vols. See Carlos Arriola's review, "Porfiriato y revolución: un libro diferente," *Historia Mexicana* 36 (julio-septiembre 1986): 173–94.

139. Alan Knight, *The Mexican Revolution:* vol. 1, *Porfirians, Liberal and Peasants* and vol. 2, *Counter-Revolution and Reconstruction* (Cambridge: Cambridge University Press, 1986), 1:x. Also see Mark Wasserman's review in *American Historical Review* 92 (June 1987): 778–80.

140. John Tutino, *From Insurrection to Revolution in Mexico: Social Bases of Agrarian Violence, 1750–1940* (Princeton: Princeton University Press, 1986).

141. Alan Knight, "The Mexican Revolution," *History Today* 35 (June 1985): 51.

Appendix

Provincial Historiographies and Bibliographies

Baja California
Joaquín Díaz Mercado, *Bibliografía sumaria de la Baja California* (México, 1937).

Campeche
Gustavo Martínez Alomia, *Bibliografía* (Campeche, n.d.).

Chiapas
Dolores Aramoni Calderón, *Fuentes para el estudio de Chiapas* (Tuxtla Gutiérrez, 1978).

Coahuila
Vito Alessio Robles, *Bibliografía de Coahuila, historia y geografía* (México, 1927).

Durango
Gustavo del Castillo, et al., *Bibliografía sobre la Comarca Lagunera* (1978).

José Ignacio Gallegos C., "Durango: la historia y sus instrumentos," *Historia Mexicana* II (octubre-diciembre 1961): 314–19.

Guanajuato
Rosalia Aguilar, Claudia Burr, Claudia Canales, Rose Ma. Sánchez de Tagle, "Guanajuato, una bibliografía comentada, 1750–1917," *Secuencia* 8 (mayo-agosto 1987): 111–144.

Guerrero
Alvaro López Miramontes, "El Panorama historiográfico guerrerense," *Historias* (Abril-Julio de 1984): 99–112.

Jalisco
Miguel de la Mora L. and Moisés González Navarro, "La historia y sus instrumentos [Jalisco]," *Historia Mexicana* 1 (julio-septiembre 1951): 143–63.

José María Muriá, "Notas sobre la historiográfia regional Jalisciense en el siglo XX," *Relaciones* 3:10 (primavera 1982): 69–85.

Jaime Olveda and Marina Mantilla Trolle, *Jalisco en Libros* (Guadalajara, 1985).

Ramiro Villaseñor y Villaseñor, *Bibliografía general de Jalisco* (Guadalajara, 1958).

Mexico

Marta Baranda and Lia García Verasteguí, "Bibliografía comentada, Estado de México," *Sucuencia* 4 (enero-abril 1986) : 78–101.

Mario Colín, *Bibliografía general del Estado de México* 3 vols. (Mexico, 1963).

Michoacán

Lyle C. Brown, "Political and Military History of the State of Michoacán, 1910–1940," in *El trabajo y los trabajadores en la historia de México* ed. Elsa Cecilia Frost et. al. (México and Tucson: El Colegio de México and University of Arizona Press, 1979), 801–5.

Joaquín Fernández de Córdoba, "Michoacán: la historia y sus instrumentos," *Historia Mexicana* 2 (julio-septiembre 1952): 135–54.

Jesús Romero Flores, *Apuntes para una bibliografía geografía e histórica de Michoacán* (México, 1932).

Morelos

Domingo Díaz, *Bibliografía del Estado de Morelos* (México, 1933).

Nuevo Léon

Israel Cavazos Garza, "Nuevo Léon: la historia y sus instrumentos," *Historia Mexicana* 1 (enero-marzo 1952): 494–515.

Héctor González and Plinio D. Ordoñez, *Bibliografía del Estado de Nuevo Léon de 1820 a 1946* (Monterrey, 1946).

Oaxaca

Rafael Carrasco Puente, Bibliografía del istmo de Tehuantepec (Mexico, 1948).

Margarita Dalton, "La historia de Oaxaca vista por los historiadores oaxaqueños," *Secuencia* 9 (septiembre-diciembre 1987): 23–41.

José Fernando Iturribarría, "Oaxaca: la historia y sus instrumentos," *Historia Mexicana* 2 (enero-marzo 1953): 459–76.

Francisco José Ruiz Cervantes, "Seis libros sobre la Revolución en Oaxaca," *Revista Mexicana de Sociología* 44:1 (enero-marzo de 1982): 341–44.

Puebla

Moisés Herrera, *Contribución para una bibliografía de obras referentes al Estado de Puebla* (México, 1943).

Queretaro

Rafael Ayala Echavarrí, *Bibliografía histórica y geográfica de Querétaro* (México, 1949).

Quintana Roo
Lorena Careaga Villiesid, "Bibliografía comentada del estado de Quintana Roo," *Secuencia* 9 (septiembre-diciembre 1987): 42–80.

San Luis Potosí
Ramón Alcorta Guerrero and José Francisco Pedraza, *Bibliografía Histórica y Geográfica del Estado de San Luis Potosí* (México, 1941, with additions published in 1947, 1950, and 1962).

María Isabel Abella Armelia, "Bibliografía potosina de estudios históricos," *Secuencia* 7 (enero-abril 1987): 70–139.

Joaquín Meade, "San Luis Potosí: la historia y sus instrumentos," *Estilo. Revista de Cultura* (San Luis Potosí) 39 (julio-septiembre 1956): 155–78.

Rafael Montejano y Aguinaga, *La historiografía potosina* (San Luis Potosí, 1974).

Sonora
E.Y. López, *Bibliografía de Sonora* (Hermosillo, 1960).

Cynthia Radding, "La revolución en Sonora y sus historiadores, una visión historiográfica," *Temas Sonorenses. A traves de los simposios de historia* (Hermosillo: Gobierno del Estado de Sonora, 1984), 207–23.

Tabasco
Ma. Eugenia Arias, Ana Lau, and Ximena Sepulveda, "Tabasco: una bibliografía comentada," *Secuencia* 5 (mayo-agosto 1986): 87–111.

Francisco J. Santamaría, *Bibliografía general de Tabasco* 3 vols. (México, 1930, 1945, 1949).

Tlaxcala
Beatriz Cano Sanches, *Estado de Tlaxcala. Bibliografía básica comentada* (México, 1979).

Roberto Ramos and Crisanto Cuellar Abaroa, *Bibliografía del Estado de Tlaxcala* (Tlaxcala, 1949).

Veracruz
Carmen Blazquez Domínguez, "Siglo XIX y revolución en Veracruz. Una bibliografía básica," *Secuencia* 6 (septiembre-diciembre 1986):61–98.

Takako Sudo and Aurelio de los Reyes, "Xalapa: la historia y sus instrumentos," *Historia Mexicana* 24 (abril-junio 1975): 607–21.

Yucatán
Gilbert M. Joseph, "From Caste War to Class War: The Historiography of Modern Yucatan (c. 1750–1940)," *Hispanic American Historical Review* 65 (February 1985): 111–34.

Gilbert M. Joseph, *Rediscovering the Past at Mexico's Periphery: Essays on the History of Modern Yucatan* (University: The University of Alabama Press, 1986)

Zacatecas

Daniel Manny Lund, "Apuntes para una historiografía de la frontera del Norte," *Revista Mexicana de Ciencias Políticas y Sociales,* 28 (julio-diciembre, 1983), 111–34.

Glossary

agrarista.	Supporter of land reform.
alcalde	Mayor, municipal president.
arrendamiento.	Rent in cash or produce.
arrendatario.	Renter, tenant farmer, sharecropper.
ayuntamiento.	Town council, municipal government.
baldiaje.	System of labor service.
baldío.	Legally vacant land; squatter–sharecropper.
cabecera.	Seat of municipal or departmental government.
cacicazgo.	Domain of a cacique.
cacique.	Local or regional political boss.
caciquismo.	System of boss rule.
Callista.	Supporter of Plutarco Elías Calles.
campesino.	"Country person," peasant.
Cardenista.	Supporter of Lázaro Cárdenas, his regime, political faction and/or political principles.
Carrancista	Supporter of Venustiano Carranza, his revolutionary cause, and regime.
Caudillo.	Military chieftain, strong man.
Científico.	Adherent of Positivism and Porfirismo.
comisariado ejidal.	Local committee that administers an ejido.
ejidatarios.	Residents of an ejido who possess land-use rights.
ejido.	Village common land; since 1915 communities established through land reform.
finca.	"Farm," ranch, hacienda, estate.
finca rústica.	Any rural property, regardless of size.

finquero.

Farmer, rancher, hacendado, landowner.

Gobernación.

Department of Government, Interior Ministry.

gobernador.

State governor.

guardia blanca.

Private military force of a landowner.

hacendado.

Estate owner, finquero.

hacienda.

Rural estate (Mexican term).

hectárea.

"Hectare," area of land equaling 2.4 acres.

jefatura.

Prefecture, political district.

Jefe Máximo.

Supreme Chief, reference to Plutarco Elías Calles.

jefe político.

Prefect, district political administrator.

jornalero.

Temporary day laborer.

latifundista.

Owner of a great estate.

latifundio.

"latifundium" (pl., "latifundia"), great estate; large landholding.

Maderista.

Supporter of Francisco I. Madero, his revolutionary cause, and/or regime.

Maximato.

Period when the national government was dominated by Plutarco Elías Calles (1928–1934).

mestizo.

Person of mixed Spanish–Indian ancestry.

municipio.

Municipality.

obrero.

Worker, laborer.

Obregonista.

Supporter of Álvaro Obregón, his political faction and/or regime.

partido.

Political party; political district subordinate to a department.

patria chica.

"Little fatherland," local region.

peón.

Rural laborer, often an indebted laborer, mozo.

peonaje.

Labor system associated with debt.

peones acasillados.

Resident farm laborers.

peso.

Basic unit of Mexican currency.

pistolero.

Thug, gunslinger.

político.

Politician.

Porfiriato.

Age of Porfirio Díaz (1876–1911).

Porfirista.

Supporter of Porfirio Díaz, his regime, or political principles and policies.

presidente municipal. Municipal president, mayor.
propietario. Property owner; elected official.
pueblo. A village.

ranchería. Hamlet, village located on hacienda property.
ranchero. Smallholder, rancher.
rancho. Small or medium-size property, homestead, ranch.

sierra. Mountain range.
sindicato. Labor union or federation.
sindicato blanco. Labor union allied with or created by business or government.

terrenos baldíos. Legally unoccupied lands belonging to state government.
tienda de raya. Company store.

Villista. Supporter of Francisco "Pancho" Villa and his revolutionary cause.

Zapatista. Supporter of Emiliano Zapata and his revolutionary cause.

The Editors

Thomas Benjamin, associate professor of history at Central Michigan University, is coeditor of *Other Mexicos: Essays on Regional Mexican History, 1876–1911* (1984) and author of *A Rich Land, A Poor People: Politics and Society in Modern Chiapas* (1989).

Mark Wasserman, associate professor of history at Rutgers University, is coauthor with Benjamin Keen of *A History of Latin America* (3d ed. 1988) and author of *Capitalists, Caciques, and Revolution: The Native Elite and Foreign Enterprise in Chihuahua, Mexico, 1854–1911* (1984).

The Contributors

Raymond Th. J. Buve is professor of Latin American history at Leiden University, the Netherlands, and editor of *Haciendas in Central Mexico from Late Colonial Times to the Revolution: Labor Conditions, Hacienda Management and its Relations to the State* (1984) and author of numerous articles, including "Neither Carranza nor Zapata: The Rise and Fall of a Peasant Movement which Tried to Challenge Both: Tlaxcala, 1910–1919," in *Riot, Rebellion, and Revolution: Rural Social Conflict in Mexico*, ed. Friedrich Katz (1988).

Romana Falcón is a professor at the Centro de Estudios Históricos de El Colegio de Mexico, Mexico City, and author of *El agrarismo en Veracruz, la etapa radical (1928–1935)* (1977), *Revolución y caciquismo: San Luis Potosí, 1910–1938* (1984), and coauthor of *La semilla en el surco: Adalberto Tejeda y el radicalismo en Veracruz, 1883–1960* (1986).

Paul Garner teaches at University College Swansea, University of Wales, the United Kingdom, and is the author of a forthcoming book on Oaxaca to be published in Mexico and several articles, including "Federalism and Caudillismo in the Mexican Revolution: The Genesis of the Oaxaca Sovereignty Movement," *Journal of Latin American Studies* (1975).

Gilbert M. Joseph is professor of history at the University of North Carolina, Chapel Hill, and author of *Revolution from Without: Yucatán, Mexico, and the United States, 1880–1924* (1982) and *Rediscovering the Past at Mexico's Periphery: Essays on the History of Modern Yucatán* (1986).

David LaFrance, is assistant professor of history at Oregon State University and author of *Francisco I. Madero and the Mexican Revolution in Puebla* (1989) and numerous articles, including "Failure of Reform: The Maderistas in Puebla, 1911–1913," *New World: A Journal of Latin American Studies* (1986).

Heather Fowler Salamini is professor of history at Bradley University and author of *Agrarian Radicalism in Veracruz, 1920–38* (1978) and the author of numerous articles on Mexican history, including "Revolutionary Caudillos in the 1920s: Francisco Múgica and Adalberto Tejeda," in *Caudillo and Peasant in the Mexican Revolution*, ed. D. A. Brading (1980).

John Tutino is associate professor of history at Boston College and author of *From Insurrection to Revolution in Mexico: Social Bases of Agrarian Violence, 1750–1940* (1986) and many articles and chapters in books, including "Agrarian Social Change and Peasant Rebellion in Nineteenth-Century Mexico: The Example of Chalco," in *Riot, Rebellion, and Revolution* (1988).

Allen Wells is associate professor of history at Bowdoin College and author of *Yucatán's Gilded Age: Haciendas, Henequén, and International Harvester, 1860–1915* (1985) and numerous articles and chapters in books including "Yucatán: Violence and Social Control on Henequén Plantations," in *Other Mexicos* (1984).

Stuart F. Voss is professor of history at the State University of New York, Plattsburg, and author of *On the Periphery of Nineteenth-Centuary Mexico: Sonora and Sinaloa, 1810–1877* (1982) and coauthor of *Notable Family Networks in Latin America* (1984).

Index